THE
GUARANTEE

P.W. with Bill and Madrue, 1917

THE
GUARANTEE

P.W Chavers: Banker, Entrepreneur,
Philanthropist in Chicago's Black Belt
of the Twenties

by Madrue Chavers-Wright

THE WRIGHT-ARMSTEAD ASSOCIATES NEW YORK

Library of Congress Catalog Card Number 86-51447

ISBN: 0-931505-05-4
ISBN: 0-931505-04-6

FIRST EDITION April, 1985
SECOND EDITION February, 1987

Braun-Brumfield, Inc. Book Manufacturers

A Subsidiary of Heritage Communications Inc.

The Wright-Armstead Associates
2410 Barker Ave, Suite 14 G
The Bronx
New York, NY 10467
Printed U.S.A.

To Benjamin and Edward

Naima, Ayesha and Shaniqua

In memory of Camille

For generations yet unborn

and

For my extended family around the world

To let you know that I
arrived safely on *Dec 23*
My papa and mama are
Mr and Mrs. *P. W. Charers*
Hoping to see you soon, I
am your new little friend
Helen Madrue Charers

1916 . . . Your new little friend.

Contents

List of Illustrations

"The world begins to be ready to receive us as a people who do not apologize for ourselves, but demonstrate our complexity as human beings, and who, at the same time, assert our dignity in that complexity."

Lorraine Hansberry
in a letter written to
the author, 1959.

Acknowledgments

This book developed out of notes written more than thirty years ago, when I was preparing to return to work after the birth of my second son. The call of career opportunity and the pressure of family financial demands lured me back to the work-a-day world, but not before considering how I could provide my sons with a knowledge of their family heritage, in a formal way. To accomplish this task, I assembled my father's papers and family pictures, and attached a three page statement entitled "Notes About Father's Life." My sons, Benjamin and Edward, were to know something about their maternal grandfather, P.W. Chavers. Although he died many years before their birth, his thinking and achievements are a part of their heritage. I felt they must know of his activities which not only reflected his idealism and creativity, but his contributions to the changing way of life and improved status of black Americans in the Midwest around the early part of the 20th century.

I had commented about his having established the first black national bank in America, and about his having written an original Congressional Bill that laid the foundation for the Federal Bank Insurance Law which guarantees bank deposits. As my son prepared to leave home to go to college in 1957, I wanted to give him something special of which he could be proud, something that would deepen his sense of identity. I showed him the newspaper clippings, the posters, the photos, and my own initial writings about my father. My son's reaction of surprise which sparked several trips on his part to the library for further research, forced me to the realization that there was a message in these documents beyond the fond memories of a daughter for her father. I sought ways of preserving them more carefully by setting up a special file. This eventually led me to discuss both the details of my father's life and the importance of the documents with several writers and friends, who urged me to write this book. The man, P.W., they insisted, was worth knowing.

Because of my closeness to my father the pain was still too great for me then to express all the incidents now related in this book. But my friends persisted. They raised sharp questions, provoking my memory and my pride. Who and what had influenced his thinking? How did he choose to become a practical spokesman in the hostile, racist climate of Chicago in the 1920's? I was reminded that in those days of speakeasies and rugged individualism, a man of his talents bent on self-aggrandizement could have done well for himself. Although I had no ready answers to these questions, I began to feel that I should share the story of his life with others. Some of my reservations about telling this story were due to the fact that as far as I knew at the time, the only proof of his activities were either in my childhood memories or the few documents in my possession. To our once wealthy family no fortune remained as proof of his vision and success. The Great Depression had obliterated any traces of it. But encouragement from relatives and associates, who still vividly remembered him, dissipated these final reservations and I began the years of research necessary to document his life fully.

This is an in-depth American saga that spans almost 50 years from the Reconstruction Period after the Civil War until the mid-Depression of 1933. It tells the story of the Chavers-Calloway-Bannister-Pannell Clans of color and their interactions and interdependencies in coping with each other and the world around them; a journey that leads from North Carolina to Virginia; Columbus, Ohio to Chicago; and finally to New York City. Much has been written of the *poverty* of pre- and post-slavery black America. Little has been written of the personal struggles, the triumphs and infighting, of *middle-class* black Americans. There was that segment that rose economically in the period following the Civil War and into the early 20th century, even in the era of

xiv

institutionalized racism. Later in the 1950's, a Civil Rights movement developed to combat the segregation laws. This brought increased interest in this facet of our American heritage. I was encouraged to feel that the world at large wanted to know more about a people who had survived, multiplied, and contributed to the American culture under all kinds of oppression, including brutal economic deprivation. A people who, though neglected and scorned in the "land of opportunity" had remained, despite this, loyal and proud of their American heritage. A wall of silence had been built around the achievements of Afro-Americans by an America absorbed in its European heritage.

From the time of the Civil War, Blacks have grown in number from 4 million to 30 million in the United States. They fought and died in America's wars. They shifted with America from an agricultural to an urban way of life, during all of this time remaining systematically excluded from opportunity through the process of legal discrimination. According to the American custom and caste system, which persists to this day, one is a Black by virtue of having one drop of this American slave blood, either visible or acknowledged. This outcast definition, a truly American tradition, was quickly perceived as a stigma and used as a divisive weapon by foreigners pouring into this country. Those eager to get ahead and assimilate adopted the mores of racist American Whites, conforming to the prevailing color codes. Thus, America has been robbed of the full expression of the tremendous contributions and talents of America's people of color: black, brown, red and yellow. This book has developed as the narrative of the personal history of one American man of color, P.W. Chavers, and his role in banking in the boom years of the teens and twenties in Chicago.

My parents so successfully shielded us, their children, from the trials and tribulations they knew during these years, that as I did the research for this book, many facets of this story came as a surprise. As I gathered facts from old newspapers, I realized that I must write not only of my parents' joys and triumphs, but of their anxieties, frustrations and sufferings about which I was now learning. Subsequently, I came to know that documentary sources in the files of the National Archives in Washington, D.C. and the Ohio Historical Center in Columbus, Ohio supplied many answers to questions raised about my father's youth and early public life. The letters to and from Booker T. Washington were especially helpful in revealing the significance of this relationship to P.W. and the consistency of his perspective in transcending the resistance he encountered in developing his ideas. This was the test of the man: how he encountered, endured, and surmounted betrayal. My parents were not a struggling young couple working together to have him achieve his goal as he had already made a place for himself in the wider community when they met. His ideas, methods, and know-how were already established before he married and had children, which was at the relatively advanced age of 37, before the story begins.

All of his life, my father was fighting several groups at one time: both the black and white self-seekers, the entrenched older generation of politicians, the shady elements, as well as the apathy of the victimized, and the betrayal of those in whom he placed unwarranted trust. Although fighting brutal injustice against Blacks in his era, he was no firebrand. He felt one had to work within the American political process in order to achieve real progress. Many will judge his optimism as the most foolish of naivete, others may see his nearly constant hope as something of great value.

I am deeply grateful to countless friends, neighbors, associates, and all of those who encouraged me over the years with their inquiries, thoughts, and suggestions about developing my manuscript. In pursuing my research methodology I sought out J.A. Rogers, the noted historian, who warned me that after I completed my manuscript I might have to publish it through private resources, just as I have. I wish to acknowledge with special thanks the help of Bobb Hamilton, the poet, who gave unstintingly of his talents, time, and inspiration during my early attempts to write a book. I greatly benefited from the interest and devotion of my friend and neighbor, Ella Silber, during those early years of typing and retyping many drafts of this manuscript. The original inspiration for this book came from my mentor and friend for years, Edith Alt, the chief social work consultant at the Health Insurance Plan of Greater New York, together with her husband, Herschel Alt, the directing head of the Jewish Board of Guardians, since renamed the Jewish Board of Family and Children's Services, a world famous mental health agency. Both were writers and internationally acknowledged experts in child development. Early on in my experiences as a social work consultant at that agency, when both were just getting to know me in 1958, they impressed upon me the value such a book would have in illuminating the world's perception of the contribution of the people of color to the American way of life. Their vision and inspiration live on within this manuscript.

I owe many thanks to all of those who answered my early letters asking for their recollections, especially Emily Brown and Rebecca Dooley whose answers strengthened my perception of my father's role as a businessman and how he related to his employees. I am deeply indebted to Helen Nixon and Essie Wiggins, our neighbors, as well as Ora Lee Morrow, our grade school teacher, for their memories of our family's role in the community. I wish to thank my brother, William Chavers, my cousins Jeanne Chavous Gwynn and Elisabeth Hawkins, as well as my childhood dancing teacher, Mary Bruce, for their practical encouragement, recollections, information and suggestions for contents of this book.

I owe a special debt to Jean Blackwell Hutson and the staff of the Schomburg Collection of the New York Public Library, to Gary Hunter of the Ohio Historical Center, to the many librarians in the Manuscript Division of the Library of Congress and the National Archives and Record Services of Washington, D.C., as well as the volunteer staff of the Church of Jesus Christ of Latter Day Saints, all of whom responded promptly to my requests for documentation and lent moral support in varying ways over a long period of time. I wish to thank all of my colleagues in the Health Insurance Plan of Greater New York, especially Chris Nelson, Ted Kaufman, and Alice Varela, who worked with me, listened to my dilemmas, and provided encouragement as I pursued this manuscript and research concurrently with my full time professional and family responsibilities. I am profoundly indebted to Mortimer Todel and Eugene Toomer of the Mental Health Association of New York and Bronx Counties, and all of the others who reviewed the manuscript and shared their thoughts with me as it neared completion. I am deeply grateful to Sara Stringfellow who took time out from her own work for discussion, collaboration, lending assistance to me in the final editing and rewriting; who, more than any one else, nudged me to keep at this work in the final stages until the manuscript completed the publication process.

A great deal of caring and sharing has gone into the making of this book. I can never repay Keith McGinnis of Braun-Brumfield and Jacqui Ashri for their devotion, guidance and sensitive work, above and beyond the call of duty, required to handle and redesign, copy edit and proofread the final printing of this book. I am deeply grateful to all those friends and associates who sustained me in various ways through the agony and uncertainty of the one year delay after it became clear that I would have to publish my own book to protect fully my literary rights and to ensure production.

My efforts have remained centered in the historical realities to which my father related and how he interacted with his environment as his life unfolded. I have used a semi-autobiographical format to present the intimate family portrait of the life and works of Pearl William Chavers, or P.W., as he was known to his family, friends, and close associates. This book is based on a true story of his life—as I knew him—and the Chicago Black Belt, as I knew it. I have fictionalized some names, certain incidents and details, and much of the dialogue, for the purposes of drama, and at times, anonymity.

I alone am responsible for the decision as to what facts to use, what interpretations to choose, what opinions to derive, and what prejudices to cherish, out of my own life experiences. My goal is to reveal P.W.'s personality, his character, his family, the fabric of the man, his impact on a given set of circumstances in his time, the outside pressures of extreme discrimination and segregation in the Chicago of the 1920's and the devastating ghetto leadership in-fighting to which he

xviii

reacted, given his convictions, responsibilities, and personal drives. In keeping with my father's words and deeds, it is my hope that in the writing of this book I will have handed to the public, to his people and to his memory, a work dedicated to benefit them in their quest for self-understanding and a more rewarding and meaningful life through a fuller appreciation and respect for their fellowman.

New York
December, 1984

1

Move to Chicago's Black Belt

We lived on a quiet little street, Forrestville Avenue, in a middle-class community of two-story, one-family greystone houses, just one-half block from the factory owned by P.W., my father. Chicago had prospered and had been rebuilt long ago, from the ashes of the Great Fire in 1871, into a city of brick and stone. It is said that Chicago's black community can be traced to the 1840's, with the coming of a few runaway slaves, when it served as a way station on the Underground Railroad. The city tolerated abolitionists and built an effective anti-slavery movement. In these early days the Blacks had been interspersed throughout the residential areas of the city. Forrestville Avenue had seen many changes. By 1920 the people of color were settled on the South Side near Lake Michigan. Between the "shanty Irish" and the railroad yards on the west, the well-to-do second generation Whites on the south, and the downtown business district on the north, was a narrow strip known as the "Black Belt."

The city had split into the white "Old Settlers," the black second-generation "Old Settlers," the white new arrivals, essentially from Europe, and the black new arrivals from the rural South. The stable, second-generation black "Old Settlers" feared that "these newcomers were making it hard for us all." And this was probably true, for the housing dilemma focused on the walling of the emerging black middle-class inside the ghetto so that, unlike other groups, they would never have access to an improved way of life in the better neighborhoods. They grew conservative as they prospered and sought to imitate the quiet, safe profile of other middle-

1

class groups. But with the increase in the black new arrivals, mainly from the Deep South, bringing their coarse untutored behavior and shabby appearance in great numbers, a black presence with an inconspicuous profile in Chicago became impossible to maintain. As these unskilled refugees from political-legal oppression of the South poured into Chicago, very few "Old Settlers" stretched out a welcoming or helping hand to the black poor "New Arrivals." But P.W., who was neither southern nor poor, established his factory and family in the heart of the Black Belt and cast his lot with the least of them, the black new arrivals, when he left Columbus, Ohio three years before.

Forrestville Avenue, tucked away in the middle of this narrow strip, was not far from the notorious 4500 Vincennes Avenue block which was rumored to contain those most fanatical against the coming of the Blacks. Our block, just one street long, linked 43rd with 44th Street in a very private, peaceful manner until that bombing of Woodfolk's home at 4716-22 Calumet Avenue the night of February 1st, 1920. Everyone felt trapped! Rumors circulated throughout the neighborhood that a terrorist had somehow obtained keys to the 12 flat building where Woodfolk lived, locked the tenants in their apartments, sprang the locks of the doors leading to the street and planted a bomb in the hallway. The explosion tore up the hallway, staircase, front entrance, and shattered all of the windows in this and adjacent buildings.

The following week, P.W. went to the mass meeting of more than 1500 people gathered in the St. Mark's Methodist Episcopal Church to hear the discussion of measures to be taken to deal with this latest bombing near our home. P.W.'s secretary, Nahum Brascher, now editor of the newly formed Associated Negro Press, had called and asked him to assist with the planning. The worried crowd milled around for a while, then settled down to hear the guest speakers report on what had happened. They listened to hear how they could prepare for the next attack.

R. W. Woodfolk, the President of the defunct Woodfolk Savings Bank, and the chief victim of the latest bombing, spoke first. Still visibly shaken, he began, "There has been great damage and almost complete destruction to the front of my building on Calumet Avenue. Now, as you know, this is very valuable property and one of the Woodfolk Bank's largest holdings."

The crowd shifted a bit noisily. After the riots of last year, many here had lost their entire savings in this privately-owned Woodfolk Savings Bank which collapsed months ago. Woodfolk talked on, seemingly oblivious to the crowd's resentment towards him personally.

"Now I live in one of those apartments in this valuable three-story greystone building so that I know what has happened to the property and the community," he went on. "I think you should know what happened in some detail, to be prepared for the next attack. Bombs were planted in the front hallways, shattering all of the front windows and ripping away most of the foundation of the front of the property. This tyrannical campaign of segregation and bombing of property by Whites, aimed at us, must stop! These people want to halt our progress and stop us from improving our position and holdings in Chicago."

The Calumet property was one of the few black owned and operated, large apartment buildings in the Black Belt. It had been in the process of transition with Blacks gradually replacing the white tenants and had been a source of pride to the community. It was also one of the largest assets of the defunct Woodfolk Savings Bank. Some of P.W.'s employees and neighbors had pleaded with him for months to help them get their money back from this bank. There were many issues at stake here: the bombings, the oppression of the black community, the housing shortage, and the recovery of the Woodfolk assets. But, tonight only the bombings were under discussion. Woodfolk was mindful of all of these pressures. He, too, had sought to fade into the background and live comfortably in a better neighborhood. This was what the Calumet property represented to this crowd. They did not know the area had recently been re-zoned from residential to commercial, to deal with what was viewed as the black invasion by politicians eager to get elected by keeping the racial ferment stirred up. These politicians were indifferent

3

or ignorant of the different life styles of the unskilled, un-tutored recent arrivals and those of the black-working class, or they did not want to be reminded of their own lowly social beginnings. Woodfolk focused his remaining remarks more sharply on the details of the destruction of the property to unite the audience to their common cause of the search for methods to deal with further destruction sure to come.

"Tenants are making every effort to comfort each other," he remarked. "Some have temporarily doubled up. They're using the rear doorways off the alley and their back porches for entrances and exits, as the front has had to be blocked off. It is not safe. The windows are being boarded up to shut out this February cold until the glass can be replaced."

"The suffering and shock to the families has been cata-strophic. It is unbelievable . . . even though I had been warned, . . . yes, yes, I'd been warned," he said in a hushed voice to the audience. "I'd gone to the police after my tenants were warned that the building was going to be bombed. I requested protection, but I got no protection; nor were any arrests made after the police showed up and the bombings occurred anyway. All of you should know that the Hyde Park Property Owners Association and the Property Owners Pro-tective Association appear to be linked to the police. We know that most of the real estate dealers in the Grand Boulevard District from 39th Street to 63rd Street and from Michigan Avenue to Cottage Grove Avenue are members of the Con-solidated Hyde Park and Kenwood Districts. We know that they beef up these slandering stories saying that letting us move into areas out south is upsetting the property values and causing them to go down. But, we are not destroying property, they are! And we are being blamed for all of this hellish bombing."

It was a grim meeting. Fears were voiced, including the fear of more bombings, fear of refused renewals on leases, and fear of real estate men preferring to let their property go idle rather than take the mounting risks. There was much more talk about the well-organized, well-to-do Whites in the sur-rounding territory, how they were preparing to squeeze Blacks into the Black Belt forever, comparisons of techniques

4

used in the bombings of other buildings, and the many ways the real estate men, black and white, were being intimidated by the powerful bitter Whites to stop selling to black families. No solutions were reached, but tentative plans were made to hold another meeting in a few weeks in a much larger hall, in view of the crowd. Someone suggested the 8th Regiment Armory.

P.W. left the meeting reflecting on Woodfolk's words and the conflicts and rage expressed, both from the platform and from the audience. "What can be done? What can I do?" he wondered. "Chicago is a bitter city with hatred everywhere. Where does one begin in a place like this?

One problem is we really do believe that Whites are more capable and trustworthy than Blacks," he thought, and he recalled the incident of the little black newsboy named Carson who came into the factory shortly after the Woodfolk Bank failure. P.W. never forgot his own newspaper boy days back in Columbus . . . he remembered the help given him. On that particular day, Carson hung around with a distant, older-than-his-age look in his eyes. The boy's attitude had disturbed P.W. for some reason.

"Son, did you lose money or a customer?"

"Oh, no sir," Carson replied, "I was just thinking!" Although he was only ten years old, he seemed much older. P.W. thought of his own young son and thanked providence that he would not have to carry such a burden and responsibility prematurely. He wondered about all the other little black boys in Chicago who, like Carson, were too busy being men ever to get a chance at being just plain little boys with birthday parties and picnics and vacations and big Christmases. . . "What's wrong, son?" he asked.

"Well, I was just thinking about something my aunt said to me when I told her that the man at the bank said I didn't have no more money there."

"You had money in the bank, son?" P.W. interrupted.

"Yes, sir," Carson's voice trembled a bit, "I had $50." He was sobbing now and P.W. got up from his desk and went to him, squatting to hold him by his shoulders. "My aunt said . . . she would have a colored preacher . . . she would

5

have a colored lawyer . . . she would have a colored doctor—
sometimes. But, she said colored bankers just can't be
trusted; they don't know how to take care of your money."

P.W. wondered where one began trying to reach the minds
of the next generation when their elders were so misguided
and psychologically enslaved. Why had this child's aunt
spoken to him in such a way? Did she realize at all how
damaging her statements had been to the little boy? Again he
thought of the turmoil and change at the time of his move to
Chicago and the riots and violence in the streets that brought
terror, panic and hunger to the Black Belt. He reviewed the
circumstances of his employees and neighbors. People had
lost money in local, privately owned black banks like Woodfolk Savings Bank, which collapsed after the riots produced a
run on their funds. It had been worse during the riots when
the white-owned businesses shut down, bringing unemployment, and most people had their money in white-owned
banks in the Loop where it was perilous for them to go. Now
depositors of the privately owned Woodfolk Savings Bank
were asking P.W. to help them get their money back, fearful
of losing everything they had.

P.W. shook his head almost in disbelief at all the misery.
"Chicago was a little village just 75 years ago. Now it is a
thriving big city as a result of countless new people: the Irish,
the Germans, the Poles, the Russians, and the Italians from
Europe, as well as the many waves of Southern Blacks from
the plantations who have come here to find a better life. All of
them have brought with their migration a vigor, zeal, and
determination—and this is good!" he said to himself, searching for an understanding of his new home, Chicago, and
hoping his young family would be safe and prosper here.

He felt his blood run fast with eagerness to push towards
something, but what, he did not know. Chicago had been built
on mud. The people had filled it in with clay from the Chicago
River. "There is a drive and a determination here which is
good, but the people don't communicate. They are afraid of
each other and this must stop! My family and my people must
be safe."

He knew there were no easy answers; the lack of loyalty

among the black people was as great as the animosity between the various races of the city. Woodfolk was a black
banker, the black banker of whom the newsboy had spoken
when his aunt said, "No colored man could ever handle my
money." How many black persons would have a chance with
this kind of anti-Negro talk circulating in their homes.

He continued driving to the house. The meeting had stirred
him more than he had expected and he was angry. How could
Woodfolk succeed as a banker when he was being undermined from within the very community he was trying to
serve? There had been too little confidence in what he was
trying to do. Which was worse . . . intimidation by outsiders
or undermining from within! He had heard grumblings in the
audience. Some had commented that Woodfolk had not yet
fully explained what had happened to their money in that
bank he had. Some whispered that he got what was coming to
him. P.W. thought that maybe someone other than Woodfolk
should have reported to the audience about the bombing of
the Calumet property since it was apparently a part of the
defunct holdings.

"We must build from within, " he thought. As he parked the
car in front of the house, he found that he was still very
agitated. Words of doubt were always annoying to P.W. In a
flash, they took him back to his childhood when he had felt
helpless and trapped in the face of doubts expressed by
strangers, both black and white, doubts about whether he
could accomplish much in life, doubts that he would have
much of a future. He had carried his experiences home to his
mother who had inspired him to be polite and sincere. She
had told him how much it meant to her to be the "mother of
Pearl" and he had been comforted to continue with his aims
and to prove to others what his place was by his performance.

He had learned early that he had to get along with Whites.
But, on the other hand, he had still refused to accept outsiders' doubts and their definition of what his place should be. As
he had risen in responsibilities, he had acquired the habit of
success. He was able to set an example and to lead by
inspiring and projecting confidence in others.

He thought of his mother again. She had taught him the

7

meaning of family loyalty and black identity. From her he had learned to respect his heritage, to be proud of himself and his achievements.

The bombings had brought in their wake pledges of unity and cooperation in the Black Belt which were, however, soon forgotten. P.W. recalled the vivid newspaper accounts of the Woodfolk Bank collapse, how stirringly this message had been brought to the black people through the Negro press. Now Attorney Lucas had told him there was little interest in the bank, and that it was only the victims of the collapse who really cared and clamored for their claims. He had observed how frightened and beaten Woodfolk had looked as he spoke of the bombings. Woodfolk had not mentioned the bank collapse, but the scars of the two great crises he had been through had been visible during the meeting.

P.W. was almost pleased that he had not addressed the audience as Attorney Lucas had suggested. Lucas was Woodfolk's attorney in his bankruptcy case and when he saw P.W. at the meeting he had urged him to make a few comments toward the close of the session. But others had been verbose, the hour had grown late, and P.W. had not had a chance to speak.

He sat at the wheel of the car in front of the house on Forrestville Avenue for a long time because he did not want to spread the gloom of the meeting over the family. "Enlightened use of opportunity is the answer, but where is the opportunity here in Chicago?" he questioned. It occurred to him that maybe he did not know enough about the details of the bank case. In many ways he was like all of the others; most of what he knew he had read about in the newspapers or heard from those around him. Maybe there were exaggerations or distortions for one reason or another. He had been a newspaper publisher, so he knew how reporting is altered and directed; one had to go to the source.

P.W. remembered the final bitter struggles of Booker T. Washington, the "Wizard of Tuskegee," who passed away in 1915, only a few years before. P.W. felt that his people were more vulnerable now than ever. He recognized their need for full legal equality, respect and protection as a group, but he was dismayed that Booker T. Washington's stress on economic survival and black capitalism was being so completely renounced.

Booker T. Washington was born into bondage on a plantation in Franklin County, Virginia to a slave mother and slave-owner white father in 1856, seven years before the Emancipation Proclamation. He labored as a child alongside his mother in the salt mines of West Virginia, and as a janitor worked his way through a Virginia trade school, Hampton Normal and Agricultural Institute, graduating in 1875. In 1881 he opened a normal school as the sole teacher for rural Negroes in a rickety, leaky church in Alabama. In between reading, writing, and other studies, he and his students together built Tuskegee Institute. Eventually it became internationally famous as a model agricultural and industrial school with 60 buildings and an endowment of nearly 3 million dollars for the education of the "head, heart, and hand" of black youth. Throughout his career he identified with the poor, untutored blacks of the rural South and remained a symbol of their hopes. He fully believed in self-help, industrial training, and the development of proper work habits for physical survival. He felt that these skills were more necessary than academic liberal arts education and that agitation for social equality in this post-slavery period was "extreme folly." In addressing the Cotton States Atlanta Exposition in 1895, the 39 year old President of Tuskegee Institute had declared, "In all things that are social, we can be as separate as the fingers, yet one as the hand in all things essential for mutual progress."

Washington wielded great power in all racial matters throughout the land for many years. His ideas were supported by governmental, industrial and educational leaders everywhere. He participated in the establishment of the Phelps Stokes Fund, the Carnegie Foundation, and the Rosenthal Fund. He secured support for the training of colored teachers, the construction of thousands of public schools for Negro children in the rural southern counties, and fellowships for Negro educational leaders in the South and

North in exchange for his compromise position on the question of social equality. He dined at the White House, was a guest of Queen Victoria at Windsor Castle, received an honorary degree at Harvard University, and money from the Carnegie Fund. President Theodore Roosevelt, in particular, hoped to develop his black political ties, to reconcile the South and the North, and strengthen the white Southern Republican Party through the use of Booker T. Washington's acceptance of the "separate but equal" approach.

But at the turn of the century, white Protestant racism was on the increase. With the rebirth of the Ku Klux Klan, the hooded night riders were terrorizing colored people, tarring and feathering, lynching, and violating civil and political rights, especially in the South. Nearly fifty million North European born immigrants had poured into the United States during the last half of the nineteenth century, competing with those Blacks emerging from the medieval slave society of the rural south for space and economic survival. After the Spanish-American War in 1898, these immigrants included millions of Southeastern Europeans of Italian, Slavic, and Russian origin, as well as Hispanics and other people of color from the Caribbean and Pacific Islands, resulting in more vicious anti-Black, anti-Catholic, and anti-Jewish terrorism spreading throughout the land, but especially in the South.

Adjustment had been smoother in Columbus than in many other urban northern areas, because Columbus was never really a city of foreign-born immigrants. In Columbus, the immigrants were "home-grown" from the border states and the rural areas of Ohio which accounted for its more stable, settled and content black and white populations, with more moderate ways of doing things. Columbus never had any race riots, bombings, or lynchings, even in the early part of the twentieth century, the most radically oppressive years in the United States. But Booker T. Washington's views were increasingly seen as a sellout to oppressive Whites by Blacks who retreated from open economic competition at the very time the Southern situation was worsening. Black capitalism began to lose favor. Washington's all-colored National Negro

Business League was denounced as a tool for personal aggrandizement even in Columbus, one of Washington's strongholds, where P.W. had been his most loyal supporter among the powerful "young boosters."

All over the nation black people and leaders, including the spokesman from the emerging National Association for the Advancement of Colored People, came forth to fight against lynching, discrimination, and segregation for civil and political rights through the courts. This new movement, led by W.E.B. DuBois, aimed to make a direct and open attack on civil and political abuses and to deal with racism through legal means in a court structure seeking to eliminate the inequities facing the struggling black masses in America within the system of due legal process. However, the sophisticated legal process was even less understood by Blacks, in general, than the marketplace laws of supply and demand. But DuBois felt that Washington was apologizing for the injustices in the North and South and opposing higher education of the "talented tenth" brighter Blacks. DuBois became one of the founders of the NAACP, the champion for academic liberal arts higher education and the interracial protest movement. These two perspectives, as represented by Washington and DuBois, might have been complementary (blue collar/white collar; vocational/academic) but, unfortunately, became antagonistic.

William Edward Burghardt DuBois, a thin aristocratic scholar, was born in 1868 in Great Barrington, Massachusetts of African, Dutch, and French ancestry. He was a scholarly student at Fisk University and had earned his doctorate as the first Black to receive a Ph.D. at Harvard University in 1895 after studying two years at the University of Berlin. Subsequently, he held three other doctorates. For thirteen years he headed the Department of History and Economics at Atlanta University where he wrote many articles and books including *The Souls of Black Folk,* a popular collection of essays, which was eventually translated abroad and went into 28 editions. Beginning in 1906, he rallied the forces of Negro militants and intellectuals to the Niagra

11

Movement, which laid the foundation for the NAACP. "We claim for ourselves every single right that belongs to a free born American, political, civil and social, and until we get these rights we will never cease to protest and assail the ears of America." The savage lynchings in Springfield, Illinois in 1909 sparked a conference of white liberals "to discuss present evils," and led to the organization of the NAACP, the interracial protest movement merging the forces of black intellectual militants and white liberals. DuBois became the Director of Publicity and Research and Editor of the *Crisis,* the official journal of the NAACP. He opposed Washington's stranglehold on public opinion and his refusal to criticize the abuse and terrorizing of Blacks which went unpunished in the South. He inspired black youths all over the world to develop their talents to the optimum, serving as an example through his writings, teachings, travels and debates with Washington.

By early 1920, fifteen years had passed since the northerly migration of laborers from the Southern farms and villages had begun, and the tensions between the races in Chicago had been building up for an even longer period. The doctrine of Anglo-Saxon superiority was being reinforced. The southern race policy of using the Negro as the national scapegoat to justify white supremacy was being heralded as the policy of the National Administration ever since the Spanish-American War with the United States acquisition of some eight million colored people of the Caribbean and Pacific Islands. Although total disfranchisement and the adoption of severe segregation laws such as existed in the South were measures never applied in Chicago, crushing discrimination practices in the labor market, in employment and in housing had been widespread.

P.W. had been too busy setting up home and factory since his arrival from Columbus, just three short years ago, to get involved with community problems. He felt he did not fully understand the situation. His thoughts returned to the bank meeting he had attended that night. Maybe he should go to the Woodfolk Bank hearings as his friends had urged him to do; perhaps there he could learn. Still, he sat in the car in the darkness of the night. The house glowed through the windows and the sounds of children's voices shifted outward. He smiled in thinking of his precious newborn daughter, Minnie Belle Edwina. She was three weeks old and mother and baby were doing fine. He climbed out of the car and went into the house to join the family.

P.W. was born to James and Julia Chavers in Columbus, Ohio in 1876, fourteen years after the Emancipation Proclamation. The name Pearl he retained through his childhood, but somehow, once he had crossed into adulthood, he was generally referred to as P.W., the abbreviation for Pearl William, by his family and close friends. He grew up in the district called "Blackberry Patch," the south end of town where most of the Blacks lived. P.W. rarely spoke of his antecedents, but I remember questioning him and was told that the Chavers family were a free colored people of French Huguenot descent who had migrated to this country as mulatto indentured servants around 1700. When there was pressure on free people of color to leave the South or revert to slavery, his branch of the Chavers family moved from town to town in North Carolina. Julia and James had eight children while living in Chatham County, North Carolina. Eventually they settled in Columbus, Ohio around 1867, where they had three more. P.W., the youngest born to them, was an infant when his father, James, passed away a few years after the family pushed northward, leaving Julia with three daughters and three sons still living at home.

At an early age, P.W. worked to help his mother with the family expenses by selling newspapers and being active in the community. He would invest in a large supply of newspapers and set up routes for other boys to deliver them, making a profit on his investment. The business knack of making a dollar was encouraged by some who saw him. "Maybe it's because I was born in 1876, exactly 100 years after the Declaration of Independence," he would sometimes say in explaining the eager independent spirit he evidenced as a child.

13

He told me of others who saw him trying to make money as a young newsboy and their comments that it was too bad he was a Negro, for his talents would be wasted, his people would not appreciate him and his chances of expressing these talents would be thwarted. He would stiffen at the thought of being expected to resent or be ashamed of his heritage. These insinuations fired in him a determination to prove this thinking fallacious and a drive to do something significant in order to refute these remarks.

While working his way through Hudson College, a private business college, studying law and banking, P.W. observed the great gap between the positions in society of his people and others in the community. Studying history he learned the real horrors of that "peculiar institution," slavery for profit, that had existed in America for 3½ centuries. When a Dutch ship landed 20 Africans in 1619 at Jamestown Colony, the African slave trade was already over a hundred years old. Black slavery had already created great wealth in Europe during the 15th century. It was a dehumanizing practice culminating in the cruelest system of slavery the world had ever experienced; a major source of capital and labor in America by the end of the 17th century. By this time there were twice as many Africans as Whites on the American continent and the Caribbean. Outnumbered, Whites lived in fear of potential uprisings. The white settlers even tried to enslave the Carib Indians, but they perished under the brutal conditions. The poor Whites, prisoners, and debtors that England had sent originally to labor in the colonies had been unsuccessful because Whites could run away and thus lose their indentured status. One reason black slavery worked was because Blacks came from African civilizations where slaves (generally acquired as captives of war) had certain rights and were conditioned to an elaborate hierarchy of social institutions that prepared them for a disciplined way of life. Often the status of slavery was not permanent. But in early America, this black slave labor from Africa (in contrast to white slaves) could not run away and escape detection because of skin color, and the supply was considered inexhaustible. The triangular trading system carried manufactured and metal goods from England to Africa in exchange for African slaves, who were exported to the West Indies and American colonies, including New England, in exchange for sugar, molasses and rum. During the 18th century, seven million Africans were abducted or sold, and slave trade was considered one of the world's greatest businesses. By 1850, three-fourths of the world's supply of cotton came from Southern plantations made possible by black slave labor. Before this "peculiar institution" was finished, nearly fifteen million Africans had been brought to North America; how many were lost en route will never be known.

African rulers supplied African slaves by raids on interior villages. Slave agents bought only healthy slaves carefully examined for strength and youthfulness. They were tied, fettered together, and branded while awaiting transfer to ships for the "Middle Voyage" from the African coast to the Caribbean or American mainland. Once on board, the slaves were stacked like log wood in the slave galley, secured by chains and packed under conditions resembling a slaughter house. They lacked oxygen and space, and were provided with spoiled food and stagnant water for the voyage which took 40 to 60 days. Slave deaths on the "Middle Voyage" were sometimes as high as two-thirds of the slave load because of suicide, dysentery, small pox, and other communicable diseases raging aboard by the time the ship reached the West Indies.

Fifty million of the youngest, strongest, and therefore the most profitable Blacks were thus taken from the continent of Africa and brought to the Americas. This traffic in human beings escalated after the invention of the cotton gin in 1793, the purchase of the Louisiana Territory by the United States in 1803, and the opening of the great sugar and cotton plantations in Alabama and Mississippi "Black Belts," a term referring to the color of the soil .

The slave uprising led by Toussaint L'Ouverture in 1791, and his defeat of the French armies in Haiti, caused sufficient panic for the United States and England to outlaw the importation of slaves by 1808. But this failed to stem the heavy flow of slaves. As prices soared, slave smuggling increased.

African slaves were landing on the American coast as late as 1859. The upper Southern states became exporters of slaves to the Deep South and the Southwestern states between 1830 and 1860, when they were completely dependent upon interstate slave trade. Slave breeding and slave rearing became the most remunerative and approved means of increasing plantation capital. Conditions worsened as the plantations grew in size. They were constantly in debt, poorly managed, and wholly dependent upon slave power since the system created and reinforced an insatiable demand for young, fertile "good breeder" slaves to multiply the value of the planter's capital. Thus, slaves were both capital and labor held in bondage. In the South, the more slaves a man owned the more he was respected.

Under this system, slaves were stripped of their African culture. They were sold away by slave traders who were sometimes itinerant auctioneers or commission merchants and sometimes entrepreneurs operating in fashionable hotels maintaining slave prisons, housing the slaves (their own and other traders) and buying and selling for speculation and resale. Here the slaves would be sold away from their mothers, children, husbands and families, stripped of their names, language, tribal customs and all rituals of feeling and belonging, bound forever to a heritage of sub-human status with no escape. The great mass of slaves worked the cotton, tobacco and rice plantation fields while thousands of others built the railroads. They labored in the quarries, coal, iron, and salt mines, built houses, docks and bridges and stoked the fires on river boats; some were blacksmiths, carpenters, and house servants. The slave-owner planter would hire a white overseer to supervise the work and a head slave-driver to oversee the slave driving in the larger plantations. The slaves knew a life of hard, unremitting heavy toil for 16 hours per day with no pay; they were driven from dawn to dusk by an overseer and the lash of the whip. On the plantation, suspicion and envy would well up between the field hands and the house servants, but their destinies were the same. They were born, lived, bred, and died in the crude shacks on "slave row" of the plantation where they slept on beds of corn shuck and ate corn meal, fat back and molasses. They were never allowed to read or write, possess firearms, visit free Blacks or Whites or to assemble. Their whole lives were spent within the plantation unless, after years of service, they were sold away again to pay plantation debts, settle a will or enhance the profiteering of their master, never to see their loved ones again. This brutal system of slave power was enforced by whipping, branding, and maiming. The slave was reduced to the sub-human status of sexually exploited chattel who performed unremunerated toil while enhancing his master's wealth on American soil. In the words of Thomas Jefferson, slavery was "a perpetual exercise of the most boisterous passions, the most unremitting despotism on the one part, and degrading submission on the other" . . . "the child looks on, and thus nursed, educated, and daily exercised in tyranny, cannot but be stamped by it with odious peculiarities."

Not all Whites lived like royalty on plantations. The bulk of the Whites, in fact, were poor tenant farmers. In the South, they were overwhelmingly old-line Protestants of Scotch, Irish, or British origin, who were consumed with arrogant pride and hatred and fiercely hostile towards anyone they saw as their natural enemies, including Whites of other than Protestant religions. These tenant farmers, illiterate and miserably poor, formed the slave patrol which guarded against unlawful assembly of Blacks. Slave revolts did occur and create great panic in the South, sometimes requiring the Federal Troops to check the insurrection excitement, as in the Nat Turner Revolt of 1831, but betrayal of other frightened slaves always squelched the revolts in the United States.

The thought of combining gradual emancipation with de-portation of free Negroes to Africa led a group of prominent white Americans to persuade Congress to purchase territory in Africa which they named "Liberia". They felt their scheme, which was based on the aim of Christianizing Africa with the settlement of free Blacks, would encourage slave holders to free their slaves. Actually 1400 were returned to Liberia by 1830, but the movement eventually died out as the value of slaves increased. Free Blacks were ordered to leave the borders of the Upper South or be reenslaved, as their presence was interfering with the more lucrative interstate traffic in human cargo. There were great slavery debates over the admission of new states into the Union, and abolition protest movements were led by white militants such as Wendell Phillips, the great orator, and William Lloyd Garrison, one of the founders of the American Anti-Slavery Society, who discovered Fredrick Douglass, the foremost Negro abolitionist, an ex-slave.

There were free-born Negroes, like the Chavers family. Some purchased their freedom and others were emancipated at the death of their master, like the Thomas Jefferson slaves. But the legal status of free Negroes was always tenuous. In the South, the free Black lived under police state conditions with his movements under constant surveillance. He was required to carry a certificate of freedom and to register his name with the police or court authorities. His migration to another Southern state was restricted or prohibited. He could not entertain slaves; his motives were suspect. He could not serve on a jury or give testimony against Whites; therefore, if overtaken by a slave catcher, he had little chance of escape. By 1835 the Constitutions in the three Southern states that allowed the franchise to free Blacks were amended to deprive him of the right to vote. The Northern response to the presence of free Blacks was not much better. Throughout the land there were legal restrictions on his movement, oppression and segregation in his use of public accomodations, and limitation to his voting rights, where they existed. Free Blacks were subjected to mob violence and haunted by the fear of reenslavement, especially as slave stealing mounted. All of the anti-slavery efforts culminated in the Dred Scott verdict in 1857 by a five to four decision of the Supreme Court of the United States: "Negroes had no rights which the white man was bound to respect and the Constitution was never meant to include Negroes."

Over the question of slavery, and its moral and economic consequences, the North and the South went to war in 1861. The Emancipation Proclamation, which was issued in the midst of America's Civil War, decreed the freedom of all slaves, effective January, 1863, in order to save the Union, to prevent foreign intervention, and to enlist world opinion on behalf of the North, which at the time was losing the war. This Proclamation freed four million slaves living in the heart of the feudal South. Thus they were freed from their masters and given American citizenship.But they were ill-equipped without education, stripped of family ties and without a tradition of communication or any means of survival as a group in a competitive, technically oriented, hostile climate. In 1863, after 3½ centuries of bondage, the American slave was officially free . . . but he knew no other homeland, no other language, no other culture and had no knowledge of how to use and protect this American citizenship. The slave was made free, but not equal, under the laws or customs of the land.

Only half the job was done, thought P.W. as he studied the history of slavery from which his people had so recently emerged. Three decades had passed since the Emancipation Proclamation.

He aimed to make use of the opportunities available to him. In college he struggled to learn all he could concerning the structures of business, law and economic processes. He learned how to form a corporation and how to float and use stocks and bonds. P.W.'s methods were typically Ohioan: orderly, moderate and gradual, applying vision geared to opportunity that he perceived in the world around him. His mind was attuned to do things in a big way, to combine business enterprise with an uplift movement and philanthropy, moving within the system, the established order, the customs and the law. As soon as he was old enough to vote he was sent to the Republican National Convention as a delegate where he met the notables of the day, including Booker T. Washington. They came to know each other, and P.W. found himself in accord with many of his ideas.

After college, P.W.'s first enterprise was the establishment of a newspaper, *The Columbus Standard*, in 1901. This was later renamed *The Ohio Standard World* which came to include supplements in Dayton, Cincinnati, Toledo, and Springfield, Ohio. As editor of the paper he campaigned for effective use of the ballot by black citizens in order to improve their position in society. As one of the "young boosters," a group of black men in Columbus with new ideas, he advocated Booker T. Washington's concept of capitalism and later affiliated with Washington's National Negro Business League. He traveled throughout the Midwest to cities like Cleveland, Cincinnati, and Pittsburgh. It was during these years that he met Nahum Brascher, a writer from Cleveland, who later moved to Columbus assisting P.W. as his secretary. They wrote and spoke about their feelings that commerce and industry were key to dissolving the morass of poverty and idleness in the black urban communities. They shared the view that the clustering of people racially and ethnically was something very natural; that people of similar heritage and common struggles understand and prefer each other in working out solutions to their common problems in a familiar way. Although legal segregation was false, repugnant, and exploitative to P.W., he felt that natural clustering could lead to a channeling of energy and thought and, thereby, to strength and peoplehood.

During these first twenty years of his career he built a reputation as a business and political leader. In addition to publishing pamphlets and a newspaper, and conducting, in partnership, his real estate business, in 1905 he established a ladies garment factory. Once his factory had been set up, he would sometimes think back to his growing up years and comment lightly on how lucky he had been to be favored by those individuals in the Jewish community who had taught him the fundamentals of manufacturing. That which people offered willingly and was constructive, he would accept and use effectively.

At one point in his Columbus career, he took over responsibility as President of the Board of Directors for the Home For Aged Colored People, raising funds and conducting mass meetings in contact with local officials who included the Mayor and the Governor. He knew how to apply pressure and how to make a strategic retreat when anticipating non-involvement by a prospect. Mainly, he knew intuitively how to salvage his gains when faced with some kind of loss.

Once, when there was controversy about one of his exposi-

Left to right: P.W. Chavers, Delegate to Republican National Convention, 1908, Rev. W. L. Taylor, Grand Worthy Master of the True Reformers, Emmett J. Scott, Booker T. Washington's Secretary (Later, Special Assistant to Secretary of War during World War I), Seated: Booker T. Washington, President, Tuskeegee Institute.

21

tions, he made a survey to get the facts and eventually used the data collected in his pamphlet, *Conditions That Confront The Colored Race, 1908*. He established independent political connections and good relationships with national leaders in Washington, D.C. such as Vice President Charles Fairbanks, Congressman Charles Dick of Ohio, and Booker T. Washington, as well as Governor A. L. Harris. He would interest them in his projects, get them to make speeches at his meetings, and ask them to give written endorsements of his enterprises. In 1907 he was most proud of organizing and developing the Lincoln Ohio Industrial Training School for Colored Youth. There he provided employment opportunities to countless black youngsters with special emphasis upon the needs of the poor, unskilled young migrant black women pouring into Columbus from the rural South. The students were taught the practical skills of dressmaking, shorthand, typing, cooking, and domestic service free of charge. Then they were placed on jobs through the employment bureau of his school. My grandmother Julia served as a matron of the institution, which accommodated forty students at a time and was always oversubscribed by a continuing flow of eager youths. Those showing interest and ability would be employed in P.W.'s factory. The food and clothing produced were sold to help in fund-raising. P.W. brought in prestigious citizens to serve on the Board of Trustees and staged large expositions to advertise black economic creativity.

Basically gregarious and materialistically pragmatic, nonetheless, P.W. seemed always to have one foot in his own idealistic world. That he could be the catalyst for the realization of progress brought him great joy. But his generosity and tireless magnanimity struck some as foolish. His first wife of five years apparently became tired of his dedication to altruistic causes. They separated when he was 25 years old and later divorced. He spent many years of loneliness before he met my mother, Minnie, when he was 35 and she 31. P.W. and Minnie looked more alike than the children eventually born to them. Each was a blend of the bloods of three continents: Africa, America, and Europe.

P.W.'s Ladies Garment Factory, Columbus, 1905

P.W.'s Real Estate Partnership, 1906

Lincoln Ohio Industrial Training School for Colored Youth,
Advisory Board, 1907

Minnie met Pearl William Chavers at a resort near Chicago when he was there as delegate of the Republican Party in 1912. Madrue Pannell, her favorite cousin, introduced them. Minnie was overwhelmed by P.W.'s elegant bearing, his persuasive manner, and noble ideas. After one year of courtship, they were married and settled in Columbus, Ohio. P.W. brought his bride to live among the folks he had always known. But Minnie found the life very insulated and uninspiring compared to life in Chicago, where she had lived

25

THE WEDDING, June 18, 1913

Left to right: Nahum Brascher, P.W.'s Secretary, Dr. Harry Garnes, best man, Madrue Pannell, maid of honor, P.W., the groom, Minnie, the bride, Tyler Calloway, bride's father, Nellie Calloway, bride's sister, George Calloway, bride's brother, Cleo Davis, groom's cousin. Front left: flower girl, name unknown.

and worked as a dressmaker for many years. Minnie's restlessness increased after the birth of her first child, my brother Bill. She yearned to return to Chicago to be near her relatives and friends. P.W.'s mother and older brother had passed away a few years earlier, hence he felt fewer family and emotional ties to Columbus.

Pressures poured in from many sides. P.W.'s thinking about future plans for expansion of his Columbus factory was being affected by the migration of unskilled Blacks from the rural South to Chicago, now considered by many as the "Promised Land." Destructive floods in the Deep South had brought the collapse of the cotton market, shifting not only labor supply, but goods and services, and therefore prices. Minnie prevailed upon P.W. to move to Chicago where he could have an even greater role in the destiny of his people and where she had some family, at least cousins. She could again become a part of the gay life of the Negro society she had known. In March, 1917, three months after my birth, P.W. packed his factory and family to make the move to Chicago.

But Chicago had changed. This move was to be, in many ways, a new beginning for Minnie too. In her entire young lifetime she had been sheltered from the ethnic and economic polarities to which she was now fully exposed by living in the Black Belt. She had known cordial relations in the quiet Morgan Park area where she lived for many years with her cousins, the Pannells. There, she was protected from the rugged Chicago life by her position in the family and by her charming ways. Now she was to come face to face with the Black Belt which she was willing to do for P.W. In some ways, P.W. had become not only her husband and companion but her father-protector as well. She was his partner and help-mate and for his sake she did not insist on living in the safe areas where she had before, like Englewood and Morgan Park. As the ultimate measure of her devotion, she was willing to live in the Black Belt, that environment completely alien to any she had ever known.

In April, 1917, as P.W. and Minnie were in the midst of unpacking the stock at the factory on 43rd Street, President

Minnie in Columbus, 1914

The Chavers family begins: P.W., Minnie and Bill, 1915

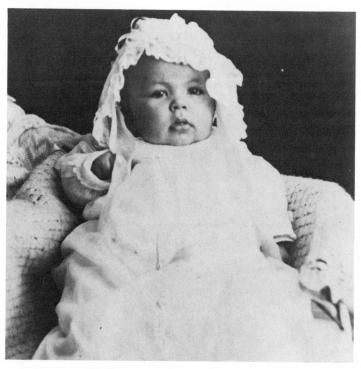

Madrue, age 5 months, 1917

Wilson's message to Congress that war had begun reached them by way of a newsboy yelling, "Extra! Extra! Extra! Read All About It . . . WAR WITH GERMANY!!!" There were proposals to forbid Negroes to fight as men in the war and to be forced to work on farms instead. Two months after the declaration of war, bombings in the Black Belt community sounded the violent outbreak of the bitter tensions between the races.

Black workers were frozen out of trade-union apprentice programs and segregated to subordinate projects with no efforts made to find jobs for them when they were not completely excluded. Or they were used exclusively as strikebreakers, as during the bitter stockyards' strike and the

30

teamsters' strike of 1905. These conditions had prevailed for many years and now were getting worse. Most black workers were porters, domestics, servants and janitors who were unable to gain a foothold in industry or in commerce. They would be laid off after strikes. Black newspapers had long recognized the exploitative white entrepreneurial practices of luring black workers from remote areas of the South, then using them as strikebreakers to intimidate white workers into submission at the bargaining table, all of which set off waves of racial conflict on the job front.

Now tension was everywhere, with those who had somehow managed to improve their economic position moving into better neighborhoods where they were openly confronted with hostility. The pattern of intimidation was well orchestrated. The real estate dealers selling or renting properties to Blacks and Negro bankers making loans on black-owned properties or financing mortgages were the targets. Systematic warnings to the community by unidentified perpetrators about planned attacks would be circulated well in advance, giving dates and places where explosions would take place, to frighten the middle-class Blacks out of the better neighborhoods. The Black Belt would ask for protection, but no arrests would be made.

P.W. and Minnie were drawn closer together, caught in this web of tensions, bombings, bomb scares and war hysteria, with their young family and a newly reestablished factory in a community alien to both. But the war caused prices to soar, bringing prosperity to them and accelerating their establishment in their new community. By July, 1919, when the bloody race riots broke out, Minnie was pregnant with her third child.

On that infamous Sunday summer day, the stone and bottle throwing at the 29th Street bathing beach on the water's edge of Lake Michigan burst into hell's fury when the police refused to arrest the young white murderers of a 17 year-old Black who had drifted into the white section of the beach. Chicago beaches were strictly segregated. It was Sunday, July 27th, and the worst race riot in the nation's history had begun. Within one week of the horrible reign of terror, mob rule and lynch law, there were 38 bloody murders, 537 persons injured, 2000 homes destroyed, and the entire city was completely paralyzed by the lawless rioting in the streets.

Newspapers of the day tell of the vicious, law-defying elements clutching at each other's throats like "mad demons and blood thirsty savages committing hellish crimes and lawless deeds." Colored men and women were dragged from street cars and shot or clubbed to death in all parts of the city by white youths encouraged by politicians who financed their "athletic clubs." Trained to invade black neighborhoods long before this mob violence started, these white youths would pull the electrified public streetcars from their wires and beat the black passengers inside, or they would roam the streets spraying bullets from their cars, intimidating black and white citizens alike.

The focal points of these onslaughts were the transfer intersections along the streetcar lines. Passengers were dragged to the exits of cars and thrown to the streets where they were clubbed or shot. The police were unable and unwilling to deal with the escalating anarchy. A streetcar strike halted public transportation, but failed to stop the riot. Blacks were hunted down, beaten, and shot as they walked to and from their jobs in the downtown business district and the stockyards. On Wednesday of that week, Mayor "Big Bill" Thompson finally called for the National Guard. It took 6000 State Troops to bring order and control to the city of Chicago.

Shocked by this anarchy, P.W. would sit in his office at the factory thinking of the reign of terror and the violence it had brought to the Black Belt. He could have been killed crossing the street one morning when a white mob approached him in front of the factory on 43rd Street, where there was a busy streetcar line. Each car that passed his factory was loaded with white youths attacking colored women and men. Minnie's fears for P.W.'s safety mounted each day as he went to the factory to keep it open as an example of stability in the tense, frightened community.

Some of his employees, who feared leaving their homes and venturing into the streets, would complain because he kept the factory open during the riots. Although production was

THE BROAD AX

HEW TO THE LINE; LET THE CHIPS FALL WHERE THEY MAY

Vol. XXIV.   CHICAGO, ILL, SATURDAY, AUGUST 2, 1919.   No. 46

Bloody Anarchy, Murder, Rapine, Race Riots And All Forms Of Lawlessness

Have Stalked Broad Cast, Throughout

Chicago The Past Week; The Vicious And Law Defying Elements In Both The White

And The Colored Races Have Clutched At Each Others Throats Like Mad Demons And Blood

Thirsty Savages. More Than Thirty Lives Lost And Five Hundred Injured.

THIRTY TO FORTY VICTIMS HAVE MET THEIR DEATH AT THE HANDS OF THE MOB THAT NUMBER BEING ALMOST EQUALLY DIVIDED BETWEEN BOTH RACES.

INNOCENT AND LAW ABIDING COLORED MEN, EMPLOYED IN HOTELS AND RESTAURANTS IN THE DOWN TOWN DISTRICT, MURDERED IN COLD BLOOD BY ROVING BANDS OF WHITE RUFFIANS WHO DELIGHT TO BATHE THEIR HANDS IN HUMAN BLOOD.

COLORED MEN AND WOMEN GOING TO AND RETURNING HOME FROM THEIR WORK IN THE VARIOUS SECTIONS OF THE CITY, WERE DRAGGED FROM THE STREET CARS AND BEATEN OR CLUBBED TO DEATH.

BETWEEN FIVE AND SIX HUNDRED WHITE AND COLORED PEOPLE HAVE SO FAR BEEN INJURED IN THE HORIBLE AND REVOLTING REIGN OF TERROR, WHICH HAS GRIPPED CHICAGO, THE FAIREST OF ALL OF THE CITIES LIKE A DEADLY MALADY.

IT WOULD HAVE BEEN TEN MILLION TIMES BETTER FOR ALL THE CITIZENS OF CHICAGO, IF POLICE OFFICER DANIEL L. CALLAHAN, WOULD HAVE DISCHARGED HIS SWORN DUTY AND PROMPTLY ARRESTED THE WHITE PERSON WHO STRUCK EUGENE WILLIAMS IN THE HEAD WITH A STONE CAUSING HIS DEATH AT THE TWENTY-NINTH STREET BATHING BEACH LAST SUNDAY.

MARTIAL LAW SHOULD HAVE BEEN IMMEDIATELY DECLARED AT THE OUTBREAK OF THE RIOT FOR SEEMINGLY THE POLICE HAVE BEEN UNABLE TO COPE WITH THE GRAVE SITUATION.

UP TO THE PRESENT TIME THE RIOT HAS COST THE TAXPAYERS OF CHICAGO MORE THAN ONE MILLION DOLLARS, WHICH MEANS THAT THE REIGN OF MOB AND LYNCH LAW OR ANARCHY IS AN EXPENSIVE THING TO FOOL WITH.

JULIUS F. TAYLOR AND A LADY WHICH HE WAS ESCORTING HOME, SAVED TWO WHITE MEN FROM BEING BEATEN UP AT 35TH AND INDIANA AVENUE AT 1 O'CLOCK TUESDAY MORNING.

SIX THOUSAND STATE TROOPS ARE NOW IN COMPLETE CONTROL OF CHICAGO AND LAW AND ORDER MUST BE RESTORED AND MAINTAINED AT ANY COST.

HON. CHARLES S. DENEEN

Former Governor of Illinois; one of the foremost citizens in this state and in the city of Chicago, who arrived home from Washington, D. C., late Tuesday evening and without wasting any time he hustled himself to see to it that all the people residing in the 31st ward and in the Town of Lake received ample police protection; that law and order must be restored without delay and maintained at all hazards

It would be utterly impossible at throats like unto madden demons and tals, cafes and at other places in the down-town district were either shot down or murdered in cold blood by roving bands or herds of white ruffians who greatly delight to redden their slimy hands in human blood in an effort to revert back to savagery.

The vast majority of the Colored lawyers and other Colored persons were forced to remain away from their offices and their places of employment in order to save their lives, and avoid running the risk of being mobbed and lynched within the very shadow of the City Hall, but every day the writer unarmed and without any police protection, while the rioting was at high water mark, wended his way through the streets in the down town district rushing in and out of the City Hall, as though his life was not worth a farthing, or was in the least danger, urging and pleading with the Colored persons to be strong or a firm stand in favor of placing the city under martial law or military rule, not for the special benefits or for the safety of any one race of people, but for the safety and for the protection of all of the law abiding citizens of Chicago.

One week ago no sane person would have permitted himself to believe that within less than a week from that time that Colored men and women would be dragged from street cars and shot or clubbed to death in all parts of the city—that decent and friendly disposed white persons would be murdered without any just cause if they attempted to transact any business or even to peaceably walk through the Colored districts and the same fate fell upon the Colored people if their business or work caused them to frequent the districts where the whites resided.

It is estimated that between five and six hundred white and Colored people have been injured one way or another, during the horrible and revolting reign of terror, which has for the past week gripped Chicago, which has always been the heaven of hope and the garden of eden for the Colored people, like a deadly malady.

The citizens of Chicago would have been ten million times better off in every way if Police Officer Daniel L. Callahan would have discharged his sworn duty and promptly arrested his

(Continued on Page 3)

reduced, the factory hummed on. But when all quieted down on 43rd Street, most of the employees admired P.W. for his decision. He would sit in the factory office at the end of the day, reviewing the day's operations and projecting the next day's schedule. Sometimes he would linger at his desk a little longer, to meditate about conditions, thinking of his Columbus factory and what he had been able to do there.

By January, 1920, it had now been three years since the move to Chicago. P.W. was not only the source of economic stability for 14 employees working in his apron and dress factory in the heart of the Black Belt, but also a spiritually stabilizing force in the riot-torn community, providing advice to his neighbors and employees. The emerging financial panic and the intense racial bitterness in Chicago had not interfered with his business, and he had managed to set an example, a small but significant one, for this troubled community, arming himself for the struggles and sacrifices ahead.

That January night when P.W. was alone, his employees' work for the day over for several hours, the telephone on his desk rang with a call from home; Minnie's labor had begun. P.W. closed the desk and prepared to go home to await the arrival of his third child. He braced himself against the cold, blinding snow for the half-block walk home. With a smile on his face, his thoughts were about Minnie now. "She is so brave," he mused. A few weeks earlier sister Nellie had come from New York to be with Minnie for the event. Shortly after her arrival she began to give unsolicited suggestions, which made her stay brief. She packed her things and moved to the Pannells, our Morgan Park cousins, just a few days before. "It's too bad; Minnie had hoped so much to have Nellie near her this time," thought P.W. as he dusted the snow off his coat outside the door.

We were already at Minnie's bedside when P.W. came in. His honey-colored face broke into a warm loving smile as he picked up my brother and me, one in each arm, to receive a kiss from his full round lips. He was an impressive man, handsome and powerful in physique, still showing evidence of the athlete he had been in his younger years. "How is my rose-bud tonight?" he asked, giving me a second kiss.

"Our baby is coming tonight," Bill announced.

"Yes, and as a special treat, you children are going to stay with Aunt Susie across the street," he said as he put us down and walked over to kiss Mother and hold her hand tenderly.

We were prepared; Minnie had told us that Rebecca, her dutiful nurse, would have to give full attention to the newcomer that night. Rebecca had worked in the factory before Minnie's confinement and would be returning as soon as Mother was able to take full charge of the household again. After bidding Mother good-night, we went across the street.

"Come in, y'all," Aunt Susie greeted us warmly with a broad smile.

The immediate problem confronting P.W. now was that of standing by while Minnie labored through the night. He went directly to the bedroom to reassure her that all was well with us at Susan's. "I sometimes wonder what we would do in a crisis without a wonderful neighbor like Susie," he said.

"Yes, dear. It's not easy to have the patience we need for the children," Minnie answered in a soft voice.

"The children help to keep us young," asserted P.W. "They have a special place in the lives of adults. Someday, I want to do something really important for children." Minnie smiled at him and yawned, as she had lost him somewhere between her pains.

He lit his customary cigar and settled back in the comfortable armchair in the parlor, listening for a sound from Minnie's room. Now he was thinking of Minnie's previous childbirths. Bill, their first, was born in a hospital after two days of labor, a hairless, walnut brown baby. Eighteen months later, I arrived, a lusty cream-colored infant with golden ringlets, who reminded P.W. of his mother, Julia. I had been in a hurry, arriving two weeks before due, two days before Christmas, and an hour before the doctor could get to the house, interrupting Minnie while she was trimming the Christmas tree. He smiled at the thoughts of Bill and me, and of the new child on its way into the world.

"There had been difficulty in Columbus too, but at least

The Family Outing, 1917

1920

me at 3½ yrs.   *Jr. at 5*

Madrue and Bill, 1920

there had been no race riots," he thought. "I have not kept in touch with my friends enough; things are so hectic here. Maybe, after the children are older, we can take a trip to Columbus to look up my family and friends." He tiptoed to the bedroom to take a look at Minnie. She was sleeping. Then he went to the kitchen where he found the box of German cookies that the Davises, our Columbus cousins, sent every year at Christmas. As he returned to his chair in the parlor, he thought of how surprised his friends in Columbus would be to see his growing family. Minnie seemed happy enough, but the changes for her had been even greater than for him. After a while he dozed off and was later awakened by Rebecca.

"Mr. Chavers, call the doctor," she urged. "It's time."

Hours later, after the doctor had come and gone, Rebecca came to the parlor door and announced, "Mr. Chavers, you may come in to see your lovely baby girl."

P.W. and Minnie were exceedingly joyous about the new baby but their happiness was short-lived. Ten nights later the Woodfolks' home on Calumet Avenue, not far from our home, was bombed. We children awoke with fright at the great roar in the middle of the night.

2

Woodfolk Bank Trusteeship

P.W.'s factory, a fine establishment for a new arrival, was located on 43rd Street, the center of traffic in a busy residential and retail area, only a half block from our home. Even on a cloudy day, we could see the large double-front windows from our house. It was the only Negro enterprise in the neighborhood.

Father had a thriving business that catered both to wholesale and retail trade. No orders were turned away. Factories would call in orders and send the materials to be made into dresses and aprons according to the season. Sometimes a company would order caps and pants for restaurant uniforms, and small repair jobs on awnings for porches or fine hand stitching on special orders, but the bulk of the finished products were wholesaled to large and small retail houses. Several times a year, some merchandise was made specifically for Marshall Field's basement sales. Business thrived, even during the race riots.

The fourteen employees were paid by the piece, at the prevailing standard, their earnings determined by their production. Twelve sewing machines lined the walls on either side of the long cutter's table from which Daddy handled the bolts of material when cutting the garments. P.W. was owner, manager, promoter, dress designer, and a very fine cutter. His employees regarded him with profound respect, even reverence, at times. He taught each as much of the business as he or she wanted to or could learn—without entertaining the thought that he might be creating competition. Few new arrivals had machine skills, for they were agricultural work-

39

ers put on simple operations in most factories. But here they were taught a skill, and this increased their earning potential. He would allow them as much time off for personal affairs as he could, always mindful of their homelife, especially in times of crisis. He became known as a benevolent employer. In the ghetto, one's reputation travels fast. People brought troubles of all types to him and at all hours; he found the time to see, hear, and help, somehow.

One evening Mrs. Hicks, a machine operator, approached P.W. with her problem. A bad check had been given to her as a refund on property she had thought she was going to buy.

"Mr. Chavers, I don't know what I am going to do. My poor children will be out in the street," Mrs. Hicks moaned.

"Well, you are talking about how to find shelter for your children," P.W. said reassuringly. He pulled out a roll of bills from his back pocket, picked up the bad check from the desk, placed it in his wallet, and handed Mrs. Hicks the amount covering the check. He continued, "We will make it up some other way; the children are waiting for you." Then he sent her on her way with a "good-night" and a smile.

Mrs. Hicks was speechless with gratitude. She wiped her eyes, gave him a quick kiss on the cheek, and disappeared out the door. Later, the employees talked of this among themselves with amazement; they had never known such kindness from an employer. P.W. never discussed the incident, nor asked Mrs. Hicks about the money.

P.W. grew accustomed to managing the factory without Minnie towards the end of her pregnancy, but he continued to share the daily events with her. She had been a dressmaker before marriage and she understood the nature of the business as well as having invested part of her personal savings to defray some of the expenses of moving to Chicago. She was involved and she liked it that way, even though she had less time to spend there now.

By spring, P.W. asked Minnie to check on various items for him at the factory again. The weather was breaking enough for her to set up visits to the factory as family outings for the children.

40

P.W. and Madrue, front of factory, Chicago Black Belt, 1919

Several times each week the three of us dressed for the afternoon stroll, first to Grand Boulevard, then around the corner and east on 43rd Street to the factory. Aunt Susie came along to keep Mother company and to watch over Bill and me after we arrived at the factory. We enjoyed these outings thoroughly as we would get special attention from the employees. We were allowed to run all over the place, usually ending up in Daddy's swivel chair at his desk in the front of the factory, watching the customers come and go.

"We will be on our way now," Mother called to us one day as she lifted the carriage down the three steps of our house. I followed close as Bill shut the front door behind us. "Today, we are going directly to the factory. We will stroll later," she continued as she turned the carriage north towards 43rd Street. "Aunt Susie had to go downtown so she will not be going along with us today. You children will help Mother a little more today. Daddy wants me to do some office work, but it won't take long."

"I'll look after the baby," I asserted, feeling like a big girl. Edwina, as the new baby was called, had been born tiny, but was growing fast and had gained weight steadily. Her alert wide-set eyes sparkled brightly against her rosy peach complexion and black silky hair. We enjoyed having Mother to ourselves, knowing that her eyes were watching over us instead of Aunt Susie's or Rebecca's when they strolled together. When Aunt Susie did the watching, Mother was free of us and chatted with her constantly as if hungry for adult companionship.

Mother laughed at my promise. She had a gay laugh which came from years of happy times and would burst forth spontaneously, radiating a charm that was contagious. We made our way down the block, fully aware that we were the leading family in the neighborhood.

It was a balmy day in May. Upon crossing the street, I saw two chairs outside the factory door; a few employees may have had their lunch out there. Bill and I romped over, climbed into the chairs and looked so proud of ourselves that mother spoke approvingly. "You may stay outside and watch your sister like Aunt Susie would, but be sure to sit still while

I run in to talk to Daddy," she instructed. "I can see through the window that he is busy at the cutting board right now. Just wave to him and remain as you are; sit still until I get back," she repeated as she placed the carriage close by the chairs. Then she walked briskly into the factory.

I looked around contentedly until the baby began to stir in the carriage. "What are we going to do?" asked Bill, in irritation, as if I knew the answer. He jumped off his chair saying he would be right back. I looked in the window to see what Mother was doing at Daddy's desk. Their heads were bent over and what they were doing looked important. Bill busied himself playing with the little dog down the street. I had a bigger concern, what to do about my baby sister now stirring vigorously and beginning to whimper. I tried to shake the carriage like Mother, but I could not see into it to find out what was going on inside. Any minute the baby would scream; I had promised to look after her.

I moved the two chairs together, pulling the carriage over, and climbed up into the chairs so I could rock the carriage and see the baby at the same time, just like Mother. Pleased with my solution, I walked back and forth from chair to chair, feeling as tall and important as Mother, and pretending I was Mother with my head in the air. The chairs began to rock. Suddenly, the carriage hit the sidewalk first, and I fell, still holding on to the carriage bars tightly. Edwina screamed. In the fall, she was thrown against the well-padded hood of the carriage, but did not spill out. I was stunned, with chairs piled on top of me, carriage capsized, and a screaming baby sister. I froze with panic.

Mother came tearing out of the factory. "What have you done to my baby?"

"I didn't mean to do it, Mother," I pleaded, shaking with fright.

"I told you to call me when you saw the baby awake," she said, then ordered, "Get her bottle!"

That did it! I began to cry, too. The employees rushed out to the rescue and one of them reached for the bottle. The baby kept screaming so I forgot about myself, suddenly troubled that maybe I had been the cause of serious injury. Daddy

P.W.'s Ladies Garment Factory, Chicago, 1920

came out of the factory, put us into the car, and drove us home.

Later that evening, after dinner, I was still bewildered that my good intentions had ended in disaster and my side of the story had not been heard. Mother looked tired after the day's stress of children and factory. P.W. was speaking reassuringly to her. "Today we had a shock about the baby, but these things are bound to happen. What started it anyway?" he questioned.

"I stayed in the factory. The children should not have been outside alone for so long," answered Minnie, blaming herself.

"Well, it's not easy for you managing both the home and getting involved in the business," P.W. agreed, "and this part bothers me."

I was too young to realize that Mother gave up the gaiety she once knew for Daddy's dreams. I could see her beautiful brown hair was greying; she was nearing forty. They spoke of their promises to each other to work unceasingly to build a good life in their new environment. Somewhere in the middle of their reassuring one another, I fell asleep.

Other things beside the factory and family began to occupy P.W.'s mind during that spring. In March, he started going to the Woodfolk depositors' meetings after his close friend, J. Grey Lucas, the attorney representing Woodfolk, spoke to him again about the complicated affairs of the Hunter and Woodfolk Banks. He knew that P.W. had studied banking and commercial law in college. It seems that during the run of depositors on the Hunter Bank a loan was negotiated with the Woodfolk Bank for the benefit of the Hunter Bank, but most of this money had disappeared causing the Hunter institution to fold. Shortly thereafter the Woodfolk Bank collapsed. Attorney Lucas was working on a solution which would release Woodfolk, but the Hunter group stood to lose even more than the Woodfolk group did. Nothing was being said about depositors' rights.

P.W. had heard whispers about the misuse of bank funds at the mass meeting about the Calumet bombing a few months ago. Banks were private domains, and bankruptcy procedures were part of the common escape for bankers and entrepre-

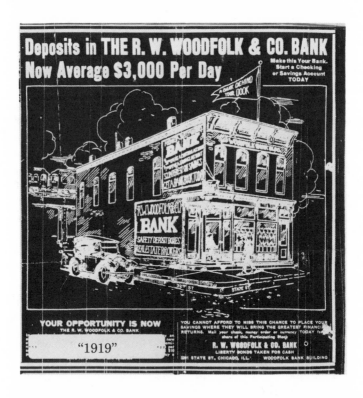

Deposits in THE R. W. WOODFOLK & CO. BANK Now Average $3,000 Per Day

Make this Your Bank. Start a Checking or Savings Account TODAY

BANK
R.W. WOODFOLK & CO.
BANK
SAFETY DEPOSIT BOXES
REAL ESTATE BROKER

YOUR OPPORTUNITY IS NOW
THE R. W. WOODFOLK & CO. BANK

"1919"

YOU CANNOT AFFORD TO MISS THIS CHANCE TO PLACE YOUR SAVINGS WHERE THEY WILL BRING THE GREATEST FINANCIAL RETURNS. Mail your check, money order or currency TODAY for share of this Participating Stock.

R. W. WOODFOLK & CO. BANK
LIBERTY BONDS TAKEN FOR CASH
STATE ST., CHICAGO, ILL.   WOODFOLK BANK BUILDING

neurs caught in the clutches of depression. He worried about depositors' protection when attending depositors' meetings to assist them in placing their claims effectively in the court.

The personal experiences of depositors were coming to P.W. from all sides now: in the factory, on the street, through friends, and with great intensity at the depositors' meetings. One evening he came home worried about a Vera Green whose situation was drastic. He was being asked to do something so she might not have to return to Alabama. "I told her to come in to see me at the factory, but I don't know what I am going to do with her there. I am not even sure why I said it, except that her story was so pathetic, and now she is alone." P.W. confessed that this time he was stumped. Vera needed work immediately.

"Has she tried elsewhere?" Minnie questioned.

46

"Well, this is the full story, as given to me at the meeting: she is a domestic and has changed jobs frequently. Things have gotten much worse for her since the depression. She can't keep a job with Whites because her negative attitude is too obvious. She is not able to keep her feelings to herself."

P.W. thought about his industrial school in Columbus, and the hundreds of youths who had gone forth with skills after their experiences in his school. It had been set up to help them avoid just such a plight as Vera now faced . . . unskilled, unemployed, middle-aged and alone in the city. She was a black woman with a defective foundation, incompetent to fill a position in everyday labor. She needed to learn a skill to be valuable in the city. A special urge to help her gnawed at him; he couldn't see how he could fit her into the factory, yet he had been unable to turn his back on her situation.

"Why doesn't she get a job with some well-to-do colored family?" questioned Minnie, responding to his concern.

"She won't work for Negroes, fearing they won't pay her enough, or that she might see one of her Negro bosses at a social function. It's amazing that she had some money in the bank to make a claim against Woodfolk, but she is on the list as one of the valid depositors," he added.

"If she's that difficult and has no particular ability, why are you so troubled about her, dear?" Minnie was thinking that perhaps she would be helpful about the house since Rebecca was getting restless wanting to return to the factory as a seamstress, her usual occupation.

"Well, it seems that Vera has had a very hard life. Actually, she is a middle-aged woman trying to start over in Chicago, and she had to make it on her own. She is one of those who had to swing from station to station to get to Chicago."

After the outbreak of World War I, European migration stopped. Northern factories had to be manned, so opportunities for black unskilled labor opened up in the North. Southerners resented losing their laborers and organized pressure to keep Blacks in the South by intimidation or any other means. Agents were hired to tell the Blacks to stay, that they were better off in the South. Railroad agents cooper-

47

ated by refusing to sell Negroes tickets straight through to Chicago or Detroit to block the exodus of cheap labor, but Blacks would buy railroad tickets from station to station until they reached one where a through ticket could be purchased. Vera had been one of the mass of Blacks who had to purchase a ticket from one station to another to make her way to Chicago, alone.

"There is a husband, but he did not want to come to Chicago. He felt it was better to stay in Alabama among familiar surroundings than risk coming here," P.W. continued with details. "Her husband predicted that they might get snatched off the train. A lot of this was going on in some parts of Alabama. He feared they might lose their money coming North, too. He just didn't trust Northerners. She came anyway. She says that is the reason they separated."

"You have to hand it to her, she has courage," commented Minnie. "I guess that is what you admire about her."

P.W. responded, "Well, she seems so confused and lost. She says she has never been able to depend on anybody, and this bank crush has taken her savings just at the time the riots broke out and wiped out her job. Her employer was looking for an excuse, she says, and the riots offered the excuse to fire her. I can understand why she would be troublesome in a close situation like domestic work. Her work may be satisfactory, but her manner is awkward and irritating as I am told she is slow. The lady of the house wants a pleasant person to share her day in the home. Vera Green is just not very accommodating—that I could tell by the way she was complaining, almost gossiping about her last boss, in explaining her unemployment to me."

"How could you possibly know what a lady of the house wants?" laughed Minnie, teasing a bit.

"Remember Minnie, I used to train girls to do domestic work and then place them on jobs through my industrial school and employment agency. Pleasant personality is important in domestic work. Things are less personal at the factory. Maybe she could try it out and if she shows any promise working at the factory, we can keep her on. Of course, she can return to Alabama if this does not work out."

Minnie sighed, "Well, if it is that complicated maybe it is better that she face going to Alabama now rather than later." She was getting tired of the conversation and wanted to tell him of the happenings of the day around the house.

"That is not the answer, dear. Vera is one of our people. She struggled to get to Chicago to improve her position like many others. We have to do every thing we can to help her get a fresh start," remarked P.W.

"Well, since we have to set the example for everything or at least you think we do, why not try her on clipping threads at the factory? Finishing details are simple enough. Try her, maybe she will work out," suggested Minnie, feeling that the only way to change the subject was to stop questioning P.W.

"A very good idea, Minnie. I will talk with her, then ask Emily to show her around the factory, and she can go to work at once," responded P.W. He was now content to hear Minnie talk about the new hat she had bought on her shopping spree with Aunt Susie that day.

Vera Green, a large, heavy-bosomed, sullen woman, made no effort to be friendly with the other employees when she began working at the factory the next week. Emily wondered why P.W. had hired her, but finally explained it to herself on the basis that Mr. Chavers keeps hoping for the best in everyone.

P.W.'s concern with the bank problem became a serious involvement. The creditors for the defunct institution, struggling to salvage what remained of the assets, offered P.W. the Woodfolk Bank Trusteeship in the spring of 1920. He eventually accepted after deliberation with Minnie about the consequences for the family and factory. In connection with the receivership, Isidore Goldman, the professional receiver appointed by the court, was working with P.W. on transfer of the liquid funds to another bank. P.W. was now developing final details so that his plan of keeping the depositors together and aiming towards the reestablishment of the bank would be approved by the court. The Woodfolk Bank was renamed the Merchants and Peoples Bank.

That summer Minnie invited Uncle George to visit us for a

few weeks. He had been her constant companion and wise confidant during her single days, and now kept a watchful, though distant, eye over her as a married woman, showing a big brother's interest in a younger sister. When George first came to Chicago as a teenager, he had found work as a porter in a men's clothing store. Being observant and personable, he mingled with the salesmen, showing an interest in the custom-made clothing being displayed and in the apparent affluence of the customers. One day he inquired how he could become a salesman. The way was cleared for him to be trained as a traveling sales representative by the manufacturer in Ohio who never before had hired a Negro in that capacity. It was around the turn of the century and George was 22 years old when he started as a traveling salesman. He eventually became one of the company's most highly successful salesmen whose customers included black men of prominence in all sections of the country. He was setting outstanding records as one of their leading salesmen of fine custommade men's clothing, winning prizes and bonuses with his firm for 20 years.

Minnie and George were much alike, attractive and highly social; they enjoyed people, travel, and adventure. Their relationship had altered because Uncle George was a perennial bachelor who traveled with the free-spending, clothesconscious race track crowd. Nevertheless, his feeling for his sister was deep and consistent. He admired P.W. greatly but remained concerned about Minnie, and she knew it.

Normally George stayed with close friends, Mr. and Mrs. Ganaway, while in Chicago. The Ganaways owned a prosperous chili parlor in the Englewood section of the South Side of Chicago where there was still a pocket of colored residents after the riots. Minnie wrote to George while he was passing through Virginia suggesting that he stay a while in our home that summer. George was our tall, slim, blue-eyed, brownskinned uncle. The "ladies man", irresistible in a suave and subtle way. The charm flowed from his natural inner warmth. But his was an adult world and our significance to him was primarily as Minnie's children. He presented us with gifts but never catered to us with the chatter which amuses children.

After a day of family pleasantries, George launched into a discussion of what he felt had prompted Minnie's invitation. All three were relaxed on the back porch. "P.W., what is this about you taking over the handling of the Woodfolk Bank receivership?" he began, stretching his long legs in the wicker chair he preferred.

"That is right, George," replied P.W., puffing on his favorite cigar. "It is my feeling that this bank dilemma could be turned into a real opportunity for our people in Chicago."

"Don't you think it is too risky a thing for you to get into at this time?" cautioned George, raising his eyebrows and shaking his head in doubt.

"Not at all, George! More of us should get into community affairs to make a place for our people. It is not enough that I am doing well for myself personally," returned P.W.

"But we have to crawl before we can walk." Uncle was quoting Booker T. Washington, hoping this might dissuade my father from getting involved.

"Well, we have to fit into the scheme of things in the big city, too," P.W. retorted, "the only way is for us to venture for survival, using our brains in the business world. That is how others got established in this country. We have to gain respect from people in business and one of the better and most effective ways is through banking." After a pause, P.W. added, "The creditors could have sought a White to handle this trusteeship; that is the way it is usually done. Instead they wanted me, even though I am a newcomer," explained P.W., feeling that George would be impressed by his popularity, if not by his goals.

This was P.W.'s discernment of a positive life cycle: community participation leads to job opportunity, advancement and eventually recognition, which strengthens family life and continuity of achievement. His experiences had prepared him for this role. He saw the bank as his challenge and opportunity to demonstrate community participation; to uplift his people as the beginning of this positive life cycle for himself

51

as well as others new in Chicago. But, he knew it would only sound arrogant speaking of these things.

After a pause, George continued, "Well, I know the story of this man Woodfolk and how he got started dreaming about a bank. He was a postal clerk for seven years before going into the banking business. I remember when he gave up his post office job to join the Hunter Banking firm in order to make it big in a hurry. There was even talk of a chain of Negro banks . . . eventually to be a big clearing house and depository for all banks to be located throughout the country. Now Hunter and Woodfolk have been wiped out! What makes you think you can get mixed up in banking matters successfully when these men, who have been here longer, could not? I'll be perfectly frank with you, P.W., I do question your getting into this so soon after coming here. The Old Settlers resent the newcomers, and resent them deeply . . . You are a newcomer, P.W.!" George felt better; he had finally said it and now they knew.

He settled back in his wicker chair relaxed, even though he felt Minnie was probably startled by his strong doubts and cautious attitude. Since he had first heard the rumor, while in Miami Beach, of P.W. becoming involved in the bank, George had been unable to shake off his fears about the risks for Minnie suffering the consequences if P.W. did not succeed in this venture. He was pleased by her invitation and had come prepared to question every aspect of P.W.'s involvement, to stress the risks for Minnie and the children, and to remain unconvinced about this bank venture.

In a calm manner, P.W. replied, "If there had been a strong Negro bank to help when I first came to Chicago, it would have been much easier on Minnie and me. I wanted to establish a branch factory here first instead of moving the entire operation." P.W. was now thinking of the difficulty he had had in securing a loan to complete relocating and financing of his factory and how he had had to abandon his original branch factory idea and eventually apply pressure through the use of his Columbus contacts to open doors for him just a little more than three years ago. "There are ways of building community confidence, and I intend to use all of them," he added. "I will spell out more of the details to you; if you have time we can look at some of the figures now."

Minnie gave no clue of her reaction to the discussion, feeling at the moment that both were right though they took opposite positions; so she got up and went into the house.

George smiled, "Of course, P.W., you know I am with you. I would like to see your point of view, if possible, though I admit banking and law are beyond me. I sell clothing to rich colored men, lawyers and doctors, the moneyed class in the South . . . I hit Miami Beach, coming up the coastline to North Carolina; all of my clientele are the rich, money-spending types. So you see, there is a big difference in what I do and what you are already doing. Your financial risks as a manufacturer are much greater than mine. As I see it, by going into this banking business you are flirting with something quite dangerous . . . the envy of others around you. I never have to risk the envy of others. These Chicago people, white, black, and in-between, are jealous people. I know, I lived here many years before you came. The Old Settlers are jealous of their position and privileges. These old-time bankers and would-be bankers are going to be against you. They all want to be the one to deal with the sinking ship, to get the salvage . . . none of these people will fully back you . . . They will watch and see that you stay in line," warned George, shaking his head by now as if he knew he could not dampen P.W.'s enthusiasm.

"It is true, George, but when they see how I handle the Trusteeship, I am sure these Old Settlers will join me. Actually, many of them sought me out. First Attorney Lucas, then Reverend Roberts, one of the staunchest Old Settlers, eventually convinced me that I was the man to handle the Trusteeship. All of these are pluses." He paused then added. . . "Someday I could enhance the assets and expand this small nucleus of depositors into a big bank, a really big one."

George jumped up and walked around the porch, sat down again, shaking his head, "I knew it . . . P.W., I just knew it! . . . Your talking about further expansion someday is just what I was afraid of . . . Once you get started in this big

money game, there is no end to it. If I were you, I would be content to set an example of financial progress and community uplift with the factory." George was thinking that P.W. was bull-headed; he'd wasted his breath. "I will have to be on my way," he announced getting up. "The Ganaways are having a card party and expecting me." P.W. and Minnie followed him to the front door walking hand in hand.

P.W.'s enthusiasm had not lessened in any way as a result of the conversation on the back porch. The following day they discussed the matter again. "If I enter into this guarantee with the other creditors to pay off liabilities on holdings at a rate of 10% each year as I contemplate, the understanding will be written that I am not personally liable." P.W. was explaining the extent of his commitment under the trusteeship, hoping to reduce George's deep concern. "You mentioned that our people now have money to spend, that means money to invest, too. I hope to build this into a bank so sound it cannot fail, one our people can feel proud to bring their money to, and a place where depositors feel welcome, at home, and well served. You'll never be sorry for seeing things our way, George."

"Your heart is really in it, P.W., I can see that. Maybe I was a little bit rough when I questioned you yesterday." George realized now that P.W. was already deeply committed to its development.

"I tell you, George, after the bank is reorganized and operating on a sound basis, it will become a mighty force on the South Side making money available for mortgages. We will be able to buy property, build factories, provide steady employment, broaden the base of a Negro entrepreneurship, and help Negro families improve and maintain properties they own."

P.W. was thinking of the one and two story houses all over the Black Belt which were turning into hideous slums with leaky roofs, poor plumbing, dilapidated porches and staircases, and rickety wooden walks, unsafe and unfit for human habitation. "I am sure you know or have heard that white banks are reluctant to grant mortgages to Negro property owners, or when they do, it is at usurious rates. That is what

54

we intend to stop. Our people have to live in this slum because they are unable to get mortgages to improve their property, or if they rent, it is impossible to get white land-lords to make repairs. Our people are jammed together by restrictive covenants on all sides; walled in further by white banks and white landlords' refusals and denials." P.W. asserted. "The assets of this bank can be used to change all this. I realize that my long range plans and hopes are too big for many of our people to understand, but I know I can make these things come true," concluded P.W.

George was silent. It was not so much that he completely agreed with P.W.'s way of thinking, it was simply that he did not know how to counter the argument any further than he had. Also he had not fully anticipated the deep emotional and intellectual investment which P.W. had already made. There-fore, for the time being, he refrained from making further statements about his reservations. Now at least he knew the direction of P.W.'s thinking. Maybe that was enough of a goal for the first visit in a long time. Then too, George was a diplomatic man who preferred to agree with people if possible and certainly wanted to keep his relationship with P.W. cordial.

Before the two week visit was over, George wished P.W. well and promised to assist in whatever way he could, es-pecially in dealing with the negative attitude he encountered among his influential friends about town. From time to time, P.W. reflected on George's words of caution, especially regarding the immigration of tens of thousands of Southern Negroes as well as the economic power struggle for control of the Black Belt. As P.W. saw it, the new arrivals were eager to prove themselves bringing fresh energy and a new outlook to the city situation. The future of the Black Belt lay in the education of black masses in the areas of self help, finance, and industry. He was driven by the potential of his dream for a strong black-owned bank in a city like Chicago. The more he thought about it, the more elated he became at being a part of the drama and the dream.

55

THE LATE BOOKER T. WASHINGTON

Founder of the Far Famed Tuskegee Institute, Ala., Who Passed Away from This Earth November 13, 1915, Whose Memory Is Still Cherished by Millions of People Throughout the Civilized World.

THE BROAD AX, CHICAGO
1921

3

Daddy's Factory Integrated

Minnie took over the supervision of the factory in the fall of 1920. Through the passage of the 19th Amendment, women in the United States had just gained the right to vote in time to participate in the presidential election. The 18th Amendment, prohibiting the manufacture for sale and the transportation of alcoholic beverages, had just begun to stimulate the return of the bootlegging industry, the smuggling and home manufacture of illicit liquor. It was Indian summer, an unseasonably hot period when summer tried to storm the autumn citadel, always unsuccessful, finally beaten back after hanging on the walls for a week or so. The black struggle was like that Indian summer, hot, torrid, and flourishing with an abundance of small business efforts being beaten back, sometimes violently, as George reminded P.W. when he spoke of Woodfolk's and Hunter's failures. P.W., by now, was so involved in the bank that he could not spend the necessary time to run the factory.

In her new capacity as supervisor, Minnie looked forward to helping P.W. in the factory, though by temperament she preferred to be the power behind the scene in an intimate setting, like home. P.W. was persuasive and persistent in finding ways of keeping her interested and involved in all of his activities. She was willing to help because she wanted to see him happy, so she prepared to step in and take over, leaving the children in Rebecca's care, and moving into the position of supervisor. With her she brought skill as well as zeal and flair to the factory. She took the attitude that this was a chance to express herself creatively, and began to consider ways of managing the factory with her own individual style. Her first task was to change the window display. Minnie felt that displaying aprons in the window would bring in more customers. She understood retail merchandising of ladies' garments more than mass production for the wholesale trade, which P.W. had cultivated. Another of her innovations was to hire a pair of elderly white spinsters as door-to-door sales representatives. George had impressed her with his talk about the profits made in individual sales through personal contact.

It was mid-morning and Minnie was poring over the stock list in the office, which had been moved to the back of the factory to shield her from annoyances. P.W. had witnessed violence from the front window during the riots and did not want her exposed to such scenes. Now, as she checked off the list, she suddenly became aware of the silence in the factory. No running machines or cutters. No one was talking. Through the office window she could see that all heads were turned towards the front window. She rose and walked briskly out of the office onto the workfloor.

"What's wrong?" she asked firmly, before she saw the two grey-haired women standing like frail white birds just inside the entrance, tentative smiles on their faces as they glanced at each other nervously. They had been looking around the factory. No one had ventured towards them. Minnie wondered what had created the situation.

"May we speak with Mrs. Chavers a moment?" ventured the taller one.

"I am Mrs. Chavers," Minnie replied, quickly adding, "Come into my office in the rear." She gave Emily a "get back to work" look. Emily, whose countenance almost screamed "What's going on?," sat down slowly and turned to her machine as the two eased past like latecomers to church trying to reach their pews unnoticed. Minnie knew that Emily was the natural leader of the workers. Once she was in motion, the others would soon follow. But Emily was not in motion yet; she sat at her machine with a worried expression on her face.

The office had been hastily constructed by placing an "L"

shaped four-foot partition topped by two feet of glass in one corner of the factory. From this office Minnie could see what was going on in the entire factory. The ladies entered through the rectangular opening, walking behind Minnie. There was no door, P.W. always wanted his employees to be free to come inside whenever they felt the need.

"Thank you, Mrs. Chavers," the taller one ventured as soon as they were inside the office.

"May I show you . . ." began Minnie, thinking they were interested in a special order.

"We were passing your factory," interrupted the shorter one, having found her tongue, "and we noticed the change in your window display. You have ladies' dresses and aprons there now."

"Have a seat," said Minnie, wondering what was coming next. Her left arm had been hurt in a fall during childhood and had been sensitive ever since. She now felt a twinge in it.

"Yes, thank you. We were saying that we noticed ladies' clothes in the window display," she began, as Minnie walked over to the desk with the roll-down top. "We think the display is just lovely," continued the shorter one from the edge of her chair.

"Thank you," replied Minnie as she sat regally on her chair. "Thank you for your interest in our business. Now how may I help you? We are very busy here."

"Yes," began the tall one, "we were wondering if you needed any more help. We would like to work for you." This was said briskly and indeed anxiously.

Minnie did not respond, at least not immediately. She just looked at them with a mixture of curiosity and amazement. What had given them the nerve to walk in here asking for work? They eyed Minnie with admiration and expectancy, as if trying to determine whether they should say more.

"We could sell," began the short one. "Oh dear, we haven't even introduced ourselves. I'm Miss Scott, and this is my sister," she nodded to the tall one. "She's Miss Alexander. She took our mother's maiden name to avoid confusion at the job where we both worked. We sold in a downtown store for twenty years, so you see we know that end of the business quite well. When we were forced to retire last year, we thought we would enjoy having a lot of leisure time. But we find we are lost without work, and it is difficult to live on our savings. We would like to have something to do but we are unable to find work because there is so much unemployment all over Chicago."

Minnie hesitated, "Well . . ."

"We hope you won't turn us away because we are white," interrupted Miss Alexander. "We're from England. You see, our plans for returning never worked out. We don't understand this rioting over here, this trouble between the races in Chicago. We know we could sell your merchandise. We have bought dresses made in your factory ourselves. We live across Drexel Boulevard on 43rd Street among the Jewish people there, and we have passed here many times on our way to the El," she continued almost out of breath. "We could take out some things and sell . . . just a few at a time to start."

Minnie began again, "Well, I have thought of door-to-door selling for our aprons. Why don't you leave your address and return tomorrow at noon?" Minnie was eager to dismiss them and yet was interested in the possibility of using their selling skills. They wrote their names and addresses quickly on a slip of paper. Minnie rose from her chair as she added, "I'll see if I can work something out with Mr. Chavers tonight along the lines of door-to-door selling."

"Oh, thank you, Mrs. Chavers. We hope you can use us. We want to work for you. We heard that your husband is starting a new bank, and we think you are so clever, taking care of three children and running a factory too. Why it's just . . ."

Minnie stiffened a little and looked down at the sisters who were still seated and apparently wished to prolong the discussion.

They rose together and walked quickly past the black and brown faces to the front door. Minnie closed it behind them as they said, "We'll be in tomorrow for your decision."

"Thank you so much and goodbye," sang Miss Scott.

"Goodbye," answered Minnie pleasantly.

As she turned around from the front door to return to the office, she could see Emily watching Vera who was signaling with her eyes and noisily cracking her chewing gum. Vera's flat brown nose was beaded with sweat as she leaned against her table with her hand on one hip cracking her chewing gum; her head tilted cockily to one side with a knowing smirk on her shining face. Minnie recognized her as a troublemaker and warily glanced up as she passed Vera. Minnie could not help but be pleased with the thought of the opportunity to try door-to-door sales.

"Come over to the counter everybody, I want to tell you something," she began, all the while looking at Emily. She had to handle this firmly, without too much explaining, before it got out of hand.

"Those women have come to us in friendship and I want you to be nice to them. They are saleswomen with talents that can be used to our advantage and they admire and want to sell our goods. I will continue to need all of you in the factory to make the things they sell if Mr. Chavers agrees with the idea. They will not be taking your jobs," announced Minnie, hoping to dispel their apprehension of white people coming into the factory to seek employment.

"But Mrs. Chavers, how do we know dey ain't jus snoopin' around to learn all dey can like many white folks do, n' en' up stealin' from you?" muttered Vera suspiciously.

"Yes, Mrs. Chavers, how do we know?" repeated Emily, as if to present the united front the workers seemed to be feeling.

"Well, there is nothing definite about all of this yet. The women just came in. I know we all have reason to distrust white people coming to do business with us, but still . . . these women are elderly and seem sincere. They've had a lot of experience selling. We can overlook the fact that they are white. I've been wanting to try out aprons as a door-to-door item."

Someone on the side snickered. Emily started to say something.

Minnie cut in with "Mr. Chavers will tell you more about it tomorrow."

Emily looked down at the floor while Minnie smiled reassuringly and swept into the office, crossing her fingers. Vera grumbled as she went back to her machine and, turning to Sarah at the neighboring machine, commented in a whisper, "Mrs. Chavers wuz pretty high-handed with us, wuzn' she? Tha's jus' like her t' hire some white folks. Why didn't she give one o' us de job o' door-ta-door sellin', if she wants ta try it out?"

"Are they going to try to be our bosses? Are they going to try to tell us what to do?" questioned Sarah timidly. She was a young girl just out of school and eager to be accepted as an adult at the factory.

"I'm not takin' nothin' off a her," steamed Vera getting louder in an attempt to impress Sarah with her bitterness towards Whites. "Ya sees what's happenin'? Miss Minnie's here one week . . . an' de whole place is changed. De factory gonna close one o' dese days. Wid her in charge, anything can happen. She an' her fancy clothes n' snooty airs . . . thinks she's cute. Did ja see her lookin' at me?" Vera was not through, "You let one a dem white folks git 'er foot in de door an' we're took over. Dat's what white folks is . . . Dey takes over folks," she muttered, turning to Emily who was passing by, then continuing still louder, as if for Minnie's benefit now.

"Emily, thought you wuz gonna be in charge when Mr. Chavers left. Stead, Mrs. Chavers is here, 'n' now she gonna bring white folks in. Dat's a joke on you, Emily. If you ain't good 'nough ta be in charge 'round here, why ain't you good 'nough to do doo'-ta-doo' sellin'? Why not you?" Vera did not intend to let up as long as she had hopes of a reaction. "You been here a long time, know de business, trusted ta open de store, to take care de chillun." She was riding Emily heavily now. "Ya, you've been good 'nough to take care o' de chillun, bu' she don't trust you no how to sell. She don't trust you with her goods. I guess dat's it!" declared Vera.

Emily listened, nodded her head, and continued on past the others to her sewing machine, without saying a word. She knew that all of the workers felt close to P.W. and missed him very much. He had hired them, he understood them, and they could talk more easily with him. Minnie, although courteous and considerate, kept strictly to the role of employer to employee. Emily, in her wisdom, knew them and the many

62

facets of their feeling and reactions and preferred to keep quiet.

Now Minnie's heart began to pound a little as she sat down behind the desk to straighten out the papers. Although excited about the possible expansion that could result from new sales, she was a little apprehensive about the possibility of her first real policy change. She could do it but would first have to convince P.W. to hire those women. How could she put it to him? How could she reach him? This problem of dealing with P.W.'s reaction to her idea loomed larger as that mid-October day wore on.

P.W. was looked upon as a leader by the community. He believed the educated Black should not merely help people of color who were less fortunate, but strive to lift the less fortunate of their race to a better standard. Hiring only his people in the factory was a practical demonstration of his policy. Minnie knew for years he had quoted Booker T. Washington, urging black Americans to "use the forces which are in their hands intelligently in order to lift themselves into a higher channel through commercial, industrial, civic and political development." He encouraged the Puritan virtues of thrift and industry as well as the values of race loyalty and self-help, fully believing this would result in his hoped for goals. He said many times that racial oppression and discrimination serve the economic purposes of the oppressors. At the core of every effort must be the thought and purpose of increasing the productivity of colored people.

"How will he take this idea of white women working here?" Minnie pondered. That which is good business may not be good politics. But she saw an opportunity to make more money on the merchandise, utilizing these white women to sell in rich white neighborhoods where they could establish contact for sales door-to-door more easily than non-whites. She was familiar with the styles and tastes of wealthy families, especially those in the area of Chicago where she had many customers years ago, before her marriage. As their favorite modiste, she had designed and created fine gowns for their cotillions and weddings. She had been recommended from customer to customer and had always worked in their homes, thus becoming fully exposed to their tastes and preferences. She was confident she could please this market and create dresses and aprons especially for these families. She then thought of all the objections P.W. would probably present to her, the color problem and the issue of setting an example. "We owe something to ourselves as a family," she reasoned almost speaking out loud. "We can't help anyone else if we don't help ourselves!"

The noon whistle startled Minnie out of her pensive retreat. The factory was now a forum with the rattling sandwich wrappers and coffee and soup being poured from thermos bottles. Emily was standing in the office doorway. "It's past twelve, Mrs. Chavers."

"What . . . Oh, yes, thank you, Emily," she answered absently. "Keep an eye on things while I go to the house to see about the children." The employees were quietly talking among themselves, except for Vera and Jack, the cutter, who were laughing convulsively at a private joke. Jack had taken over P.W.'s job as a cutter for Minnie could not swing a cutting machine through layers and layers of material because of her ailing arm and delicate physique.

These elderly women had come by the factory just that very morning and their visit was still vivid in everyone's thoughts. Minnie knew a decision would have to be made very soon. "I'll see you this afternoon. Have a good lunch," called Minnie and walked through the front door.

As soon as she was out of earshot and down the street, Vera, in a sarcastic voice, mocked, "Oh, thank you, Miss Minnie . . ." A thunderclap of laughter shook the factory. Everyone may not have been laughing with Vera, but they all welcomed the chance to let go. It had been a rough morning and everyone in the factory was wondering what would happen with the white ladies.

Emily, still standing at the door, turned around to the workers and commented, "Mrs. Chavers knows what she's doing. There are some good white folks too."

"That's right! We been listenin' to Vera grumble long enough," someone from the rear of the factory shouted.

The afternoon dragged on hot and humid. All of the fans

were going, and the door was propped open giving a full view to the street of the feverish activity of the employees working steadily within. By now their fears had been channeled into their assignments, and they were making up for lost time. By two in the afternoon Minnie had returned and sat working the rest of the day at her desk with the last three pages of inventory. When the factory stopped work, she breathed a sigh of relief. Well, she could finish this tomorrow. She wanted to see her children again. She had to talk to P.W. and must somehow find a way of reaching her star-chasing husband who was so wrapped up in his own activities she felt he sometimes forgot his family.

That evening we were all in the parlor. After dinner, Mother had a terrible headache. Bill was busy with his toys on the floor, of no help to her headache with his vocal dramatization of trucks and engines. Nor was I of any assistance clambering over Daddy's knee then hanging on his neck, while pulling at the anti-macassar on the couch. "Stop annoying your father," said Mother looking at me desperately. "Go with Bill to his room and play. Daddy and I want to talk."

Daddy winked at me but nodded his agreement with Mother. "You know, Minnie," he began, as I went reluctantly with Bill through the door of the parlor, "we will soon be more than just a handful of depositors. Oliver Stewart, the President of the Citizens Trust and Savings Bank, is willing to help. I spoke with him again today to confirm the understanding we arrived at several months ago. In fact, now I can safely say he is with us."

"Do you mean Oliver Funston Stewart?" questioned Minnie as she moved over to the couch to be near P.W.

"Yes," he replied, "Oliver Stewart will be advising us more openly in the future." Then looking at Minnie intently he continued, "He has experience and influence in banking circles which will be invaluable. He has contacts. We can't let his being white get in the way of business."

Oliver Funston Stewart was the grandson of an abolitionist, son of a Presbyterian minister, and President of a thriv-

65

ing bank located in the heart of the hostile area adjacent to the fringe of the Black Belt—the very neighborhood that black families were "invading." He had retained his compassion for the plight of oppressed people in general and for black Americans in particular. He was a fourth generation white Protestant American who had not lost his interest in these people as he had risen in the financial circles of cynical Chicago.

Stewart's family was proud of their grandfather's heroic efforts in the days of the Underground Railroad when he withstood the scorn of peers for his principles. He harbored and counseled the runaway slaves, assisting them on their journey further north to Canada or helping them settle in and around Chicago. Stewart, in his younger years, remained quiet about his attitude towards the Blacks because he had had a personal problem in establishing himself securely. He had arrived at a position of power in financial circles at an early age which engendered jealousy and envy in some of his elders. His type of philanthropy might have been used very effectively against him by jealous and ambitious colleagues. However, as Stewart matured and his position became secure beyond question, he became less adverse to open expression of his concern. Then, too, other philanthropists, rich Jewish philanthropists, were beginning to invest openly in the self-help movements within the Black Belt largely by subsidizing or subscribing to the Chicago Urban League or the NAACP. Stewart wanted to do his part. P.W. had known him for years so rekindling their friendship was easy.

"We can't let his being white get in the way of business," P.W. repeated for emphasis. "I know it's going to be hard in convincing others this is a wise move," P.W. puffed on his cigar. Minnie felt he had anticipated her delayed objections, answering questions she might have, and therefore further prepared herself for the reactions of others. She was his constant sounding board for ideas. This time she did not challenge his thinking but smiled broadly as he went on. His face was animated and beaming as he voiced his hope of creating a sound bank and that Stewart could be useful in this enterprise. He paused to knock the ashes off his cigar and Minnie took this opportunity to clear her throat; she felt better already.

"You know, P.W., today must have been special somehow because I was just going to tell you about my having a similar experience. There is a market for our aprons in the exclusive white neighborhoods of Chicago," she said, drawing herself up, "so I have tentatively hired two white women as door-to-door salespeople. You know none of us could do business out there." She moved on through the details of how the women had approached her this morning asking for work, then added, "I agree with you that we can't let the race issue get in the way of business."

P.W. crushed his cigar and looked up at the ceiling. You could almost hear him groan. "Oh, Minnie, what are the workers going to say?"

"Probably the same thing your associates are going to say about Stewart joining you openly," she replied confidently and calmly, the headache now completely gone.

"That's just it, Minnie. Now they will really think I'm selling out. The workers always thought of the factory as a place where they could work comfortably without the pressure of white peoples' eyes and ears; it's like home," he said giving her a look both intent and tender.

"I told them, dear," continued Minnie, "these women won't be replacing anyone in the factory because they will be on their routes most of the time. I can get $5.00 per apron or $1.75 more on each item in this way than by wholesaling. And the merchandise will move quickly, I am sure" said Minnie, explaining her approach to him.

"Well, Minnie, I did say that you could run the factory," he replied. "Oh, it will be all right, dear."

"But you might drop in tomorrow just to reassure the employees," said Minnie as casually as she could. "Now, I am going to make you some tea."

"Yes, I could use some," said P.W. His mind raced madly as she left the room.

Later in the evening as Mother prepared us for bed, Daddy

sat in the parlor alone meditating for a long time. He did not resume the conversation but remained pensive and preoccupied until later, thinking through the answers, not so much for the words to give to the employees in dealing with them, but in search of the position he could and should take to live with himself. His conflict had not fully emerged until Minnie presented him with the same proposal of integration for the factory as he had contemplated for the bank, but in a less conspicuous manner. Her plan might have a damaging effect upon all he was trying to do by building up the community through his serving as the bank trustee. Pride in race, self-direction, and self-respect through accomplishment were his constant aims for his people. Would the community as well as his workers misunderstand? Would they question whether he practiced what he preached as they watched Whites coming and going, so conspicuously, as employees in his factory in the heart of the Black Belt? As he pondered these questions, it again became clear to him that there were gaps in the relationship between his people and the Whites, not so much because of the recent race riots but for a deeper reason: the fact that they actually lacked experience in mingling in each other's daily world in the city. The race curtain in Chicago was thick, as though it had been meant to last forever, so that neither race would ever be comfortable in the other's presence.

One of the advantages he had known as a youth in Ohio was a healthy, respectful and reciprocal relationship with Whites. As a result, he learned whom to trust among them. His people, lacking such experiences now that they were no longer physically enslaved and dependent, were trying to make it in the city—an impersonally cold place, at best. Blacks had to learn how to deal with Whites on a different level in Chicago. They had to learn how to discern friend from foe among Whites here. As things now stood in Chicago, they either hated Whites violently or loved and followed them blindly, still psychologically enslaved. Yes, this was another dimension of freedom which he had always taken for granted. His people must learn how to mingle among all kinds of people, at least on a business level, in the city. They must have this freedom to choose associates brought about by common interests and mutual experiences.

But, he asked himself, if there has been no background of positive exposure but only negative encounters such as avoidance, hostility, violence, and rejection in the city of Chicago since the war, and even worse in the South, how could they learn? How could they extend friendship if it was extended to them from nowhere? He reasoned further that if these white women were really as friendly and as open as Minnie had assured him—if they weren't prejudiced—this would be an opportunity to expose his employees to a relationship between black and white people that would be positive and therefore unlike anything they had ever known before. It seemed to him that all they had ever known was the Negro in a subservient role to Whites as employees of white employers. This hiring of white employees would offer a chance to show an alternative. Their seeing a Negro in a business man's capacity with white employees functioning under his direction could serve to sharpen their motivation, to give them a different outlook concerning possibilities in life to break stereotyped roles.

The next morning Minnie sat at the desk, more relaxed now, with her ledger before her. There was really nothing to do now but wait. Everyone was on the job at exactly eight o' clock, diligently cutting and sewing and then stacking the fresh finished work. Minnie knew P.W. was busy settling matters about the bank, but she hoped he would be able to come in before the two spinsters returned. Suppose they decided to come in early or P.W. was tied up and could not come at all, she thought. She especially wanted him to dispel any doubts Vera might have stirred up in the last twenty-four hours. And, of course, there were the loyal ones like Emily and Jack, who still needed reassurance. Our people are still edgy with the recent and bitter memories of the riots and they naturally resent any white person, thinking they will be a threat to their tenuous security, she thought. Of course, Vera spoke things the others felt but left unsaid. Just then, Minnie saw P.W. come through the front door.

"Good morning, Mr. Chavers," Vera announced loudly.

"Good morning, Mr. Chavers," echoed the rest of the workers as they turned their heads towards the door and then back to their tasks.

"Good morning Vera; Good morning everybody," P.W. replied pleasantly.

No one stopped working, but everyone kept one eye on him and the other on their work as he walked calmly to the office. They were happy to see him. He had not stopped by for over a week since Minnie had taken charge. It cheered them to see his confident smiling face. Minnie was standing behind the desk as P.W. entered the office. He spoke to her a moment and then they strolled up the middle of the factory floor together with a confident air.

"I want to talk to all of my helpers," he began speaking over the hum of the machinery. The work stopped and everyone looked at P.W. attentively, then moved closer to him.

"As you know, Mrs. Chavers is managing the factory now, and she decided to try two white women as sales ladies. If this trial is successful, there will be more orders for more work and therefore more money for all of us," announced P.W. Then pausing a second time he added, "Now, can I count on you to pitch in and help make this thing work right?"

"Well, if you say it's all right, we'll do it and be nice about it. We just don't like white folks rooting us out of everything," said Emily. "You know how it is, Mr. Chavers. They get work where we can't. Even when they act friendly, they're always trying to take something from us."

"I'm glad you said that, Emily," P.W. continued. "What is important here is that these women are useful to us. They can open up an important market if we handle this right. They can't take anything from you that you have or need; all they can take away from here is a picture of colored people being productive and doing a good job. Maybe they have never seen anything like this before. When they go into rich white neighborhoods, they may speak of our factory to their customers and tell them about this place where colored people all work together pleasantly. Whites should see us in our true light." He looked around at the workers and added, "We are a warm, spontaneous, and sharing people! No one can take your skills and achievements away from you. If you stick together, pooling your resources, everyone's respect can be gained. If those rich people in Beverly Hills like the way you cut and sew garments, there is no reason not to sell to them, is there?"

"That's right, Mr. Chavers," said one of the male workers, needing only P.W.'s words to push him and all the others across the line of indecision.

P.W. spoke emphatically about the oppression of all people, black and white. He did not encourage his workers to be superficially polite nor would he tolerate the possibility of their being arrogant with the elderly women. In his mind this new development, as Minnie envisioned it, would be an exchange of talents and he wanted his workers to see this fully and know that he expected them to treat these women in a respectful manner. To him this was the only way to get along with others. Later that day, the two elderly spinsters arrived and began to work.

THE BROAD AX

VOL. XXVI   CHICAGO, ILL., SATURDAY, APRIL 30, 1921.   No. 82.

The Temporary Home of the Nurses of the Fort Dearborn Hospital, 3818 Grand Boulevard Bombed; Several of the Nurses Being More or Less Injured

The Colored People in This City Are in a Pitiful or Deplorable Condition, In Relation to Bombing of Their Homes, for Their So-Called Leaders Seem to Be Indifferent or Bewildered When It Comes Down to Planning Any Relief for Them

Nurses Home Bombed, 1921

4

The First Black National Bank, 1921

That winter was severe even by Chicago standards. Storms swept out of Canada and across Lake Michigan. Icy gales galloped through the overcrowded tenements to add to the misery already wrought by the 1921 depression, which has today been obscured from the national memory by its devastating successor, the 1929 Great Depression. But in 1921, the homeless and jobless were visible everywhere. Thousands of men slept on floors and chairs in poolrooms and police stations. This was a difficult time to try establishing a bank.

As Trustee of the defunct Woodfolk Bank, P.W. had hoped to unify the depositors and eventually insure a 100% return on their deposits rather than seeing the bank's insolvency deprive the depositors of a full return. Assuming the management of the Woodfolk holdings, P.W. hoped to salvage a bad financial situation to the benefit of the depositors who were the victims. As Trustee he was not personally liable for the monies involved; however his main duty was to place the trust property in a proper state of security, and to handle the proper distribution of it. His powers, by law, superceded those of Isadore Goldman who was the court-appointed receiver. P.W. was the spokesman for the creditors . . . but at the same time he was subject to the pressures of the creditors. His initial belief in the creditors' interest and good faith was, however, not wholly well-founded. Attendance at the defunct Woodfolk Bank claimants' meetings was sparse, and the response to letters attempting to locate claimants was slow.

But his enthusiasm for banking continued unabated. Although deeply involved in the Woodfolk bankruptcy, P.W.

moved ahead in his plans to develop a new national bank in the community. Now that the factory was in Minnie's hands, he could more fully begin to work on ways of involving all working people in the community with his idea of a sound black-sponsored and operated national bank. This was to be a Peoples' National Bank!

He spent one evening in November outlining the first of a series of speeches to be given at the Bethesda Baptist Church. What with Minnie poking her head through the study doorway with refreshments or questions about how he felt, he worked late into the night on his manuscript, oblivious of the hour until Minnie asked when he was coming to bed. Actually, he worked through the night and before he realized it, Bill and I were up and bouncing around the house. Mother fed us in the dining room so Daddy could be alone with his thoughts. She knew when to stop interfering with his work and how to keep us busy, distracted, or out of his way at these times. She quickly arranged for Rebecca to take me to school with Bill as an early morning outing. Bill was delighted by my coming as it looked better to his friends to have me as the excuse than for Rebecca to take him to school alone.

"Rebecca is taking both of them this morning," explained Minnie realizing P.W. wondered what was going on. "It seems as though you've been up all night," she continued, implying that it was getting late and she wanted to know what he was up to. Although she knew he had worked long hours on a project many times before, she never knew him to work straight through the night and into the morning without a break.

"Well, here's what I've been doing," P.W. said. "I have simplified the bank movement so the average person can understand the importance of supporting it." Tapping with a pen, he continued pointing out the passages and phrases he planned to use to strengthen his speech at the Bethesda Baptist Church.

Minnie knew she could never be an intimate part of this side of his life. She felt a little sad that the deep companionship they had known in establishing the factory in Chicago would somehow be changed now by his involvement in the bank. She listened attentively but could not bring herself to say what she was thinking. She was too moved by the happiness radiating through his tired, sleepy eyes as he spoke on. "We will have this information in the press someday, but right now we must rely on program ads at local social affairs and on speeches at big mass meetings. We plan to get this message across to our people so they will know that the next big move for us is economic freedom!" said P.W. emphatically. "I hope I'll make the bank sound worthwhile enough to make each person want to invest in the purchase of stock. That's really what I'm after now." He was yawning with exhaustion and Minnie could see he needed rest.

"I think you'll reach them, honey; it's very clear even to me." She urged him to get some sleep, then kissed him goodbye for the day and hurried off to the factory.

Minnie smiled as she walked to the factory in the bitter cold. Their days were spent apart now, each busy and productive in handling separate tasks. When night approached they welcomed the hour to return home. Minnie usually arrived first in time to get the children settled in their evening routines and to look over the dinner preparations Rebecca had made. Settled like a housewife for a comfortable evening at home, she listened to us tell of our experiences with each other during the day. Edwina was walking now and beginning to get into mischief around the house.

This evening, P.W. was knocking the snow off his rubbers and spats when Minnie came into the foyer to take his overcoat. "Haven't seen a December like this since we've been here," he said. He was very cheerful, not at all in keeping with the way others were complaining about the weather.

Minnie sensed some new development as they walked arm in arm to the dining room table. As usual, we children were called, the blessing was said, and the transit of steaming dishes began. After serving the meal Rebecca joined the family group at the table, telling of amusing incidents with the children during the day. Daddy and Mother were always eager to hear Rebecca's additional comments of happenings at home and the reports allowed Bill and me to get into the conversation freely. That evening after dessert, lingering over his coffee, P.W. began, "I'm sure we'll get the permit, Minnie. The Douglass National Bank will be the first of its kind, owned and operated by our people."

"I thought so. In fact, I just knew so!" exclaimed Minnie, her big hazel eyes widening.

"How do you know we'll get the permit? We have a long way to go. You must be a mind reader, Minnie," answered P.W., a little startled by her reaction.

"I'm not talking about the permit," she interrupted, "I mean I just knew you'd put the bank under someone else's name, instead of yours. You do all the work and you never get the credit!" P.W. looked at her half-smiling and half-solemn.

"Now Minnie, don't look at it that way. The bank is the beginning of a protest movement against economic slavery. This thing is too big to name after a local man. Everyone knows who Douglass was and those who don't will learn from the literature I'm preparing. His name, like Washington or Jefferson, is a symbol of the protest movement in this country. We must take pride in honoring our own."

"I realize that," answered Minnie, "I admire and respect Douglass . . . but the people here know you; they see you every day. When a man does something outstanding, he should get the credit. Woodfolk named the bank for himself and you are one of their own, too."

"I hadn't seen it that way, dear. Let's go into the parlor as we're in Rebecca's way," said P.W. recognizing the discussion was to be a long one. He had not spoken about the naming of the bank with Minnie before and felt she was reacting partially to his oversight.

Once in the parlor, P.W. began again, "I felt that a famous black man's name with historical significance would sell more stock more quickly and that the buyers would relate to his accomplishments. We must recognize that our people have become very panicky about investing in Negro ventures after the Woodfolk Bank failure, not because of the name, but because of the run on the bank caused by riots. The whole thing was handled in too personal a fashion; having seen the conditions of the records, I can tell. Choosing one's own name is self-serving and too immediate. That institution was handled more like a social club than a money or banking firm. No one can say that the man Douglass was a failure. He stands for integrity, dignity, and self-respect for our people." P.W. used logic again and it seemed his logic well disputed Minnie's point.

But Minnie persisted. "When a man does something important, he should name it for himself to protect it from those who would steal it . . . would steal the credit. A man's work is part of himself . . . I still feel you should name it Chavers National Bank." P.W. leaned back in his chair and puffed hard on his cigar as if to throw up a dense screen for protection against Minnie's protests.

"I've been warned many times about fanning jealousy in Chicago. Remember what your brother George kept telling me? There is too much in-fighting among our people already; I don't want to incite any more."

Minnie got up and walked about the room. "I am more afraid of a thief than I am of a jealous competitor. I remember my Uncle Grieffe . . . the way he used to demand that those white people in Danville call him Mr. Bannister. They were jealous of his wealth and tried to be familiar with him, belittling him by calling him Grieffe or Bannister, but he never tolerated that. He insisted they recognize not only his wealth but his manhood by calling him Mr. Bannister. He believed in claiming what was fully his, and manhood was fully his." She paused, "There is power in a word and in a name."

"Minnie, there you go again, talking about your uncle in Virginia. We are dealing with a different climate and time here in Chicago." He smiled again as he watched her sit down, secretly pleased with her protective efforts. After a pause, he continued, "My name simply would not provide the effect I seek; it could be used by others as a reason for withholding help from me. This bank named for Douglass will help to build community confidence. If we are to survive and live with dignity as a people, the base must be laid for greater economic opportunity, especially for the young, to give them hope and direction. Minnie, it is not the accomplishment of myself or any one single man alive today that is

77

significant in the development of our people. We must awaken to our potential power. We must recognize that we can do a lot better than we have done in the past as a people working together to achieve in the American economy." Minnie smiled. Love for him welled up in her again.

"Dear, I just don't want them to hurt you. You place too much confidence in the good nature of all men, but I see you have made up your mind about the name."

"That's right, Minnie. Our people must learn the value of work, achievement, and the wise use of money. They must be shown this is the way to a better life. I don't intend to make this bank a monument to myself."

In his dual role as organizer of the national bank and Trustee of the Woodfolk receivership, P.W. sent Rev. William R. Roberts, head of The First Methodist Church, a notice to come in to discuss his claim. P.W. was sitting in his office on the second floor of the old Woodfolk Bank the following day awaiting the arrival of Roberts, when Al Young, the secretary of the bank, appeared at the door. "Rev. Roberts is here, sir."

"All right, Al, send him in," answered P.W. looking up from his pages of notes. Al returned with a square, mustard-colored man with thinning dark brown hair who dismissed the cashier with a wave of the pudgy hand he extended P.W.

"Good afternoon to you, Reverend," continued P.W. shaking hands with the preacher. Roberts was a Methodist minister and always made sure to inform strangers, "We stuck to the 'mother church,' we didn't pull out." He took pride in the "we." The innuendo referred to the "pulling out" of Rev. Richard Allen from the Methodists in 1827 after tiring of the humiliation of being pulled off his knees at worship by white churchmen. Roberts' church catered to the needs of the black middle-class Christians in Chicago who found the fervor of holy rolling black Christians "primitive" and embarrassing. His First Methodist Church was the church for the black establishment of the day. Others than the middle-class had gone there two or three times but were not "snatched off their knees." Instead they were "frozen out" or ignored.

Roberts sat down before Chavers could finish saying "have a seat, Reverend" and began, "Well, P.W., I came over as soon as I got your letter. I want to congratulate you on the way you smoothed over all the doubts those folks had about bankruptcy procedures and your handling of the Trusteeship."

"Thank you, Reverend. I am pleased you've been following what we have been doing. This is a very complicated procedure we will have to take before the courts, and I want to get your claim processed properly. I hope you brought proof of your claim so I can turn it over to Mr. Young, the young man who showed you into my office," answered P.W. getting right to the reason for the meeting and letting his guest know that Mr. Young, in charge of checking accurately and carefully all the books and records of claimants, was no ordinary office boy to be waved away peremptorily.

"Yes Chavers, I am still marveling at the way you really pulled it off big, taking over this Woodfolk mess," Roberts began again. "You know all of us were concerned about how Woodfolk allowed this thing to get out of hand. Now you needn't worry about the proof of my claim. I would have brought the books with me if I thought they were necessary." Roberts leaned over, getting very confidential. P.W. had heard something of his rise to prominence and was cautioned by some to beware of dealings with him. However, P.W. made up his mind to remain open about involving Roberts, despite the gossip.

Rev. William Roberts had arrived in Chicago fifteen years ago. He was not a graduate of any college but had received public and high school education in the South and had been the pastor of a number of churches in Kentucky during the years before he came to Chicago. He was 49 years old and considered an established "Old Settler," having climbed the ladder of success within the Black Belt on the strength of members of his large congregation. He now owned a prosperous bakery and the financial transactions connected with it had been handled at the Woodfolk Bank in Reverend Roberts' private account.

Roberts had become known as the largest depositor of the defunct Woodfolk Bank, threatening to sue for his assets shortly after Goldman had been appointed receiver. But later he reached out to Chavers to take over the Trusteeship. He saw in P.W. a shrewd entrepreneur and assumed P.W. would have an interest in gaining a foothold within the inner circle of financial power inside the Black Belt. As a favor, he had hoped P.W. would handle his claim without publicity.

The Old Settlers wanted a new arrival to handle the situation, an experienced businessman, a black man who comprehended the machinations of the secret world of finance which is built on non-disclosure. A new arrival, if he failed, could be disclaimed, and if successful, could be absorbed. Some thought Richard Owens, who was also a newcomer, had a prosperous factory and knew how to mind his own affairs, should take over the Trusteeship. But Roberts sought P.W. because he had a flair, a dramatic quality attractive to people. He counted on P.W. to play along.

P.W. could see that Roberts was a key figure in the community. His factory could probably do wonders for our people as an example of industry and self-help, he reasoned.

Economic stability as a lever or key to political rights and social equality was a concept shared by prominent Blacks since 1865. Storefront banks like the Woodfolk Savings Bank were scattered across the country. Since white banks refused to get involved with the risky ventures of financing black enterprises, such as small retail stores and businesses, these black-owned banks were to be found wherever black people lived in sufficient number to have fraternal and burial societies which flourished after the Civil War. These banks became the depositories for these organizations, but they became economically incestuous. Lip service was given to "doing good," but the chief aim was to "do well personally." Books and records were not kept scrupulously and there was a limited sense of accountability.

"If you bring in your proof and turn it over to Mr. Young, he will give you a receipt and process your claim." P.W. wanted to make it crystal clear that the Trusteeship process was to be followed to the letter of the law in every single situation.

"Of course, P.W." was Roberts quick answer. He settled

back further in his chair, troubled about what was really going on.

"Not that I want to change the subject," said P.W. "but I would like to talk with you about another matter, a part of this situation that may be of interest to you."

Roberts shifted in the chair again. "Yes, go right ahead."

"Reverend Roberts," P.W. said with a cajoling tone. "I need your business knowledge and experience to back me up at the bank." Roberts relaxed now but was still worried about P.W.'s aims.

"It was you who persuaded me to take on this position, and I am glad I listened. You're successful, prominent, and interested in making a better life for our people," continued P.W. Roberts' vanity overcame him and his eyes lit up.

"Thank you, Chavers," he said. Getting back to himself, he smiled and shifted in his chair. "Well, I want to be in on anything that affects my claim!"

"My idea is all part of the same thing. I want you to look at these papers. They contain a rough outline of the general plans I drew up about how to put what's left of the old bank funds to work." P.W. handed the papers to Roberts and leaned back in his chair while Roberts read.

The papers contained the speech outline he had gone over with Minnie. Now he used them to sound Roberts out. The speech explained the new banking law, the meaning of shares and Chavers' plan to form a national bank. Roberts pulled his neckless head further into his ample shoulders as he read. Everything was spelled out in an uncomplicated manner so that those who could not read would certainly understand the spoken words of P.W.'s speeches. They would all know how the bank would be run, the duties of the board, and the rights of all depositors both large and small. Roberts read intently, eager to catch up with what Chavers had been doing and delighted he was being given this confidential picture of the plans. The further he read, the more he looked like a snapping turtle in a preacher's suit and collar. By the time he finished, he was beginning to think that maybe he had made a mistake in button-holing Chavers to handle this Trusteeship. His concern regarded his assets only and in assuring that these would be refunded—not in creating a *new* bank. Had he made a mistake by not going to the depositors' meetings where his physical presence might have stopped Chavers from going this far? He could have raised questions publicly, planted doubts about reactivating the bank, and pressed for speedy distribution of the remaining assets.

"They're not going to trust you, Chavers," he finally said, "no matter what you say or do." He was thinking that Chavers was gifted, but idealistic and foolish. "You're an outsider, I may as well tell it to you," he said with emphasis. "For the most part, these Chicago Negroes are ignorant and comfortable in their ignorance. They don't want to learn anything; they don't want to understand anything. They follow the leader and are suspicious of anybody that wants to teach or help them."

"Reverend . . . Reverend . . . " P.W. interrupted, "I know what you mean, but our people have got to catch up with others in learning the power of the dollar . . . and the wise use of it, as the path to self-respect in America." He was wound up now, "I've spoken to Congressman Madden and to Stewart, the President of the Citizen's Trust Bank. Both of them are sold on the idea and have political connections that could smooth the way, but we must show them the community wants this first." P.W. looked for a glimmer of understanding of this point in Roberts and pursued, "What we need now is a show of unity amongst ourselves to back up this new plan for a National Bank to be owned, managed, operated, and supported by Negroes. We can show them we are able to run a bank, manage, and finance businesses just like anyone else."

Roberts was silent for a time. The mention of Stewart and the white Congressman impressed him.

"Who have you selected to be on the Board of Directors?" he questioned.

"I would be happy to consider you," answered P.W., pleased that Roberts had asked. "This young institution would benefit by your active support on the Board. I am looking for men of established and solid experience."

"Well I'll have to think about it. My claim against the

Woodfolk Bank is sizeable and I have a good stake in the way all of these assets are handled, you know." Shifting his eyes from P.W. to the papers still in his hand, Roberts questioned further, "Who else do you have in mind for the Board?" then quickly, "I like to think about matters like this before jumping."

"I'm sounding out different individuals for their abilities and interests," returned P.W., wondering whether Roberts actually grasped the magnitude of the movement; whether he had stirred Roberts' imagination and reached deeply enough to inspire this ambitious man.

Roberts was puzzled. He thought P.W. very clever to move into the Trusteeship of the defunct bank as a means of breaking into the inner social circle of the Old Settlers, but had anticipated that the liquidation of the remaining assets would be his only role with some of the usual manipulation of funds that went on as part of carrying out this type of duty. Now he knew it wasn't so much that Chavers was not going to play along in the usual manner, he was going to change the entire game. Chavers was putting his major effort into starting a new national institution and holding on to the assets to keep the small bank depositors feeling confident about the ultimate goal of a national bank. Roberts rose to leave the office after hinting that Dr. Morris might be a possibility. He said he had to talk this over with someone and perhaps Earl Morris, the dentist, was the best one.

"Chavers will have to be carefully watched," Roberts mused to himself as he approached the front door of the office. As he started the car, Roberts decided he would definitely call Dr. Morris. Together they could watch what Chavers was going to do about a new bank since that's what he was aiming for. "Without the Old Settlers, he can't do much," Roberts concluded, smiling to himself as he pulled away from the curb.

By the beginning of 1921, P.W. had gained the cooperation of Roberts, Morris, and a number of business people in the community for the common effort of starting the Douglass National Bank. He soon mailed the formal application, including a draft for $100.00 covering expenses for an in-

83

vestigation, to the Comptroller of Currency in Washington for a permit to organize "The Douglass National Bank of Chicago." In his covering letter, he acknowledged that none of the applicants for this proposed institution had any previous experience in the banking business. It was their purpose to select men of proven experience in that field once the organization was under way. A copy of the application was forwarded to the Illinois Auditor of Public Accounts, then referred to the Chicago office for investigation. The subsequent preliminary report submitted by the local bank examiner to the Comptroller of Currency revealed that there was a demand for a national bank in the proposed neighborhood of an estimated 75,000 colored population. In this same area there were four banks, one of which, The Binga State Bank, was operated by colored people and had no protest against the proposed bank.

But the bank examiner, in his report, questioned the capacity of the applicants to handle the management of a national bank because some lacked substantial credit standing and all were inexperienced in banking. He proposed a white man be placed in charge, a man of sufficient experience and integrity, to manage the institution. The examiner feared, however, that the organizers might dismiss any such experienced man shortly after the granting of the charter, taking charge soon thereafter, and leaving the federal system with a bank conducted by inexperienced men. One month later when the final reports from the Field National Bank Examiner, the Chief National Bank Examiner, the Federal Agent, and the Illinois State Bank Examiner were received, all recommended rejection of the application on the basis of their doubts and questions.

Thus the application was caught in the vicious cycle of "no prior experience," which P.W. had acknowledged from the start. In those days, there was no national policy of affirmative action for expanding opportunities available to inexperienced and disadvantaged people although a reservoir of men with power and prestige, who wished to alter social injustice, did exist. The Comptroller of Currency did not reject the proposal outright. He read the fully documented reports carefully and noted the application had not been referred to a member of Congress for opinion even though one report stated the applicants were all active in politics and expected to be able to succeed in this venture through applying local political pressures. After weighing all the facts and opinions before him, the Comptroller qualified the decision by recommending "a hold on the approval until experienced men join the application," and notified P.W. accordingly.

P.W. spent the next few months checking on the Woodfolk claims, attempting to keep the expenses of the Trusteeship at a minimum and following up on all details. He used this time to hunt down more Woodfolk claimants who had not come forth with satisfactory proof of their claims to present to court. The response was slow and the latest letter from the Deputy Comptroller in Washington was a big disappointment. It stressed that the banking experience criteria had not yet been met by the two new applicants whose papers P.W. submitted. One of the white applicants was investigated and found to be a general bookkeeper of fair ability, not a bank official as he claimed on the application. The other was contacted over the telephone by the Chief National Bank Examiner and quoted as saying he did not intend to give any time to the organization or management of the bank but would serve on the Board for one year and meet with the Directors if they invited him to do so. The general feeling around the Comptroller's office continued to be that the applicants had no idea what constituted competent bank experience. It was forecast that a national bank would be used for the applicants' own benefit, and the rest would be mismanaged due to incompetency.

In the meantime, P.W., pressed from many directions, recognized that he would now have to go to Washington to complete the formal application procedure. Before going, he would have to secure the written endorsements of Congressman Martin B. Madden, the member of Congress from the First Congressional District of Illinois within whose district the Douglass National Bank would be located, and the United States Senator from Illinois, Medill McCormick, for their support in handling his national bank movement. He continued searching out prospects to smooth things along and to facilitate the demonstration of community support for the bank as well as preparing material for distribution at meetings he organized and chaired. He was pleased that the largest asset of the defunct Woodfolk Bank, the Calumet property, had not reverted to the previous owners at a loss to the creditors. This was accomplished by contract to purchase the property through the courts. He was able to effect an agreement, as the Trustee of the Woodfolk Bank, to guarantee the creditors 100% reimbursement of their deposits over a 10 year period with the date of maturity, March, 1931. This came to be known as the Chavers Contract on the Calumet Property.

Although February had been unusually warm, the fierce March winds were now blowing. P.W. opened the door, thumping and shaking the snow off his overcoat. This night he had come home with the idea of a trip to Washington on his mind, hoping for a good time to discuss it with Minnie. He realized he had to stop springing surprises on her after the way she took the decision about the name of the bank.

Dinner was over and P.W. and Minnie were sitting in the parlor, she with her sewing basket, he with his cigar and newspaper. It did not seem like a good time to bring up the trip. Minnie looked troubled. Even though it had been a good day at the factory, something was bothering her and P.W. sensed her mood. It did not help for him to remain behind his newspaper. Minnie was concentrating on her own thoughts, occasionally sighing as she pursued her sewing, when the conversation veered away from the discussion of the day's events.

"I've been thinking about the Calumet property, Minnie," commented P.W. "I was over there today looking into some of the tenants' complaints. Those apartments are very spacious; I was surprised. This was the first opportunity I've had to go into one of them." He put the newspaper down and took a long puff on his cigar, settled back in his armchair, and began. "In spite of the harsh weather, I went over," he repeated for emphasis.

"Is that so?" responded Minnie, not looking up as she

continued sewing on buttons that had popped off Bill's clothes during the fight in the school playground that day.

"Yes," P.W. continued, "the apartments seem to be clean, however the Negro families are quite bunched up because they rent space to strangers. The Negro and White families living there now appear to get along well. The bombing of the Calumet property last year tore it up pretty badly and many of the tenants are new. The Negro tenants are proud to live in a Negro-owned and operated building." P.W. went on to discuss with great enthusiasm the good race relations existing in the area at large, in spite of the bombings last year. He talked with the shopkeepers about his observation and in their opinion the races got along well because "they minded their own business, respected each other's ways and helped each other when a family was in trouble." He hadn't intended to dwell so long on his discovery of the true conditions in and around the building, but Minnie had not interrupted.

P.W. shifted his thoughts to the damage done to the property by the bombings, which was partially repaired; the inside staircase ripped up by the explosion was hastily restored although it remained unpainted. The walls of the hallway where the bomb was planted had not been restored and the brickwork around one of the entrances remained hazardous. "At least the shattered windows have been properly restored," he commented.

"Is it safe?" Minnie finally questioned, continuing to sew.

"Oh, yes. Some of the brick torn away has been replaced. It's not unsafe, it's just that the building is unattractive because of the incomplete work. There must be at least five windows with 'Room for Rent' signs in them. That's a shame because it's a very impressive building, but all of those signs take away from the appearance of the property." He talked about what he learned of the practice of renting to single men by many families who lived there. These families felt single men would pay more, use less gas and light, and make less use of the rooms. It seemed to him this practice tended to overload the property with transient men and was a prelude to depreciation of the building and neighborhood. "In some cases, two and three families doubled up to share one apartment in order to save on rent expenses. I don't know which is worse, but those 'Room for Rent' signs in already rented apartments will have to come out of those windows," he commented.

P.W. paused suddenly, observing that Minnie was now sewing more intently without stopping to talk with him. "What are you doing?" he asked.

"Your son had a real fight at school today in the playground in all that snow. His clothes were nearly torn to shreds. Sanfelice told me as much about it as she could. Bill won't talk about it. Didn't you notice how quiet he was at dinner?" Minnie continued sewing and never looked up.

"Boys will be boys," reassured P.W. "You mustn't worry too much about his school fights. We all had them as a part of growing up. By the way, how do the children like our new maid?" he questioned in an effort to change the subject.

"But this boy was so much bigger than Bill," Minnie protested. She was not to be deterred and continued, "It started when a much bigger boy jumped him in the playground. The boys were throwing snowballs in fun when this bully jumped him. I get the feeling Bill is being singled out because of his appearance; he's always neat, clean and well-dressed. Maybe that's why they pick on him," Minnie went on. "I do wish our children could go to a better school than Forrestville Elementary School; it's changing very rapidly and the children are rough. There have been a couple of other fights I haven't mentioned to you." Minnie sighed deeply as she put her sewing aside, relieved that she had finally said what she wanted to say ever since Bill had started school last fall.

Minnie felt uneasy about the changes in the neighborhood. Our little street, Forrestville Avenue, remained the same, but many middle-class families, who formerly lived on the adjacent streets and sent their children to this school, had moved away, some as far south as 55th Street. There were signs here and there that the "sporting element" had begun to move into the neighborhood. There was the cluster of men who hung around the corner drug store across the street from the factory, their language, clothing, and general idleness bothered her. She felt the children in the playground were mimicking the street behavior they heard or witnessed in their homes. Every time Bill got into a fight with one of the local toughs, this uneasiness returned to her. "We must find a decent place to live and bring up our children," she said to herself.

Schools of those days, as today, reflected the preferential attitude of the Chicago Board of Education towards the needs of children from educated families. Wide latitude in the expression of bias by the individual principals of local schools was permitted; some principals would shift the Negro children to more rundown schools with low operating budgets and teachers of below-average skills. Forrestville, now 25 years old and showing signs of deterioration, had a large percentage of children from uneducated families and twice as many Negro children enrolled as there were Negro families in the entire school district. The white principal, a firm believer in segregated schools, readily cooperated with other principals to perpetuate segregated schools elsewhere in the city.

Minnie did not know these statistics, but her observations and intuition helped her discern that Forrestville was deliberately being allowed to deteriorate. P.W. always believed in the positive aspects of segregation in schools, all other things being equal: Negro teachers for Negro children, early encouragement in the feelings of identity and belonging, and a sense of pride in one's own racial and ethnic background. This may have stemmed from his having attended integrated schools in Ohio as a child, his long and lonely search for communion with his own people, and his always having to prove himself with Black and White. Minnie pointed out to P.W. that because of segregation in the Chicago school system, the academic program of the Negro schools was substandard. She dramatized the influence of these low standards on the children and he acceded to her preference for integrated public schools.

"Bill will have to learn to defend himself no matter where we are or where he goes to school, Minnie. That's the way a boy learns to become a man," P.W. insisted. "The pity of it all is that he wants these children who bully him to like him."

Minnie did not want to ignore P.W.'s earlier question totally so she added, "Sanfelice does pretty well with the children, but of course she's not as tender as Rebecca was with them."

P.W. then suspected some difficulty with our new house-keeper, Sanfelice, who had been placed in our family's cus-tody, on a trial basis, from a girls' reform school. P.W. was not at all sure the arrangement would be satisfactory even though she was a relative of one of his employees, but he believed in helping people who got into trouble by giving them a second chance in life. It was generally known that young, homeless, colored girls like Sanfelice were looked upon as fair game in the underworld of Chicago, often ending up as servants in the "call houses," "reefer dens," or the gambling parlors where employment agencies would send them. An unwritten law forbade the sending of white girls to work in brothels and, as a result, practically all of the male and female servants were people of color. Saloon and gambl-ing housekeepers were friendly with the local politicians and hooked up with the police. The most noted of all black gambl-ing kings, a college-educated undertaker, ran his gambling games in his undertaker parlor not too far from the home of Mayor William Hale Thompson. Although the undertaker was known to control vice houses of prostitution, bootlegging, cabarets, and the crap, poker and "policy" gambling games early in his career, he was nominated for County Com-missioner. He subsequently became Second Ward Com-mitteeman appointed by Mayor Thompson, and later was appointed a member of the Illinois Commerce Commission by Governor Small. Such was the intricate network of vice and politics awaiting those whose existence was precarious in the ghetto of Chicago.

There was no protection for young, attractive, homeless, colored girls emerging from reform school, the breeding ground for brothels. It was clear that Sanfelice would be swallowed up by these undesirable forces, so P.W. had agreed to her being placed in our home on a trial basis, with the understanding that she would be expected to respond to the environment of our family life while working as a sleep-in

90

maid. Minnie noticed that Sanfelice spent more time looking in the mirror than watching over us but P.W. was relieved that the trouble for the evening was about Bill in a school fight rather than about Sanfelice, which he had expected.

"I am going to see the teacher tomorrow to find out what is really going on at school," continued Minnie. "I'll take time off from the factory."

"Of course, dear . . . maybe we should move," P.W. responded to her deep concern. "One of the apartments in the Calumet building will be vacant soon."

"That's not far enough south," countered Minnie who dreamed of living in a more exclusive area. Secretly, and for some time now, she had hoped that when they finally moved it would be to where she could express her tastes and their accomplishments amidst people who were beginning to arrive, the more elite group to be found in the southern-most tip of the Black Belt near the Hyde Park area of Chicago. But she continued, "What's the neighborhood like around there?"

"As I told you earlier, Minnie, the people get along well. You weren't listening to me, were you dear? I was over there and looked around. The people seem to be seeking security and I don't think the neighborhood will deteriorate . . . not for many years. We can at least look into it."

P.W. had not seriously thought of moving as he felt their interests would be better served remaining where they were for the time being. He had only brought this into the conversation to soothe Minnie's irritation. His mind was more genuinely occupied on how to initiate a discussion of his pending trip to Washington. But, he reasoned, if they moved to the Calumet Avenue building, they could oversee the remodeling he was planning, so he added, "There may be many advantages to moving there, Minnie."

After a few minutes she asked "But can we move while you are campaigning for the bank?" She listened as he reassured her that it might be better for him with the family there. Everything would be more easily supervised.

The conversation had a paradoxical flow that evening. In the beginning, much of what he said Minnie had not heard and what he wanted to talk about most went unsaid. In the end, he decided not to bring up the subject of the trip for fear it would spoil the evening further. Eventually P.W. went to Forrestville School, spoke to Bill's teacher and was convinced that a change in neighborhoods was best for his children. They were both pleased and happy about the moving plans.

A few weeks later P.W. received a letter from Washington stating that the application would receive further attention. Congressman Madden and Senator McCormick had responded to P.W.'s pleas for endorsement of the new bank, recognizing the need for the institution, and verifying the banking experience and credentials of the two white applicants as having been connected with successful state banks. Both telephoned the Comptroller's office and pressed for early consideration for approval of the application in view of the total situation in the financial circles of Chicago. In his call to the Comptroller of Currency, the Senator said he would like very much to see the Douglass National Bank approved, if at all possible. He pointed out that it was planned to be located in a section of Chicago densely populated by colored people who were experiencing considerable friction and antagonism in their dealings with the controlling bank officials. By this time P.W. had secured the endorsement of the Mayor, the U.S. Postmaster, several judges, and had completed the selection of the Board of Directors.

The Board included: an assistant U.S. District Attorney; a retired Major in the Illinois National Guard; an undertaker; Rev. Roberts, a pastor; Dr. Morris, a dentist; O.F. Stewart, President of the Citizens Trust and Savings Bank; and P.W., a manufacturer, as President of the Douglass National Bank. Resolutions were adopted by community groups at mass meetings all over the neighborhood, supporting the efforts of P.W. and his associates. These resolutions poured into P.W.'s office daily now. He used them to follow up on other contacts in getting additional support he needed. Through black presses in other cities his appeal was extended to the black communities across the nation, emphasizing the opportunity to the individual and the colored race to join "in the mighty campaign for economic freedom for ourselves and our posterity."

92

More than 1500 black citizens voted unanimously to support P.W.'s enterprise at a meeting at the South Side African Methodist Episcopal Church. He felt ready to go to Washington to deal with the remaining questions and doubts through personal contacts with governmental officials. The quality of support received from the community and knowledge that the application for the permit was still being given attention served to increase his confidence that everything about the bank was moving in high gear.

The evening before his departure for Washington, D.C., late in April, was spent quietly at home discussing with Minnie the tight schedule and making last minute arrangements for her well-being in his absence. Their lives were so inextricably interwoven that the pain of their first separation descended on them that evening. Their words were reassuring, but their hearts were heavy with concern for each other. P.W. fought to overcome his feelings as he spoke. "We won't have time to write each other, but if a real emergency comes up, call me." She reassured him with gentle concern. They had collaborated on everything; this would be but another test for Minnie in making it possible for P.W. to reach his goal.

The following morning he left for Washington, D.C. in the family's eight-passenger Pierce Arrow. Jack, the cutter at the factory, was at the wheel. He had come into our lives very unceremoniously. He had stopped by the factory one day looking for an opportunity like all the others. He had bragged to his family back home about how well he was doing and he told P.W. he could not go back as his family expected him to send for them. The county sheriff in Alabama was gunning for him on a fake charge because he had hopped a freight for Chicago after a skirmish down there with some white men. P.W. liked him immediately because he displayed courage, honesty, and an easy smile throughout telling his story. He seemed willing to do any type of work to make an honest dollar and was eager to learn more if given the opportunity. He could drive a car, cook a meal, clean a house and had many handy skills. P.W. needed a cutter in the shop and Jack needed a break, which P.W. gave him and never regretted.

93

Jack now served as P.W.'s chauffeur for this long trip to Washington, D.C. Our good-byes were tearful that morning because this was our first separation from our father. We knew he would be gone for days. Bill, who had just turned six years old, stood at the door waving at P.W., looking pensive as tears rolled down his cheeks. I cried and pulled on Daddy as he swung his luggage into the back seat of the car.

"I want to go too, Daddy," I kept repeating, crying loudly while he continued arranging his luggage. When all was in readiness, he stopped and scooped me up in his arms, then spoke to me.

"Now Rosebud, my little Rosebud, you mustn't cry. Help your mother all you can while I'm away. I'll be back very soon." He then kissed me and took me over to Mother who stood near the car with Edwina in her arms. "Minnie, I'll be back in one week," he said as he put me down near Mother and kissed her tenderly. Although upset, she stoically remained reserved, not wanting to disappoint P.W. She had wanted to be with him on this momentous trip.

Minnie contented herself with watching for announcements in the newspapers. Every night she brought home a copy of each local paper to scan for news of him. It was in this way that she learned whether he was successful in his mission. On April 27, 1921, the Chicago Daily News carried a long article with a big headline announcing his success. It read in part:

"The Douglass National Bank of Chicago received its permit for organization from the Comptroller in Washington, D.C. today following the visit there of P.W. Chavers, local colored leader. Chavers operates a women's garment factory at 534 East 43rd Street."

She read on through the article as she sat alone in the parlor that evening, looking occasionally at P.W.'s empty chair. The article told the history of the institution going back to Woodfolk's voluntary receivership days and the experiences of Negro banks in the South. It emphasized that never before had colored men become heads of national banks. She smiled, thinking that her managing of the factory had made all of this possible, though she continued to be a little sad because

94

she could not be with him to experience these great moments of triumph. By the end of the week, after scanning dozens of newspapers, she noticed that only local white papers heralded this as a great feat and wondered why.

P.W. returned with gifts for all. It was a warm and loving welcome home, with the opening of gifts and packages around the dining room table. Minnie was so moved that she began to cry.

"Oh P.W., you should not have bought all these expensive things," she said. "We're very proud of you, dear, just having you home again is gift enough . . . but, they are beautiful," she said in between sniffs. She didn't know what to say. She was happy to have him safely home again and finally able to express her true feelings.

For Minnie he brought a diamond lavaliere, for Bill, a train set, and for us girls there were big dolls. It was like Christmas again in early May. "From now on nothing will do but the best for my family," said P.W. as he fastened the clasp of the lavaliere at the nape of Minnie's neck. He insisted she try it on, wanting to make sure she would wear it and not just keep it in the jewel box. "This is special, Minnie," he said looking at her, "just like you." How proud he felt of his accomplishments and his family. He beamed as he told Minnie about the people he had met and promised he would take the entire family to Washington someday. He settled back in his comfortable chair that evening with the bundles of newspapers Minnie had saved for him. She had kept them knowing how he treasured his scrap book.

P.W. spent the rest of the spring traveling around Illinois and the Midwest. The family got used to his short overnight trips. Stock-pledges were coming in fast because of the national publicity and he was met with openness and endorsement everywhere he went. Black newspapers in cities other than Chicago were carrying the story with interest; the grapevine was whispering the message swiftly. His ideas received wide attention.

Once, when P.W. returned to Chicago to catch up with local news, the headlines screamed "More Than Forty Death-Dealing Bombs Hurled at Homes of Decent Colored People,"

THE BROAD AX

More Than Forty Death Dealing Bombs, Have Been Hurled at the Homes of Decent and Law Abiding Colored People Since January 1, 1918, to the Present Time and Seven or Eight in That Length of Time, Have Been Thrown at the Homes of White People, Who Sold Property to Colored People; and So Far, Not One Single Arrest Has Been Made by the Police.

May 1, 1919, the Home of Mrs. Ernestine Ellis, 3401 Indiana Avenue, Was Bombed and Her Beautiful Little Daughter, Was Blown Through the Roof.

IT IS REPORTED ON GOOD AUTHORITY THAT HON. ROBERT E. CROWE, STATE'S ATTORNEY OF COOK COUNTY, HAS RECENTLY EMPLOYED A DETECTIVE AGENCY TO HUNT DOWN THE GENTLEMEN WHO HAVE FOR THE PAST THREE OR FOUR YEARS BEEN PLEASANTLY ENGAGED IN BOMBING THE HOMES OF COLORED PEOPLE RESIDING IN THE SECOND WARD OR ON THE SOUTH SIDE.

Hon. William A. Bither, the Able and Brilliant Attorney for the Board of Education, in His Race in the Spring of 1920, for Republican Committeeman of the First Ward, Informed the Colored People Who Attended His Meetings that He Had Sufficient Evidence to Indict and Send to the Penitentiary at Joliet, Ill., Some of the Men Who Had Been Bombing the Homes of Colored People; that Hon. Maclay Hoyne, Being a Hateful Democrat; that He Would Not Raise His Little Finger in that Direction.

Mr. Bither Was Stating the Absolute Truth at that Time and Was Not Endeavoring in the Slightest Degree to Pull the Wool Over the Eyes of the Colored People. It Could Be Very Timely if He Would Turn His Evidence against the Bombers Over to Hon. Robert E. Crowe, Who is a True Blue Republican.

Monday evening, April 25, the building at 3818 Grand Blvd. was bombed and all the nurses belonging to the Fort Dearborn Hospital who occupied the building were tossed from their beds and the following nurses were severely injured: Miss Florence C. Lyle, Miss Josephine Harris and Miss Lillian Wood, and it was no fault of the bombers that all of the fifteen colored nurses were not murdered in cold blood.

Friday night, May 6, the six-flat building at 701,703 E. 50th Street, owned and occupied by colored people except one flat which was still occupied by a white family who had been unable to find a flat, was bombed at night time. No arrests made by the police.

Other bombings of the homes of other property belonging to colored people without the dates of occurrence, follow:

Appomattox Club House, 3632 Grand Blvd.

Jesse Binga, 5922 South Park Ave.

Chas. Burgess, 3710 Grand Blvd.

William Woods, 6600 Maryland Ave.

William Jackson, 446 E. 44th Place.

Powell Wilkinson, 5223 Indiana Ave.

Apartment building, 4030 Calumet Ave.

Apartment building, 4119 Lake Park Ave.

T. Y. Powell, 423 E. 48th Place.

Creol Hubbard, 4331 Vincennes Ave.

Apartment building, 43rd and Grand Blvd.

Apartment building, 740 E. 45th St.

The following homes and property belonging to white persons have been bombed for selling property to colored people:

M. A. Conner, 6557 Bishop St.

June, 1920, W. E. Austin, white realty man, 102 Bellview Place. Window broken. Rented property at 4807 Grand Blvd to Richard R. Harrison, a Negro.

Dec. 6, 1919, white real estate firm, Hobbs & Grubbs, 454 E. 47th St. Suspected of renting to colored Negroes.

Dec. 12, 1919, home of Harry J. Coleman, 418 E. 45th Place. Wealthy man said to have sold property to Negroes. Sister attempted to put out bomb, seriously injured. Hurled through door, limb badly burned.

Feb. 1, 1920, William Austin, 103 Bellview Place. Rented property to Negroes.

Feb. 10, 1920, Mrs. W. D. O'Brien. Had sold property at 3632 Grand Blvd. to Appomattox Club. Had not moved at time of bombing. Windows broken.

Feb. 11, 1920, South Hamlin Ave. Damage: $1,000. Aimed at Alexander Gibblen, said to have sold real estate to Negroes in white localities.

March 11, 1920, Morris Fox. Sold property to Negroes. Damage: $1,000. Had not moved yet

The maliciousness of the practice is self-evident. There has been offered no defense to one by any of the Chicago colored citizens. They live beside themselves, attending to their own business, patronizing extensively among themselves. They have their own hotel, some relations, their own social clubs, and their own little colony. They are satisfied with their own, and are unable to remain to themselves.

This isolation does not seem to appease the bloodthirsty element of whites who are not content to remain to themselves, but who are bent upon visiting upon the colored people all kinds of desires, hates and fury. They practices as bomb throwing and bomb planting can thrive in Chicago is certainly a reflection upon the city police authorities, to say nothing of our keen loss civilization.

Such disaster as was visited upon colored people within the past few weeks is calculated to stir race feeling to the breaking point. If race trouble ever does break out now in Chicago, the people

Mrs. Ellis and a few of her friends wended their way to the City Hall to see some of the big colored leaders, but being unable to find them, she came in contact with our people, who stood close up to the powers that be and she was requested to tell her troubles in relation to the untimely and horrible death of her beautiful little daughter to some police men, but so far the police have utterly failed to make any single arrest of any of the bombers.

THE DOUGLASS NATIONAL BANK

Will Soon Throw Its Doors Open for Business at Thirty-Second and State Streets

Within the past two weeks the promoters of the Douglass National Bank, which will have the distinction of being the only national banking institution controlled by colored people, secured its charter from the comptroller of the currency at Washington, D. C., authorizing it to transact a national banking business.

Its capital will be $200,000; surplus $50,000.

Headlines summarize Chicago violence, 1921

96

with lines that read "The State Attorney of Cook County employed a detective agency to hunt down the gentlemen engaged in bombings." Nevertheless, that night from the pulpit of the Pilgrim Baptist Church, P.W. delivered an optimistic speech stating, "We believe our efforts will result in showing that the best class of Anglo-Saxons not only desires, but is anxious, for Negroes to reach the highest point of civilization."

Someone cried out, "You must ain't read today's paper, Chavers." Everyone turned around and some snickered and stomped their feet. Then everyone started laughing, first one, then two, then ten, until soon the church was romping with laughter, hoots and whistles. P.W. stood still, his face impassive, but his thoughts raced in confusion. He saw he had to regain his audience. This group was even larger than the one at the Methodist Church back in April. The ruckus subsided abruptly. There was something about P.W.'s manner that fascinated people, not necessarily admiration all the time, but a blend of curiosity and awe that made them want to learn more about what was going on inside this unruffled man.

"Yes, I did read the papers today, and my doubts were as strong as yours," he said calmly, adding, "but, I also read in the same papers that we were close to being oversubscribed. That means we have more pledges than we have shares to sell. We will not permit the detractors to stop us. We are going to keep on building. If we stick together, we can rebuild so fast they will finally get the idea that we are not going to give in to them."

"Let's give brother Chavers a hand," said one old man near the front. There was a torrent of applause. It seemed he had won this round and felt grateful even while he knew there would be other challenges. What he didn't know at the time was that the most severe ordeal he was to face would be put to him by his business associates, some of whom he was about to introduce as the next speakers.

From
Physical
Slavery
To
Economic
Freedom

Shall The
Negro
Live
Or
Shall He Perish
Economically ?

The Douglass National Bank

3201 SOUTH STATE STREET
Phone Douglas 5898
CHICAGO, ILLINOIS

CAPITAL $200,000.00 -- SURPLUS $60,000.00

TOTAL $260,000.00

P. W. CHAVERS, President

Do you know—That the Douglass National Bank is the first **COLORED NATIONAL** Bank ever authorized by the United States Government?

Do you know—That its officers and Directors have passed the most rigid scrutinizing investigation possible by the Comptroller of currency?

Do you know—That now for the very first time you are given the opportunity to purchase **NATIONAL** Bank stock?

Do you know—That the Directors, in order that you may own at least one share, have arranged payment on a part-pay plan?

If you will phone Douglas 5898 or write into the Bank, a representative will be sent to see you with full information

Stock is selling very fast — You must act **AT ONCE**

Shall the Negro Live or Shall He Perish Economically? 1921

5

Bank Stock Campaign

At that moment, George was driving up Lenox Avenue in New York and thinking of P.W., Minnie and the bank stock campaign. George was doing his share . . . he was planning how he could get sister Nellie to buy stock. She did not easily part with the dollar and would have to be sure of the solidness of the investment before she would put anything into it. As he drove up to the door of her new co-op apartment on West 120th Street in Manhattan, he frowned as he thought of the rivalry between Minnie and Nellie. But Minnie's request that he sound Nellie out had not fallen on deaf ears.

In fact, all winter while traveling throughout the South he had thought about his prospective visit to New York during quiet moments, remembering the conversation last summer on the back porch. P.W. had told him how important it was to have their support, and Minnie had asked him to speak to Nellie about P.W.'s Trusteeship role at the bank. George wanted to make some kind of contribution for he was proud of P.W. and Minnie's determined efforts. He knew that P.W. had gone ahead with his plans and that bringing Nellie's reaction to Chicago would be a positive step he could take to encourage them, although his doubts about the timing of this venture continued to haunt him. He felt that P.W. was a stubborn, bull-headed man, difficult to dissuade; but he admired his courage, so that he did not want to appear indifferent or uninvolved. Where Minnie was concerned, he could never be uninvolved.

His last stop before heading to New York had been Washington, D.C. where he had visited with Cousin Gabrielle, renewing family ties, catching up on the developments in the Virginia branch, and visiting his favorite lady friend,

Josephine. They were a perennially engaged couple always talking about getting married but doing nothing about it. Gabrielle had been surprised to hear that he was going to New York until she realized that Minnie had asked him to see Nellie and get her support.

He climbed out of the car, sounded the buzzer in the hallway of the building, and then waited for a few minutes at the front door of Nellie's ground floor apartment. However, it turned out that the front door was never used for Nellie was afraid of being burglarized. Then he saw her peeking coyly from the door under the staircase.

"Hello Nellie, how's my baby sister?" he sang out, rushing to give her a kiss as she backed away from him automatically. She had long ago developed a way of holding everyone off from her in self protection. Nellie was the youngest of the three and the loss of their mother due to cancer had apparently affected her the most. This early deprivation had made her wary of others. Determined to make his stay with Nellie short but pleasant, he struggled with his valises to hide his disappointment.

She asked, "How have you been?" adding quickly, "How is Minnie?" Before he could answer either question, she continued almost compulsively "Oh George, I am so happy that you really came to see me. I just moved here a few months ago and once I had a city job, I needed a permanent home in Manhattan." Nellie was proud of her cooperative apartment on the ground floor of this five-story walk-up brown-stone building, which represented a tremendous social advancement to her. "Let me show you around," she added as soon as he was well inside the apartment with all of his luggage.

He had wanted to put the suitcases away and rest for a little while, but in order to avoid any unpleasantness, he agreed and congratulated her on her choice of a home. Nellie's apartment had six rooms which led off one side of a long narrow hallway, with a kitchen at one end and a parlor, kept locked, at the other end, which had a connecting door to Nellie's room so that she alone could use it. The lodgers had access to their rooms and to the kitchen which remained unlocked; the dining room was rented to a roomer who work-

100

ed on the railroad, and was therefore rarely home. George's things remained in the hallway of her apartment until he had met all of her upstairs neighbors and one of her roomers, a widow, who was home that afternoon.

George was not too confortable about settling into the room they entered by means of a pass key which opened the doors to all rooms in the apartment. "Just in case of a fire," she would explain to her roomers. Now she was putting George into the railroad man's bedroom, the converted dining room, and his uneasiness at this trespassing was obvious.

"It's all right, George. Mr. Smith is a very polite young man. He gave me permission to let you use it in his absence," explained Nellie.

He wondered whether the rent was more than Nellie could afford, and whether she was trying to "keep up with the Jones's," renting rooms to earn more money. Then he remembered again how tight Nellie was with a dollar so that she would naturally try to get as much as possible from her investment. It was dark; the windows were off the court. "They stuck Nellie with the worst apartment in the building," he thought as he sat on the side of the bed and looked around the room. He hoped she had got it at a bargain. In fact, he reasoned, more than likely she took it because it was a bargain.

Everything looked well worn, but comfortable. The place was furnished with "antiques," as she called the second-hand furniture she had found here and there. George knew it was second-hand furniture, for she had no furniture previously. She had recently left Bordentown, New Jersey, where she had been a teacher, and board and room had been supplied. Having a knack for style, George's taste was offended by the fact that the furniture was not matched. Then he smiled, saying to himself, "But it is useful, and it fills up space in the many rooms."

He felt a little sad. "What kind of a life is this?" he asked himself, but he knew it was too late. Nellie was now a thirty-eight year old spinster, tall and awkward, living alone in New York; she would never marry and would never change. He sighed and thought, "Maybe I should get married and stop worrying about my sisters' affairs." He thought of Josephine and became restless. Anyway, Nellie had seemed genuinely happy to have him there as she busied herself in the kitchen preparing dinner.

Trying to be cheerful as he entered the kitchen to watch her finish dinner, he commented, "You're happy here, Nellie; I can see that." He bent over to kiss her lovingly, but she drew back embarrassed at his expression of spontaneous warmth.

"Be careful, George! I'm frying chicken," she responded. "I want this to be just like when we were children and I had you all to myself. But mostly, there was always Minnie tagging along."

"Don't start that, Nellie." George had been wondering what they would do to get out of this gloomy place after dinner. "What shall we do tonight? I would like to get a little rest after dinner and then we can go out on the town if you want, Nellie," he added. He did not intend to be trapped in Nellie's apartment of locked doors while she indulged herself in gossip about Minnie.

"Well, there is a concert down the street that I was thinking about going to. But you might not like it," said Nellie, looking out of the corner of her eye mischievously as if prepared for rejection as usual, but delighted with herself and completely unaware of George's discomfort.

"I haven't changed, Nellie. I still don't like that stuff. I like people and action. We can just stroll down Seventh Avenue as far as I'm concerned," he said, taking a seat at the kitchen table to be out of Nellie's way as she raced from the stove to the sink to the ice box, lined along the wall of the narrow kitchen. "But let's do something. A man from Chicago has to be able to talk about where he went and what he saw in New York when he gets back."

This time she got the message. Nellie had hoped they would settle into a long conversation in the parlor if he would not go to the concert. But she wanted to please him so, after dinner and a rest, they went for a stroll. It was Sunday evening and she would be going to work the following day, then he could get more rest from his long drive.

Actually, he managed to keep her busy going places for a

few days before she began to complain of gas pains and foot trouble so that he eventually had to content himself with sitting out evenings in the parlor. It bothered him that he could go into the parlor while the child who lived in one of the rooms in the apartment could not. A widow and her 7-year old son lived there and they seemed like well-mannered people who would not misuse Nellie's "fine antiques" with which she had decorated the place, thought George, but he made no comment. He would smile at the boy, and move on, not wanting to evoke a situation he could not deal with.

That evening in the parlor Nellie felt like a duchess entertaining her favorite suitor. "Let's play pinochle," she suggested, trying to sound worldly.

"Oh, that's a good idea. When did you learn the game, Nellie?" asked George, delighted that she had volunteered such a pleasant pastime. Of course he knew that with Nellie one could never be sure of the ulterior motive; she may only have been wanting to save wear and tear on her antique sofa. He was amused to watch Nellie as she set up the card table and chairs in the middle of her highly polished parquet floor.

"At Bordentown the boys taught me," she answered with a twinkle in her eye again. "You know, George, I was always more like a boy than a girl anyway. I mean, I always liked to do the things the boys did and learned them easier. Maybe that's why I did not get a man." She laughed at her own joke about herself, squirmed all over provocatively, and then watched piercingly for George's response as if he might have some special secret.

George looked around the room then answered in a mock-serious tone, "You must not lose hope, Nellie. With a fine apartment like this, anything can happen now."

"I am too busy with my work. I don't have time to be bothered with men. They are all right to talk to, but I don't have time to be serious about a man," answered Nellie quickly, while shuffling the cards.

"I was joking, Nellie. You have a nice job, and a nice home, some man will surely come along. But let's play cards," said George, thinking that the apartment was really too large for a single woman who worked all day and surely spent some time socializing outside. But he did not mention it because he was beginning to feel guilty that he had remained so far from Nellie and had not kept up with what she was doing.

As the card game progressed he again wondered why she had roomers, and why she had made a permanent investment in something like a cooperative apartment; but he was pleased that she had not scolded him, so far, for his negligence in not visiting her more frequently. Every time these questions occurred to him he would remember that it had been five years since his last visit to see how Nellie was getting along. It surely had not been easy for her as a spinster teacher at Bordentown, the school for wayward boys in New Jersey. Yet, he did not want to scold himself anymore about this either. He forced himself to concentrate on the game, mindful of the fact that he had not as yet brought up the matter of the bank. In the meantime Nellie was winning the game, delighted with the compliment about the apartment as added bait for getting a man some day if she put her mind to it.

She suddenly broke the silence with a barrage of words. "I was bragging to those awful Irish down on the job today about my handsome brother, and you should have seen them perking up their ears. 'Shanty Irish' that's what I call them. It's hard for a Negro woman on this job. The Jews and the Irish fight all the time until a Negro comes around . . . then they gang up," declared Nellie, getting to her favorite subject, the tensions and warring among the different ethnic groups on the job.

"What do you care! This is New York, the great melting pot. There are all kinds of people here," answered George, hoping to cut short the discussion. "They don't pay your salary. You are civil service, aren't you?" He wanted to show an interest in her job and accomplishments.

"Yes, but you have to fight back. You have to let those Irish know that you are somebody too, by fighting back, or they will walk all over you," replied Nellie, bent on prolonging the conversation. The second hand of pinochle had been dealt, but she had not picked up her cards for she would rather play racism than any other game.

"You were somebody here when they were nobody in the old country and don't you forget it. You were here first, so don't let them bother you. Just do your job," answered George, deciding to stop agreeing with everything Nellie said and to start talking like the big brother he was. Family matters were the only serious discussion he cared about, and George could be emphatic when he became concerned about Minnie and Nellie. "Just do your job," his voice echoed across the room again. Then, to soften the impact, he added "Do you like it? I mean . . . the work."

Nellie hadn't really meant to trouble George, she was trying to entertain him. She quickly shifted, "Oh yes, I'm an investigator with the Department of Hospitals. I take care of Bellevue Hospital patients," she explained with pride. Then she went into another catalogue of complaints about her cases and the flights of stairs she had to climb to see her patients, adding that they always seemed to live on the top floor of a walk-up tenement.

As she talked on, George thought that even with a college education, Nellie had less class than Minnie. No wonder he preferred Minnie's company. He decided to make the plunge . . . he had tolerated Nellie's antics long enough.

Watching for a change of expression, George asked, "Have you heard the big news about the bank?" He pretended to look at the cards. Nellie's smile turned to a scowl because she did not want this tete-a-tete interrupted as it always was with a discussion of Minnie. He added, "Here's a chance for you to make some money. P.W. intends to get as many people as possible into this."

Nellie had wanted to start talking about Minnie. In spite of her antagonism she was really interested in her; unfortunately her interest always came through in a negative way. Minnie always seemed to dominate George's thinking; it was obvious he was never Nellie's exclusively, and for this she never forgave Minnie. She led with a card, and the game began again. Suddenly, Nellie broke through coyly as she answered, "No, I'd like to know more about it. How does Minnie see this new bank of P.W.'s?"

George was determined. He did not intend to get caught in

105

the trap he felt was being baited, so he countered, "P.W. suggested that I speak to you about what he is trying to do. We had a long talk before I left there last fall. P.W. wants us to invest. He's the president of this proposed bank, you know."

"And who is the vice-president, Minnie?" asked Nellie teasingly.

"Minnie is managing the factory," answered George in a matter-of-fact manner. "That's her part in all of this." He was not going to allow Nellie to provoke him into a discussion about Minnie so he quickly added, "P.W. really has the whole load on his back. We are the only family P.W. has, you know. His parents are both dead, and his brothers and sisters have gone their separate ways." If he could handle the appeal to Nellie on the basis of her love for money and compassion for lonely people, maybe she could see P.W. alone in this, and maybe she might come through with some family coopera- tion, for a change. He repeated, "Yes, P.W. really has the whole load on his back. I could feel it when we talked about the bank situation."

Nellie smiled to hear George's plea for his brother-in-law. She liked P.W. but she shied away from him because she did not understand him. They were cordial but P.W. was a gentle- man, and you can't fight with a gentleman, she thought. Somehow she knew Minnie had put George up to approaching her, for P.W. would not consider her participation vital. She reasoned that George was letting her win at the card game too, in order to soften her up. She smiled as the thought occurred to her that everything began to make sense, for she enjoyed intrigue. She enjoyed the thought that Minnie needed her. Then she suddenly asked, "Are you sure there is money in it, George? Are you investing?" Her smile became sardonic and she held her cards under her nose like a fan.

"Yes, I have decided to purchase twenty shares as soon as I reach Chicago. They are talking about the bank all over the South," answered George, and, using his skills of salesman- ship added, "Haven't you heard about it here in New York yet?"

"I did read something about it in the *New York Age*,"

replied Nellie. "Maybe I should look into it more, especially the quality of the stock. Is it a good buy?" She was being more reasonable now. She continued, "You know I have spent a lot of money on this apartment, and these roomers don't pay me enough. I did not realize that I could have charged them more. But, I want more information about the bank. After I get the details and when I make some extra money, I'll invest in Minnie's bank."

"In P.W.'s . . . not Minnie's . . . It's P.W.'s bank." Nellie smiled and dealt another hand.

The three children, George, Minnie, and Nellie had been born to Tyler and Mary Jane Calloway of Henry County, Virginia. Minnie was born in Bristol, Virginia, in 1881, a few years after the formal end of the Reconstruction Period in the South. Tyler Calloway was known as the "bridge builder" of Henry County; and although his mother was a slave, he was a scion of one of the most distinguished families in Virginia.

The Calloways had a history going back to the 14th century in Cornwall, England, and were one of the oldest families in Virginia, closely identified with the development of land and institutions in many counties of Virginia, Kentucky, and other states. They were noted for military, public affairs, entrepreneurship, and civic attainments, but above all, for strong family ties and devotion. According to genealogists, this Calloway family had been prominent for four centuries on both sides of the Atlantic. Tyler's grandfather, Colonel James Calloway, was the eldest son of Colonel William Calloway, the most successful of the first generation of the Calloway brothers who founded this Virginia dynasty. Like the other Calloway brothers, James served in the French and Indian War and the American Revolution; he became a man of wealth and influence. He married three times and eventually had twenty-two children, of whom John Calloway was the fifth of eight sons who survived, married, and left children. In many ways, John's life was the most tragic of the sons.

Tyler's father, John Calloway, migrated from Bedford County to Henry County, Virginia. He had survived two wives and was a lonely widower when he met Eliza Baker, the vibrant young mulatto slave girl living on the Widow Baker's plantation. He visited the area to watch over the property belonging to his disabled son and to periodically see his granddaughter who married into the Widow Baker's family. For years after the death of his second wife, America Hairston (adored daughter of George Hairston, a wealthy Virginia planter) John Calloway longed for the companionship and tenderness that he had once known. The early death of his first wife, Mary Polly Hairston, followed the death of their last-born child. But he remarried in 1821 . . . and his new wife was America Hairston (the first cousin of Mary Polly). Both Mary Polly and America were descendents of the Hairston slave- and land-owning Hairston clan. Their slave empire extended from Virginia through North Carolina and Mississippi. Mary Polly lived only nine years after marriage, bearing three children; America, his second wife, died suddenly after bearing two children in five brief years of marriage. John knew fifteen years of loneliness before he met Eliza around 1840.

John was descended from a family unaccustomed to defeat. Now more than sixty years old, he had to deal with the increasingly harsh realities of his situation. Both wives were many years dead, two of his three sons died of sudden illnesses, and a few years before his remaining son, George Hairston Calloway, was permanently injured by a wooden bat blow to the head while playing at school. His youngest daughter married a Reverend George Pannell and moved to Henry County. He resigned himself to devoting the remaining years to his disabled son. In his loneliness, he decided to move from Bedford County, where he had been born and had lived his entire life, to Henry County, where he could be near his youngest daughter and granddaughter. There he also could keep a closer watch over the property left by George Hairston, the wealthy grandfather to the grandson. But this grandson, George Hairston Calloway, now grown but incapacitated, was subject to periodic seizures and tantrums, requiring constant care. This land, left by the wealthy grandfather, lay adjacent to the holdings of the Widow Baker.

At first, John lived in the home of his granddaughter on the Widow Catherine Baker's property. There he came to know Eliza, the young slave girl. Later, he moved to the adjacent land belonging to his son, built a house, and cultivated crops. The Widow Baker would send Eliza over from time to time as a housekeeper. Eliza's family had been inherited by Catherine Baker when her husband passed away a few years earlier as part of the Baker Estate, a modest holding of small farm lands and a few slave families who remained on with the Bakers for generations, never being sold from each other, as was increasingly the practice. Eliza, now a beautiful young mulatto girl, was fair with short kinky hair and warm thoughtful ways.

John came to care about her and to depend upon her. Their stable relationship lasted almost twenty-five years, produced nine children, and apparently fulfilled John's longing for companionship. He outlived his granddaughter, most of his brothers, sisters and contemporaries, and freed many of his slaves. He was active and alert, and towards the end, arranged for the life-long care of his ailing son; provided for the children of his deceased granddaughter, and the education of his children born to Eliza before he died at age 84 in 1865.

Even though it was illegal to educate a slave under the system, this practice was superseded by John Calloway's love of family and knowledge that the children had to be nurtured if they were to be prepared for adult life. Apparently, John felt since he begot nine children who would be handicapped by their slave heritage, he had a special responsibility towards them. Tyler, their first-born son, was taught the trade of a stone mason. Each of the others were taught a special trade, too.

Tyler was the only son of John Calloway and Eliza Baker to carry the Calloway name. He was twenty years old when his father passed away. Three years later Tyler married Mary Jane Bannister.

For several generations prior to the Civil War, the Bannisters, a free colored family, lived as small tenant farmers in Patrick County. Later, they moved down the road from the Widow Baker in 1840 and continued as tenant farmers. They

Mary Jane Bannister Calloway, 1887

inherited the shrewdness necessary to endure with dignity as free colored people and to hold on to the property in Danville left to Nelly Banister, Mary Jane Bannister's mother, by a Civil War colonel.

Mary Jane and Tyler Calloway were married more than ten years and had three sons, James, John, and George— before Minnie, their first girl finally arrived. Minnie was a welcome sight to the family. Tyler, a lovable husband and father, and a good provider, traveled from place to place because of his work as a stone mason. Minnie could remember her mother being alone with the children often or packing and unpacking as they moved about with Tyler wherever he went to work. Most of his jobs were building bridges, although he also constructed the Hotel Roanoke, in Roanoke, Virginia. That quaint building still attests to the craftsmanship Tyler put into his work.

Mary Jane developed warning signs of a serious illness, cancer of the breast, a few years after Minnie's birth. Nellie, the last-born, was affected by the illness. She rejected Mary Jane's milk and developed rickets. Eventually, Mary Jane was sent to Johns Hopkins Hospital in Baltimore, Maryland, where she was diagnosed and treated, her expenses paid by her brother, Grieffe Bannister.

Grieffe Bannister increased the value of the holdings when he came into his inheritance, until he owned several blocks of property, a general store, a seat on the Stock Exchange in Danville, Virginia, a textile center which recovered more rapidly than some other areas in the South during the reconstruction days. He was a loyal brother to Mary Jane, placing the finest medical care available at her disposal. In spite of his best efforts, Mary Jane passed away when Minnie was nine years old and Nellie was six.

Saddened by her demise, Tyler nevertheless continued in his work. He traveled about building bridges in Virginia but, unable to keep the family together alone, he finally sent the children to live with their Uncle Grieffe in Danville. But they soon began to react to the changes in their lives. The boys found Grieffe to be a benevolent despot, a stern patriarch to his children, and a philandering husband to his wife, Sally.

Minnie's older brother, James, ran away to see the world, becoming an itinerant cabinetmaker, passing for white, and never settling anywhere. Soon, the second brother, John, left for Boston where he learned printing before joining the Army. Minnie and John stayed in touch by letters, especially after he was shipped out to the Philippines. George, the third brother, stayed on with Minnie and Nellie in the Bannister household for seven years until the three of them were old enough to face the world together.

Shy and sensitive to being motherless, Minnie grieved. She was constantly bullied by Nellie, who despite her poor beginning, outgrew Minnie in a few years. Gabrielle, the eldest of Grieffe's many daughters, watched over Minnie, observing that she was unable to cope with Nellie's aggressiveness. Minnie drew closer to Gabrielle and George, and looked to Aunt Sally for warmth and guidance. Sally developed an intense interest in the arts, compensating for the lack of Grieffe's companionship. Although Minnie dearly loved her Aunt Sally and admired her Uncle Grieffe for his acomplishments and proud aristocratic bearing, she remained keenly sensitive to the unhappiness between Grieffe and Sally, reflected in every family routine.

Grieffe was stricken by a heart attack which took his life within days after a shift in the Virginia tobacco market threatened his holdings. The family was again split. Minnie and George, 16 and 19 years old, went north to an older cousin, John Pannell, a merchant who lived with his young family in Morgan Park, a suburb outside Chicago. Tyler was brought to live with his married sister in Englewood, a section of Chicago. In this way, Minnie was once again reunited with her father. Nellie was but 13 years old and, rather than be further obligated to other relatives, she was sent off to boarding school with Minnie and George promising to pay her expenses.

As a mature woman Minnie was attractive, petite, and fun-loving, with an aristocratic bearing. She had the proud Calloway presence and the cultivated tastes of her Aunt Sally, which blended with her natural artistic inclination. She appeared younger than her years and her high spirit and girlish laughter lent a childlike quality to her adult charm. Her turned-up nose, thin lips though generous mouth, and high cheek bones, along with her caramel-colored skin, gave her a strikingly Indian appearance, belied only by her hazel eyes and long brown finely-textured hair which she wore in a bun at the nape of her neck.

Minnie remained dutiful to Tyler, ailing with a heart condition. She visited regularly to see how he was getting along in the home of his married sister and her family while she lived in the home of other cousins in Morgan Park. She was swept into the gay social life of the Negro "Talented Tenth" and the "Old Settlers" of Chicago, which centered around church activities. She became the belle of the Baptist Church, escorted and courted perennially by the popular minister, but avoided marriage as the type of life she recalled her mother having, with children, sacrifices, and a complete loss of personal freedom. She cultivated a rich clientele as a much sought after "modiste," designing and making fine gowns for the wealthy in Beverly Hills. In the home of the Pannells, she became a carefree, happy person among loving relatives. It was to this style of life Minnie longed to return during the few years she lived in Columbus. Such had been the tapestry of family life for George, Minnie, and Nellie.

A few days later George was out on the road, heading for Chicago. He had just completed one of the most difficult transactions he had ever attempted. He felt good that Nellie's personal involvement in the bank had been secured and he had fulfilled his allegiance to Minnie.

While George was in New York, P.W. and Minnie were busy planning the one promotional affair for the bank they were to work on together. P.W. was pleased when Minnie offered to help with the decorations for the Douglass National Bank at the Eighth Regiment Armory Dramatic Festival, an annual affair sponsored by the local civic women's group. Minnie wanted to help and this occasion seemed most appropriate. She assisted in setting up the booth, and selected the furnishings and fabrics as background for the artwork. Months ago, P.W. had commissioned a promising black artist

113

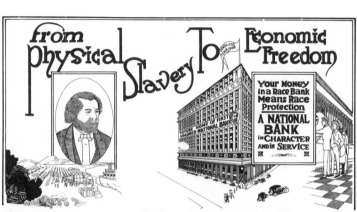

from
Physical Slavery **To** Economic **Freedom**

Your Money
in a Race Bank
Means Race
Protection
A NATIONAL
BANK
in CHARACTER
and in SERVICE

DOUGLASS NATIONAL BANK
CHICAGO ILL.

From Physical Slavery to Economic
Freedom, Bank promotional literature,
1921

named Scott to paint a full life-size oil painting of Fredrick
Douglass and a smaller portrait of himself. Eventually, these
paintings would be moved to their permanent home, P.W.'s
office at the Douglass National Bank.

There were many pretty booths at the Festival. It was
well-attended on weekends by crowds of adults and children.
On the opening day a huge crowd went to the bank booth for
the unveiling ceremony in the early afternoon. Alderman
R. R. Johnson, one of the Board members, gave a brief speech
in glowing terms about the purpose of the booth . . . to illus-
trate the economic opportunities which would be available to
the black community through the bank. P.W. and Minnie
mingled with the crowd. S.T. Moses, another Bank member,
did the actual unveiling, commenting about the exhibit having been designed to portray the history of the colored
citizenry from slavery to the present with emphasis on three
great steps of "physical freedom," "industrial freedom," and

114

What Is a National Bank?

AND

What the Douglass National Bank Means to You.

BY

P. W. CHAVERS, Pres.,
Douglass National Bank

HOW A NATIONAL BANK IS FORMED

FIRST, a formal application must be made to the U. S. Comptroller of Currency at Washington, D. C. The signers of the application must be known to be reputable business men of sound business character and financial standing.

This application must be endorsed by a Judge, the U. S. Postmaster and the Mayor of the City.

Upon receipt of the application, the Comptroller of Currency sets his machinery into motion for the most scrutinizing and complete investigation of each and every officer and proposed member of the Board of Directors; requiring a schedule of their net financial worth; satisfying himself as to their business ability needed in the safe and successful management of a bank.

None having been involved in financial difficulties can affiliate with National banking. In other words, each and every officer and director of a National Bank must not only be of good repute, but he must be of absolute proven ability in character. For all must prove themselves to be as "clean as a hound's tooth".

What Is a National Bank, 1922

"economic freedom," in the progress of the colored race in America. The pictures were arranged in a semi-circle.

A hush came over the crowd as they looked to the left at the portrait of Fredrick Douglass, standing six feet tall within a 9-by-7 foot canvas frame. There he stood, magnificent, head erect with piercing eyes, his hair flowing like a lion. He typified "physical freedom." Oooohs and aahs could be heard in the audience. The crowd felt his presence and the majesty of the black leader as they gazed at his portrait. P.W. was exceedingly pleased. The people crowded closer while the photograph of the second great black leader was unveiled. The center portrait revealed Booker T. Washington, typifying "industrial freedom." This huge photograph showed Washington years earlier as he sat relaxed and self assured. It was borrowed from our home and would be returned to us after the festival was over. "He looks handsome," someone said. Then P.W.'s bust portrait was revealed on the right showing "economic freedom" which completed the exhibit. P.W. had spared no expense and was delighted with the crowds' reaction. He listened intently to all comments and discussed the response with Johnson and Williams when the ceremony was over. After a few days, interest was running so great that he had to send some bank employees to help service the booth. They answered questions and distributed information about how stock could be bought. Minnie assisted in servicing the booth on weekends. She enjoyed listening to reactions from the crowds and working to promote the bank. In fact, she reminisced about this experience weeks afterward. It seemed for the first time to give her a closer acquaintance with P.W.'s bank efforts and its significance to the community.

After the Eighth Regiment Armory Festival, P.W.'s campaigns were stepped up, taking him and his Board all over the Midwest and into Washington, D.C. The city newspapers continued to be more receptive of what he was trying to do than the black-owned press, even after he had secured the permit.

6

The Campaign Escalates

The two British women were doing exceptionally well with their door-to-door selling and by now Minnie seemed quite proud of her direction of the entire factory operation. They were coming back with such a big profit, Minnie was encouraged to let them have more and more merchandise as samples. Some of the wealthy clients the white women secured were submitting repeat orders and requesting uniforms made to order for their maids and nurses. They would return to the factory with interesting stories about the people they met while selling the aprons. On one occasion, a customer asked for advice about preparing a meal and they proceeded to prepare the meal for her while selling the aprons. Minnie had just given Miss Alexander a package to take to one of these customers earlier that day at the factory, when the white landlord, Mr. Thompson, unexpectedly dropped in.

Minnie had seen him once or twice before at the old Wood-folk Bank when P.W. was signing papers. She had disliked him instantly, and later had told P.W. how she felt. But he had laughed and given her one of his "Now Minnie" looks. However, Minnie was sure of her instincts; there was something about Thompson's sharp nose, the smirk on his face, and the way he was always shifting his large grey eyes around that made her distrust him. He might be considered handsome, had it not been for a sinister quality about him. It was as if Providence had given him a tall frame, wavy hair, and a deceptively youthful appearance and then as an afterthought had decided to warn his fellow men who might otherwise be taken in, by putting that smirk on his face. Well he did not fool Minnie Belle. She always knew by the time you're forty you have the face you deserve. P.W. never looked at it that way. He was trusting of everyone, ready to give them the benefit of the doubt.

It was strange he would come by the factory, Minnie thought as she arrived home that evening. P.W.'s footsteps broke her train of thought. "P.W." she called out as he came into the parlor, "Mr. Thompson came by the shop today."

"Oh?" he replied, frowning a little. "He was probably just looking around."

"Looking around for what?" her eyes were flashing now. She got up from the sofa and walked across the floor to close the sliding door. "What's he snooping around for?" she repeated, adding "with that horrible grin of his!"

"He probably just dropped by to look around," P.W. said again.

"That's just what he said," she rang out. "Since when did he start making social calls?" Minnie was very aware of positions, categories, and social boundaries within which people were assumed to operate.

"But Minnie, honey, he is the landlord. He might have been looking around to see if the building needed any repairs."

"Oh P.W.," she said as loudly as she dared, looking over her shoulder to see if the door was really closed, "You just can't see anything about people. Sometimes I think you would trust a water moccasin if it could talk. Nobody's bad in your eyesight."

"Does looking over one's property make one bad?" he questioned, using his logic on Minnie now. She didn't mind when he used his soft sweet approach to get next to her, but his logic made her furious when she couldn't handle it. She felt helpless and insecure when relating to people she did not intuitively like. She sensed that her man and her family were being threatened now. It was not something she could put her finger on or articulate, but a nagging foreboding had been with her for awhile now.

"Dear," she said softly, with a tremor in her voice as if still another thought had suddenly burst through to her. . . "Did you renew the lease on the factory?"

"No Minnie, there's plenty of time. Thompson and I have a verbal agreement and it's done automatically every year. No hurry," P.W. answered reassuringly. He was moving towards her with outstretched arms, but Minnie tossed her little head and turned on her heels. She was completely unable to answer his logic with logic and was angered by his confidence in Thompson.

"I'll put your dinner on the table," she announced as she swept out of the room.

True, the lease on the factory was renewed every May, as had been done for the last four years. Now it was June. "I must look into that as soon as possible," said P.W. following her into the dining room.

It was during the summer stock campaign that signs of internal jealousy began to crop up among Board members. The meetings were carefully thought out, with a format for presentation of the bank stock as the black man's opportunity for financieal investment and security in an institution sensitive to his needs. Dr. Morris usually handled the introduction, setting the tone of the meeting. P.W. followed with details about the bank plan and development, stressing his hopes for the Fredrick Douglass National Bank. In his pinstripe suit and cutaway coat, using bank terminology, P.W. projected the confident style of a bank president, carefully describing financial concepts in relationship to the individual. Later, he would introduce a guest speaker, usually a prominent white politician of the locality with a reputation for supporting the best interest of Blacks. These were huge meetings conducted throughout the Mid-west. The possibility of the white politician garnishing votes was not to be overlooked as their eloquent words rang out to black masses. Few powerful black politicians existed in those days, and white politicians, somewhat sympathetic, tenuously represented politics in the democratic process during these rallies. Barnstorming from city to city, the format for the Board of Directors became smoother, but Morris always made it a point to correct or elaborate on some item P.W. brought out when they spoke on the same platform and the internal jealousy behind the scenes began to fester like a boil.

Before the end of the summer we packed to move to Calumet Avenue, farther south on the periphery of the Black

Belt, where the more affluent families were concentrated. The change was more than in location for all of us. This was a large luxury-type apartment building; we no longer lived in our own home. The move into the Calumet property created further rumblings within the Board and intensified the growing envy of P.W.'s stature and popularity in the community. Although when it took place, the move appeared fairly uneventful on the surface.

The factory employees, including Rebecca and Jack, helped us move into this elegant, three-storied, grey-stone, twelve-apartment building. Uncle George agreed it was a good location for the expansion of P.W.'s activities, near the corner of 47th Street, a main thoroughfare lined with small retail stores, busy street cars and heavy pedestrian traffic. The elevated train with a main station nearby added to the convenience and the emerging commercial atmosphere in the area. Yet Calumet Avenue was sufficiently protected for the family because the trolley cars stopped a short block away at another main thoroughfare, Grand Boulevard, later called South Parkway, and now known as Martin Luther King Drive.

We children soon became aware that our daddy was in charge of the entire building, not because we heard any discussions of this at home, but because he opened a real estate office on the first floor. There he handled his transactions with tenants, listening to their problems, collecting rents, ordering repairs, replacements, and supplies, hiring workmen, and the other countless duties in managing and planning for the care of the property. The large front window of the first-floor apartment was gold-lettered, "P.W. Chavers, Mortgage Banker." We could see well-dressed people with a business-like air coming and going into his office, and with childish pride we thought of him as the "Chief"; we swelled with pride whenever we passed his office. We loved climbing the wide mahogany staircases that terminated at our third floor apartment and were busy making friends in the building and neighborhood. A few weeks after we moved, Daddy took time off to enroll me in the Willard School.

Now, at my mother's insistence, I was to start the long

educational journey which would begin in a non-segregated school. The Calumet property was located in the same district as Willard School, a new, modern school with better facilities, assembly halls on the first and second floors, a separate gymnasium on the third floor and a program planned as a series of experiences in the development of the complete child. The percentage of Negro children accurately reflected the number of Negro families living in the district, an indication of the unbiased, more socially responsible attitude of the principal. P.W. and Minnie had reason to feel content about the quality of education in store for us. Academically it would be at least adequate, if not outstanding. As we drew near, the school came into view as a huge, three-story, nearly block-long building, with many gaily colored, draped windows. We must have lived far away, on the fringe of the Willard School area; at least it seemed very far away for a little girl of four years and nine months just ready for kindergarten.

I remember how proud I felt walking into the school building that morning hand in hand with my daddy. Mother had curled and ribboned my hair and dressed me in a pleated skirt with a ruffled blouse. For a long time I had looked forward to school and catching up with brother Bill. As Daddy and I entered the principal's office, we found ourselves alone except for the school clerk who was blond, blue-eyed, plump, and efficient. She spoke sharply, inquiring how Daddy wanted to register my name. He replied, "Helen Madrue," but she looked up with a cold bureaucratic stare and let him know that no child could be called by two first names.

He seemed a little surprised. His discussions of school plans with Mother covered every detail, but they had not anticipated a question about first names. Daddy paused, looked down at me as I sat on the school bench, then spoke to the clerk again, "My little girl's name is 'Helen Madrue.'"

"But, Mr. Chavers, it's against the rules of the school to call a child by two first names. We make a notation of both names for the record," replied the clerk.

"My wife is probably going to be upset about this," he continued, "but, if you have to use just one name, let's ask my little girl which name she prefers." Turning to me, he asked,

"Which name do you want to be called in school?" His voice and manner were gentle and reassuring.

I looked at the clerk, and then at Daddy, "Madrue," I replied. Daddy was surprised again. At home, Mother called me "Helen."

When we got home and explained what happened, Mother became annoyed, just as Daddy expected. She insisted that "Helen Madrue" was phonetically very beautiful, and should have presented no problem to the teachers.

School life at Willard was pleasant and I quickly made friends in kindergarten. Shortly after school started I was enrolled in dancing school operated by a nationally famous dancer, Hazel Thompson Davis. There, children from aspiring black families were sent to learn dancing as well as to develop social amenities and contacts. Eventually Mother filled all of our days, adding music and elocution lessons both in group and private sessions as well as costume fittings and recitals, keeping us busy in a constant whirl of acquiring "culture." As I look back now, I realize that our heavy schedule was set up not only to perpetuate Mother's standards of self-expression and expose us to the value of the Negro middle-class, but to keep us away from the other tenants' children whom Mother considered beneath us. It was also a diversion from Daddy's growing absences from home, due to long trips to other cities on behalf of the bank, and the promotion of other causes in Chicago.

The first stockholders' meeting in the late summer culminated in an even greater stock campaign. A call was issued to more than three hundred pledges with an announcement of an offer of one hundred dollars in prizes to be given to the stockholder who got the most new buyers in the next thirty days. Of the local black press, only *The Broad Ax* had provided full coverage, but the newspapers throughout the nation carried the story in sufficient detail for the black population in the larger cities to follow. Citizens' committees in many of these cities were formed to invite the Board to visit and bring their message. To encourage full participation, P.W. financed the expenses of the trips out of his pocket, and had never accepted any compensation for his services either

122

as President of the Board, or Trustee of the Woodfolk Bank holdings to which he was entitled, even in the absence of such a provision. By fall the Board took its message to Joliet, Illinois before a capacity audience. In St. Louis, they also spoke to an overflowing audience.

Then P.W. had to make a hurried trip to Washington, D.C. to settle the approved opening date for the bank and to submit the final organization papers required by the Treasury Department. He returned home bringing gifts for all of us, fur coats for mother, Edwina and me, and a gold watch for Bill. Minnie was radiant in the leopard jacket, carrying the beaded evening purse he brought her and modeled them for us. There was a full length squirrel coat for me, and a white rabbit fur coat for Edwina. We felt very precious and were delighted, but we saw even less of Daddy after that.

Twenty-five officers and staff of the bank took off with P.W. for Indianapolis, Indiana for a massive last lap drive which resulted in the subscription of thousands of dollars worth of stock. At each meeting P.W. became more determined to project his message. He was factual and specific about the importance of the great economic crusade being waged, about the lack of financial progress because of negligence in supporting black-owned enterprises, and about the plans to make extensive alterations on the old Woodfolk Bank building to make it the most handsome building in the city of Chicago owned by colored people. Now, as the campaign wore on and gathered momentum, his speeches became even more dramatic. He was bent on arousing his people to action, telling them that "the immortal Abraham Lincoln took the chains from more than four million slaves fifty years ago, giving them physical emancipation," telling them "today, nobody could give the Negro American economic emancipation, he must win this for himself through thrift, honesty and good judgement."

He stressed that the Negro American had been preyed upon and exploited by every sort of stock swindler, scheme promoter, and confidence man in the country until he didn't know whom to trust or whom to suspect. He must now use his intelligence to find trustworthy men who could be trusted, and then help his brothers by being trustworthy himself. Sometimes he would confide in his audience, "Ever since childhood I have trained for this job. It has been my lifetime ambition to found a successful Negro bank." He wanted them to know how fully prepared he was to give of himself in this effort, and how dedicated to their cause he felt.

But by late fall, P.W. began to show signs of fatigue. With all the planning, speeches, travelling and the maneuvering behind the scenes, the toll was showing in his face. He was deeply troubled by the undercurrents of dissent and the examples of sabotage he noticed here and there, especially the snide remarks made by Roberts and Morris about how Chavers was "grabbing all the credit in the white press releases," and how "the whole campaign was sure to fail anyway" since no real big money came from certain key people in Chicago. These people expected special invitations, but the pitch had been to the little man with emphasis on having the stock held by the masses of poor Blacks. Part-payment plans on their pledges extending over an eight-month period had been set up to allow as many as possible to become involved. Roberts was annoyed with this strategy which required that they stage many meetings and work diligently. He felt it could have been done quick and easy by opening the campaign with a pitch to a selected few of the wealthier black Old Settlers.

One day P.W. overheard Morris say to Roberts, "P.W. must think he's a white man, trying to be a banker is a white man's job. Somebody's going to teach him his place as a Negro in this town." This comment troubled P.W. more than any of the others. His intent was being misunderstood and distorted. The whispering campaign began simultaneously with the bank stock campaign wind-up. Because of this chaos it slowed down and P.W. had to write to Washington periodically requesting an extension of the permit.

The Comptroller of Currency received letters from Chicagoans asking whether or not a permit had been granted. The answers confirmed the legality of the bank drive and satisfied some doubters. Some checked with the federal authorities to make sure the proper credentials to operate a national bank had been submitted. P.W. was notified of each inquiry and he shared with the Comptroller copies of newspaper clippings about the bank developments.

It was around this time that P.W. was made aware that some of the Board members were meeting secretly with Owens, the wealthy insecticide manufacturer, whom they felt had plenty of money to handle the purchase of a huge block of stock. Richard Owens was nearing 60 years old, had studied and worked hard and long, saved his money, and was determined to achieve, making every move count to become a wealthy man. He had started the insecticide factory in Mississippi, then moved his small operation to the Chicago Black Belt about ten years ago. It had prospered almost immediately. Although he had been born a mixed-blood slave in the Deep South before the Emancipation Proclamation, Owens had prospered as a self-made man in the "Promised Land" of Chicago. His factory made insecticides and household cleaners which were sorely needed in the overcrowded Black Belt. Owens was known for his shrewd manipulation of time, space, men and money.

Roberts was spreading rumors to get others to dissent openly. He had become obsessed with the idea of bringing Owens in to simplify the stock campaign and to stop P.W.'s crusading. "I told Chavers a long time ago they weren't going to trust him; these ignorant people were like sheep. Because they clap their hands at these meetings doesn't mean they're going to honor their pledges. You can't stir up enough of them to support the bank! We've got to get Owens. He has plenty of money and the right connections with the big down-town banks. He has already promised to buy a big block of stock. We Old Settlers can show Chavers we know how to get a job done without a lot of work, time and complications."

P.W. did not know how far the discontent spread. He struggled to take the bite out of these rumors as he wrote letters to Washington, submitting Articles of Association of the Douglass National Bank, acknowledging that his methods and plans were a little slower than the ordinary ways of making a bank, and continuing in consultation with the Deputy Comptroller, obtaining instructions about preparing the organization certificate, the certificate relative to payment of capital stock, the by-laws papers, and the application for stock in the Federal Reserve Board. He refused to back down from his goal of reaching the masses and reproached the restless and short-sighted for stirring up the fears of others, reminding them that these mass meetings had not been side-shows. Many seeds had been firmly planted in the minds of those who attended. He was sure the mass meetings had helped many oppressed Blacks to dare to dream the American dream of "getting ahead," and that they would eventually purchase stock even if they were not prepared to do so immediately. Despite all of his eloquence and pleading, the dissenters continued to make trouble.

In desperation, P.W. went to see O.F. Stewart for a private talk. He was serving as Chairman of the Board with the intention of staying only as long as necessary to get the bank operating and had refrained from participating in any of the public meetings to avoid clouding the racial issue, but he knew what was going on. P.W. knew Stewart to be a man of good will and a friend of the black people. They went over details of the sales campaign and how P.W. had tried to deal with the growing unrest of the Board. They agreed that because Stewart was white, he would not be effective in settling any behind-the-scenes squabbles. Any interference on his part would only serve to aggravate the distrust and bitterness germinating in the minds of some Board members. Together they planned how P.W. could convince the Board to present a united front at the next mass rally in order to solicit the necessary final pledges, as well as a tentative plan for the opening celebration. Both men felt it would be effective to have a parade along State Street inviting the more than 5000 members of various Churches, Sunday Schools, and Businessmen's Associations to participate in the triumph anticipated. Although this parade never came to be, the idea bouyed P.W.'s spirits. It was as though a marching band, banners for a common good, cheering crowds and colorful balloons all floated through his imagination, leaving him extremely hopeful on the bleakest streets in the worst of times.

With his convictions reaffirmed by Stewart's encouragement, P.W. faced his audience at the next meeting with increased confidence, telling them "We are making history. This is the first time a black man has held any position in a national bank above that of janitor." The crowd roared. "This is the first time a national bank in the United States is being completely officered by Negroes; the first time bank notes will be signed by a man of color. There can be no race question after the colored race is freed to grow financially," he continued. "Last year, three of the top graduates of Ohio University were black men. Two are working as pullman porters, the other is driving a truck. This bank will begin the long task of reversing the trend of serious underemployment for the many colored men like these three. This bank will provide business opportunities to deserving men like these three Ohio University graduates that will be in keeping with the level of their education and ability. We must all work together to assure our people of these opportunities."

One evening, early in December, Dr. Morris paid an unexpected call to our home expressing regret that he had not called in advance . . . the matter seemed urgent. Mother joined them in the alcove off the living-room where they continued to speak in hushed voices. Dr. Morris was saying that he was unable to pay for enough stock to qualify as a director of the bank. This shocked P.W. who considered Dr. Morris a financially responsible director.

"Earl, we'll have to work something out. This is a pretty bad time, so close to the bank opening, and so near Christmas," commented P.W. He wondered why Morris had waited so late in the campaign to speak of his inability to meet the requirements to be qualified as a director. He had subscribed right away, but had not paid up. There had been plenty of time, several months had passed. In other cities where they travelled together, he had never discussed his inability to pay or seek an alternative. Why had Morris waited?

"If you would loan me a certain amount P.W., I could qualify," said Morris in a casual tone. "Times are hard and many patients are unable to pay me."

P.W. knew some of Morris' private aggravations and wondered if he was in a position to take care of his responsibilities

127

or if he was faking. Morris' snide remarks during some of the campaign meetings and his private discussions with Roberts also came to P.W. as he now studied Morris intently.

"Well, I could resign from the Board" said Morris, breaking the silence.

"What would that accomplish?" questioned P.W. He realized that the Board composition being disturbed at this late date would be a reflection on the stability of the Board.

Earl Morris made no further comment about remaining on the board; instead he continued speaking of his patients. "You just can't trust them. They tell me all about times being hard and Christmas being near. I just can't force them to pay me." P.W. knew that dentists were often not paid when patients were short of money and he did want to be fair about Morris's situation. But somehow, the request did not ring true to P.W. Was Morris putting on this "poor act" to intimidate P.W. so he would feel compelled to let Owens on the Board? Or was Morris really less affluent than he appeared?

This time Minnie broke the silence, "I really don't know what you should do."

Finally P.W. decided, "We have got to see the bank opening through as planned. Everything hinges on our presenting a strong united front to the community and to Washington!" He paused for a moment, "We can't have word getting around that one of our directors is financially unable to meet his commitments. How much do you need?" P.W. asked slowly.

"One thousand dollars would be enough of a loan, Chavers," said Morris. This was the amount he originally agreed to purchase, the minimum to become a director. He did not look at Minnie, but addressed his remarks completely to P.W. as if to see what his reaction would be to this demand.

P.W. showed no reaction. Instead he said, "I'll have the money ready for you in the morning." Morris immediately thanked P.W. for being so understanding, urging that this be kept confidential.

"Naturally, Dr. Morris, I wouldn't care to tell too many people that one of our directors couldn't meet his minimum stock payment. To speak publicly of how we worked this out tonight would make a joke of all we've been trying to do," responded P.W.

As soon as the door closed behind Morris, Minnie opened the conversation with, "This was a strange thing for Morris to do. This bank promotion is really bleeding us, P.W., when will it end?" They talked as they walked through the house together to the bedroom; P.W. sat on the edge of the bed and removed his shoes.

"You're right, Minnie, that was an unusual request. I wonder what gets into these men at times" continued P.W. very puzzled.

"We've been over that many times," Minnie sighed. She did not feel like talking about the bank; she wanted to talk about how the campaign would all end, but she continued, "Well, it won't be long before the opening. I've planned a birthday party for Madrue that will have to be cancelled, I suppose, because of this loan."

"Madrue will have her party," returned P.W. "but there is something about Morris' coming here tonight that annoys me." A frown furrowed his brow as he stood up and began restlessly moving about the room.

Minnie was pleased, and almost sang out, realizing she wasn't going to be disappointed about having this one social function she'd been looking forward to for so long. "I have the invitations all addressed for the party and it would have been a shame to disappoint Madrue; she's so proud of becoming five years old."

P.W. tried to concentrate on Minnie's words, but the terrible shock of Morris' demand preocccupied him still. "More should be done for our people when they are young. I hope to do something really significant for all Negro children some-day," he commented. "We won't have to worry about ours doing well. We'll see that they have a good life." But Mother's eyes revealed a deep exhaustion.

"P.W., if you keep throwing away what we have for our children on others, there won't be anything left for them," answered Minnie. "That's my biggest fear when you talk about what our people need. But let's not go over it anymore

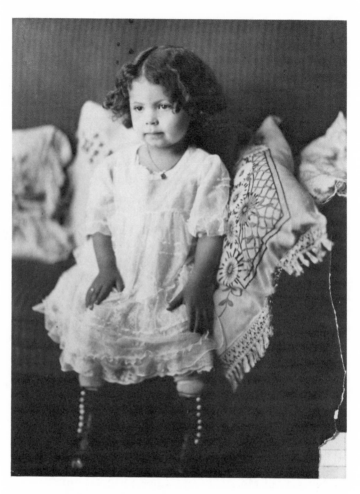

Madrue at birthday party, 1921

tonight," she added, completely tired, turning off the lamp to go to sleep.

Mother took great pride in preparing for my party. She arranged the lavish favors, decorations, refreshments and party games to encourage the constant gaiety and movement of the guests. Our apartment easily accommodated the fifty or sixty guests who attended; the large foyer, dining room, living room, and alcove flowed into one another without doorways, which made mingling possible in that part of the house. The guest list read like a Who's Who of the Black Belt, and they all turned out that afternoon. I recall the excitement of being among so many people, most of whom were adults and strangers to me. There were mothers and fathers dressed in fancy clothes, busy doing things to please each other and a great many unfamiliar, but attractive children. I remember feeling that I would have had more fun if I could have invited more of my school friends. It was my party, but Mother had made up the guest list.

I was dressed in ruffles from shoulders to knees, pearl-button shoes, pink ribbons in my curly hair, like the belle of the party, but somehow I knew it was more Mother's party than mine. She seemed more interested in trying to impress those fancy strangers. Nonetheless, I played the party games and finally took my place at the head of the children for the parade around the house before the big birthday cake and refreshments were served.

Looking back, I realize it was actually a joint celebration of the anticipated bank opening and my birthday which accounted for the serious discussions and the lack of interest in the children. But I did enjoy being with so many children and the party was a social success by adult standards.

Daddy spent most of the day following Christmas in solitary meditation in the office, reviewing his accomplishments, reflecting on the many situations he had been able to deal with, where his errors had been, especially in his dealing with the Board. Reverend Roberts and some of the others had not yet paid up their pledges. They had put off final payment with various excuses. "Wait until after Christmas," "times are hard," were some of their answers when he had urged them to pay up. Suddenly his thoughts were interrupted by a call from Morris to wish him a "Merry Christmas."

P.W. sat in his office trying to put these maneuvers in their proper perspective, but his concern had deepened in the past month as payment on pledges slowed down. He had been notified that the charter would not be issued until receipt by the Comptroller's office of a certificate from the officers and directors covering payment of at least 50% of the capital and the required amount of the Federal Reserve Bank stock had been paid. A few days later the *Chicago Defender*, the powerful black news weekly, featured a lengthy article about the forthcoming opening of the Douglass National Bank with comments by Jesse Binga, the black president of the state bank in the Black Belt, about his attitude towards the possible competition, and raising the question: "Does the Negro community need two black banks? In the article, Binga was quoted as answering directly that the Negro Community could support two black banks. "This is a real breakthrough," thought P.W. as he read the news item. "This newspaper article reflects community support by a nationally known and respected black businessman, Jesse Binga, at a time when we very much need it."

P.W. telephoned Attorney Lucas, his friend, to draw attention to the article and discuss his reaction. Lucas, Woodfolk's attorney in the original bankruptcy case, had removed himself temporarily from active public participation in these affairs because of some family matters, but he kept in close contact with P.W. around the bank developments over the months. He listened as P.W. pointed out the significance of the article appearing in the *Chicago Defender* from his perspective. "I see that Binga has put the figure at $15,000,000 representing 1,000 black business people who have deposits in white banks. . . . He's telling it just like I do . . . "When you work for your money, you should see that it works for you . . . that it builds your community" P.W. read on, as Lucas agreed. "Binga is quoted as saying 'A Negro commercial bank is needed to keep our resources where we can use them, and a national bank can do this where a state bank cannot.' This is a great day, Lucas . . . Now we can show the world that Negro Americans can get together and set up a national bank!!"

Lucas cautioned P.W. about the motives of some local community men in their thirst for power and control of the community, but this new development was deeply gratifying to both of them. The thought of the Defender supporting his

132

efforts so belatedly made P.W. sad momentarily. On the other hand, he felt this recognition could only be interpreted as an acknowledgement that the national bank movement was too significant for any faction to ignore any longer.

The Broad Ax, Chicago, Ill.

THE DOUGLASS NATIONAL BANK

The officers and directors of the Douglass National Bank, headed by the genial president, Mr. P. W. Chavers, reached the city early Tuesday morning after concluding a very successful out-of-town stock selling campaign, with a big mass meeting at Indianapolis on Monday evening.

The meeting was held in the auditorium of the new Phillips Memorial Temple, just completed at a cost of $110,000, the finest structure of its kind ever owned by our group. The population turned out "en masse" to welcome the bank representatives and indicated their interest by subscribing and paying for a large number of shares. The meeting which terminated so profitably was held under the auspices of a citizen's committee of one hundred, composed of the leading business and professional men and women of the city.

Similar meetings have been held in St. Louis and Detroit and Mr. Chavers and the board are much elated with the evident awakening of the race to its industrial and commercial needs and predict that within a short time we will attain REAL freedom: That of economic emancipation.

All necessary equipment, such as pass books, check books, etc., and office appliances have been ordered and will be installed as soon as the contractor completes the renovation of the building and makes it ready for the formal opening early in January, 1922.

Douglass National Bank to Open Jan. 1922

7

The Journey to Washington

The formal opening of the bank, scheduled for January 2, 1922, had to be postponed. Newspaper releases were sympathetic, clarifying the reason for the delay as a result of remodeling the building. This gave P.W. some hope that unity was finally gathering within the black community, but this was short-lived. P.W. knew Roberts, Morris, and some of the others had kept in close touch with Owens, flattering him openly, in the hopes that the delay in subscribers' payments on stock pledges would open the way for Owens' admission to the Board. Owens was now taking the position that he would not advance any money for the venture as long as P.W. was still President.

The required legal documents were submitted and all necessary procedures were completed. Now, because of slow subscription payments, P.W. was forced to face the possibility of losing his Board. Word was passed around the community that Washington probably would not issue the charter to P.W. "They know his type can't be bought, and they want a black man they can handle, one of those 'safe ones' . . . the kind they can give medals and awards to for doing their bidding." When P.W. had a discussion with Rev. Roberts about this crisis, he came out openly with, "P.W., you'll just . . have to face it, Washington does not want you in there as President. Owens is their type. With him all of this would move faster. You would still be leader, but his money would move your plans into action. He is ready to join the Board, but is holding up on this because of you." P.W. approached Dr. Morris who claimed times were getting more difficult for him, he was still unable to repay the $1,000.00 loan. He had nothing to add to what P.W. already knew. "P.W., the best thing for you is to work with the Whites and give up all of this community business. The Board, in particular, does have misgivings about you."

By early February, Roberts was explaining to P.W. that he was involved in some grave situation, and was being pushed to consider a career offer in New York. He said he had been unable to keep up with his sermons recently and thought he might step down from the Douglass Bank Board and other community commitments altogether. A few weeks later, P.W. wrote to the Deputy Comptroller of Currency requesting another 60 day extension of the permit to complete the organization of the bank. This time he elaborated on the details of the situation . . .

"My dear Mr. Fowler:

I wish to report to you that owing to the fact that quite a few of our subscribers, because of the industrial depression, have been unable to make their payment promptly on their subscriptions; their inability to pay has retarded our progress. Our part payment plan makes it easy for our subscribers, but it is a very slow method for us.

You are familiar with the conditions under which we are laboring and, for the above reasons, I must again ask that you grant us the customary sixty days extension to complete our organization.

Most all lines of business here are beginning to slowly pick up and a large number of people are going back to work. I find that most all of the business people and working people are optimistic and hopeful and that within the next few months, times will again be normal.

Thank you for the past favors, I remain . . .
Respectfully yours,
P.W. Chavers

From time to time, and more openly now, Minnie and P.W. talked over the stalemate in the bank's development and the conditions in the factory to relieve each other's mounting apprehensions.

"What the hell is the matter with these men?" P.W. exploded one evening when they were exchanging thoughts about the pressures they felt.

"Vera hasn't shown up at the factory all this week," said Minnie a few nights later. P.W. just shook his head.

But several days later, P.W. was totally shattered by the appearance of the police at his real estate office. He was arrested and taken to the Stanton Avenue Police Station to be arraigned as prescribed in a warrant taken out by a Reverend J.P. Cooper. Once there, P.W. was advised of the charges made against him . . . that he was allegedly operating a confidence game and accepting funds for the insolvent Woodfolk Bank. Although in shock from the outrage of these accusations, he remained outwardly calm and silent for a few minutes while searching for ways to respond to these treacherous charges designed to intimidate and discredit him in the community. Then he moved stoically to telephone Attorney George Adams, his personal lawyer. His heart pounded; it all seemed a nightmare, illogical, surreal. While waiting for Adams' arrival, P.W. found himself in a harshly lit room filled with many police milling about; then he caught a glimpse of Vera, his worker who had been absent from the factory. "What is she doing here?" he thought. A few minutes later it became apparent that she was with this Reverend Cooper, the neighborhood store-front minister, who had taken out the warrant and had come prepared to press charges; but the procedure had been stopped when P.W. requested counsel. Attorney Adams arrived shortly, talked with the police about his witnesses, and made the plea of "not guilty" before the Judge who was brought in. The hearing was then scheduled to continue the following week.

All the way home P.W. was confused about the entire experience and deeply troubled about Vera and her role in all of this. Over and over he asked himself . . . who was in back of this move to intimidate him? Were the Blacks in the ghetto turning on him, ready to discount and degrade him, showing no consideration for his family and his efforts? Was the loose talk of the doubtful Board Members feeding fears to the community people? Vera was definitely with this minister that had sworn out the warrant against him, but why? P.W. could not be sure he had never seen the minister. He was not sure of what or how the connection existed between this Reverend Cooper and his Board, but he was certain it did exist.

At the hearing the following week the case was dismissed on the grounds of lack of evidence. Although he was still shocked and unclear as to the terrible motivation of the act, P.W. attempted to explain to Minnie what had happened by this time. With unusual quietude she accepted what he said, realizing how painful this unfortunate experience must have been for him to endure. She was alarmed, chagrined and deeply hurt as P.W. told her of the arrest and the charges, but she struggled with herself not to allow her feelings to show. Her heart went out to him and she did not scold as he had somehow expected she might do. P.W. knew by her silence that she was suffering too. Now at least he knew what was at stake, and how far envious and jealous people were willing to go to destroy him.

"All of their fears, discontent, and acts to undermine my authority will end as soon as I have that bank charter in my hands," P.W. reassured Minnie. The arrest made him resolve to complete his mission and helped him to realize the only thing left was to go to Washington in person and investigate the delay, to confront those responsible, and to demand the immediate release of the charter so the bank could open its doors to commence operations. It was just a question of who would go with him and when to make the trip so that the impact would be conclusive and effective.

A few weeks later, at Minnie's request, P.W. purchased tickets for the opera. In the foyer he met Harry Garnes who had been the best man at their wedding. He was alone in the audience; his wife was singing on the stage that evening. Harry was now a socially prominent dentist, settled in Chicago and married to Antoinette who passed for white to get and hold her job in the chorus of the Chicago Grand Opera. The old friendship was quickly rekindled. Harry and P.W. were somewhat alike, both born and brought up in Columbus, Ohio, but Harry had remained much the same as when they had graduated from high school; concerned about his popularity and his small circle of close friends. As the world measures success, he had all the trappings; professional training and status, a fine middle-class home and a wife who was "in-opera," and passed for white. He told P.W. that they entertained quite a bit and believed in enjoying their position in life. They were a handsome couple, Antoinette was delicately beautiful, talented, and self-contained; Harry was handsome, personable and affable. It was after their marriage that Antoinette joined the chorus of the Chicago Opera Company. Her earnings enabled them to buy their home. However, they had no children.

The following week P.W. took Minnie to a gala party the Garnes held in their home on 42nd Place, where she met Antoinette for the first time. However, Minnie could not warm up to Antoinette. It was not so much because she was so aloof and condescending in her manner, or because she was taken for white, pretending to be what she wasn't, but because she openly showed her anxiety about P.W. and Minnie's interest in her life at the opera, fearful they might reveal her true identity. Minnie always felt Harry wasn't in P.W.'s class as a human being, but she tolerated Harry because of P.W.'s fondness for him. The two men looked alike, smoked the same cigars, and enjoyed talking of old times, bragging about their Columbus exploits in general without getting personal, at least in Minnie's presence. But Minnie's antipathy towards Harry's wife grew more open and obvious each time they met. Antoinette made no effort to extend herself which could have added to the pleasure of the friendship the husbands shared and contributed to their common interest in the opera. Minnie felt that if the men were to be good friends, and it was obvious that they enjoyed each other's company, to her, wives had the responsibility of being cordial. But she simply could not abide Antoinette's attitude towards P.W. and herself.

After numerous unsuccessful efforts to bring their wives together, P.W. and Harry began to seek each other out at times and places where the wives would not have to be involved, usually at P.W.'s Calumet Avenue Real Estate office, or occasionally at Harry's home when Antoinette was out of town travelling with the opera.

Aside from the slight relief brought by a more active social life, Minnie and P.W. continued to live out their routines, but now, each day they were confronted with new inquiries from anxious well-wishers or smug doubters. Meeting Harry again helped to temporarily lighten the stress of waiting, but no amount of frivolity could lessen P.W.'s deep concern about the Bank's future. P.W. felt that if a delegation of the Board Members went to Washington to handle this together, the subscribers would pay their pledges and the matter would be taken care of. But by mid-March, he knew he was wasting his time.

Roberts was now cautioning him not to expect anything, that cash in the pocket was what counted. "P.W., you have not been able to put this thing over, something is missing. You are alright at persuading people in high places in Washington, because of your Ohio contacts, and you have the ability to reach high-minded Whites whom the community doesn't really trust. You dazzle them with your manner and approach, but this doesn't mean anything in the Black Belt. They don't believe in Negro enterprises and won't invest another nickel in this bank. We're going to have to take Owens in. He has money we need, and is willing to invest in it heavily. We can use his money to put this over. With his investment, he can fulfill what you say can be done through this Negro Bank."

Owens never called P.W. about any of this directly. His interest in the bank was relayed to P.W. through Roberts and Morris, and hinted about by other Board Members. P.W. was determined not to reach out to Owens. In a moment of contemplation, P.W. realized that his deep attachment to the idea of a Black National Bank created a definite anguish, a fear of loss, that a man like Owens could, by the use of his wealth, undermine his leadership position. Perhaps this was selfish, he mused, but he had himself put much time, effort and money into this creation. He sensed that what he said to Roberts and Morris was being taken back and exaggerated. He felt no matter what he decided on, the bank movement would collapse if the power-play continued. Roberts once emphasized to P.W. "Washington is not going to grant the kind of power that exists in the giant banking industry to a Black National Bank, and you, P.W., should face this. Maybe even Owens coming in will make no difference. There are ways of getting around governmental procedures Washington uses if they wanted this bank movement to succeed."

By late April, the loss of confidence in the government's willingness to grant the community the right to run a Black National Bank reached such proportions that P.W. felt he had no choice but to allow Owens to come on the Board. He decided Owens' presence might sustain the hopes of others and encourage the subscribers to meet their stock pledges. On the last day of April, Owens attended the Board Meeting. He was quietly introduced to the Board Members who voted to accept him. Yet, as weeks passed, Owens becoming a Board Member seemed to have little influence.

One night Roberts came over to see P.W. He was definitely pulling out of the fight over the opening of the bank . . . he wanted to have nothing to do with it. The idea of a Black National Bank was too ambitious. . . . The community was not ready for it. Owens was not the answer.

Later, P.W. said, "Minnie, Roberts is a tight little man. I realize he's having a hard time explaining this delay to his church members, especially those that have pledged and paid for their stock, but it's not easy on any of us Board Members to face our customers." P.W. felt he could make no further demands on such a limited human being. "Perhaps he had to pull out," mused P.W. to himself, "remain uninvolved and protect himself, preaching words about loving and giving with no understanding of their true meaning."

That night P.W. received a call from Attorney Lucas. "You have no idea, P.W., how much I admire you. You belong at the head of that bank." The conversation was gratifying to P.W. who had taken several blows to his self-esteem in the past few months. He needed these words of appreciation and encouragement from someone he admired and respected. He needed the reaffirmation that at least one other person felt as he did about his idea.

P.W. was uneasy about the possibility that with Owens on the Board the direction of the bank policy would shift from his idea of having the bank owned by the common black man, but he felt powerless in preventing the shift. Owens made a sizeable investment, more subscribers paid up, and the certificate of payment for 50% of the capital stock of the Douglass National Bank was eventually forwarded to the Comptroller's Office in Washington. But the delay in granting the charter for the bank continued. P. W.'s main concern was not so much that Owens was on the Board, but a haunting sense that the delay in granting the charter was a political tactic to defeat the entire movement in Chicago because of its racial implications. After all, a National Bank would be a true show of strength of the black community in Chicago, since the purpose would be to increase the purchasing power of those in the area it served. Was this another case of Whites sitting back waiting for Blacks to fall into disarray over plans they dared to create? P.W. didn't want to believe men in Congress would deliberately cooperate with those lesser forces in America bent on perpetuating the myth of the "Great White Father." Yet, he could not be absolutely certain how much of the difficulty stemmed from possible strings being pulled in Washington to stop this bank movement. Was the movement's emphasis on awakening the black man to the possibility of the wise use of money and unity through purpose causing the delay? P.W. now realized he must go to Washington without his board members. He must deal with this situation just as he had started it . . . alone. There he would demand the release of the charter to open the bank and thereby restore the confidence of the community in its leaders and itself. The trip would take about ten days.

P.W. and Minnie agreed to take all of us. We would first go to Buffalo, take in Niagara Falls, then drive on to Washington where he would attend to obtaining the charter while Minnie visited with her cousin Gabrielle. Rebecca and Emily gave assurances that they would keep things going at the factory. The more P.W. thought about it, the more he was pleased with the Buffalo stop-over. It would allow Minnie and him to relive the happier days of their honeymoon. He considered a stop-over in Columbus on the way to Buffalo but dismissed this idea primarily because most of his family had

142

moved away. It was five years since they had left, and their only contact had been with distant cousins. Finally, he acknowledged that Columbus was also the place where he had lost his first wife who, unlike Minnie, could not go along with his enterprises, his community and civic activities, and his wish to do something constructive about the plight of his people.

We set out in the Pierce-Arrow on June 15th, headed for Washington, D.C. In her mind, Minnie relived the romantic cavalcade to Niagara Falls and Buffalo. Dr. Garnes, the best man, Nahum Brascher, P.W.'s secretary, and Nellie, Minnie's sister and maid of honor, motored to Buffalo with the bride and groom in a very crowded car. She thought about Garnes and Brascher who were present in his life again, for P.W. began stopping by Garnes' home or having long discussions with Brascher in the downtown office. Since he preferred not to bring it home to her if he could avoid it, he talked over his problems with them and whiled away many pleasant hours as a relief from the tension built up by the difficulty and delay in the bank opening. Nahum Brascher was now editor of the Associated Negro Press and rising swiftly in prestige in the Black Belt. He had been P.W.'s secretary in Columbus, had married and had come to Chicago soon after P.W. and Minnie were settled in Columbus. He was active, and like Garnes, took a great deal of pride in the functions of the Ohio Society, a group of middle-class Blacks who gave dances and social affairs regularly. He believed in making the color-blind world of business the vehicle by which black people could enter the mainstream of economic life. Brascher was a college-educated intellectual, a writer and editor for many years, who joined P.W.'s staff in Columbus after the collapse of the Cleveland newspaper for which he was working in 1911. They shared many common interests and discussed at length the philosophy of Booker T. Washington. Recognizing the value of this relationship to her husband, Minnie would extend herself graciously and remain pleasant when found in Brascher's company, for intuitively she understood the role of an entrepeneur's wife.

Minnie would have welcomed a vacation from her children

and the factory, but this would have to come later, after the bank was fully established, when she could begin to make P.W. exclusively hers. As the car with Jack at the wheel sped along the highway, Minnie kept reminding herself that P.W. was only fulfilling his promise to take the family to Washington. She was grateful he had not included a stopover in Columbus, which she feared he might. She thought of how those first four years of their marriage had been for her, living in a town where she knew his friends looked on her as the "second Mrs. Chavers." Minnie was not used to being second to anyone in any situation, so this was difficult for her. Although she never mentioned it to P.W., she was relieved when he decided to move to Chicago.

Her reverie was broken by Jack's sudden question, "Isn't it strange, P.W., how you got into this, 'n' how it's turnin' out now?" All three were lost in their own thoughts as the children slept, and the Pierce-Arrow made its way along the lonely road in the early evening. We were nearing Buffalo where we spent the night. P.W. lit a cigar and puffed on it awhile before answering.

"Yes, it is. I'll admit I am filled with mixed emotions as we approach the end of this journey, son."

"Yessuh, it sure is strange," Jack repeated as if to get the attention of both at the same time. He was proud and happy to be at the wheel, doing his part to make the trip possible.

"There have been a lot of set-backs, it's true. This trip is crucial." Daddy didn't know I was listening in the back of the car. I pretended to be asleep, but had been awakened by a sharp turn many miles back. I liked to listen to grown-ups talk. Mother and three of us were piled up in the rear of the car almost wrapped around each other as the car sped along the road.

The Pierce-Arrow was an open touring car, a forerunner of todays' convertible. We felt adventurous in it and liked to travel long distances. Now six of us were travelling to Washington with enough paraphernalia for two weeks. I looked around to see Mother still dozing. She usually kept vigil, rarely relaxing this way in the car. When P.W. was the driver, she was navigator or the overseer of the children.

144

With Jack at the wheel, Daddy was the navigator and Mother rested. She was now curled up on the rear seat with Edwina tucked close to her and Bill and I were on the floor with the pile of pillows. Yes, we were very snug in the back of that Pierce-Arrow as it headed into Buffalo. "This is so special," I thought, "How can they sleep all the way?"

"Two night's rest here in Buffalo will put us in Washington Tuesday," announced P.W., smiling confidently. He was glowing with anticipation as we pulled up to a hotel. Climbing out of the car proved a big undertaking. We were still sleepy, dishevelled and somewhat car-cramped. Daddy made the arrangements at the desk and we were shown to our rooms. "What fun," I thought. Every minute something different was happening. I got used to the hotel mattress about two in the morning. The following day we went sight-seeing through several parks in Buffalo, then took a long drive to see the plunging waters at Niagara Falls.

Daddy, full of enthusiasm, wanted a photo of the family, and although mother protested, he located a photographer with a Niagara Falls setting just a short walk away. The photographer was plainly disinterested in business at this early hour and mumbled that he just happened to be in the front of the store, that this was no time to take a good picture and that he could not promise satisfactory results.

"It doesn't have to be good," remarked P.W. as he went through the door with the three of us. "Just prop us up in front of some scenery, take the picture, and mail it to me in Chicago. Here's my card."

We were ushered over to the prop. Daddy took his place behind us, as the proprietor located a stool for Edwina. Only brother Bill was presentable. He was dressed in a blue middy blouse shirt with black tie and his hair was well groomed, but he wore a sleepy expression like the rest of us. Edwina and I were quite rumpled, our ruffles crushed, our curly hair tangled. Mother did not have time to groom us. "That's not important this morning," Daddy asserted. The photographer worked underneath a black cloth making an effort to get the proper angle for us. We became aware of the magic moment, peered curiously at the three-legged machine, then a flash of

Niagara Falls, enroute to Washington, D.C. 1922

light, a scream from Edwina, and the picture was taken. Soon we were off again.

From the rear, Mother took over as navigator instructing Jack about turns in the road. Our breakfast was quickly ordered and eaten enroute. Mother was eager to see her cousin Gabrielle, currently between husbands and working at the Mint. They had too few opportunities to see each other and talk over experiences they had shared in childhood.

We settled in for the final push to Washington, looking at all the sights along the way. Jack reminisced about when he had first come to know us and the lucky break he had had stopping by the factory and asking for work. "A fella has to get up courage 'n' ask for what he wants in this world," he said, "if he wants to git ahead." His happy mood blended with the beauty of the morning on the open road, the clear sky, and the bright sun in the heavens. P.W. spoke very little of his anticipations in Washington. He had saved many of the country-wide newspaper clippings about the bank story, and kept them in one of his valises. At one point along the road, he reached into the valise, pulled out a big black scrap book, and started scanning the clippings in preparation for his presentation the next day.

"What are you looking at, Daddy?" I asked curiously. I was familiar with his scrap book, though I had never handled it. I had, however, observed him cutting, pasting and inserting clippings.

"Rose-bud, this may be my most valuable possession, the newspaper record of the bank's development," he answered.

"Please read them to me," I begged.

"Of course" he said as he began reading, stopping occasionally to check on my attention. At one point I reached over the front seat and hugged Daddy tightly around the neck.

Once Jack broke in with "You'll have to watch your step when you git back to Chicago, P.W. A lotta people listed in that article have turned on you."

"They really didn't know what they were doing Jack, it will be different when we get the charter."

We soon pulled up to our Washington hotel. There was little conversation about the bank now. As soon as we were settled in our rooms, Mother busied herself on the phone with Cousin Gabrielle who told her she had arranged several tea parties and outings for us during our stay. To us, Cousin Gabrielle was someone our Uncle George visited every year when he passed through Washington. When she came to the hotel that evening to see us, we knew at once why Mother spoke of her with such reverence.

Cousin Gabrielle was the picture of royalty, all five foot nine inches of her. Her style of speaking, carefully chosen words and commanding mannerisms were matched only by her graceful movements and exquisite taste in wardrobe. Her honey-brown complexion was heavily made up to conceal the evidence of her middle age. She appeared much younger than mother, though in age they were only a few months apart—my Mother never wore make up. We trembled in awe of Cousin Gabrielle. She was a grandiose priestess and well-aware of it. Minnie again became that little girl growing up in her Uncle Grieffe's house, and Gabrielle, who had been his first-born daughter and favorite child, became her proud protectress again. It was obvious we would be engulfed in the elaborate entertainment plans she made for us, freeing Daddy to attend to business.

There had been delay in Washington over issuing the charter even after the necessary stock subscriptions had been paid and, like most complicated financial matters, the reasons were many, intricate and interwoven. Warren B. Harding had been President for more than a year. When he had been nominated at the Republican National Convention two years ago in Chicago, P.W. had just begun to think about getting into the bank movement and had been inspired by the success of an "Ohio favorite son" whose philosophy of the "best minds" had influenced P.W.'s thinking over the years.

Harding entered the White House after surviving a vicious campaign which included the accusation of his having Negro Blood, which Harding never denied, and his patience and silence throughout the slander had apparently contributed to his landslide victory. Harding brought his friend, Daniel Crissinger, a local Ohio banker, to Washington to serve as

Comptroller of Currency. In fact, the "Ohio Gang" was now running Washington. This turned out to be a fortunate combination of circumstances for P.W. and had encouraged him in his efforts to create a Black National Bank from the beginning. P.W. knew well how Ohioans were moved by such slogans as "the self-made man" and "the best minds should run institutions and governments."

Several times P.W. met with Charles G. Dawes when he was available in Chicago. Dawes was now Director of Budget, appointed by Harding to handle the tough job of cutting government spending in all departments during this tight-money post-war period. Their discussions during this trip centered around the future of the new bank. Dawes was President of the Central Union Trust Company of Illinois and a staunch, behind-the-scenes, supporter of P.W.'s efforts to establish a Black National Bank. He had talked with Stewart when in Chicago and had urged Crissinger to deal seriously with the bank application for the charter when in Washington.

It is true that P.W. was reluctant to transact business exclusively with the local Chicago national bank officials throughout this entire affair, sensing their doubts, resistance, questions and fears about his being able to organize and handle a national bank. In dealing with these attitudes, P.W. let it be known at the Federal Reserve Bank in Chicago that he was influential in politics in Columbus, Ohio, and was acquainted with powerful Congressmen, which included Senator Willis from Ohio, who would see him through in securing the charter for the Douglass National Bank. This confident approach was not favorably received by the Chicago Federal Reserve Bank. Each time papers and inquiries were handled, the processing of these items would somehow be delayed right up to the final step of the bank's application for, and purchase of, the 72 shares of capital stock, the required stock in the Federal Reserve Bank of Chicago needed to secure the charter. This took many months of negotiations. The delays would be explained away by the Chicago branch on the basis of the National Bank Examiner being absent from his office for an extended period of time, or that he had no commissioned representative to consult with on the matter. In their correspondence to Washington, they were always careful to repeatedly point out that the President, P.W. Chavers, was colored, and that the Board of Directors were colored and inexperienced. Part of the technicalities related to questions of recognizing P.W.'s preliminary expenses of $10,000.00 for bank furniture and fixtures, as bank assets, and why the check for deposit with the Federal Reserve Bank for membership was drawn on a state bank rather than the Federal Reserve Bank of Chicago. The Federal Reserve Board was insisting on a transfer of funds from the state bank and recommended a thorough investigation of the source of these funds before granting the charter, which prolonged the delay.

Crissinger was new in office and had proven himself, but he raised many questions including whether or not the black community had the ability to meet its obligations. His position was that "a bank thrives best in a stable community." The depression, just beginning to subside, fed into his apprehension. Also, the internecine bickering of the Board of Directors of the Douglass National Bank had somehow leaked out. This news didn't help convince the Comptroller of Currency of the United States Treasury that the Chicago Black Belt was prepared to take on the responsibility of so great a burden as the directorship and management of a first-class commercial bank.

Within a few days, P.W. met with the Federal Reserve Board in Washington and the necessary conditions were satisfied. P.W. was issued a certificate of the amount held by the depository bank and then arranged for the transfer of funds to a national bank after he was reassured that his bank would be given every courtesy of the national bank system. An investigation of P.W.'s certificate was promptly handled by a Western Union Telegram delivered to the Comptroller, verifying that the Douglass National Bank's capital stock was unimpaired by loans and was on deposit in a National Bank. Thus P.W. was able to deal skillfully with each of these sensitive areas. It helped that Crissinger was from Ohio as they found they had several mutual friends. P.W. spent a few moments reminiscing with him about the old days in Columbus which they had both enjoyed. He vouched for the bank's integrity and its intention to make this a genuine community institution that would belong to the people it served.

We saw little of Daddy, except on the evening of June 27th when he lingered longer than usual at dinner to talk about the signing and obtaining of the bank charter accomplished that day. A notice had already appeared in the Washington daily paper heralding the signing as a big event, and P.W. regaled Minnie, Gabrielle, and Jack with the details of the confusion in taking pictures of him and the Comptroller during the ceremony. A few days later, P.W. hired a limousine to take all of us to the White House to meet President Harding. Minnie questioned the necessity of hiring a luxurious car for the occasion, but P.W. pointed out that the Pierce-Arrow was being checked for the return trip to Chicago and, more importantly, he wanted his family to have this experience of arriving at the White House in elegant style. Years later, Bill told me how embarrassed he recalled feeling, at age seven, when Daddy introduced him to the President as the boy who would someday become "first Negro President of the United States." I remember more of the trip enroute to and from Washington, but Bill recalled every detail of our introduction to the President in the East Room of the White House. Harding's predecessor, the war-time President, Woodrow Wilson, kept the White House heavily guarded and barred the public from admission. Allowing the public to come into the White House and meet their President was a new American tradition introduced by President Harding that P.W. did not intend for his children to miss. This innovation has largely been forgotten as attributable to Harding.

P.W. telegrammed the Board of Directors in Chicago immediately after the signing of the charter to let them know it had been secured and that business could commence at once. He was confident again of the future of the bank and his voice was filled with pride and elation as we planned our departure from Washington. Minnie was exhausted but pleased as much with her renewed family and friendship ties as she was with P.W.'s business triumph. Despite the oppressive July heat, she would gladly have spent an entire month with

151

Cousin Gabrielle and her socialite friends. P.W.'s triumph at the Treasurer's office had made her somewhat of a celebrity at all the Washington teas and social gatherings. We children were very tired after seeing so many new faces frequently thrust before us, with the necessary hugs and pats. As we finally started on our journey home, we slept fitfully on the back seat and on the floor of the car.

"Jack," said P.W., excitedly musing about the future, "in two or three years we might have branches all over Illinois, wherever our people have settled." Then he added thoughtfully, "But I think we should put up our first branch right here in Washington, D.C. You know Douglass had his bank here."

"Yes suh." Jack mopped the sweat from his forehead as he braked the car to wait for a green light. "I think we are on our way, if them high-fallutin' niggers back home don't sell us out to the white folks."

Mother dozed. P.W. lit a cigar and puffed on it silently for a few minutes. He hated the word "nigger" and he hated it even more when colored people used it. For a moment he felt angry with Jack for using this word. But he realized that Jack was speaking from his heart, saying what he himself knew to be the fears of poor colored people who thought the way Jack did about upper-class Blacks. P.W. stiffened, his jaw set, and he gazed out of the side window away from Jack, composing himself before he answered.

"We must show the Whites who believe in us what we can do for ourselves. The Board Members will see this as their duty and responsibility and live up to the law of the land. This is democracy," he added.

"Well, I know 'bout democracy," insisted Jack, grasping the steering wheel desperately. "It didn't stop Whites from shootin' us mens 'n' draggin' our women off them streetcars, 'n' beatin' folks near to death in the riots. We wasn't startin' no banks then, jus' goin' to polish them cars, 'n' trim them hedges, 'n' wash them clothes."

Mother awoke and shifted in the seat to get more comfortable, then cleared her throat sharply. We were on the open road now, headed northwest. "Dear," she interrupted irritably, "may I see the letter again?" She was referring to the document transmitting the charter and authorizing the Douglass Bank to commence the business of banking. Proud and pleased with P.W.'s achievements, she felt he had earned the respect and appreciation of his people for having made so great an accomplishment over almost insurmountable obstacles. Minnie did not intend to allow Jack to try to cut through the elation he was feeling. "Do you have it handy?" she asked again.

P.W. pulled the official document from his vest pocket and, as he gave it to Minnie, he said to Jack, "This is what is respected by the influential people in America . . . the law, and the intellect behind it . . . what I have here represents truth and justice and they will always win out."

"Yessuh," said Jack automatically.

AO   No. 12227

TREASURY DEPARTMENT

WASHINGTON

COMPTROLLER OF THE CURRENCY

ADDRESS REPLY TO
"COMPTROLLER OF THE CURRENCY"

June 27, 1922

Mr. Pearl W. Chavers,

President, "The Douglass National Bank of Chicago",

Chicago, Illinois

Sir:

Inclosed find certificate authorizing

"The Douglass National Bank of Chicago"
to commence business, which should be published for sixty days
in a Chicago   city or Cook   county newspaper,
as required by section 5170, Revised Statutes of the United
States. Evidence of publication of the certificate should be
sent to this office on the accompanying blank. Please state
the date on which the bank begins business, a blank for which
purpose is also inclosed.

Application should be immediately made to the Federal
Reserve Bank of your District for stock in that bank in a sum
equal to six percent of the paid up capital stock and surplus
of "The Douglass National Bank", Chicago and this office advised
when the application has been made.

Respectfully,

W. J. FOWLER,

Deputy Comptroller

Form 1933   7-28-20 --1000

Charter secured: Letter of confirmation, 1922

154

8

The Coup

P.W was back at the bank, ready to meet with the Board in a few minutes. Despite the heat, Chicago was bustling with activity on that July 10th. The weatherman promised thundershowers, a relief from the hot humid pall that had hung over the city for several days. The Douglass National Bank had opened its doors for business on June 29, 1922, immediately after the Board had received P.W.'s telegram advising that the charter had been issued. The high volume of business reflected the interest of the community. Immediately on his return, P.W. had called a Board Meeting to legalize the business the bank had already commenced doing and to formally present a report to his Directors. He was at his desk, preparing for the meeting, making notes and gathering papers, confident that the doubtful Board Members would become more determined to follow his lead in making the bank a successful institution when he told them how he had accomplished everything necessary to secure the charter.

As P.W. readied himself for this meeting, his thoughts were on the constant internal warfare among his people. How could he cope with his Board Members to stop this waste of energy? Despite his earlier misgivings, P.W. had accepted Owens on the Board since the others wanted him to come in. "We can use his talents for our benefit," he thought, but he found himself wishing it hadn't been necessary to let Owens in just to have access to his money.

The door of his office opened and in walked Vera Green dressed in her finest, with a satin hat, high-heeled shoes and a rumpled silk dress. She stood on the threshold, her manner brazen and offensive. This devious, fraudulent side of her was made evident to P.W. when she had appeared as a material

155

witness against him in the police station many months before. At that time Vera, who had disappeared from work a week prior giving no notice whatsoever, had seemed unreal to him, like a bitter and furtive ghost, when he had faced her accusation of fraud which had sparked his trip to Washington to get the charter. She had dropped from sight again, but now she was once more before him, leaning over his desk, presenting a startling picture, cracking loudly on the gum she chewed.

"Yes, Vera?" he asked quietly as he picked up his ledgers and legal folders.

"I wuz lookin' fu' yu las' week; I saw Owens here, bu' he claimed you wuz down in Washington, somewhere," Vera said, still leaning over his desk with her arms folded. "I wanna talk 'bout my claim."

"I can't discuss the matter with you right now. I have a meeting with the Board, but I want to see you," responded P.W. walking towards the door. The thousand details of his presentation to the Board whirled through his mind. But one question jutted forth, "Why did you press those phony fraud charges against me, Vera?"

"I wanna get my money." Vera blocked his movements momentarily, then gave way and followed him out of his office. "I'll be back, suh! Don' you fo'git. I'll be back!" she called out loudly.

Two hours later the door of the conference room swung open, releasing a dead silence into the hallway of the Douglass National Bank. A brown hand, trembling slightly, pulled it shut. The man began walking rigidly erect and with great effort down the marble floor to the front entrance, down the steps to the sidewalk, shaken into a dazed numbness by the granite hardness of what had just taken place. He shivered as he walked towards the corner . . . "Justice, truth, integrity," these Victorian standards kept repeating themselves in his brain over and over, as if to reassure himself he was still alive, still P.W., still in the world.

"P.W.!!!!" George was yelling and honking his horn as his

156

canvas-topped roadster roared over to the curbside. "Whewww, it's hot!" he said. "Hey, P.W., over here! I've been cruising this street for the last half hour waiting for you to come out. I told Jack I'd pick you up since he was over here twice looking for you."

P.W. suddenly became aware of Minnie's brother. "Hello George," he responded absently and slumped into the car wearily; George pulled away from the curb and kept talking.

"Did you bowl them over with that charter report, P.W.?" P.W. sat silently staring ahead into space as George continued, "I had my doubts about a Negro getting one of those charters in this bank business. You can sell colored people cars, houses, or clothes, like I do, but this bank and community involvement business is too much, too advanced. I mean, it's not something you can see or show off after your mortgage or your down payment. I can sell a suit in twenty minutes, but this is the future, this stock buying business, a little beyond most of our people; but you did it anyhow, didn't you? How does it feel to be President of the first colored national bank in America, a bank of your own? Tell me how does it feel?"

P.W leaned his head back on the seat, sighing wearily. "I am not the President. I am not even a member of the Board, George," answered P.W. in a voice that sounded as though it came from far, far down. An angry coldness swept over George. He slammed on the brakes for the red light, and when it finally turned green, he pulled over to the side and parked the car . . .

"Tell me what you are talking about, P.W." he demanded.

"I mean there is, at this time, no place for me at the Douglass National Bank," said P.W. slowly, "I mean the Board Members elected another President as well as Chairman of the Board, and ousted Stewart from the Board while I was in Washington." P.W.'s voice rose slightly now in anger.

"That's impossible." You have the Trusteeship of the old bank assets, you reorganized the whole thing and set up the entire Douglass . . . the whole Douglass National Bank . . . and now?"

"I'm telling you George," interrupted P.W., "this was done while I was in Washington! I have been pushed out of my policy position."

"That's impossible," George repeated, gripping the wheel. "But you'll still be able to run the bank?. . . You've got the charter. It's in your name."

"No, George, I don't have the charter, it belongs to the bank . . . it belongs to the bank. The Board wants me out of the actual operation; they offered me the Vice Presidency, an honorary position without pay. I refused the position. Then I walked out of the meeting. The charter belongs to the bank. As of today, I'm out."

The strategy of the Board Members was to first remove Stewart from the Board, then to offer the Presidency to Owens, while P.W. was still in Washington. He told George that the meeting began with the Board pressuring him to write his own resignation, demanding that he submit it to the Directors, even before he had a chance to make his report or show them the letter authorizing the bank to commence business. He said that when they offered him the Vice Presidency, their attitude was that he had acted for the bank in securing the charter like an ordinary political emissary and had had all of the credit for more than a year, but his role, as such, was drawing to a close. P.W. felt that what they offered him was tantamount to offering him nothing and that they knew he would be too embarrassed to accept. They had promised Owens to squeeze him out of his own creation, even after he had kept his promise and delivered the charter, knowing it had cost him and his family so much time, money and energy. They looked upon him as a disgruntled aspirant for the presidency of an institution he had created. P.W. found this incredible; he was appalled that these men, who were supposed to be leaders in the community, could dispatch him so easily after so much work, and could be so short-sighted.

A change in leadership now would have a ruinous effect on the institution in the eyes of the banking establishment. It could open an attack on the bank and reinforce the myth among Whites that Blacks would not comprehend the value of cooperation and authority, and that they are not ready for the right of self-determination. P.W. was still in shock as he considered all of these ramifications and the possible consequences of the actions taken by the Board.

At first, George, livid with rage, wanted to curse the Board Members and P.W. when he thought of Minnie who had so much faith in him. Instead, he started the engine and pulled off. "You could have whipped them, brother," George half-shouted. "You had the ace in your hands and let it go."

"What could I have done? Perhaps I should have seen the signs earlier," returned P.W.

George thought of his sister Minnie again. Then he looked at his idealistic brother-in-law, now beaten by the acts of men he had trusted. To walk out in the middle of the meeting must have been painful for him. He suddenly realized how P.W.'s faith in these men was broken and what this must mean to him. He felt a sudden deep and anguished sorrow.

A newsboy approached them, and George signaled for a paper.

"Yes sir!" beamed the newsboy as he ran up to the parked car. "Do you want one, too, sir? he asked P.W. as George gave him a coin.

"No son, I'll read this one."

"Minnie will be waiting with dinner for us," commented George as he drove off again. "Are you planning to tell her before we sit down with the children, or do you want me to tell her?" asked George thoughtfully. This annoyed P.W. even though he knew George was being protective of Minnie who held George up to P.W. as an example of the well-to-do businessman whose business was uncomplicated by race consciousness. She never put it to him directly, but hints would crop up at times. P.W. took her comments in good humor, realizing that George had certain admirable qualities. However, he would not allow George to take his place tonight.

"No, brother, that's my job. This situation was my making; I can take the consequences," declared P.W.

"I didn't mean to. . ." started George.

P.W. interrupted, "We better go in now or dinner will be cold."

The door swung inward just as they reached the third floor landing and they could see Minnie silhouetted against the soft dim light from the hall. She saw George first, then looked at her husband, and then back to George again, as they slowly climbed the last few steps to our apartment. Bill and I were pushing and elbowing each other, as well as Mother, in our efforts to get to Daddy.

George suddenly commented that he had left his newspaper in the car and started back down the stairs. "I'll be right back, folks, I'm hungry," he called over his shoulder. George picked up the *Chicago Defender* from between the two front seats and sat down in the car to read the bold face typed front page column:

"NATIONAL BANK TO OPEN ON SOUTH SIDE
PIONEER INSTITUTION TO HAVE FORMAL OPENING: OWENS HEAD"

All the Board Members were listed. George went through the list carefully name by name. Owens was President, P.W. was listed as one of the Board Members but O. F. Stewart was not listed at all. Perspiration rolled down George's forehead. "Plans being made for a new building to be ready for occupancy by the end of the year." It was all spelled out, George thought. "This newspaper was already out in the streets while the Board Meeting was going on; while P.W. was being stabbed in the back." George tried to drop the paper, but it clung to his sweaty palms. He flung the wretched newspaper vehemently and it lodged between the front seats.

We were climbing all over Daddy; he tried hard to enjoy the rough-housing we put him through. Minnie had prepared a very special dinner in celebration of the first Board Meeting after receipt of the charter. She decided not to ask any questions about how the day had gone. This was P.W.'s day; she would await for his presentation of the details.

Dinner was eaten in the dining room on the white linen table cloth with Sanfelice shuttling between dining room and kitchen with steaming dishes from the stove. As the meal progressed, Minnie wondered about P.W.'s continued trancelike silence, and noticed George didn't seem eager to talk about the Board Meeting either. Minnie offered second helpings each time there was a lull between George's accounts of his recent escapades, talk about the intense heat of the day, the children, or the telephone calls from workers at the factory to say they were happy to know she was back in town. She rose above the uncertainty and worry that was mounting, and chattered on about unpacking from the trip. Tomorrow she would be returning to the factory; she was pleased to know that the workers had missed her.

Then, finally, P.W. spoke. "It was a mutiny, Minnie. That's all I can say; it was like a mutiny," he repeated dully.

Bill stubbed his toe on a chair and went into his room to look at the bruise while I lingered and listened to adult talk.

"I knew it all along . . . they don't appreciate you," said Minnie, shaking her head. "They don't deserve you." She couldn't help but think that she had known they were deceitful all along.

"They turned on me. No one, not one single man spoke up for me. To think I personally selected each one, except Owens, in whom they now place their confidence," continued P.W. I shivered to hear my Daddy sound so distressed and so crushed. "The Board Members agreed to vote Owens in as President and Chairman of the Board while we were away. They had agreed in advance on their strategy, and they staged the meeting today to get me to hand over the presidency. They were not interested in learning how I had secured the charter."

"But you alone were responsible for getting the charter, as their President, while they were scheming to vote you out of office. . . ."

"I know Minnie, but they had already acted in secret and made their decisions. I saw it in their faces and heard it in their words and the tone of their voices, so I walked out of the meeting," answered Daddy, looking at Mother as he talked. Not even Uncle George spoke; he sat quietly, looking down, as if he couldn't bear to look at either my mother or father in their agony.

"Suppose you hadn't secured the charter?" questioned

161

Mother with anger. "Suppose you had failed in Washington? Where would all of their secret meetings have led them? What could they have done?"

"They evidently counted on me securing the charter," responded P.W. George suddenly announced that he would have to leave and asked them to let him know how he might be helpful.

The next morning, P.W. asked Jack to bring the car to the front of the house. Minnie watched him anxiously; she knew he was going to the bank to get his papers and personal effects. "Why don't you just send Jack to get your things?" she asked as P.W. handed Jack a valise and brief case.

"Wait in the car for me, Jack, I'll be out right away," P.W. said turning to Minnie. "They wouldn't let Jack go into the office. Besides, he wouldn't know where to look for things even if he could get in."

"They might not let you in the office either, P.W." said Minnie. "Did it occur to you they may have removed your things?" Her voice tightened. She worried that P.W. might be faced with another unpleasant situation.

"I still have my keys. There were two keys made originally, and Young has the other," responded P.W. Minnie kissed him tenderly, then pulled away and left the room.

P.W. and Jack drove up in front of the rectangular two-story building where the bank was housed. The big glass window sported new red velvet curtains hung across their width on round horizontal poles of brass. Jack jumped·out of the car and came around the front to open P.W.'s door, but P.W. was already out. "Get the bags," he said to Jack, "and follow me."

It was quiet and there were no customers inside the bank; only Young was seated at a desk, closed off by a mahogany wainscott, facing the doorway. He looked up from his ledger as the two men walked in. "Oh, good-morning Mr. Chavers," he stammered, rattled by P.W.'s unexpected appearance.

"You've done a good job since you've been here," said P.W. recognizing something more than embarrassment in the young man's attitude. "You are an excellent accountant,"

P.W. added. "I just came down to pick up my personal papers and effects. I will send someone over with a van for the heavier things. Come on," P.W. said as he walked past him into the room.

"Excuse me, Mr. Chavers, these letters came for you. I intended to mail them to you." Al backed out, wringing his hands and perspiring, while Jack was busy taking down books and papers from the shelves, putting them into valises. P.W. glanced at the envelopes, one had the Senate's seal on it in the upper left-hand corner. Below the seal was neatly printed, "Honorable Furman B. Warren, United States Senator." He tucked it into the inner pocket of his frock coat.

Scooping up the other letters and papers on the desk, tying them together with a piece of string, Jack quickly cleared the surfaces, then asked, "Will that be all, P.W.?"

"Yes, Jack, I think so," P.W. said looking around the room as he opened the bottom drawer of the desk, then straightened up. "Lets' go out to the car." P.W. wanted to leave as quickly as possible now.

After they left, Young fumbled for a kerchief in his breast pocket and mopped his face and neck. "That letter," he said aloud, "had a government seal on it. Maybe I should call up Owens and tell him everything."

"Tell me what?" said Owens standing before him with Price, his handy man.

"Oh, Mr. Owens, sir, Mr. Chavers was just here. He and his man took a lot of books and papers and drove away." Owens gave Price a glance, then laughed.

"That's alright, young man," returned Owens, "we got everything we need."

It was early afternoon when P.W. and Jack arrived at the house. Minnie had dressed Bill and me to go grocery shopping. "I am leaving Edwina with Sanfelice," Minnie said as she went into the office. She knew P.W. would want to be alone for awhile to think things through. She also knew she was in no condition to hear anything else about the bank, even though she was worried about how P.W. was feeling.

The door was shut at last; everybody was gone. In solitude, he sat a long time at his desk, leaning back on his chair, his

163

back to the bay window. Once in a while the chair creaked in protest to a slight movement. Now and then there were sounds of footsteps in the hall, a voice from outside the building, the sound of a passing vehicle, or a tune being sung by a tenant in the hallway that would pierce his thoughts, but only for a moment. Twenty-eight hours had passed since the treachery of the Board Members was revealed to him. He now reconstructed the terrible ordeal and felt a brief wave of relief from the pain he had held in, the burden he was forced to cast off. The first shock of the meeting had subsided. His emotions were spent, his body drained of energy. Suddenly it occurred to him he didn't ever have to go back to the bank building again and a secret pleasure at no longer having to present the public image of the crusading bank executive comforted him. This weighty role of explorer through alien financial territories that he had had to present to the world could now be dispensed with.

At the same time he felt this relief, he also felt sick and depressed. He searched for some resolution of these conflicting emotions; it was intolerable to contain two such contradictory and equally strong feelings simultaneously. How could he derive solace from the thought of never going back to the bank he had dreamed so long of creating and worked so hard to establish? Even Minnie, with all of her understanding, was going about her business with the shopping, the children, and the house. The silence that a moment ago was relief now became a reminder of how expendable he was, how his world stood still unless he pushed on alone. Once again, he felt anger arise. He had believed he was handling the situation right, that his perception, skill and effort would show them the way and that the men on the Board would follow his lead and cooperate once he had attained the charter.

In his agony he thought that no one had warned him, no one on the Board, no one. No one but Minnie, and he had refused to listen to her. Now, for the first time in his marriage, it was painful to think of Minnie. Not only had he failed himself, he had failed his devoted wife. He thought of her words about naming the bank, how she had wanted him to

164

name the bank for himself. Now he reminded himself that George, too, had tried and again he had refused to listen. P.W. sighed suddenly and shifted in his chair. Why hadn't he heeded them? He confessed that he didn't know why. There were things logic could not explain, things that Minnie knew and he didn't, and it brought great pain.

When he could no longer stand the self-torment and self-pity and hoping to find something to distract himself, he began to read his mail to pull himself out of his depression so that he could deal with all the rest to come later. The sound of crackling paper caught his attention. He absently touched his coat pocket, reached inside, and pulled out the Senator's letter. He stared at the envelope for a long time before reaching for the letter opener on his desk.

Walking through the door to the smaller office he came face to face with the portrait of Fredrick Douglass looming large on the far wall. Somehow the picture added a razor's edge to the irony of what had happened. In the beginning, Fredrick Douglass' trail-blazing was an example to him in forming and naming the bank. The portrait had been unveiled at the Armory to inspire the community, as part of the bank stock campaign, more than a year ago and had been scheduled for transfer to the lobby of the bank when the bank would be formally opened. He remembered Fredrick Douglass and Booker T. Washington, both forcefully represented in portraiture at the Armory. Now the portrait of Douglass seemed to be presiding over his demise. Almost absently, he slid the black letter opener into the envelope and slit it across the top.

July 10, 1922

"Dear Mr. Chavers:

I have just learned that on Wednesday, July 12th, the formal opening of the Douglass National Bank takes place. I take this means of congratulating you, your stockholders and your depositors on this auspicious event. The organization of this splendid banking institution, planned, and officered by colored men, is a second Emancipation Proclamation so far as the economic welfare of Afro-Americans is concerned. I have no doubt it will be a success and that it will be largely patronized. I am glad to have had a humble part in aiding you to secure your charter from the government. I have every

165

confidence that the work of this institution so auspiciously begun will be productive of great good to all people in your section of Chicago.

With good wishes to yourself and all those interested in the Douglass National Bank, I am,

> Yours very truly,
> Furman B. Warren"

Again, the letter was a reminder of all he had hoped for. He had obtained the charter, the first ever secured by a black man in America. Everything he knew about banking would be lost to his own creation. His experiences in dealing with the Federal Reserve Bank, Federal Reserve Board, Treasury Department, Comptroller of Currency, the courts, the Congressmen and all that went into making his creation would not be available to the bank.

"I've succeeded and failed all at once," he muttered to himself.

A few days later, George left on P.W.'s desk a copy of the *Defender* he had purchased the day of the infamous board meeting. As P.W. read the article about Owens heading the bank, noting the date of the newspaper, he realized the release was submitted while he was still in Washington. "They were moving ahead with their scheme even before I had received the charter," he thought bitterly. He read on, "The present location, corner of State and 32nd Street, is a temporary one; plans and specifications are being drawn up for a building to be known as the Owens Professional Building that will be ready for occupancy about the end of the year."

"Where are they going to get the money?" P.W. groaned. Throughout the campaign, the Board had promised an ample surplus would be maintained to allow for any anticipated run on the bank ... protection for the depositors, a sort of insurance. "How will the depositors be protected now?" he wondered.

It was late afternoon and P.W. put his head down wearily on the desk and fell asleep. He was awakened later by his own snoring, stood up, walked slowly back to the big desk in his front office and sat down.

"Sanfelice, bring me a pot of coffee," he called, reaching for a pen and blank paper in one motion. Sanfelice brought the coffee. He drank a cupful and commenced to write; the entire situation became clear to him as he wrote page after page. He began to formulate an idea of insurance as security on bank savings.

"Banks must be made secure for depositors. Insurance on deposits will guarantee that people will be protected and they can be confident in those institutions in which they save their money." He threw away several sheets, starting again and again. There must be no mistakes this time he thought to himself aloud as he wrote on and on. When he finally went upstairs it was dawn. He had finished his proposal:

"The Chavers Plan for Guaranteeing Bank Deposits" it began:

"This is an act designed to require all national banks to furnish surety bonds for the protection of depositors. It is intended that all national banks furnish bonds signed by reputable surety companies and approved by the Treasury of the United States. . . . thus guaranteeing the safety of all deposits. A bank, upon its organization, will be required to furnish a bond in an amount equal to the total amount of the capital stock the first year, and each succeeding year thereafter, giving the surety companies the right of examination of the bank for which it acts as surety . . . together with such powers as are incident thereto. This will inspire the confidence of depositors in all banks, regardless of size, which will endure beyond any construction changes, such as personnel, new investments, new competition and all other elements that now tend to hamper or interfere with the bank's enjoyment of the full confidence necessary for the growth and prosperity of a bank, especially the small bank struggling in the early stages of its beginnings. The depositors in the smaller banks, under this act, can rest with the same feeling of safety and security as depositors in the largest banks now doing business."

P.W. felt better the following day. Writing down his thoughts and forging his new ideas into words had helped. He placed it in his safe and reflected that he would watch with interest any of the changes the Douglass Bank Board made in its commitments to the community people.

Several weeks later when the *Race Relations Commission Report and Recommendations* was released, he read the newspaper story of the commission's recommendations that $100,000.00 be paid to the survivors of the 1919 race riots. P.W. and Minnie talked about the irony of his developing the bank out of the distress created by the riots and that a handful of victims would now be identified and vindicated by the payments to families of these victims. They also discussed the absurdity of making such vague recommendations as the "fostering of improved understanding between the races through the enlightened civic conscience of the community" as suggested by the commission after the three-year study of race relations in Chicago.

"What the average white person has to comprehend, and somehow must be made to feel, is that the American Negro was here prior to the founding of America, as both slave and freeman, and has the right to settle, as American citizens, anywhere they have the money to pay their way. Terrorism and the threat of death in Chicago cannot stem the tide of migration from the rural South, since to stay there means to die." The second Ku Klux Klan, the Knights of the Ku Klux Klan, had originated in Georgia after World War I and was ravaging the black communities of the South.

He wondered about the effect of the riots on his own life as he shared his thoughts with Minnie. If the riots had not occurred, would there have been such a run on the Woodfolk Bank as to force it to close? Would he have gone into the banking field? Even though he realized his ouster from the bank was a grievous blow to Minnie, he said to her, "I'd do it all over again, Minnie. I would build a national bank for our people and our community all over again. Without the things I did, my people could not benefit from the bank today."

"I can't find it in myself to forgive those thieves for stealing all the credit and honor from you," replied Minnie. "Sometimes I just don't know you."

"I will not just let it go," he reassured her. "I am proud of what I did to make it possible, and I am not going to turn my back completely. I plan to watch how the bank is managed and how its policies develop to make sure that all the work I've done is being put to some constructive purpose."

"Oh, but you're taking it so calmly. Those people have robbed you of the respect and recognition you have earned" said Minnie shaking her head.

P.W. answered her quietly. "The essential thing now is that it remains open. I still have a function to play in this situation because of all the work I've done, and the confidence the community people have placed in me. But beyond what has happened to me, the bank itself is a vital institution and it must continue to flourish."

The next few months P.W. concentrated on reorganizing his work schedule and his priorities. The Pierce-Arrow had served us well for years, but now aging, it was replaced with a more luxurious hard-top sedan known as the Velie-8. He took the family on long Sunday outings, travelling about the countryside, and evening drives around Chicago's Lake Front and Outer Drive to escape the heat, and somehow found time to see more of Dr. Garnes, especially while promoting his real estate business. P.W. completed negotiations for one-half interest in a 15 year leasehold on a 21 "flat" (apartment) building at 4901-3 Calumet Avenue, a 100 room structure of red brick, which he looked upon as income-producing property and the first big move in the expansion of his real estate holdings. One day in the early fall, as Bill and I returned from school, we noticed the change in letters on the window of Daddy's office.

The gold letters now read:

"P.W. CHAVERS
MORTGAGE BANKER
FOUNDER OF THE FIRST NATIONAL BANK
ORGANIZED BY COLORED PEOPLE OF THE
UNITED STATES."

The next morning after breakfast, P.W. sat in the parlor with his usual cigar and the morning newspaper. Occasionally Minnie interrupted his thoughts with comments about how well the factory was doing. Her chatter was cut short by the sudden clanging of door chimes. A tall square built man in a grey pinstriped suit stood at the door.

"Yes?" said Minnie, looking him up and down.

"I'm Mr. Brass of the Keystone National Detective Agency. Is there a Mr. Chavers here? A Mr. Pearl William Chavers?" A meaty hand flashed a small calling card.

"What is this about? I am Mrs. Chavers."

"Yes, I'm Mr. Chavers," P.W. said coming up behind Minnie. Apparently P.W. was expecting him. "Come in, I received your letter and your call." Minnie stepped aside as the heavy-set man with horn-rimmed glasses, a manila folder in hand, moved forward smiling politely as he walked past her. P.W. and Brass stood chatting in the hallway for several miniutes, then went downstairs into the office.

"Well, Mr. Chavers," Brass began after accepting a chair and a cigar. "We have the information for you but it took longer than we expected." He shifted in his chair, "Uh, well, we had to hire special people to do some of the work. Anyway, here is your report." Brass, an experienced West Indian detective and proprietor of the only colored detective agency in America, had a national reputation. He was retained to investigate some of the most sensational cases in Chicago, working for both Blacks and Whites. The nature of his investigations caused him to proceed with caution.

"You have my retainer. Send me a bill for the balance and I will send you a check by return mail," responded P.W.

"Yes," said Brass as they both rose and he followed P.W. out. The detective had been hired to check on rumors P.W. had heard about financial machinations that the bank directors were selling stock to Whites at a lower price. He hesitated about becoming involved, hoping the detective would find the rumors were not true.

As he sat reading the contents of the report after Minnie had left for the factory, he realized that the rumors were true, and he grew both sad and angry. White agents bought stock in the bank at twenty-five dollars less than P.W. had sold it, while Negro agents were told that all of the shares were sold. This manipulation occurred because Whites would pay in full instantly, while Blacks paid on installment, which was slower. The arrangement was being kept secret. The surplus in the bank had declined, and there were reports of other secret machinations as well. Rereading the report, P.W. wondered if the regulatory system of national banks was at fault, but he had to do something about this situation and there was no one else to force disclosure to the community. He reviewed once again all of the ignominies heaped on him, starting with intimidation by the arrest, then the questions and delays in Washington, and ending with his ouster from the Board. Roberts, Morris, and others had been part of it, but they were misled by their fear of failure and the lure of Owen's wealth. He realized that banks are a part of an industry that fears disclosure, but everything was moving fast; he would have to do something . . . he would have to request an investigation through the Federal Court. To remain silent now would in effect make him an accessory to these secret dealings, because of his knowledge. He couldn't allow this to happen. Washington would have to take responsibility to diligently supervise this bank as they claimed they would do when he founded it. The Douglass Bank was to be a beacon light of financial stability for his people, whether he was part of it or not. To P.W. it was that simple.

He thought about the way to handle this matter with Minnie. She had complained about how removed she felt from what he was doing and the additional expenses of his over-concern for the bank. He decided to proceed without telling her in order not to burden her further. He did not see this as making a choice in loyalties, but as a means about how to proceed with what he had to do. Action had to be taken. He would accept and handle the consequences of this decision.

On a warm Autumn day about two weeks later, Bill and I were playing in the back-yard . I was overdressed, as Mother insisted that I look proper even in the backyard. Bill had on overalls and could more easily join with the other kids.

"Wait for me, Bill," I called as he crawled under the porch.

The backyard, about 50 feet deep from the porches to the back fence and alleyway, was an ideal play area. Children could play ball, tag or other action games in the yard as the adults seldom used it. However, on hot or rainy days, children

171

Madrue playing in the backyard, 1923

crawled under the porches to play. Bill had joined his friends there. I stooped down awkwardly to get under the porch as my clothing hampered my movements. "Wait for me," I protested again.

"Oh, come on in and stop yelling," Bill insisted. "Girls are such pests," he added, looking at his friends. The other boys were over on one side of the hideaway with a forbidden deck of cards, playing "Everlasting." I looked around for some girls but there weren't any.

"Mother told you to look after me," I protested, letting the boys know I was Bill's responsibility. "I want to play cards too."

"You're too young and you can't even count," Bill grumbled, angry at my insistence. I gave him a long, hard look, thinking he had been happy just a few minutes ago with my company as we scampered down the three flights of stairs to join our friends after wheedling mother's permission. I then began to amuse myself playing in the dirt about fifteen feet away. I noticed a puddle of water near one of the basement windows and crawled to the water to make mud pies. I suddenly became aware of activity inside the basement.

At first I couldn't believe my eyes—shadows seemed to be moving inside. When I wiped the window with my dress to clear off the mud, I saw a number of men hauling huge pieces of machinery into the basement and setting them in place. I crawled up close to the window, pressing my nose against it.

"Look, Bill, there are a lot of men in our basement," I whispered.

"What do you want now?" snapped Bill.

"Bill, there are a lot of men in our basement . . . Come and see," I yelled out, then added, "Please!"

"Girls!!!" roared Bill to his friends, throwing down his hand of cards. "Why did I have to get two sisters when I wanted a brother?" Finally he turned towards me, still grumbling, "What do you want now?"

"Come and see," I persisted.

"Gee, those look like sewing machines," said Bill. "What are they doing putting sewing machines in the basement?"

"I wonder what's going on," I said, puzzled.

173

"We better go find out, Madrue," declared Bill reaching for my hand. "See you later, fellows," he called to the boys as we crawled from under the back porches. "Come on Madrue, something is happening and Mama should know about it."

We dashed up three flights of stairs to find Mother, but only Sanfelice was there with Edwina. She was pulling things out of the front bedroom as if making space. We did not stop to ask questions; she never had any answers for us and we wanted our Mother. We dashed down the front stairs to the first floor office where we found Mother and Dad.

The men continued to file into the basement with the sewing machines from our factory. My heart sank when I saw the expression on Mother's face.

"We're storing the factory equipment for a little while," explained Daddy. "We hadn't wanted you to see this, but maybe it's just as well."

"Why didn't you stay in the backyard?" Mother began to scold.

"We saw the men through the window in the basement," said Bill, sensing the tension our parents felt. "Do you want the machinery there?" asked Bill. During the bad weather, when he was allowed to roam with his friends, they often played cops and robbers in the big basement with only the janitor looking in occasionally.

"No, this is not going to be the factory. The machines are being stored here for just a little while until I find a better location for the factory," Daddy told us calmly.

Mother noticed my dirty clothing and decided to take us upstairs to clean up. As we left, I overheard one of the moving men comment, "It's a shame this is happening to Mr. Chavers." What did he mean? I wondered but did not ask, for I sensed our parents wanted us to know as little as possible about what was going on. Later, the huge showcases full of dresses and aprons from the factory were hauled upstairs to our home and placed in our parents' room, now to become the storeroom. We stood around watching with amazement and uneasiness as Daddy and Mother gave directions to the men filing in and out, placing boxes, cartons, bolts of materials, the small factory equipment and other merchandise into that room. Row upon row of merchandise, slowly reaching the ceiling, grew before our eyes.

While the factory equipment was being brought into the apartment, our parents were discussing the sleeping arrangements for us. They seemed to agree that the apartment was large enough to keep the equipment and to use the room planned for Edwina as their bedroom, and that Bill and I would not be cramped in the new arrangement. Then Mother commented that Edwina could eventually be moved in with me.

This was October 3rd. Two weeks earlier, on September 18th, the landlord had told P.W. the factory would have to be out by October 31st; he had leased the property to a new tenant after the old lease expired. . . . P.W. protested the insufficient notice; Thompson told P.W. he could keep the rent for October in lieu of that.

The lease for the factory was a verbal agreement that P.W. expected Thompson to honor. It had always been continued by Thompson, even after it had legally expired, until P.W. and Thompson were able to get together to sign papers. Then the landlord would date the new lease to cover the time from the expiration date of the old lease. One year ago, when P.W. called Thompson a few weeks after his visit to the factory, P.W. remembered the landlord as being cordial and having spoken only reassuring words. Three days later, before leaving on a trip to sell Douglass National Bank stock in Marquette, Illinois, and now eager to firm up the contract renewal, P.W. had stopped by Thompson's office to discuss the factory lease. At first glance Thompson always seemed friendly; P.W. recalled how coyly he had smiled while agreeing about the lease. That day P.W. had talked a good deal about how well the bank stock campaign was going and Thompson had listened nervously. He was one of those "Good Neighbors" of Irish descent who talked about what a shame it was that the colored people were walled off into the ghetto Black Belt. He had been curious about P.W.'s factory, even in the early days during the war, wondering how it had managed to prosper. After the race riots in 1919 he had attended the bank depositors' meetings at the Old Woodfolk Bank and the Hunter Bank out of his interest in what was happening to his "friends," as he called the ghetto people. When he showed up at these depositors' meetings, no one asked him questions. He owned several houses in the red-light district and property along the other side of 43rd Street, in addition to the factory site, and was known as "Mr. Landlord." He was close to Isidore Goldman, the professional receiver.

Several years ago when the judge assigned the receivership to Goldman, this was a favorable sign to encourage the friendship. Thompson had an eye on the Calumet property even before P.W. moved the family into it. P.W. paid the rent for the factory that day in Thompson's office, and asked him to discuss the terms of the new lease. He remembered that many months had passed before the factory lease was signed last year. Thompson repeatedly assured him there was no cause for concern, he knew P.W. was busy at the bank and with his new apartment house, so the matter hung, with Thompson offering congratulations and wishes of success "to you and your people" everytime they talked.

But now P.W. refused to accept the offer of one month free rent. He prepared the employees for termination with the understanding that he would recall them as soon as the factory was relocated. Minnie always found it hard to say farewell to close ties; endings were painful for her. She had grown fond of her job and her dealings with the factory employees, their many customers, delivery men, and the salesmen. All had come to know and trust each other like one happy family. Now saying "Good-bye" to the ones she might never see again, like Miss Scott and Miss Alexander, was agony for her. P.W. and Minnie were so concerned about handling the separation of their employees, and moving the factory equipment out of the building, that they hadn't anticipated the effects of this drastic change on the daily routine of their family life. Now, with us standing around watching moving men and asking questions, they were forced to face up to the effect of this upheaval on our home, stirring up tensions between them that lasted for several weeks.

The general conversation around the house, usually initiated by Minnie, was about the new arrangements . . . the

176

inconvenience of it to our family and the callousness of Thompson in forcing such an abrupt factory shutdown. Minnie was volatile and much of her wrath was directed at P.W. for not pinning Thompson down and getting the lease renewed on time. In retrospect, he could clearly see there were indications that Thompson had evaded drawing up a new rental contract for the factory. He became ashamed of his negligence in the matter, arising out of an old problem of trusting everyone, as well as putting all his zeal into the bank campaign. Minnie often told him that he sacrificed his family on behalf of the black race; perhaps she was right.

The machines were idle, not producing work or putting out goods. Minnie had found an outlet for her creative energies by running the factory. It was good for her and now it was gone, taken from her by his negligence and concern over matters she felt were of only secondary importance in their lives.

The pressures that beset P.W. came from all directions. P.W. found time to handle the employees' separation from the factory in an orderly and considerate manner but could not offer any certainty regarding the future. Mrs. Hicks, whom he had befriended several years ago, left P.W.'s office in tears and rushed over to see Mrs. Emily Brown, the trusted factory employee, who had become close to her since that early incident.

"Come in honey" said Emily. Mrs. Hicks told her of the talk with Mr. Chavers and how frightened and sad she felt about the factory being shut down and not working for Mrs. Chavers any longer. The employees experienced a sense of loss . . . not only that their jobs had vanished, but that their employer, who had been unusually generous, had been so cut down.

"Mr. Chavers was always thoughtful, kind, and a very fine person," commented Emily. "When I came to work for him my husband had just passed away and I was a young widow in this strange city, but he taught me the sewing trade free of charge, and let my children come to the factory after school. Now, I don't know how I'm going to handle the children after school. At least I have a good trade, and I'll be thankful to him for the rest of my life." Mrs. Hicks recalled P.W.'s making good on the bogus check passed to her when she was new in the city.

"I'll never have another boss like that . . . I have never had a boss who trusted me before, Emily."

"When it rains it pours" was the way the former employees of the factory and other people in the Black Belt put it whenever they met on the street or in their homes, talking of P.W. News of the bank battle and factory shut down swept through the city via print and word of mouth. Public charges were made in the newspapers that the bank capital was being depleted and at the same time stocks were being sold to white subscribers at $25.00 less than the going rate. With information acquired through the detective investigation, P.W. was about to present the charges in court when, unexpectedly, Thompson sued P.W. for the October rent on the factory.

Legal papers were sent to P.W. by mail. Looking over the charges he frowned, thinking of Thompson. The sudden leasing of the factory site, followed by a false suit for unpaid rent, confirmed P.W.'s suspicion that Thompson was part of an elaborate conspiracy to discredit his name even further in the community. Things began to fit together now . . . the newspaper article appearing the same day as his confrontation with the Board, being served with an eviction to move his factory and now Thompson's suit only two days after P.W. had applied to the courts for an investigation of the banks. As P.W. sat in his office with Thompson's letter at hand, he became fully aware of the power play going on, not only in the black establishment, but definitely linked with certain Whites who could also benefit from the ignorance and poverty in the Black Belt.

178

9

The Attack

In 1871, in the wake of the Great Chicago Fire, large numbers of underworld characters deserted the burnt-out areas of the world famous red-light district of Chicago, the "Wicked City," for the miraculously unharmed black neighborhood. Prostitutes, pimps, and other characters took refuge, then decided to remain among the Blacks after Chicago rose anew. The Old Settlers said the holocaust was God's vengeance for what the Union armies did to the South during the war between the states. The local ministers said it was God's vengeance on the City of Sin and on the Whites for having mistreated Negroes. The Black Belt was the area in which Joseph Price was born in 1884.

He grew up amidst the struggle so common to the Black Belt with its "resorts," brothels, saloons, gambling houses, spiritualists, prostitutes, pimps, panderers, over-crowded flats rampant with disease, unemployed, relief cases, and the "policy" number writers that flooded the streets. By the time he was fourteen, more Blacks were streaming into Chicago. The Old Settlers were compelled to witness the brazen display of vice and official protection rendered by the political powers. Although the newcomers could not brag of their family connections or education the way the Old Settlers could, they had a fresh vigor envied by the established elite. Many eventually formed the new leadership as policy kings and constituted a powerful political machine, establishing businesses and becoming the seed of a new middle class. Deals were made between white politicians and these black men because they were the most powerful men in the Black Belt, holding the extreme confidence of the poor street people. The tangled threads of politics and racketeering choked the

179

energies of black inhabitants in Chicago in an inverse ratio to their possession of power and wealth. The weakest paid the highest dues in terms of demoralization, deprivation, and defeat. The "call houses" and "reefer dens" flourished, honeycombed with shooting and cutting scrapes and the dance halls, with shrieking ragtime piano playing, stayed open far into the night. In such a murky, polluted swamphole, the goldfish perish early and the catfish thrive. Joseph Price learned early how to become a catfish. In the winter of 1921, one of Richard Owens' contacts introduced him to Joseph Price.

By this time Owens was widowed and left with a young daughter. He had become even more determined to increase his wealth, aiming to become a highly successful businessman in the million-dollar class. In the late spring of 1922, when Owens first joined the Douglass Board of Directors, he had remained quiet, waiting for others to approach him. But now as Bank President, events moved swiftly. The Black Belt was a gold mine for money and power. Owens was impressed with Jesse Hull, a young lawyer, after he successfully handled a negligence suit brought by an injured factory employee. He saw in Hull a potential ally that could be bound to him as a kinsman. When Owens arranged to have Hull meet his daughter at a dinner party in their home to celebrate the court victory, Jesse noticed all of the affluence in the expensively furnished house along with Owens' tone when he said "son," and picked up the hint. After a six-month courtship, they were married.

Owens, a short, balding man with stooped shoulders, walked briskly into the office of his son-in-law carrying a briefcase, preoccupied with his thoughts. Behind him walked a dapper little man sporting grey spats, a black derby, a red carnation in his lapel and a toothpick sticking out of a row of teeth rimmed in brassy gold. "Jesse, this is Joseph Price, my private investigator," Owens began. "He is just the person you need to get the job done."

"Well, good evening, Joe," responded Jesse, getting the hierarchy straight. "Sit down."

"We don't have time, son," interrupted Owens. "Now Price

can look into this Chavers business for us. We have got to stop Chavers' influence."

"Chavers is suing for an investigation of the bank," Jesse announced. "Now we will have to fight fire with fire. We are going to have to turn this whole fight around so he won't be able to investigate us. We are going to turn his creditors of the Woodfolk Bank against him."

"Yes, but . . ." Owens hestitated.

"The job in the beginning will be to arouse suspicion," continued Jesse, outlining his strategy. "An insinuation here, a well-planted doubt there. Before you know it, and before Chavers knows what's happening . . . he's going to have his creditors clamoring for their money."

Owens walked over and gave him a friendly punch on the arm. "But Jesse, as far as I know, Chavers doesn't have a bad credit rating," Owens replied.

"He will . . . he will dammit, by the time your man Price and I finish him off . . ."

"But these people are not his creditors. . . They are the creditors of the defunct Woodfolk Bank and Chavers is the Trustee." Owens whipped out a handkerchief and wiped away his sweat as if to wipe away his agitation. "Of course, Chavers made some statements to the papers that were completely out of line. If he had any complaints to make, he should have come to us. I was induced to take charge of the bank affairs by the Board after he struggled for more than one year and it became evident that he was not going to succeed in raising the money. The Board sought me to finance the bank, and I agreed to supply the money on the condition that the Board would see to it that I was made president at the proper time . . . Now Chavers wants to play headlines. Well, we'll give them to him, hot and heavy. It's not his bank anymore, it's mine, and I'll run it the way I see fit."

"Somehow we've got to beef up a clamor for those old claims on the Woodfolk Bank," continued Jesse who had given this a lot of thought.

"I know . . . I know . . . all about that!" Owens interrupted, and his voice rose to a high pitch. "Strategy is what counts, son. We have got to shut Chavers up."

181

Hull walked over to the closed door to make sure it was shut so no passerby could hear, then walked back to his desk. "You know Dad," he began slowly, "Chavers has records of all his dealing with the depositors of what happened before we got involved with the bank."

Price snickered and Owens broke into a laugh. "No, he does not have the records. He does not have the records," Owens repeated for emphasis. "He was in such a hurry to get out the day he came to the bank, he didn't check to see whether any of his own records of the payments he made on his own shares of stock were included. He left his records about his stock and personal investment in the bank and we threw them out; we didn't need them. He lost his factory because he was so busy playing God." After a long pause he added, "It's up to Chavers to prove his own case . . . to prove us wrong, right counselor?"

Jesse nodded. "We can put Price here to work on several angles." Settling back in his chair, he continued, "If we can get enough people worried about their money, we can get the Trusteeship from Chavers. We know the courts have done nothing about reviewing those old claims because for more than two years those claims have been on file. Lawyers with their postponement schemes can delay and delay. They don't care about claims on a Negro enterprise. They let the claims sit until useful. Well, we can blame Chavers . . . say he doesn't want anything done about them and that 'justice delayed is justice denied'."

Owens smiled and commented, "Remember, what's good for me is good for you, son . . . This is a big business enterprise, not a burial society. We are out to make some money!"

Jesse looked at Price and jerked his head towards the door. "Do you think you can handle this?" he questioned. Price nodded. They were all in accord. Then Jesse watched them go out the door and overheard Owens telling Price that education wasn't everything, "What counts is mother wit." Jesse felt a sudden revulsion, not sure if it was for Owens, Price or himself, but shrugged it off. The important thing was to get ahead.

182

Price, now in his mid-thirties, had parlayed his talents and standing with big-time gamblers into providing an "intra-party detective service." A few days later he strutted into Ben's Barber Shop, an old place with a potbellied stove in the middle of the floor. A checkerboard was at the disposal of waiting customers and hangers-on, and a table stood just for card games. Ben was relaxing in a chair with a newspaper over his face as the shop door opened and in walked Price, chewing a tooth pick and looking like a dandy in his tan shoes, grey pin-striped suit and white silk shirt with pearl cuff-links. "Can a fella get a hair cut an' treatment here?" he asked coolly. Ben sat up quickly, almost falling off the swivel chair.

"Man, give me a massage an' manicure, then a haircut," Price began again.

"Yes, sir," Ben managed, adding in a whisper, "What's a manicure?"

"Filin' and polishin' my nails. Men gits it done down in New Orleans an' they gits it done in Paris too."

"We'll have it next time," Ben cleared his throat.

"Okay ... Okay ... Start with my haircut ..." Price replied, climbing into the chair. "I was down at the pool hall, they was talkin' 'bout how this Chavers fella opened the bank without no money to back it up. Then he started sellin' stock to pay his bills. He had to give up his factory 'cause he couldn't pay the rent. I hear folks are takin' him to court."

"Well, I don't know about that kinda talk," Ben paused, holding his clippers in mid air, "but I believe Mr. Chavers is a good man. I read something about frauds and legal suits in the papers, but I'll wait an' see what they say in court."

Price turned his head, "That's all part of the game. You can't trust them college Negroes, no kin' a way. They get slick in them schools."

"Well, at least Chavers paid his help decent, or so I heard," said Ben.

Price ignored the reference. "If it was me an' I'd given that dude some of my money I worked hard for, I'd tell the judge to put him behind bars."

Ben broke in, "I don't know about that either, 'cause there's two sides to every story." Ben was stirring up his shaving brush in its cup when Price took out his gold watch, checked the time and said he had to leave.

"Well, for my part," Price said, "I hope they runs 'im out o' town." He pulled out three one dollar bills and pressed them into Ben's hand. "That's for your time, even though I didn't get the whole works," he added with a chuckle and went out to the jangle of the door bells.

News of the smear campaign got back to P.W. and his lawyers. Someone acquainted with both sides stopped P.W. at the County Court House and told how Price was circulating gossip and rumors to influence the community against him, to make him drop the investigation, and was bragging that he planned to keep P.W. in court as long as he lived. He let it be known that he was working for Jesse Hull who was out to get Chavers for "meddling" in the bank's affairs. He and Hull were going to have P.W. out in the streets one way or another.

By this time Owens had met with Roberts and Morris to see what they knew about Chavers' case pending in Federal Court. "We've got to find a way to teach him a lesson for good now," Owens began. "It rankles me to hear those depositors and even some of the employees in the bank still talking about what Chavers did, and what he's saying."

Roberts and Morris looked at each other; both wanted to protect themselves in an open fight with P.W. "The trouble is . . ." Roberts finally spoke up, "even those who aren't his friends respect him."

"Well, there are ways of changing all of that," responded Owens.

"What about his family?" questioned Morris.

"What do you mean 'what about his family'?" asked Owens.

"We can get to him through his family, if that's the only way," countered Morris.

"But you can't expect his brother-in-law to turn against him," said Owens, his eyes wide with amazement, yet annoyed to have these men spelling things out for him.

"And why not?" questioned Roberts. "At least we can plant the seeds of doubt about Chavers' motives by writing the

184

relatives a letter. If they bite, we are ahead. If they don't, they'll be thinking about it. We know this man Chavers is a dreamer with his head in the clouds; he's not to be trusted because he is not a practical man. . ."

Owens agreed. "We're out to win . . . that's the reason you brought me into this. I agreed to come into this bank deal on the condition that it be run my way."

"Where do we begin? What do we say?" questioned Morris, reaching for paper and pencil.

"Well, enclosed with the letter, we can send them a copy of the newspaper clipping showing the new Board Members," explained Owens. "We will reassure them there is no double jeopardy involved for them, even with the changes on the Board . . . We've got other things to think about now," continued Owens. "The payment of the capital stock on the Douglass National Bank has to be completed; only 50% of the required capital was paid in at the time Chavers got the charter. We've got to raise the rest of that money, and we don't need this extra aggravation."

Morris began drafting the letter while Roberts went out for refreshments. Owens sat motionless watching every move Morris made. Roberts rejoined them with three cups of coffee. He was uneasily quiet as Morris and Owens edited the two letters with care, rewrote them in ink, then Owens prepared to leave.

"This should create one more obstacle for Chavers to overcome. If this goes to court, having someone's own brother-in-law and sister-in-law among the people clamoring to protect their investments should make a tremendous impression," summarized Owens, tucking the two letters into his coat pocket. He was pleased with himself. His separate conferences with Price and Hull at his son-in-law's office and this meeting with Morris and Roberts in the latter's study would keep everybody and everything moving.

He knew how to solve business problems, and profit from the confusion of black and white problems. By early 1923, the City Council voted unanimously for the Douglass National Bank to be designated as a depository for the funds of the City of Chicago.

That winter P.W. pursued his plans to remodel the Calumet property after his survey of the neighborhood and observations of the habits of the local people. In these prohibition days, entertainment was either in a ragtime speakeasy or in the home with a victrola or player piano. P.W. decided to set up a tearoom in the first floor apartment of the Calumet property where people could get light meals in a homey atmosphere. The carpenters were busy tearing down walls and enlarging rooms in the apartment across from P.W.'s office. Rebecca was chosen to be hostess and manager of the tearoom which would be named for her. P.W. had confidence in her quiet ability and her willing and pleasant attitude when serving people.

The big opening was announced on engraved invitations. Many people crowded into "Rebecca's Tearoom" and we were allowed to come down for awhile that evening. I vaguely remember looking around and being tempted to run under the tables decorated with white linen tablecloths and fresh flowers. An atmosphere of prosperity continued to surround us. There was a constant flow of people on the first floor, either in the real estate office or the tearoom, which eventually became a social gathering place. Rebecca took on the role of hostess with a real flair.

Minnie enjoyed the new venture at first, but more and more she felt uneasy about the changes occurring in her relationship with P.W. Her time was spent in the supervision of her home and children, taking us to dancing class and to other places, and participating more actively in the Parent Teachers Association and ladies' clubs. Around this time she became involved as a Board Member in the neighborhood plans to open a private school. Even though P.W. was somewhere on the premises every day, Minnie felt they were becoming estranged from each other. She also had more time to observe Sanfelice and her inadequacies. Sanfelice, the flapper type in the flapper era, had been in our home for more than one year, arriving as another of P.W.'s projects. But she had grown less attentive to the children and had not responded to the environment as Minnie had hoped. This irritated her. Sanfelice remained a beautiful woman but was cold, selfish, withdrawn and unresponsive. There had been no overt incidents of which she knew, but being a watchful mother, Minnie thought it best to avoid future domestic problems by quietly replacing her. "What's the use of discussing it with P.W.?" she questioned herself. Realizing he would only find another young girl to rescue from a reform school, she decided to go about replacing Sanfelice in her own way.

Minnie started to leaf through the "Want-Ad" section of the newspaper one day, and was idly turning the pages, when she noticed the following announcement in the lower-left section of the last page:

"NOTICE CREDITORS"

Be advised that the creditors' petition to remove P.W. Chavers as Trustee of the property of the Woodfolk Savings Bank is set for trial Saturday March 10th at 9:30 AM, Room 707, County Building. Judge Herbert Mann.

The criminal case against P.W. Chavers is set for March 14th at Criminal Court, 625 So. Clark St., at 9:30 AM. Kindly be present without further notice.

> Very truly yours,
>
> Jesse Hull,
> Attorney at-law

P.W. If any additional information is desired, telephone Victory 5324 and ask for Mr. Joseph Price.

The term "criminal" in legal parlance is often not intended to be as severe as the term sounds to a layman. Minnie did not know the fine points of law and probably it would have made no difference to her if she had. It was upsetting in itself that her husband was a defendant in a court case. She realized this was another attempt to crush P.W. and she had to talk to someone about this latest trick. "If only George were here," she thought as she began to walk restlessly through the apartment.

What could she do, she wondered, realizing someone would

have to talk to P.W. but didn't want to be the one to break the news to him about this, if he hadn't already seen it. She felt some sense of bewilderment, thinking how far the situation had gone, and how lacking in knowledge she really was about the happenings to P.W. She was troubled. Perhaps she was the only one among his close friends, associates and relatives who knew. She decided to write to George and reached for a pen and paper in her little desk in the alcove. As her thoughts and feelings welled up in confusion, she was again in torment. Crying, she tore up the first draft. When she finished, her letter read:

"Dear Brother George:

I don't like to trouble you while you are on the road, but something is going on that frightens me and I don't understand it. I just read a notice in the paper, which I am enclosing, that Jesse Hull is calling all the Woodfolk people together, labeling them P.W.'s creditors, and announcing a hearing in Criminal Court.

It all sounds so terrible! I can't believe my eyes, seeing P.W. referred to as a common criminal. There must be something dreadful behind all this. I'm afraid P.W. doesn't know anything about this and I'm too upset to talk it over with him. What should I do? I am besides myself with worry. Have you heard anything about this while on the road?

Would you please call P.W. and tell him of this notice? He needs someone to talk to. He is such a proud man and being labelled a common criminal may prove too much of a shock. I can't ask you to cut short your business trip and come, although I need you. It will be enough help if you can call and talk to P.W. You can't imagine how the thought of my husband, such an honorable man, having criminal charges brought against him is affecting me.

Please call as soon as you receive this letter and clipping.

Affectionately, as always,

Your sister, Minnie"

George postponed all appointments as soon as he read Minnie's letter. He arrived in Chicago before the end of the week, only to learn that, despite Minnie's fears, the efforts made earlier on March 10th to remove P.W. as Trustee had fizzled out by default; no one showed up in court to make a claim. When George arrived on Thursday evening, he stopped first at P.W.'s office where he found him in conversation with a tenant who was showing him a letter just received from Hull. It urged him to be present at the second hearing now postponed until March 17th. "What are you doing in Chicago in March, brother George?" asked P.W., helping George with his valise.

"Minnie sent me a letter telling me these scoundrels are after you," answered George forthrightly. He went on to tell P.W. that he had received a letter signed by Morris a couple of months ago that he didn't like, didn't understand, and to which he didn't respond. But when Minnie's worried note arrived with the newspaper article, he decided to come at once to see what was going on. Hearing of Morris' letter stirred P.W.'s protective instincts regarding the family.

"Trying to manipulate the family against me, that's what they're up to. I still can't believe men can stoop so low," P.W. said, then added, "But George, why didn't you write and let me know about the Morris letter? You shouldn't have been pulled off the road for this. Those people are just trying to see how much confusion they can stir up, but I'm glad to see you! Minnie's upstairs and will be delighted."

"I'll just leave my valises down here, P.W. I'll be going to the Ganaways' later."

"One has to let some things go, George. Life is a matter of priorities, and you can't win every skirmish," P.W. philosophized that evening, sitting in the parlor with George and Minnie.

"That's true," answered George, "but I hope you're fully aware that you're tangling with a very tough bunch."

Wanting to see and hear for himself what the charges were, George accompanied P.W. to the hearing in Circuit Court before Judge Mann. Jesse Hull arranged for reporters to be present and rounded up a few claimants and spectators so that the courtroom was crowded when they entered. Both sat quietly through the legal gymnastics. Hull perspired and strutted around with thumbs in his vest armholes and an exaggerated arch in his back as he addressed the bench in flowery sentences.

"Our most damning proof of the defendant's misconduct is that one Nellie Calloway, sister of the defendant's wife, is among the claimants who demand the removal of P.W. Chavers as Trustee of the . . ."

"Objection, your honor!" shouted Batts, P.W.'s lawyer, rising from his seat. "Your honor, counsel for the claimants is implying that the petition of my clients' relative by marriage, who lives over a thousand miles away from the scene of the alleged crime, should carry more weight than those here in Chicago."

The Judge sustained the objection and subsequently dismissed the case on the grounds of insufficient evidence. P.W. and George left the courtroom silently, both fully aware that though this was a legal victory, it was nevertheless a severe blow to the family.

"I just can't believe Nellie would do such a thing," Minnie repeated over and over again. "She probably panicked and didn't realize how they would misuse her request," broke in George as they discussed the situation at home later.

"And to think of all we did for her! I guess you can't change a person, college education or not," Minnie went on. "Nellie was always contrary and mean, even when we were children. Now she's joined the enemy against her own flesh and blood."

"Some of the other depositors did the same . . ." started George, but Minnie interrupted . . .

"They are not my blood!" she shouted, her voice breaking. Minnie began to cry; she could hold back her tears no longer as her anger with Nellie dissolved into pity for herself. She was suddenly that little girl of long ago, without her mother to comfort her. P.W. rushed to hold her in his arms and kissed her tear-stained cheeks.

"Minnie dear, remember the charge was thrown out of court," he said tenderly. She was grateful for his gentle

190

concern, but did not like herself for being so despairing. She straightened in her chair, threw back her head and smiled.

George took this opportunity to prepare to leave. "P.W.'s right, Minnie. Nellie didn't hurt his case, in fact it may actually have swung the judge in favor of dismissal. Why don't you forget it?" Minnie could not forget it; many years would pass before she and Nellie would be friendly again.

On his way back to Washington, D.C., driving along the lonely road, George felt his presence at the hearing had helped. As he pushed Southwards, his thoughts turned increasingly to Josephine, the school teacher who had never married because she was too involved in taking care of her sister's family. The sister had four children from a husband who eventually had deserted the family. Josephine was a devoted family member whose salary allowed them to live comfortably. George earlier, and Josephine now, were in a way involved in the same kind of impasse, and may have found each other because each had the same excuse for avoiding marriage. Josephine's self-sacrificing ways increasingly appealed to George as he neared Washington, and he thought of her as a haven from life's problems.

Much talk in the Chicago Black Belt centered around the news of Hull's defeats, one by default and the other by dismissal. As word reached the outside, the sentiments of the community turned openly in favor of Chavers. People felt it was not fair to allow a man to put an awful lot of time and do an awful lot of work, much more than the rest, into something like building a community bank, then turn on him. Others voiced the opinion that he should have submitted a bill for his services. His time should be paid for and weighed along with the money investment of the others if they put in more. Some felt that he was being undermined and should have continued to be President of the bank that he had created. He had saved them from losing their money in the defunct Woodfolk Bank and they let their feelings be known to him.

P.W.'s Federal investigation suit led to a conference with Crissinger, Comptroller of Currency. The bank was found to be solvent with the remainder of the cash due on the account of the capitol stock almost fully paid. Although the rumors about the bank stock price inequities were apparently found to be untrue, Isadore Goldman, the receiver of the defunct Woodfolk Bank, was found to have manipulated moneys in hundreds of cases including the cash funds of which P.W., as Trustee, had legal custody. The investigation was being continued with P.W. scheduled as a chief witness in a forthcoming hearing.

It was during this time that he placed his claim before the Circuit Court of Illinois in the form of a petition for the 50 shares of Douglass National Bank stock which he had paid for out of his personal funds. The Douglass Bank officials, without cause, had refused to issue the stock to P.W. in a retaliatory move. P.W. felt that he was being wrongfully denied his entitlements which had come into being by virtue of a charter he had made possible and secured.

A few days later, the bell rang at the front door and Jack ushered a federal marshall into P.W.'s office. After identifications were made on both sides, the marshall extracted a paper from the inner pocket of his grey suit and commenced to intone in a sonorous voice from beneath a matching grey hat:

"To Pearl William Chavers, greetings,

For certain causes offered before the District Court of the United States of America within and for the Northern District of Illinois, as a court of Bankruptcy, we command and strictly enjoin you laying all other matters aside and not withstanding any excuse, that you personally appear before said District Court to be held at Chicago, in said District on the 14th day of May to answer a petition filed by EDWARD MORRIS . . . REVEREND WILLIAM ROBERTS . . . VERA GREEN.
In our court, praying that you may be adjudged a bankrupt; and to do further and receive that which our said District Court shall consider in this behalf. And this you are in no wise to omit, under the pain and penalties of what may befall thereon."

Holding the document, then handing it to P.W., the Marshall turned and quickly left the room. P.W. read the subpoena over several times, but these names seemed to leap at him from the page. As he looked at Morris' name on the petition, he thought of the night the "socially prominent" dentist came to borrow money to become an eligible Board Member. Now Morris was charging *him* with indebtedness. Then his eyes moved to Roberts' name, the Reverend Roberts, the church leader, a man of the cloth, using his pulpit to mislead the community, permitting his name to appear on such an infamous document. He thought of the machinery in the basement, rusting and gathering dust. He hoped to reopen the factory as soon as the Goldman case was presented to the court. This had to be completed because it impacted on his Woodfolk Trusteeship. Now he was faced with another trumped-up charge.

P.W. asked himself, "What are they being promised?" He remembered their attitude at the public meetings before the bank opened, how they had accused him of exaggerating the benefits of such a bank to the community as a means of glorifying himself. "My own people, seeking to destroy me at the very time justice might be done." He thought of his beloved Minnie who had gone along with all his enterprises and goals, even when she hadn't approved of them. She believed in him, brought out the best in him, inspired him, and brought joy and family fulfillment to him. Where had he gone wrong? He realized the problem was that no one with any real influence in the community cared. "But, then, why do I?" He got up and paced the floor leaving the subpoena on his desk. "They see, they know, but they don't really care." At this point he knew he must fight for his reputation and his family. The only trouble was, he was now beginning to feel the limits of his strength.

He must fight to protect what he had built during his entire lifetime as a promoter and entrepreneur. The name on the petition that upset him more than the other two was Vera Green, the woman whom he had befriended when she had arrived from the South. He remembered hiring her because she seemed so grim with no one she could turn to for help. She was now repaying him by supporting his enemies. "What's her name doing on a Federal petition charging me with bankruptcy?" he wondered.

10

The Defense

P.W.'s relationship with his lawyers was a multi-faceted mix of mutual friendship, admiration and professional biases. Years ago he had hired the firm of Batts, Payne, and James, two seniors and one junior partner, to handle his real estate and business legal work. All three admired him for his logic, depth of insight, and courage, but admitted privately that P.W. was not an easy client. The youngest partner wondered why Chavers hired counsel at all. In the legal profession, truth and justice are relative and sometimes even tenous concepts. The aim of counsel is to win his client's case. Let the opposition counsel pick up the missing pieces, or object to the presentation, if he wished.

P.W. had a businessman's working knowledge of law, the role of the lawyer, and the courtroom drama. He did not care for the theatricals of some court presentations, but he was not averse to the spelling out of details about the motivations of his opponents. P.W. determinedly clung to his philosophy of justice, and a belief that man's reason could grasp and accept truth if it were properly presented to him. But he was hesitant about separating the "legally useful" truths, as his lawyer put it, from those which might be damaging to his own case. He was not convinced that style could be more decisive in the courtroom than the substance of a case. As a result, many hours would be spent by the four men in long and sometime heated discussions of what should and should not be broached in court by his lawyers.

He was thinking about these previous sessions with his lawyers as he headed towards 31st Street the following day. P.W. had telephoned his lawyers, after the shock subsided, alerting them to the new development. This meeting had

195

been scheduled as a conference on the case against Isidore Goldman, but would now have to be changed to a discussion of the bankruptcy charge. The closeness of the date that they had to appear in Court to answer the charges made it mandatory to spend time preparing his defense. The request he had placed before the Federal Court many months earlier had resulted in the conference in Washington regarding the solvency of the Douglass National Bank and an agreement that further investigation of the manipulation of hundreds of bankruptcy actions on Goldman's part, including the maneuvering of the Woodfolk funds, was indeed necessary.

"You know, Mr. Chavers," said Jack, "I think you shoulda hired some white lawyers fo' this case." P.W.'s only reply was a soft, sad chuckle as the car pulled off up the street. "I know you believe in usin' your own folks, bu' you got to be a little more practical 'bout the position you're in. The way I sees it, in the law's eyes, this is jus' a fight between colored folks an' Owens does have some downtown connections. I hear tell the only way you kin win is to git some white folks on your side. Less you give somethin' back to them white folks, like hirin' their lawyers, you ain' goin' to git no justice at all in this town. Colored lawyers is all right for' crap games, and those Southside street fights, bu' this is big time."

"We have many brilliant lawyers, Jack. Someday, we'll have a Negro judge," returned P.W.

"Bu' that's not goin' to do you no good now. You need somebody who's white and knows the game. Your folks gits panicky in front o' those white judges," continued Jack.

"Our folks," cut in P.W.

"Nossuh! 'your folks'. Look at Vera. You took her in off the streets, showed her how to sew dresses, and now look what she's done."

"Well, you can't give up because of a few." P.W. was tired and did not want to argue with Jack.

"But you got to look out for number one, Mr. Chavers," returned Jack. He sounded strangely like P.W.'s middle-class friends who had warned him about the possible problems when he first started talking about a national bank run by Blacks. Maybe it was this cynicism, this deeply imbedded

196

cynicism, that partially explained the behavior of all the people directly or remotely involved with the bank, from Owens to Vera, and including Jack. How did he, Pearl William Chavers, feel about it all? At the moment, as he glanced sideways first at Jack and then at himself in the mirror on the windshield, he wasn't quite sure about how he had escaped the stigma of this cynicism.

Jack eased the car up to the curb directly in front of a complex of stores on East 31st Street. The law offices occupied the upper story of a converted store, rented by a physician, adjacent to a funeral parlor. The sun reflected tranquilly on the gold letters of the second-story window front that spelled "Batts, Payne, & James, Attorneys at Law."

"Don't bother to wait for me, Jack. This will be a long session," P.W. sighed as he climbed out of the car with his briefcase. "I've told Mrs. Chavers not to hold dinner for me." Impatiently Jack nodded, started up the engine and pulled the car away. P.W. climbed the flight of stairs to his lawyer's office, thinking of the subpoena and his conversation with Jack.

Batts came into the library and sat in silence, struggling with his thoughts and his breathing, as Payne and P.W. talked. "It looks like a late session tonight," P.W. began.

"Well, we might as well get started," said Batts, "say, we petition for a dismissal on this bankruptcy charge."

P.W. bristled. He thought of what Jack said earlier about the scope of legal work done by colored attorneys. True, Batts handled notary jobs, petty ghetto law suits, small claims, mortgages and other minor legal matters, but this was an issue with ramifications far beyond the accusation of bankruptcy. The bank was a chance for the colored men of talent and vision to demonstrate and prove their ability to run a substantial business and to gain experience in high finance. Although P.W. hadn't initiated it, this charge provided him with an opportunity to have a hearing in a federal court to prove the integrity of dedicated colored men in a competitive society; and Batts was asking for a dismissal! Without a clear cut legal victory, there would remain a serious doubt about the ability and skill of colored men in business. P.W. shared his thoughts with his lawyers and Batts walked into the front office for a cigar. Payne was smiling and shaking his head when James entered. Batts came back into the room smoking and looking solemn.

"This is simply a legal tactic, Chavers," Batts said quietly, with some effort. "We need more time to prepare this case."

"We don't expect to have it granted, but we're sure of getting a postponement out of a petition for dismissal. We can use the time," cut in Payne, "remember, we have two cases to work on now."

P.W. stood up and walked over to the wall lined with heavy law books filled with torts and misdemeanors, from floor to ceiling, corner to corner. He walked slowly back to the square of four chairs that James had drawn up for the conference. He thought of the pamphlet on Self-Reliance and the Colored Condition he wrote years ago. "We know we're going to lick them," he said slowly. "Truth is on our side, gentlemen."

"The machinery of justice has to be oiled, and that's what lawyers are for," Batts interrupted. "Justice is a poker game and you've got to bluff until you get another deal of a few more cards. We can use the postponement the judge will give us after he rejects our petition for dismissal."

It came to P.W. that in the beginning he thought that the case should be pressed through to the end, but Batts had said "petition for dismissal." Now his lawyer was agreeing with him but was somehow not in the same camp. Winning the case would mean the triumph of truth to P.W. but to them it would mean the triumph of tactics. P.W. had no misgivings about the integrity of his attorney, but he was upset by his counsel and the rules it was based on; "yes" meant "no" and "no" meant "maybe." First he turned to Payne, his longtime personal friend, who was knowledgeable about the entire case and well-versed about intricate court deals. Then he turned to James, the youngest in the group, ambitious, aggressive, and quick of mind. He realized that here were three entirely different men, somehow united and of one mind about how his case should be fought.

"I wish I knew the key to race unity," P.W. mused.

"The colored race will not be on trial," James looked away as he spoke.

"Are you sure, young man?" P.W. answered.

Payne leaned forward. "If we are all on trial, then it's even more important that we use every rule in the game to make sure we win. Success is what determines a judgment and success is not always achieved by a head-on attack."

"Let's get on with a response to the subpoena!" suggested Batts. "A plain, sensible, legal response, yet hard enough for the other side to deal with . . . I suggest our petition for dismissal as the first step, Chavers," he said turning to P.W., "and we can use solvency on your part as the basis for this plea."

P.W. nodded his agreement, but thought to himself, "Vera's role may reveal something about the opposition as yet unknown to me and my lawyers," and he hoped they would cross-examine her thoroughly.

In their response, the defendant, P.W., denied bankruptcy and asked that the charges be dismissed and that he receive damage payments and full recovery for the expenses entailed in the court case on the defendant's part. P.W. thought there should be some further statement about attempts at defamation of character, but his lawyers objected, saying such questions could be handled in the cross examination.

Reminding them that they had another trial to plan for, James brought up the Isidore Goldman case. Their energies were immediately channeled into reviewing the facts revealed by the Federal investigation: Goldman took funds of which P.W. had legal charge, and through questionable legal tactics, forced the Oak Park Bank to surrender these funds. He was involved in more than 300 cases, the Woodfolk cash fund of $8,000.00 being one of the smallest. The initial probe had opened a tangled skein involving double deals in cases amounting to almost one third of a million dollars and the judge took it upon himself to appoint officials to succeed Goldman as receiver in all of these pending cases. The discussion brought forth no dissension, except for Batts who sat back breathing hard again.

199

"P.W., I think we should limit how much time we put into the Goldman case and the Federal investigation from this point on," he advised. "We've worked on our presentation in court now, so let's be prepared to go along with what the judge's decision is and concentrate on this new development, the subpoena."

"Why do you say that, Batts, when we've got Goldman right where we want him?" questioned P.W., acting out of his responsibility as Trustee of the Woodfolk holdings.

"Right now I'm thinking of you, personally, as my friend as well as my client," answered Batts. "After all, P.W. you're a family man and have others to think of."

Payne added, "I agree. You have to think of what you are going to get out of this court action, P.W."

Batts cut in, "You can't do it all, P.W. You've started the legal machinery rolling, now let the judge's decision be your guide, and let the courts deal with Goldman after this hearing."

Exhibiting some of the same singlemindedness so characteristic of him, P.W. frowned. He appreciated their solicitude and thought about them as friends trying to get around him for his own good. But he kept remembering his original intention in requesting the Federal investigatin, to protect the young bank he had founded, and now the courts were bogged down with the revelation of the crooked Goldman receivership in which he also had a stake as Trustee of those Woodfolk funds. "We have many scores to settle here, gentlemen. We cannot appear to publicly accept less than complete justice for our community."

"But P.W., you owe it to your family to put your energies into this legally more important case. This subpoena goes beyond whether this receivership is crooked or not, it strikes at you. You are being legally accused of having engaged in shady dealings with the depositors when you were in charge. As far as you and your family are concerned, if this isn't handled right, your reputation will be ruined. You'd better listen to my counsel!!" cautioned Batts.

"There will be added costs for research on the new charge

too, Mr. Chavers," added James as he watched P.W. prepare to leave.

"I fully realize this is a dirty case, gentlemen," P.W. answered. Then, as if speaking to himself, he added, "Even in victory there are elements of defeat because the enemies we are dealing with are members of our own race, and this is hard for me to accept."

As he rode home that evening, it occured to him that many of those prosperous colored men against him were all family men first. They were fighting him tooth and nail, more concerned about themselves than about the welfare of the colored community, as he seemed to be. He persisted in believing in the value of his philosophy which held that if poverty and ignorance in the Black Belt bothered you, then you, as a more fortunate man of color, had a moral responsibility to work, teach and enlighten. This could be done only if the more fortunate Blacks were willing to sacrifice time and money on behalf of the less fortunate. Apparently, very few affluent black men in Chicago shared his conviction.

As the taxi neared the house, a final question nagged at him. "If economic rise is the basic answer, why had it not changed those middle-class colored people who arrived? They still were racked by insecurity, jealousy, selfishness and petty covetousness." Was it always to be that only a handful did the spade work while the rest stood aside? Even those who showed some concern did little more than give it verbal expression: "Poor P.W.! Whata shame!"

In spite of his legal troubles, P.W.'s real estate holdings had now expanded to include equity in a subdivision of property located at 38th Street, as well as the 4901-3 Calumet Avenue building and the 4716-18-20-22 building where we lived. Jack was kept busy securing apartment listings, showing prospective tenants available "flats," collecting rents, and expressing his flair for handling business transactions. The day came when Jack began to work full-time as a real estate agent in P.W.'s brokerage, and another chauffeur had to be hired.

Frank, the new chauffeur, was a tall, red-haired young man with grey eyes and a face full of freckles. My adulation for him remained my secret because his girlfriend, Cleo, became my "big sister." Cleo lived in our building with her widowed mother and teen-aged sister. She was petite with olive complexion and grey eyes, had a direct, refreshing manner, and adored my mother. For some time now I had noticed the difference in age between my friends' mothers and mine. What I once thought of as mother's beautiful long grey hair now embarrassed me as it was a sign that she was older than the mothers of my friends. I felt she was removed from my world and I needed to bridge the gap in years between Mother and me, when I met Cleo. Our families were brought close together and would take long drives through the nearby forest preserves and the Michigan farms with Frank entertaining us by playing his ukelele whenever we stopped for refreshments.

One Saturday morning, after we crowded into the car, P.W. began speaking of land in certain sections of Michigan that was supposed to be cheap. As we headed in that direction, he talked about developing a camp for children someday, and the importance of social and cultural opportunities for the young. Minnie rolled her eyes heavenward, but said nothing. Daddy and Frank located a suitable picnic area deep in the country-side. After we ate, Bill went off with Daddy to explore the woods; when they returned there was much talk about several acreages they had looked over. On the way home that evening, the conversation turned to P.W.'s camp idea again.

"It really would be wonderful to have a camp," Cleo began. "There's nothing for kids to do in the summer but go to the shows."

"Mr. Chavers always has such inspirational ideas," observed Cleo.

"My husband has some project in mind. I've learned from our life together that planning for new possibilities keeps him happy." Her voice rose significantly to make sure Daddy had heard what she said. P.W. smiled.

Bill and I were up early one morning wandering about the

house. Sanfelice's door was open, the room empty, her bed still not slept in. She was usually the first one up in the morning, but remained in her room puttering around until Mother called her for some chore, a point of contention between the two. We looked everywhere for Sanfelice. Daddy called the police and requested a missing person's alarm.

Returning home a few days later, we found the lights on in our apartment. Daddy checked each room while we stood in the doorway. We had been robbed! The place had been ransacked; we were struck with horror! P.W. reported the burglary to the police and reassured us that he would get detectives on the job. Mother voiced fears that Daddy may have been careless about telling what valuables we had in the house. Edwina began to cry. Bill and I, frightened and motionless, sat around the dining room table with our coats on until the police arrived. I remember the heavy, sure-footed police looking around our apartment, asking Daddy and Mother questions.

"This must have been an inside job, Mr. Chavers," the sergeant said.

"We found a trunk open," commented another patrolman.

Mother gasped. "Minnie don't go in there. It's best you stay right here and tell the police what was in the trunk," commented Daddy. The storeroom was Mother's little domain, entered occasionally as if she were still keeping store. Among the factory equipment was her trousseau trunk where she kept her treasures. In it were gifts sent by her brother John from the Philippines, her wedding gown, her finest linen, a handmade quilt sewn by grandmother Mary Jane, family pictures, and her jewelry.

"My jewelry is in a velvet box in the corner of the second drawer of the trunk: 2 diamond rings, a ruby clip, a diamond lavaliere, a large solid gold bracelet, and a string of pearls," Mother told the police. The police went back into the storeroom to search for the items. Returning, one of them said, "Mr. Chavers, we searched again and found nothing, no velvet box, no jewelry anywhere."

"Whoever stole it knew where to look," said the sergeant.

"The footprints leading from the jimmied kitchen window show the thief entered your apartment in the rear. Are there any relatives or roomers we can question?"

Mother was irritated, "We don't have roomers but we do have a housekeeper."

Daddy decided to cut the interrogation short. "We're pretty tired," he said, not wanting to implicate Sanfelice until he was sure.

"No need to question you further, Mr. Chavers. we will put in a report of the missing items," said the sergeant as the police left the house.

Sanfelice was apprehended and brought into the police station several days later. She was wearing Minnie's gold bracelet and confessed to being an accessory to the burglary.

"Mr. Chavers and his wife will have to come down to press charges against you," said the sergeant.

"Please call only Mr. Chavers," Sanfelice pleaded. "I just couldn't face Mrs. Chavers," she said as she broke into tears. Sanfelice was certain P.W. would be more lenient with her, especially when she told him she had eloped with Anthony, the janitor.

"The sergeant just called, Minnie told P.W. "He wants us to come to the station to file charges against Sanfelice. She wants only you to come. I suppose she hopes you'll let her off easily." Minnie told P.W. he should make Sanfelice come to the house and explain her actions in front of the children; this betrayal of trust and abandonment was seen by Mother as extremely upsetting to us.

As it happened, P.W. did drop the charges and signed the custody papers to release Sanfelice after admonishing her. Then, turning to the sergeant, he asked, "Will you release Anthony to my custody too? He's been in my employ for sometime."

"Yes, they can both be released to your custody. Your wife's jewelry has been fully recovered. I'll provide you with an escort," he said, then motioned to one of the police officers in the rear to bring Mrs. Chavers' jewelry in the velvet box.

As bad as the robbery was, Minnie felt the worst crime committed by Sanfelice and her husband was that of violating the trust everyone placed in them. "The greatest offense adults can commit," Minnie said, "is abusing the trust of little children."

It was as though in allowing Sanfelice to take care of us for so long, Mother was guilty too. After the incident, we began to speak of all the cruel things Sanfelice had done to us. Bill told of her twisting his arm to make him obey. I told how she put me in the closet as punishment, and her kissing and petting with the janitor whenever Mother was away. Daddy and Mother were horrified as they listened to us tell of one abusive episode after another.

"Why didn't you children tell me these things a long time ago" asked Daddy.

"We were afraid of her," I answered.

"I wasn't afraid of her, maybe you were," Bill piped up. "I was afraid of that big janitor always hanging around. Sanfelice said she would have him beat me up if I ever told on them."

Mother seemed so hurt when she finally spoke. "You children knew we wanted you to be safe. I only wish you'd told us what was going on." Her tone was soft, anguished.

I continued, "but Sanfelice was always threatening to hurt us if we told." Then I recounted, in detail, how she had put me in the storeroom closet where I became frightened, fearing I might smother to death surrounded by heavy coats and equipment which left little space for me. Since we were not allowed to go into the storeroom, Sanfelice had committed a double offense in Mother's eyes. Continuing to unburden ourselves, we were completely oblivious to Mother's reactions. We told of the frightening stories she told us whenever Mommy and Daddy left us in her care. We were glad she was gone and we did not want her back.

Later that evening, Minnie and P.W. spoke of their disappointment in Sanfelice and her misuse of their benevolence. Out of hurt, indignation, and anger, Mother said, "There will be no more crusading in my house at my children's expense. P.W., I know you are concerned about the problems of homeless young colored girls and the prejudice against them in finding jobs which forces them to become prostitutes, and their having to live in such immoral conditions, but-but—I cannot help that!!! My children must never be subject to this kind of treatment again."

"This will never happen again," Daddy said reassuringly.

"That's right, this will never happen again," Mother echoed, adding "This is the end of your philanthropy in *this* house."

Because of her fear of causing further harm to her children, Minnie's refusal to continue acting on P.W.'s theory about self-help within the race resulted in the hiring of Mrs. Morgan, a pleasant elderly lady whose chief claim to fame was her son, the pharmacist. The first day she came, Bill and I watched her with suspicion as we had never been in the care of an elderly person before. She had a pleasant voice and called us "darling" and "dear," so that by the end of the day we decided not to protest. Before long we could see that Mother was pleased as she began to depend on her ideas about what to have for supper, what to do for an upset stomach, and how to handle aches and pains.

"A little warm tea," Mrs. Morgan would say, or "a little epsom salts will cure most children's ailments." Then she would set about proving her methods, which would work surprisingly well. The all knowing wisdom of Mrs. Morgan soon earned her the love and status usually accorded a grandmother. As she put on her hat and coat to go home each night, we would gather about her with hugs and kisses.

The housing shortage all over Chicago had increased during the years since the war so that by early 1924 it had reached extreme proportions in the Black Belt, although the Great Migration from the South was beginning to show signs of winding down. But there was no relief from the housing shortage for those arriving from the South with their families. Property owners were converting attics and basements into living quarters. Three and four families were doubling up in apartments, and others were moving into partially completed accommodations. All were paying exorbitant rents. P.W. was proceeding with the remodeling of the Calumet building at 47th Street, as one by one the apartments became available when a tenant moved away. Some of the original bomb damage of four years ago still had to be restored and there were twenty apartments of eight rooms each which were to be divided into smaller units, furnished, and rented by the week.

Remodeling of the apartments had reached the third floor on our side of the building when a lady, who needed the apartment opposite ours right away, moved in before it was completed for occupancy. That evening Mother learned that the tenant had no gas for cooking and offered her the use of our kitchen to prepare her evening meals. "It's so nice of you to let me into your home to use your kitchen," said the lady, surprised at Mother's generosity.

We had watched the carpenters and plumbers coming and going and, with a growing sense of excitement, we used to play in that vacant apartment opposite ours. Now, wanting to explore it for the last time, I seized the opportunity of having Mother busy in the kitchen with the new neighbor to make my way across the hall alone. I didn't stop to find Bill who usually accompanied me on such explorations of unoccupied apartments. Once inside, I locked the door as if to lock out the new tenant and anyone else who might try to interrupt me. I tiptoed down the narrow hallway to the rear of the apartment where I found a candle and matches on the floor of the closet. I lit the candle and began to dance while looking out of the window and was pleased with my dancing exhibition. As I whirled about, I imagined the entire empty room was my stage and beyond the two windows my audience sat watching. I became so enamored by my own reflection in the window that when suddenly my hair caught fire, it was burning for a few seconds before I noticed. Then I smelled the smoke and felt the flames as they leaped from my hair, moving closer to my clothing. Frightened, I threw the burning candle down and screamed for my life while holding tight to my eyes with my left hand. I felt my way along the dark hall, feeling for the wall, until I reached the main door and unlocked it. There was Daddy coming upstairs from the office. On hearing my screams, he climbed the remaining steps three at a time. Whether he realized at first that it was I who was aflame, I don't know, but he moved in quickly to protect me. The fire singed the hair on his hands as he smothered the flames. He then picked me up and carried me into our apartment. My crying ceased almost immediately when Daddy put his hands to my head. He laid me down gently on the couch in the back parlor and went to call the doctor. Mother paced the floor with Edwina in her arms, moaning about what a sight I was. I appeared to be burnt to a crisp from the neck up. She cried hysterically, "My baby is going to die, I just know it! My baby is going to die."

The neighbors came over to see what happened when they heard Mother's frantic moaning. I couldn't really see any of them but I heard Cleo's voice. Someone called the fire department and the sirens could be heard outside from blocks away, adding to the confusion. I was in great pain. At one point mother touched my forehead trying to comfort me. I smiled faintly to acknowledge her loving concern and knew I would not be scolded for having brought on this catastrophe. Mother would forgive me, her touch told me. The doctor finally arrived and the neighbors began to leave quietly, offering sympathy and help to Mother and Daddy in case they needed any assistance.

Dr. Howard, an elderly physician with great tolerance for the restlessness of children, treated the third degree burns on my scalp, face and both hands with skill. He came everyday for many weeks and with each visit my bandages were changed in various ways to give a more pleasing appearance, making me feel pampered. Somedays I was wrapped in a turban, on others little bunny ears perched on my head and later I looked like a gypsy as my hair began to grow out. For several months I enjoyed all of the attention, such as having my meals brought to me, constant questions from neighbors and relatives out of concern and the special visits from Dr. Howard.

One day I overheard a conversation between Mother and Mrs. Morgan about what a problem it was shopping for Edwina and Bill because of their dislike for many kinds of foods. "Bill can't eat eggs, Edwina doesn't like spinach," then Mother added lightly, "but Madrue will eat anything." I sensed that perhaps I was not picky enough about the foods I ate, or how they were prepared. I solved this apparent dilemma of indiscriminate consumption by announcing shortly afterwards that I did not like foods cooked with salt. Mother went into a panic; she had to prepare separate dishes of all foods for me! This announcement improved my position in the household. I was now recognized as being the most finicky person in the entire family. I felt like a seven-year old princess . . . did I not now have the secret path to my Mother's affection?

For three months, school, music and dancing ceased to exist for me. But this unexpected vacation came to an end when Mother began to complain about the expensive medicines that I was taking when I was well on my way to recovery. She questioned the necessity of so many doctor visits and wondered how I would make up all the lost time from school. Mrs. Morgan spoke of a special medicine she could get through her son, free of charge and in large quantities, that could complete the job of healing my hands. She reminded Mother repeatedly that, after three months of Dr. Howard's constant care, the worst was over. My scalp had healed, my hair had begun to grow back, and Mother's fears that I might be bald for life were proven groundless.

I doubt Mother consulted Daddy about the decision. He spent long hours away from home and would frequently come upstairs long after supper in time to kiss us good-night before we fell asleep. Many household decisions were made without his knowledge because of his growing involvement in business affairs, court trials, and the drafting of the bank bill. Mrs. Morgan was persistent in actions that would speed my recovery. Nature's way of curing burns, she insisted, was by exposure to the air. With her son's special medicine, I would soon be well and free of scars. Mother eventually agreed to try her shortcut cure.

Sitting on the back parlor couch early one evening between Mother and Mrs. Morgan, I watched the slow removal of the bandages which revealed two raw red hands covered with salve, the left more damaged than the right. Dr. Howard had kept me amused to divert my attention as he changed the bandages so I hadn't seen my burned hands until this mo-

209

ment. I stared, frightened. Mother reminded me of how smart I had been to protect my eyes during the fire with my hands and told me how lucky I was that my eyes were alright and that my hair was growing in again. Mrs. Morgan kept assuring Mother that the air and her son's medicine would completely cure my hands. I would be good as new again.

We waited for many months but the scars on my hands were never to fully disappear. Mrs. Morgan was at a loss for an explanation as to why her son's remedy had failed. Mother ceased to complain about the scars as soon as full function returned to my hands.

The memory of Daddy, his presence, and how he saved me in my moment of horror and panic was never to leave me. I realized I owed my life to him. I also realized that Mother and the neighbor would never have heard my screams from the kitchen in time to save me from even more severe burns. Thus, the fire episode crystalized the idea in my mind that Daddy was a hero and my special knight in shining armor who loved me more than anyone in the world. For hadn't he magically appeared there on the landing at the proper moment to protect and reassure me that I would live? This special feeling about my father was with me for months, long after I was able to return to school, and indeed has remained with me ever since.

P.W. continued with renovations in the Calumet building as well as working long hours on drafts of the bank bill, convinced his bill was the hope for guaranteeing deposits in small neighborhood banks. All that spring he concentrated on spelling out the provisions to project in his proposal, treasuring the hours he could have sufficient privacy for the flow of his creative thoughts. His friendship with Stewart of the Citizens Trust and Savings Bank had grown. In a day when bankers were authoritative, resentful, and fearful of any regulation by the national government, he and P.W. were believers in a government that protected the people. They talked about P.W.'s deep concern about regulating banking to benefit the economy of the Black Belt of Chicago, and how this might find a ready audience in the larger financial community through one such as Charles Dawes, the banker and philanthropist, who might be counted on at the proper time.

Alone in the office one day, quietly working on his proposal, P.W. was interrupted by a knock at the door. It was Dr. Harry Garnes.

"I was in the neighborhood attending to some business for the Ohio Society and I thought I would stop by to say "hello."

"Come right in, Harry," said P.W. while drawing up a chair. "It's good to see you. How's Antoinette?"

"Out of town travelling with the Opera. She'll be preparing for another church recital whan she returns," answered Harry, now the President of the Ohio Society, a group of Ohio-born Blacks who met to maintain ties while enjoying their new homes in Chicago. He wanted P.W. to become a member, but each time Garnes approached him on the subject, it turned out P.W. was too busy with projects and business ventures. "Pearl, why do you bother with all of this bank business?"

"I know what you mean, Harry," P.W. interrupted. "Sometimes I question myself . . . why I do it and where will it lead me?"

"Of course, you keep busy, but there is a time to stop and say 'Hello' to old friends, just like I am doing now," commented Harry puffing on his cigar and whirling it about his mouth. "By the way, Pearl, that one family house next to me is going up for sale. Have you ever thought of living on a quiet street like mine?"

P.W. shook his head in a vague sort of way.

"It's right next door to us," said Harry, "Why don't you think about it for yourself? It would be great to have you for a neighbor," persisted Harry, reaching for his pocket watch to look at the time.

"A one-family house for us?" P.W. mused. "Minnie might like that someday." He reflected on the tenants' complaints and the business activities and how they interfered with the privacy of her present home.

"I'll call you about it, P.W. Regards to Minnie," Harry made his way out of the office.

P.W. watched from the office window as Harry climbed into

his car. "Dear old Harry." He thought about the different worlds men find themselves in as they spin out their lives and the differences that draw them apart. P.W. longed for an interested ear he could trust; he knew Harry cared about him as a friend and could be trusted, but he knew Harry could not share his dream. "Harry has never wanted to know what's happening in the world about him." P.W. was thinking back to their childhood in Columbus when Harry seemed to be the spoiled kid, but the indulgences he had known hadn't really spoiled him, they had just kept him uninvolved, a sheltered person. Harry was not interested in uplifting the community, enterprises by Blacks, or in bills to guarantee bank deposits.

Once alone, P.W. pulled out the written material and looked it over again. He was satisfied with the outline: "surety companies guaranteeing deposits have the right of examination of national banks, and other powers now conferred exclusively upon the Comptroller." He resumed writing. "By the enforcement of this act, prospective depositors who might ordinarily be patrons of small local banks but who go to the other banks because of their size and other considerations effecting the question of safety, would patronize the banks in their locality." He read these thoughts over and over, adding a few words here and there. "I want to encourage banking among my own people. They robbed me of my bank but they can't rob me of my banking dream," he mused.

Encouraging banking would have to come from afar, he knew, but he wanted to say more about this as an objective in insuring deposits against bankruptcy. He wrote on and on, late into the night, until he was satisfied not only with his concepts, but also with the way he projected his purposes. He felt his message would be understood as he read the last draft.

"Under the federal law now in force, the federal government requires bonds to protect *its* funds and deposits placed in depository banks. Why shouldn't the little man, the average depositor in banks, be granted that same protection?"

"This act will cause millions of dollars, now invested elsewhere because of lack of confidence, to be placed in banking institutions where the owner can enjoy the satisfaction of financial safety and know that the bank officials cannot float securities with their money because of this protection."

"It is difficult to estimate the enormous financial business now conducted outside of banks, in other investments, by persons concerned about the lack of safety of deposits with banks. A large portion of this business would be attracted to banks and banking institutions under this protective system of insurance."

"The far-reaching effect of this proposed law will revolutionize bank methods leading to an enormous increase in banking prospects and opening new avenues of accomplishments and prosperity to banks. Coupled with the imperative need to protect depositors, the inauguration of a system in conformity with this plan is wholly justified."

As Stewart predicted, P.W.'s bank proposal was well-received by Rep. T. Doyle who praised him for his diligence in completing his project and saw in this bill an effort to affix national responsibility in the safekeeping of depositors' funds and to abolish the failure of national banks. Rep. Doyle warned P.W. about the oppositions such a bill would face by those opposed to any federal controls. Nevertheless, he was prepared to present the bill on the floor of the House of Representatives, commenting, "Just getting the Congressmen to think and talk about 'depositor's protection' will be a great step forward."

By late spring, when I returned to school and the house had taken on all the outward appearances of normalcy, P.W. received the news that his bill had been presented by Congressman Doyle on the floor of the House of Representatives and was referred to a committee for study. P.W. and Minnie discussed the bank legislation and we children became aware that something important was happening when Daddy announced that it was referred to the Committee on Banking and Currency and ordered to be printed and distributed for further consideration.

11

The Trials

Six months earlier, in the fall of 1923, the preliminary hearings on the alleged bankruptcy charges against P.W. had begun in the District Court of the United States for the Northern District of Illinois with Judge Arthur Lenback presiding. P.W. had to permit his lawyer, Payne, to testify in order to clarify his relationship with Dr. Morris, the first witness. This he realized would legally disqualify Payne from further participation in the bankruptcy proceedings as his attorney but Payne reassured P.W. he would continue to follow the suit as advisor to the other attorneys.

He performed admirably that day on the witness stand. After being sworn in before Judge Lenback, Attorney Payne declared, "I wanted to collect the money owed to Mr. Chavers without going to court, if possible. Morris acknowledged that he had received the loan from Chavers, and assured me he was going to pay it back, so no action was taken against him. He is still in Chavers' debt for that amount." The Judge dismissed Morris' claim on the basis of this testimony and set the date for the next hearing with the understanding that Roberts would be expected to come forth to state his claim at that time, if he had any. Payne's testimony resulted in P.W.'s sacrificing part of his legal team at the time when he could least afford the loss. Then Batts became ill. The hearings dragged on with James doing the best he could, requesting postponements and continuations throughout the winter, hoping Batts would recover.

In the spring of 1924 the hearings resumed and steadily gained momentum. Batts' health had improved and he insisted on handling more of the hearings. P.W.'s denial of bankruptcy and his lawyers' subsequent petition for dismissal were countered by Hull's seizing the initiative and hiring Gustaf Wagner, a white attorney, as the moving counsel in the name of Morris and Roberts. Wagner promptly posted a document detailing charges called, "The Creditors' Petition." Hull and Wagner based their petition on the narrow technicality that P.W. showed preference by making a final payment to Thompson for the factory rent. P.W. and his lawyers went to a preliminary hearing to request the petition be dropped, bringing records of accounts pertaining to his property, stock certificates in the Douglass National Bank, bankbooks, cancelled checks, and statements about the missing records of purchases made by him for the Douglass National Bank. His books showed the value of the factory furniture, equipment, and machinery for manufacturing women's wearing apparel that were stored in the basement, and the raw materials and manufactured goods from the factory that were stored in our home. This proved his worth at $30,000.00 in frozen assets alone, exclusive of his income from real estate holdings, his substantial equity in the Calumet property, and his personal property. The challenge was that the claimants prove bankruptcy, or the case be dismissed. In light of these facts, the plaintiff's claim of preference for a $50 rent payment to Thompson looked ridiculous and provoked a visible show of dismay by Hull and Wagner. The case was heard before Judge John Crawford in Judge Lenback's absence. Wagner came up with a counter proposal asking that a Special Master be appointed to study the defendant's evidence, which resulted in delay of P.W.'s petition for dismissal to allow time for the requested study.

Frank Wade, a Special Master in the District Court of the United States for the Northern District of Illinois, with whom Wagner had connections, was appointed to consider the argument. Ten days later, Wade issued his report which distorted or ignored the facts and overflowed with slanderous accusations. The report began:

"A petition in bankruptcy was filed on behalf of three petitioners, the aggregate of said claims being upward of $3,000.00.

The acts of bankruptcy alleged were that the said Chavers, while insolvent, did, within four months next preceeding the filing of the petition, pay over to Walter Thompson, a creditor, the sum of $50.00 with intent thereby to prefer said creditor over his other creditors of the like class."

In his four-page document, Wade concluded that by paying Thompson in full, P.W. *showed preference over his other creditors*, so they had the right to demand full payment immediately.

Somehow, the fact that Thompson, P.W.'s landlord, was paid rent not really due him and not concerned with any of the contracts negotiated with the Woodfolk creditors was arrogantly ignored by Wade. The October rent in question had been waved by Thompson because of his demands that the factory be moved on short notice. Thompson later reneged on this agreement and sued for the rent, which P.W. paid rather than be further harrassed.

P.W.'s lawyers were notified of Wade's report accusing him of vagueness, insufficient evidence and making accusations based on his bank-book in Minnie's name. It was made available for examination in the court with notice that objections could be filed within five days. P.W. felt he must prove unquestionable solvency. His counterclaim stated, "The findings, conclusions and recommendations are contrary to the evidence introduced at the hearing," reiterating that he did show books listing his property with cash values of $43,000.00, including personal property with cash values this time; all of which spelled out "Chavers was not insolvent at the time he paid Walter Thompson the sum of $50.00 and the rent payment was not made with any intent to prefer him over any other creditor."

Wade did not answer P.W.'s counterclaim but simply placed a note on P.W.'s petition that the objections should be overruled and further review of Chavers' evidence should continue. The penciled note on the petition was an expression of Wade's highhandedness in dismissing P.W.'s efforts.

The courtroom was well-packed as P.W. took the witness

stand. Batts sat stolidly listening to the arguments, distortions, and accusations of the lawyers across the room. P.W. thought again about the contents of his request for dismissal of the charges. "Now, perhaps, I can apprise them of the injustice of this litigation from the witness stand."

Wagner, in his cross examination of P.W., constantly cut off response beyond "yes" or "no" to the questions he put to P.W. Batts' objections were to no avail. Each one was overruled by Judge Lenback. When Batts objected to the unfair phrasing of Wagner's question about property in Minnie's name he was gavelled down and threatened with a contempt citation. "Your witness, counselor," Wagner said, apologizing to the judge for the uncooperative manner of the defendant and his lawyer.

"Your honor, I could not in good faith call myself an attorney nor could I continue defending my client without registering at least a protest against the manner in which this hearing is being conducted, and the flagrant manner by which my client is being cajoled," began Batts.

"Counselor, are you making a summation now?" asked the Judge as his face changed from bright pink to pale white.

"No your honor, but if it may please the court . . ."

"It does not please the court. Get on with your defense!"

Batts stood for a moment dumbfounded. In the chill of the silent courtroom, an old woman in the back moaned, "Laud, Jesus, they crucifyin' Mr. Chavers. . . ."

"Put her out," the Judge shouted to the bailiff. All heads turned to the back of the room. The bailiff stalked to her bench and grasped her arm. "Thank you suh, I ain't feeble in body or in mind either," she said haughtily, leaving the room.

Batts leaned on the railing in front of the witness stand. "If it please the court, I would like to clarify the intent of my client, Mr. Chavers." He turned to P.W. "Will you state, in reference to the Thompson judgment, under what circumstances you paid it?"

"I had a legal dispute with Thompson about his claim for rent of his property the last month my factory was operating. Thompson was awarded a judgment of two hundred dollars with a stipulation that I pay $50.00 within four months of the judgment. But I talked with his counsel and by agreement I paid him $200 in full for his claim. That judgment was paid in full on May 7, 1923, and I was confronted with this bankruptcy charge four days later, on May 11, 1923."

"And was that judgment paid with any intent on your part, at the time you entered into the agreement, to pay it to prefer one creditor over another?"

"No. . . That judgment was paid to terminate a landlord-tenant relationship involving my factory. This preference charge is a joke!!" P.W. sighed to contain his irritation.

Batts turned to the Judge. "If it please the bench, I would like my client to tell the court in his own words what this case is all about." Wagner and Hull were on their feet to object, but Batts continued. "Your honor, if my client cannot defend himself in these hallowed halls in the face of such a grave accusation as this, when his name and reputation are being bullied, where and to whom can he turn? The touchstone of our judicial system is that the accused is innocent until proven guilty." There was applause and stomping until the judge threatened to clear the courtroom.

P.W. began his testimony with a heavy heart. He recounted how he took over the Woodfolk holdings as Trustee through State court proceedings. He mentioned how a surety bond was put up to cover all claims, the efforts made to locate the creditors of the defunct Woodfolk institution, and the verification procedure requirements he established in the handling of such claims. He told of how he defended the Trusteeship after his request for a Federal investigation revealed the Woodfolk cash funds were being manipulated by a court appointed receiver, how this revelation led to an exposure of hundreds of other manipulations of funds in other banking institutions by this same receiver, and how in the handling of all this he was able to preserve the integrity of the Woodfolk Trusteeship. He spoke of how he set up a ten-year repayment agreement with the Woodfolk creditors, known as the "Chavers Contract," keeping the real estate and other assets intact under the Woodfolk Trusteeship. He recounted how he conceived the national bank as a showcase of self-help and industry among colored people, and a vehicle through which

219

he could keep the Woodfolk depositors confident about the banking system and how it could work for them. He told of the campaign, how the bank's Board was set up, and how he loaned money to one of the accusers in this court action to purchase stock so that he could qualify for board membership. He reviewed the entire history of his bank dealings and his business contacts with Thompson, who was not a Woodfolk creditor in the sense implied by the plaintiffs.

He led the court and the spectators step by step through his travails. The proceedings up until now had given him little hope for victory, but now he anticipated that after he explained everything fully and carefully the Judge would consider the case seriously. As he stepped down from the stand, he silently wondered if perhaps the judge would see the real stakes in his grim game. The courtroom was a bedlam of spectators milling about discussing the proceedings.

The day Batts cross-examined Roberts the courtroom was electric with tension, full of his church members whom he had stirred up against P.W. Hull temporarily stepped aside to allow Wagner to consolidate the courtroom thrust, but he arrived early to set the tone for his team. Wagner came in carrying a heavy brief case. He now had a dual responsibility to Morris and Roberts as attorney for their bankruptcy charge, and as attorney for the "Petitioning Creditors" as the agitated Woodfolk claimants were labeled. Wagner brought all of the bankruptcy-charge papers to make sure he did not lose ground today. He strutted into the courtroom, winked at Hull and took his seat with an air of confidence. They watched Batts come in with P.W. at his side and James following. There was a loud commotion before the Judge gavelled the courtroom to order. Roberts took the oath as a witness to verify himself as a creditor against P.W., who sat calmly through the first part of the examination. As the hearing proceeded, it became clear that Roberts' claim arose from a contract he said he had entered into with P.W. in September of 1920 as one of the Woodfolk creditors having an interest in the Calumet property assets, but which was not this court's responsibility.

Batts wiped his forehead. "Have you any papers of any kind

showing your deposits in the bank down there?"

"Yes, my personal checkbook," answered Roberts smiling broadly and shifting his rotund bulk in the witness chair.

"Will you bring those papers to the Court? The Judge asked you to do that but I have never seen them," demanded Batts beginning to lose his breath again as he pushed Roberts to make a commitment. He struggled to cough; a silence hung in the courtroom. The Judge picked up the questioning to keep the hearing in motion.

"Does he have the papers?" asked the Judge.

"If he wants to see them, I have my book," answered Roberts with a smirk on his face, looking down at Batts, with an air of contempt at his physical distress.

"What kind of book is it? A deposit book?" asked Batts, still panting a little.

"Show him the book," the Judge said to Roberts, irritated now with his stalling.

"It's a bank book," answered Roberts, handing it to the Judge, ignoring Batts.

"This book merely shows certain deposits made on six different dates; it doesn't show at all whether there was any balance on deposit after the date of January 7, 1920," said the Judge, after scrutinizing the book.

Batts seemed fully recovered as he spoke up. "That's just what Mr. Chavers has disputed, your honor. As a result, the matter was referred to a referee by the other judge." Batts was appealing to the Judge now, hoping he would comprehend the manipulation.

"It doesn't show anything at all except the deposits," repeated Judge Lenback looking over the item again.

"Your honor, that's the thing we were trying to determine in the other court," Batts repeated. "A surety bond has been put up to cover this man's claim, if he has one, on the Woodfolk assets. The deposits in this bank book have nothing to do with his being a personal creditor of Mr. Chavers. I don't know what more a person can do to clarify this. It is a . . ." Batts was breathing hard, but he felt he was getting through to Lenback.

Wagner had rehearsed the whole defense with Roberts, but

something had gone wrong. He stood up, "Your honor. . . your honor. . ." but the Judge did not recognize him. Instead he kept looking at what was handed him as evidence of a personal claim against P.W.

"There has been no personal claim proven by this," the Judge finally said slowly. "A man might dig up bank books and it wouldn't mean anything unless the withdrawals are shown . . . Both sides of an account have to be shown as valid evidence in this court."

"That is what we have not been able to ascertain," Batts returned. Wagner could stand it no longer and burst out, "The contract entered into and offered in evidence showed Roberts was a creditor." Pointing to Roberts he continued, "Here is a contract where Chavers agrees to pay the Woodfolk Creditors."

"Now the court is requiring proof," Batts added quickly, showing no surprise at Wagner's outburst.

"This court has nothing to do with that," explained the Judge. "This hearing is to determine the validity of the alleged bankruptcy charge, not the Woodfolk claims. If the witness produces proof of Chavers' personal indebtness to him, that is what I am talking about."

P.W. was recalled to the witness stand. He remained calm and factual, responding to Wagner's blustering questions. At one point he calmly replied, "Mr. Young found out through one account, Roberts handled his bakery transactions."

"Mr. Chavers, just what are you trying to say?" questioned Wagner in his best effort to intimidate P.W.

"I am saying that I have never had a personal financial transaction with Rev. Roberts. All of our business related to validating his claim against Woodfolk and establishing the Douglass National Bank. I brought him into my Board at the bank while organizing that institution."

Batts spoke up, "Your honor, What Mr. Chavers is trying to say is that Roberts is seeking to have this court determine his claim, that whatever it is should be paid at once and thus break Mr. Chaver's contract as the Woodfolk Trustee. . ." He began to breathe harder, "Your honor, this would be a grave injustice as the ten-year period has not elapsed and a grave injustice to the Woodfolk creditors if Roberts were allowed to come into this court and secure annulment of the Chavers Contract. Particularly so inasmuch as Roberts was the complainant in the State Court precedings .... and ... and ..." Batts reached for his chest and gasped for breath... "The Chavers Contract was entered into at Robert's instigation... He brought Mr. Chavers into the Woodfolk Trusteeship!" Batts shouted, then collapsed on the floor.

Everyone rose to their feet. P.W. sprang from the witness stand and ran to Batts. "Call an ambulance," shouted someone as Judge Lenback pounded for order, bending over the stand, watching for a sign from the court attendants.

"He's unconscious, your honor," said one of them.

"This case will be adjourned until further notice," the Judge announced. P.W. accompanied Batts to the hospital. Leaving the courtroom that day alone, James was a solemn young man, feeling the weight of the world. Perhaps he should have insisted upon taking the case today, but he had deferred to the pride and determination of his senior associate. He was prepared to cross-examine Roberts. Maybe he would not have exposed Wagner as Batts succeeded in doing, but he would probably have spared the ailing attorney another heart attack.

James sensed he might have to carry the case through unless Batts rallied, this time allowing himself more time to convalesce. "His dogged determination to run for judge in the next election keeps driving him," thought James.

But Batts did not live to see the next election. Soon after the heart attack he died. This was a great blow to P.W., both personally and professionally. However, despite the loss of Batts and the forced withdrawal of Payne, P.W. did not wish to bring in a new legal team. He decided to depend solely on James at this point in the proceedings. But James, early in June, was called to Topeka, Kansas to conclude some unfinished legal matters Batts had handled there. While James was away, P.W. was adjudged a bankrupt by default because he did not reach the court at the appointed time when the case was being heard. This judgment by default occurred because no notice of the hearing to review the Special Master's final report was ever received by P.W. or his attorney. This undelivered notice clinched the outcome of the bankruptcy charge, and although he had no knowledge of these proceedings, P.W. was adjudged a bankrupt by default on June 10th, 1924 by order of Judge James Wilson who heard Frank Wade's recommendation in Judge Lenback's absence. According to Wagner it was mailed on June 7th, which was insufficient notice. James was already out of town, and even if it had been received, no action could have been taken by him. The lack of any receipt of notice and the decision, based on default, forced P.W. to feel that his oppressors and the court had worked in conjunction to unduly bring his defeat. This was particularly bitter to him as he had placed great faith in the concept of legal justice.

On his return to Chicago early in July, James submitted a motion to vacate the Order of Adjudication, as well as submitting a Petition for Review, and mailed a notice to Wagner stating that he would appear before Judge Henry Clifford to present these requests. In his requests, James pointed out the nonreceipt of notice:

"Now comes P.W. Chavers, by his attorney, W. H. James, and moves the court for an order of setting aside the Order of Adjudication. Petitioner and his counsel knew nothing of the intention of the Attorney for Petitioning Creditors to procure the approval of the Master's report and adjudication and so no notice of that fact was given for sometime subsequent to the said 10th day of June.

Petitioner desires that he be heard in review of the finding of the Master, and that upon the hearing he be given an opportunity to present his objections filed to the Master's report and that he desires to be given an opportunity to be heard in that regard as there is merit to his objections.

The filing of the Creditors' Petition was the result of a conspiracy between certain persons and for the purpose of injuring P. W. Chavers in his social and business standing. The petitioner is wholly solvent and has committed no act of Bankruptcy within the meaning of the Acts of Congress, and Amendments, thereto, pertaining to Bankruptcy."

The court upheld the decision anyway, accusing P.W. of concealing assets and of gross delay in the judicial process. With this last blow, P.W. knew he was being smeared systematically. Betrayed by his Board, tricked by the preference charge, further doomed by the loss of his lawyers, and now the undelivered notice upheld by the court, P.W. wondered how his oppressors had managed to circumvent the spirit of the law which was supposed to provide safeguards for the rights of men. The scale of Justice had plunged in favor of his opponents. P.W. was reluctant to admit this, although he now could see that he was up against a giant powerblock, rooted in the economy, and hopelessly reinforced by the mores of the ghetto which revered the powerful.

Defeated in court because he lacked legal counsel, P.W. hired three white lawyers who submitted additional affidavits to support the motion to set aside the Order of Adjudication. It saddened him to seek white counsel but his opponents were moving in for a kill, recognizing their advantage. Jack's words about the need for white lawyers who knew white court strategies, especially in the big money cases, now took on profounder meaning for P.W. Unless this order could be set aside, his Woodfolk Trusteeship would be dissolved, the ten-year Chavers Contract with the depositors would be broken, his business reputation defamed, and his family crushed by such a series of events. He was determined not to let this happen.

As it turned out, by hiring white lawyers, P.W. brought encouragement to James who was spurred to further action in spite of a personal tragedy. His father was seriously ill in Cleveland, Ohio and by mid-fall he was spending a great deal of time at his father's bedside, but P.W. did not dismiss him from the case throughout the ordeal. James was able to pursue his notion of tracking down Vera Green, whom P.W. had wanted brought in earlier. But she had disappeared without a trace.

P.W.'s defensive moves were distorted by Hull and Wagner, implying some kind of delay in justice to the Woodfolk creditors. First, they prepared a petition demanding a sufficient valid bond of at least $10,000.00 against loss of claims due to delay required by P.W. whom they accused of taking advantage of the summer court vacation by seeking to have the Order of Adjudication set aside. By mid-fall, they had charged P.W. with recklessly disposing of his assets, living off the rents of the Calumet property, enjoying the profits in luxury and ease by keeping his bank accounts in his wife's name and thus preventing creditors from recovering their claims.

"Unless a receiver is appointed, Chavers will make further disposition of his assets." Hull pressured the judge who granted appointment of a receiver for the Calumet property by Thanksgiving. Bruno Hummel, a professional receiver, was appointed. He called at P.W.'s office demanding all assets be turned over and threatened further court action unless the Calumet property was surrendered at once. P.W.'s new legal team advised him to ignore the harrassments or deal with them as they arose. In the meantime, they collected affidavits from witnesses to support P.W.'s claim that the "Creditors Petition" was a conspiracy to defame him and to destroy the Chavers Contract.

Despite this, early in December, 1924, Hummel began to take possession of the factory machinery in the basement of the Calumet property, removing ten sewing machines. One morning while we were out, the janitor, too frightened of Hummel and his legal documents, allowed the receiver into the basement. The machinery was gone by the time we returned.

"What will become of all of us?" Minnie cried out, wrenched by the loss.

"I must get you and the children out of this sordid fight. I can't bear having you see all of this," P.W. responded to her fear and anguish.

"Those wicked people are going to tear you apart for not letting them have their way about that bank . . . and those Woodfolk creditors demanding their claims intend to strip you, to destroy you. Nothing will stop them." Minnie was becoming hysterical. "Oh, my poor children . . . what will become of them?" Minnie dimly realized how much her tears

226

and hysteria were hurting P.W. She wanted to stop adding her anguish to his problems but she was torn with despair. The factory was her domain, a personal part of her, and now it was gone, perhaps forever.

"You're right, Minnie, we must think of the children. We must protect them." P.W. spoke of the one concern he knew which would motivate her to remove herself from the distress he was causing her. He was forced to tell her more of the details she had to know. "Hummel has hired a lawyer to assist him in taking possession of this property as the court-appointed receiver. I have to fight to keep him off these premises." Minnie was stunned . . . silently, stoically, she listened as he went on. "My lawyers assure me that with further evidence, the entire matter will be thrown out of court. Until then, we must protect our little family. This litigation was brought on us, dear, but now the fight is being brought right into our home."

"My life's savings have gone into this property. I should be in the fight too," Minnie answered.

"That's what has kept the receivership away, the property is in your name, dear. They can't take it away from you."

"If we did move, where would we go? We couldn't live in that 49th Street building, the apartments are too small, and I refuse to go down to that big house on 38th Street. The thought of those places distresses me. I'm so tired of all this," Minnie moaned.

"Dear, there is a one-family house I've looked at on 42nd Place. You would be more comfortable there, on a quiet side street away from the noise of a busy thoroughfare, and the house is next door to Harry and Antoinette Garnes," answered P.W.

"I don't want to move back into the heart of the Black Belt! It seems just yesterday we were living on Forrestville Avenue, around the corner from 42nd Place, and the neighborhood was becoming run down then," Minnie cried out, weeping. "You know I detest that area."

"But dear, Antoinette and Harry would be nice neighbors. Antoinette is a cultured person."

Later, after Minnie and the children went to bed, P.W. sat

alone in the parlor thinking of the stolen machinery, his hope to restore the factory and of his former employees who told him of their bitter experiences since his factory shut down and the wretched conditions they found in other factories where they had been forced to pay for needles, thread, and even the use of the sewing machines. They remembered him as a kindly employer, never driving them to exhaustion or fighting and squabbling with them, so they continued to hope he would reopen the factory. Why hadn't he restored the factory? He reproached himself for his own procrastination. It had been two years since the factory eviction and the machinery had been down in the basement rusting away all of that time, but he had been preoccupied with these endless law suits, hearings, the remodelling of the property, opening the tearoom and other projects. His thoughts went back to his life in Columbus where his career as a manufacturer had begun. He had sewing machines that he willingly shared, an active factory operating with eager, promising employees, and customers for the merchandise he created. The machines that had been a way of life for both him and Minnie and had produced so much for him and others were now gone.

Looking around the basement after the machines were removed, P.W. could hardly believe they really were no longer in the basement awaiting a new location to begin humming again. He thought of the kind friends who had helped him get started because they believed in his ability, and how he tried to help others get a start in life as a means of showing his gratitude and to repay these opportunities. He would design the dresses and aprons and select the colors that so many ladies found exciting; his wild use of oranges, reds, and purples were very popular. He smiled, remembering he was able to please the trade because he never discerned this flashiness; he was color-blind, but his limitation led to his success. This had taught him a lesson that had remained with him and now came to him as he mourned the loss of the sewing machines. He would have to triumph over this loss and recover the machines. Maybe the move to 42nd Place would turn the tide for him. Actually, he had not looked at the property. Even though he had heard no more from Harry since their last visit, and Minnie had refused to consider the move tonight, he would pursue the thought.

One month ago, Albert George, the first black Judge in America, had been elected to the municipal court of the City of Chicago. Since a municipal court judgeship required city-wide support, this had been heralded throughout the Black Belt as the beginning of a new era of justice for black men, not only in the City of Chicago, but throughout the nation. Behind the scenes there were demands for a recount in an effort to stop his being seated, but he was installed on the judicial bench along with the white judges which was perceived as a show of strength for the Second Ward Republican Organization.

P.W. hoped the new municipal Judge would be an asset to the black man's quest for justice in America. He was confident that black lawyers were as able as white attorneys to preside over our court system and merely needed the chance to prove their ability. Would this judge use his influence behind the bench to further the cause of justice for his people or would he become another unconcerned, apathetic observer as many other black men had become once they rose to power? P.W. knew the great powers over men and property that judges wield in the closed circuit of the judiciary. But his own distress was acute and his problems were multiplying; he now had little time for public matters.

James was again called to the bedside of his ailing father in Cleveland and this time, after his father's death, he stayed for two weeks. Through his other lawyers, P.W. petitioned the court for additional time to prepare their case. His aggravation and grief over the inhumanity of man took its toll on P.W.'s health and he was stricken with pneumonia. His physician ordered him to bed.

James located Vera Green before he was called to Cleveland. She had changed locations every month or so, but James finally found her in a small rundown rooming house in Chicago. The landlady eyed him suspiciously as he knocked on the door.

"It's a young man to see you, Vera," she volunteered with a

229

mixture of warning amd mockery. "A Mr. James to see you. . ."

"What young man? I don't know no . . ." Vera stopped in mid-sentence and opened the door slightly.

"I'm Mr. Chaver's attorney," said James handing her his business card. "I'd like to speak with you for a few minutes."

Vera looked angry for a moment, then said, "Oh, alright, come in."

"I'll be downstairs . . . if you need me," the landlady called out.

"It's alright, Mary," replied Vera stepping back as James entered the stuffy, windowless room with it's smell of burnt hair, grease, and sterno.

James explained the reason he'd been searching for months to find her. Vera told him she was on the move for a long time "cause dat dapper dude, Price 'as been worrin' me near to death 'bout signin' mo' papers fu Hull. I ain't talkin' to nobody no mo' 'bout nothin', no siree!" she said defiantly looking at James then turning her head to the door wondering if Mary, the landlady, was standing outside.

"I am not going to have you say or do anything you don't want to, Mrs. Green." James looked intently into her eyes, realizing he couldn't afford to antagonize her. After a moment of silence he added, "I just want to know if you can tell me anything about this bankruptcy charge against Mr. Chavers since you did work for him and you see what has been happening to him."

"Mr. Chavers is a nice man" she finally said, "bu' . . . I wuz concerned 'bout my money. . . I ain't as young as I look," she spoke a little regretfully and defensively as if she hadn't heard the question about the bankruptcy charge. James cleared his throat as the closeness of the small room, the smells and the dimness of the light bulb, continued to make breathing laborious.

"Have a seat, Mr. James," she said as she pointed to an apple crate that stood against the wall. James moved over and sat down, fumbling in the breast pocket of his suit for a handkerchief and a pencil. She studied him again then walked across the bare floor to the door, opening it wide until it banged against the wall. She then told James, "I'm ashamed dat my name is being used on dat bankruptcy petition, bu' I nevah signed no such papers. I signed some papers dat I wuz told would he'p ta git my money back. I got no grudge 'gainst Mr. Chavers."

"But how did you get in this with Roberts and Morris?" questioned James, groping for relevancy in her remarks.

"I got scared 'bout my money 'n' evahthin' when de bank di'n' open. I wuz 'fraid evahthin' wuz goin' 'gainst Mr. Chavers, 'n' if I stayed on his side, evahtin' would be goin' 'gainst me."

"Well, how are things going for you now?"

"Oh, suh, I jis' don' know whut I'm goin' ta do," confessed Vera, suddenly breaking into uncontrollable sobs, too lost in her present predicament to worry about what this young man was thinking of her or to talk about what she did to P.W.

James was not prepared for this. He waited silently and patiently for a few minutes, then spoke in a low, comforting voice. "Now Mrs. Green, we must think of our friend, Mr. Chavers, who is being victimized after all he's done for so many people. You know what he's done for you and you know what it's like to be deserted in your hour of need. Let's think about Mr. Chavers for a few minutes. . ."

Vera looked up, dried her eyes slowly on her apron, then looked out of the corner of her eyes at James as though trying to see inside him to determine his sincerity. "Don' mean ta talk 'bout myse'f . . . bu' I jis' can' he'p it. . . I feel so terrible 'bout whut I did ta Mr. Chavers . . . bu' I know fu' sure . . . I di'n sign no bankruptcy papers . . ."

"Well, just tell me what you know and what you did do and leave the rest to me. I will make it all right with Mr. Chavers so you can be friends again. He is a very understanding man, Mrs. Green."

"Tha's his trouble, I guess . . . he's too understandin'."

"Well, just tell me what you know that will help him, Mrs. Green."

Vera took a deep breath and looked straight ahead as she began her story. It started innocently the first day Thompson stopped by the factory, when Mrs. Chavers was supervising the work, over three years ago. Thompson wandered back to her machine. It seemed he had flirted first with Mrs. Chavers and then with her. She remembered his attentions, though brief and superficial, and that Mrs. Chavers had greeted him coolly. She was too busy taking care of customers to notice Thompson's attention to her or his conversation with Vera. Later, at the rear of the factory, while he was pretending to be looking at a crack in the ceiling, Thompson asked Vera a few leading questions.

"Do you really think Mr. Chavers can establish a bank?"

"Course he can," Vera had answered.

"Well, I wouldn't be too sure." He said it seemed to him that Mr. Chavers was more concerned about what he could get out of starting a bank than he was about his workers in the factory. "I saw Thompson a few weeks later, right after de holidays, in his office. He as'd me whut kinda work I done 'fore I came ta work fu Mr. Chavers. I tol' him I done cleanin' work, washin', 'n' ironin'. When I told him whut I done at de fact'ry, he wanned ta know how I liked my boss," Vera paused and looked out towards the open door. "I tol' him I liked Mr. Chavers, bu' he'd stopped comin' ta de shop, 'n' Mrs. Chavers had been runnin' things fu a long time, 'n' I di'n like dat woman . . . 'cause she wuz always walkin' 'round with her nose in de air, like she's bettern us . . . ."

Thompson warned her to let her friends at the factory know that things did not look too good for Mr. Chavers and that he, Thompson, had an offer for the property that he might have to accept and that her friends might find themselves suddenly out of work if they didn't begin to look around for other jobs.

"I guess he could see dat he scared me near ta death." After Thompson warned her to look out for herself, he gave her a $20 bill as a friendly gesture and hinted, as she left his office, that she could help the others by passing the word among them. For a long time she fretted about having to return to Alabama and Thompson's comments to her that "the workers could all lose their jobs if Mr. Chavers didn't take better care o' de factory," haunted her from day to day, serving to en-flame her constant anxiety about holding a job. The following week she voiced comments here and there in the factory to warn the employees, "bu they di'n pay no 'tention to me. Some o' dem jis' laughed at me 'n' said I wuz always complainin' 'bout somethin' or otha'."

As the days passed, her uncertainties and questions about her future grew. When The Douglass National Bank didn't open, Thompson's doubts that Mr. Chavers could really establish a bank were confirmed for her. "Eva'one wuz so 'fraid 'bout whut Mr. Chavers wuz goin' through . . . de delay in de openin' 'o' de bank. . . . Eva'body felt it. Not dat Mrs. Chavers said anythin', bu' we all knew somethin' wuz wrong somewhere. I di'n say goodbye' to anyone when I left so dey maybe di'n even miss me," remarked Vera. "I went straight ta Mr. Owens' factory, hopin' dat my runnin' wuz ova an' he gave me a job as cleanin' woman fu de upstairs offices in de bank. Dis seemed like a nice, easy, steady job," she went on. "Den Price began ta seek me out afta work. I nevah knew whut dey wanted wid me 'til dey started afta me 'bout chargin' Mr. Chavers wid misuse o' my money. Price said it wuz de only way I could git my money back from Mr. Chavers, 'n' dat I would be he'pin' a lotta innocen' people. I dunno, suh, why I lissen' ta dem," she pleaded, "I'm so 'shamed 'o my part in it, Mr. James."

"You are sure?" questioned James.

"Oh, yessuh, I really belonged on Mr. Chavers' side all along. I wan'ta say somethin' 'bout all o' dis when I saw Mr. Chavers at de bank. I wuz happy it wuz open 'n' dat he had got de charter, 'n' I wuz sorry 'bout havin' anythin' ta do wid his arrest on dat confidence charge. I really wanned ta talk ta warn him 'bout what wuz comin' next. He shoulda taken time ta talk ta me dat day in de bank bu' it wuz all my fault. . . . I jus' said I wanna talk 'bout my claim . . . bu' I wuz too mixed up by den," Vera confessed further.

"Will you say that in court?" asked James taking notes as fast as he could in the dimly lit room. The possibility that Vera was the link in this entire chain had crossed his mind many times before, but he felt he could never prove it in court. Now he realized that this frightened, lonely, bitter woman who sat across the room from him might be the one to vindicate P.W.'s reputation against all of these slanderous charges . . . *if* only she could be relied on to come through for him in the bright daylight of the courtroom as strongly as she did in this dim, drab, windowless room where they sat at the moment. James asked her to go over some of the points for his clearer understanding. He went over detail by detail with her, then paused to ask Vera again why she remained in hiding. All of her tears, and even her confession, did not explain her complicity. Why had she continued to allow herself to be used in case after case? She must have known the Woodfolk case and the fraudulent bankruptcy preference charge were being used to defame Mr. Chavers. It was all over the newspapers. "You must have realized what was really going on. Why did you stay away?" he finally felt compelled to ask. "Why didn't you come to Mr. Chavers' aid then?" He was testing how she would stand up in open court under the extreme pressure of Wagner's cross examination.

"Like I said, Mr. James, I jus' di'n know whut ta do," she said pleadingly, looking into his eyes.

"But what has changed for you now? Do you understand that you will have to justify what you say, clearly, in court? Your name is on that bankruptcy petition." James was searching to measure her stability. "What moves this woman?" he asked himself, "fear or something else?" He was looking at her intently now.

"Oh, I'll be glad to he'p Mr. Chavers," she repeated nodding her head excitedly. "I jis' di'n know how ta git outa dis mess. I'd even thoughta goin' back ta Alabama. It wuz gettin' ta be too much fu me here. I'm so glad you came, Mr. James."

"I'm glad I came today too. I only hope it's not too late. So much wrong has been done to Mr. Chavers and since you were a part of it, you'll have to be ready to tell all of this. I want to fully understand how you could have done the things you did, Mrs. Green. We will have to talk about this again. Remember, you took out a search warrant against Mr. Chavers, acting under instructions from Price. This and everything else you did will be brought out in court. There is no place to hide there."

234

"I know dat I wuz wrong . . . bu' I don' need ta hide . . . or run no mo'.'"

"You will have to make this clear in the court."

"Yeah, I wuz wrong in whut I did do," repeated Vera, "bu' dat wuz den 'n' dis is now. I don' think dat way no mo'.'"

James assured her that what she told him would be held in strictest confidence, and that they would go over every detail of her evidence again before he brought her in to testify on Mr. Chavers' behalf. He realized that she hadn't fully answered his questions, but he felt he had pushed her enough for their first encounter. Vera agreed to submit an affidavit that she was not a plaintiff in the bankruptcy case, and to testify in court about how Hull had conspired to undermine P.W.'s reputation.

"You tell Mr. Chavers dat I'm sorry 'bout the things I said 'n' don' want ta make his troubles worse fu him, bu' dat now I will make it all up ta him if he'll jis' gimme de chance."

James reached into his wallet thinking "she is really down and out," but immediately changed his mind feeling any money he offered her could only be considered a bribe in retrospect. He prepared to leave her small windowless room, assuring her he would take her message to P.W. She smiled in relief as she closed the door behind him.

This was the first real break in the case. James hurried to telephone P.W., letting him know he had located Vera and that she had agreed to cooperate.

During the next few weeks, P.W. lay seriously ill with a high fever. We all moved downstairs to the three-room apartment behind the real estate office so that Mother could manage his general affairs. I remember stopping at his door and looking helplessly at him, listening to his loud breathing; there was so little I could do. I just wanted to comfort my Daddy, I had never seen him ill before. P.W. and Minnie discussed their plans for our future during his convalescence and I had a chance to hear some of their serious conversations.

P.W. spoke again about the house on 42nd Place where he had wanted us to move, "just for a little while." Minnie listened, mostly to comfort him in his illness. "I should have known more about what was going on with you all along, P.W.," Minnie said reproachfully.

"That would only have upset you more, dear. It's best this way."

"But I know I could have helped you."

"You can help me now by settling the family over on 42nd Place. Minnie, I've been thinking of our newly elected Judge and the importance of political strength. I've decided some-day, when all of this is over, I want to run for Congress."

"Oh, P.W. . . . you're not going to run for Congress too?" She was thinking how like P.W. it was to be lying sick in bed, almost inundated with legal problems, and talking about running for Congress someday. Because of that he wanted her to move back into the heart of the Black Belt!

"Yes, dear, running for Congress could help rush my bank bill through the House of Representatives," he answered.

"Are you going to give your life to banking, P.W.? Look at all the trouble your banking efforts have caused you already. We should have stayed in Columbus with the factory there." It seemed that for a moment Minnie had forgotten that the move had been at her suggestion.

"It's not that I am so determined to stay in banking, dear, it's that in a capitalistic country, money rules." He watched her expression change as he added, "The passage of my banking bill will stabilize my career and bring stability to the Black Belt."

"You're a good man," Minnie said in deep admiration, "but you must remember that I'm just a woman trying to bring up her children in a healthy way."

"Our children," he corrected her gently. "I'm not trying to be presumptuous, Minnie, but we need our own representa-tives. I lie here all day watching and listening to you carry on for me. I hear the tenants' problems about money and their requests of you to wait for the rent. This has me thinking again of what must be done to get our people out of this mindless exploitive cycle . . . this economic slavery."

"Yes . . . I'm trying to follow you."

P.W. continued, feeling he had enlisted Minnie's attention.

"While lying here my whole future has become clear, Minnie. I know running for Congress as an independent candidate is the right thing for me to do. The Deneen faction has talked with me. They think I would strengthen their reform ticket and have asked me to let them know when I am ready to run."

"Yes, I am trying to follow you," Minnie answered gently. "You're feeling better dear, aren't you?" Struggle as she might against P.W.'s convictions and determination, Minnie knew she had little chance of dissuading him.

"I'll be out of this bed, back on my feet, and at my desk soon," P.W. smiled. "I've got plenty of work to do. I enjoyed being a manufacturer because I was creating work and earning a living for myself and others. But political and economic strength go together and we are living in Chicago, the pivotal city of America. What happens here is important all across the land. Now, others in America make every effort to force our people to feel obligated and indebted to them so they can wrest all the rewards of our labors . . . and Minnie, the worst of it is . . . we cooperate in this; unknowingly, we cooperate. Our people are like a great sleeping giant needing to be awakened to feel his full strength. I know no white man can represent me or my people better than a colored man."

In the days that followed, when they were alone together, he would resume his talk about his vision of combating the myth that a white man is better qualified to represent black people and his growing outrage that the American Blacks had years ago been systematically excluded from Congress. "We've got to change this racist thinking," he would say to her repeatedly.

One day Minnie finally replied, "P.W., you know I won't stand in your way. I convinced you to come to Chicago and, now since all of this has happened, I have promised myself that I will never try to influence you again." Her voice sounded strained.

"Then you accept my suggestion to move?"

"Just for a little while," Minnie laughed. "I really don't want my children in that neighborhood when they get to their teens, and I won't permit a change of schools. Their schooling must not be interrupted."

"Then we agree completely, dear." He felt all along that Minnie would eventually accept this idea. She had cooperated, sometimes actively, sometimes silently and hopefully, in all of his endeavors.

During one of their talks, P.W. told Minnie that he wanted the children to participate in his campaign when the time came for him to run for public office. "We must awaken in them a sense of their part in the community life; we must awaken race pride in them . . . and pride in the history of our race." She wondered what the children could possibly do in a political campaign. They are so little.

"I am determined to make a place for my children in everything I do," he said firmly as if to make a commitment to himself too.

When P.W. fully recovered, the family returned to the third floor apartment. We were happy to be back in our own home, but we had enjoyed the stay behind the office too. On his return from Cleveland, James went directly to P.W.'s office and talked about the value of Vera's evidence. P.W., still convalescing from his illness, became hopeful again that his case would be tried fairly.

"Yes, I'll work on this quickly. If Vera comes through with that affidavit, and I think she will . . . Mr. Chavers, take my advice, sir, you should not stop with this Petition for Review, in the higher court. You should sue for defamation of character and name Roberts and Morris as co-conspirators. Everything those people have done to you has been for the purpose of defrauding, injuring, damaging, harrassing and embarrassing you. Vera's testimony will blow their case wide open now."

P.W. nodded in agreement. "We may have to confront them with their own motives to discredit me in the community. You will get the help you need to carry this through to conclusion."

P.W. hired an experienced Negro lawyer, Neville, who had a reputation as a brilliant trial lawyer among his colleagues and who had followed the case with interest, in the press. Together, P.W.'s legal team prepared an elaborate document

with affidavits from various persons, including Vera. The
Petition for Review began:

"P. W. Chavers, the petitioner, is the organizer of The Douglass
National Bank, a national bank devoted to the interests of the
colored population of Chicago, organized in the Spring of 1921, and
doing business since then on the South Side of the City."

It went on to cite the refusal of The Douglass National Bank
Board Members to repay P.W. the money owed to him and the
refusal to issue his 50 shares of bank stock, the pilfering of
the bank records and the debilitating, groundless suits being
pressed by Hull and his associates in this and other courts
making claims for debts already paid or not owed at all. The
petition spelled out every detail of the history of P.W.'s
involvement with the "Chavers Contract," the Calumet property, the Woodfolk creditors, and The Douglass National
Bank.
    "It will take a long time to obtain a ruling on our petition
because complete transcripts of all the records will have to be
reviewed by a number of judges," explained Neville, as they
went over the final draft before submitting it to the United
States Circuit Court of Appeals.
    "Let's all have a Happy New Year in the meantime,"
suggested P.W., ever the optimist.

12

The Unveiling

Early in the year, P.W. began negotiations to purchase the house on 42nd Place. He met with the present owner, Mrs. Neal, a widowed, childless, wealthy white woman who seemed pleased to offer the property to him at his price even though her attorneys advised her to make as big a profit on the sale as possible by selling to Blacks. She was charmed by P.W.'s description of his young family and felt they would enjoy the property and enhance the neighborhood.

There was something different about this little side street on 42nd Place, a homey quality that pleased him. It was two blocks long, running east and west, connecting Grand Boulevard and St. Lawrence Avenue. It was lined on each side by a string of one and two family frame and brick houses, interspersed with an occasional more impressive greystone house here and there, a few multiple dwellings on the corner of the alleyways, and Fuller Elementary School on the corner of St. Lawrence Avenue. The Garnes moved into the block around 1915 as the first "upper-middle-class" black family. It is likely that Antoinette did the initial negotiations back in 1915 since she passed for White, or a foreigner of one type or another, and they had been accepted easily into the white milieu of the block. P.W. pointed out these factors to Minnie as a good omen.

Shortly after, Minnie began to complain about the racial tensions increasing at Willard School. When February arrived and Edwina was not promoted from kindergarten to the first grade, she was determined not to wait to test out the attitude of the white teachers about encouraging the potential of colored children. Before the end of the month, Edwina entered private school. Now, every morning, a big bus labelled "Mason School for Children" on each side rolled up Calumet Avenue, stopped at the entrance of our building and waited for Edwina to trip out, wrapped in her white fur coat, to join the black elite on their way to school. Years later we learned that Daddy had advanced the school a loan to purchase this special bus.

One day Minnie was approached by a tenant who heard of her dissatisfaction with the dancing school we attended and told her about Mary Bruce who was starting a dancing school. "It may be better for our girls to study ballet with a young teacher than a former Broadway performer whose main concern is producing more professionals. An appreciation of the arts, a finishing school touch, is really all I want the girls to have," she said to P.W. later that evening, thinking of her Aunt Sally.

On a deeper level, Minnie's anxiety about the mounting pressures on P.W. turned her thoughts to her own mother, Mary Jane, and the memory of the pressures that she knew with Tyler, her father, moving about to earn a living as a stone mason. Minnie did not intend to be like Mary Jane with destroyed hopes of a stable home. With no one to share these thoughts and fears, Minnie questioned the desirability of the house on a little side street.

But P.W. had no time or energy to make further efforts to appease Minnie by answering all of her questions. He listened, grateful at least that some of her complaining ceased about Edwina's school situation, and he did try to keep her apprised of what was happening in court. He told her about the first meeting of the Woodfolk Creditors held at Hummel's request in Referee Wade's Court, the various notices placed in the Chicago Evening Post, and how he had challenged these moves because none of the 23 claimants that showed up had a provable claim against him. He knew this and he was filing objections against all of them.

What P.W. could not have known was that even before the first creditors' meeting, Hull, Hummel, and Wagner met to plan how Minnie's assets in the Calumet and other property could be declared a part of the Bankruptcy Estate. Hull agreed to finance all litigation to accomplish this task. Hummel agreed to become Trustee, taking on more power than his receivership and requesting that the court allow an attorney to be appointed. Immediately after the first creditors' meeting, Hull hurriedly prepared a petition to the Honorable Frank Wade, Referee, which read:

"Bruno Hummel, now Acting Trustee, bond fixed at $2,000 employed no attorney as receiver. Numerous hearings before the Referee and the District Judge on the question of solvency were held and in said hearings Gustaf Wagner represented the various creditors, became familiar with Chavers' affairs and the title to various property in which he claims to have an interest. Further litigation will be necessary to prosecute this action. An attorney not familiar with the proceedings which have taken place during the past year and a half, would be at a disadvantage and possibly not sucessful in prosecuting said action in the best interest of the general creditors of this estate. Wherefore, this Trustee prays that he be given leave to employ Gustaf Wagner as the attorney and to pay said attorney a reasonable fee for said services from the funds of this estate, the amount thereof to be subject to the determination of this court."

Referee Wade granted this request. Hummel now had no intentions of filing P.W.'s objections to the fraudulant claims submitted at the first meeting of the creditors. Instead the deck was stacked for the case of Hummel vs. Minnie B. Chavers, unbeknown to P.W.

Within two weeks, Minnie was shocked to receive a summons to appear in court to answer questions that might be put to her concerning the assets and property of P.W. Chavers. She was at home alone with Mrs. Morgan when the summons arrived.

"Now they are going to try to scare you, honey," Mrs. Morgan said.

"But P.W. already explained what my stake in all of this is," Minnie spoke helplessly as she sat down to read the summons over again.

"That's not enough for those people," Mrs. Morgan answered patiently. "They want to strip your husband of everything . . . reduce him to a beggar!"

"Well, they won't succeed," snapped Minnie. "I'll never

243

forget my uncle and the way he took on those white people who tried to intimidate him. 'Poor white trash' he used to call them. I may not understand any of this legal business but I know what it means to stand up to a bully," she continued.

"Don't get all riled up about this, Mrs. Chavers," Mrs. Morgan cautioned.

"What is mine is mine in my own right," responded Minnie... "My money in the South Side Savings Bank is my own property. I have had that bank account since 1917 when we first moved here from Columbus. Some of that money I earned before I knew my husband. They are not going to steal from my children."

"They don't care about your intentions, Mrs. Chavers. They're trying to bluff you so you will begin to weaken Mr. Chavers' stand against them, plead with him to give up the fight.... If you can be frightened, they know Mr. Chavers will fall."

Minnie began to cry unashamedly. All of the ploys being used to wreck her husband were more than she could bear. "He's such a good man. Such a fine character ... all he thinks about is others ... never himself," she muttered over and over between sobs. Mrs. Morgan stood silently for a long time while Minnie had a good cry, then she spoke, "They're convinced that every Negro has his price and can be bought off, but Mr. Chavers is a champion, they hadn't reckoned with his will. So now they want to test you."

"I'll give them something to talk about when they see how I stand up to them," returned Minnie.

"Mr. Chavers will probably object to your being questioned by those people, but don't worry, Mr. Chavers will take care of it," replied Mrs. Morgan.

"No, that's not it! Going to court isn't what is bothering me. Looking at this summons, something is coming clear to me... I know we must move from here. They don't intend to grant my husband any justice. There will be no justice for him! They intend to crush him because he built that bank and they don't care whom they slander or hurt to do it. Next they'll try to bully my children in some way," said Minnie in a slow deliberate voice. "Now I know we must begin to pack and be

244

ready to move as soon as P.W. closes the property deal on 42nd Place." Minnie was exhausted, her emotions ran the gamut searching for ways to respond to this challenge.

Confusion still lingered in her face and Mrs. Morgan saw it. "Somehow . . . I wish Mr. Calloway was here," said Mrs. Morgan.

"No . . . it's best that George not know. I've bothered him enough," answered Minnie. Mrs. Morgan busied herself with chores so that Minnie could not see her embarrassment. They didn't speak for some time, avoiding each other's eyes. "If I write to George, he'll write back about P.W.'s bullheadedness," Minnie sighed, mentally noting that she didn't want to hear anything negative about her husband from her relatives. She herself had been negative enough recently. She loved her husband, she loved them both, but she knew George wasn't P.W.'s equal and she didn't want to be the source of another confrontation between the two. . . George would have compromised long ago, returning to the factory before the fight reached this point. Not that he was more reasonable than P.W., he just did not see the larger picture.

Minnie spoke to P.W. about the summons, that evening after dinner, while the children were playing upstairs. P.W. observed the slight tremble in her head, hand, and voice as she talked. He did not speak of the outrage he was feeling towards his enemies in daring to attack his trusting wife, and struggled to hide the anguish and guilt he felt about burdening Minnie. He held her hand tenderly as they talked in restrained voices, out of concern for each other, aware of the alarm both felt about Minnie now being subjected to questions in court over her role in P.W.'s business affairs. He told her that she had been very brave all along and that he hated what these trials were doing to them and to the children. Minnie's trembling stopped as she listened to P.W. say it would be best for her to answer all the questions as simply as possible, many of which would be harsh in an effort to intimidate her. He told her not to challenge them, that this was yet another legal trick which he would deal with appropriately. Minnie felt reassured in listening to his words just as she always felt secure in his presence and somehow knew

245

that everything would be alright. By the time they stopped talking about the summons, and turned to other topics, Minnie was able to be philosophical about the forthcoming court experience . . . She finally said that she had wanted to help in some way all of these months and that appearing in court would now give her a chance to do just that.

Dressed in her finest for her day in court, Minnie walked with head held high to the witness stand. She was sworn in and sat fully poised as Gustaf Wagner began to bark his intimidations at her. Looking directly at the Referee, she declared she was unable to understand what was wanted of her or what she was expected to do. With her head held even higher, she repeated emphatically that she was answering every question to the best of her ability and that she had answered truthfully and honestly every question put to her. Her appearance and poise in face of the onslaught had a disarming effect on Wagner who began to question her about her intention to cooperate in the future. "Will you produce any documents or records within your possession concerning the property of the "Bankrupt," Wagner shouted at her.

"I will do everything to clarify this charge against my husband, P. W. Chavers. I will produce all records in my possession," Minnie responded quietly and with great dignity.

"Then you are implying that you have more records than The Bankrupt has already produced?" questioned Wagner sharply with emphasis on the words "The Bankrupt."

"I did not say that," returned Minnie evenly.

"Well, what did you say?"

"I said I have not refused to answer a single question about the property and assets of my husband."

"And what does that mean?" continued Wagner looking at the Referee who smiled one minute and squirmed the next. "You know Mr. Hummel has been appointed Trustee for the bankruptcy proceedings and that these hearings are necessary and very expensive because your husband has concealed his assets in your name." Wagner watched the Referee scrutinizing Minnie, observing her closely. "These hearings are adding to the cost of these bankruptcy proceedings." Wagner's voice became shrill, but Minnie sat calmly through the tirade. "This court has been very patient with your husband." Wagner was squinting at Minnie now, attempting to upset her.

She cleared her throat and lifted her head as she reiterated, "I am ready and willing to comply with all lawful orders of this court."

Wagner shook his head and turned away. He had not been able to break Minnie under cross-examination. "That will be all, Mrs. Chavers," the Referee said after Wagner finally conceded.

"Thank you," she said in a quiet voice, smiling pleasantly.

A few days later a contempt of court order was received, addressed to Minnie. The Referee had taken Wagner's side though he had appeared somewhat sympathetic to Minnie during the trial. Now, more puzzled than ever, she talked the matter over with P.W. "I don't know what they wanted of me, dear. I thought nothing further was required." P.W. kissed her tenderly. "Nothing further is required of you, Minnie. I will handle this." He assured her that his Petition for Review submitted to the higher court should soon result in a reversal of all this torment.

"But P.W., you are right . . . the family is no longer safe from their harrassment and intimidations." She began to pack in earnest now.

Minnie took time off to explore the new dancing school that the tenant had spoken to her about a few months ago. Bill refused to be a part of any dancing school "sissy stuff," but agreed to take violin lessons, and was now tolerating the necessary practice without too much pain. That evening Minnie told P.W. "I found Mary Bruce to be a delightful person, so young and full of exciting ideas. She is an imaginative youngster, planning a recital at the Eighth Street Theatre this June."

"I am glad you liked her," commented P.W. "I liked her approach to dance! She is very serious about wanting to develop young children artistically," continued Minnie. P.W.

smiled, knowing Minnie was always pleased with herself when she began to sound like her Aunt Sally, the serious patron of the arts.

By late March, 1925, everyone was geared for the move to 42nd Place. The spring thaw promised good weather, only to be broken by a gusty last snow of winter's fury. Bill and I left our apartment home for the last time that cold morning with instructions from Daddy that he would pick us up after school. We would not be returning to Calumet Avenue, but we felt little loss when it was upon us that morning, because Mother had so designed our social contacts that we were involved with children from many areas, from our music and dancing class members and our scattered school friends to our Morgan Park relatives. We were never dependent on or too closely involved with the neighborhood children. Light-heartedly we set off for our new home that day after school.

Rounding the corner with Daddy in the Velie-8 , we could see our house in the middle of the block. It was set back from the sidewalk about twenty feet with a porch stretched across the front entrance like all the others, except for Dr. Harry Garnes', whose lawn was fenced closed. We scampered up the steps still partially covered with snow in spite of the movers and the warm March afternoon sunshine. Mother was trying to locate more dishes and pans for Mrs. Morgan who was in the kitchen preparing dinner. As soon as we greeted Mother, we bounded upstairs to explore the bedrooms, the bathroom and hall closets, in clocklike fashion. We peeked into the back parlor where the full-length picture of Frederick Douglass was propped up against one entire wall. It was the only piece moved from Daddy's office with our household furnishings. There was little room for anything else besides Frederick Douglass, the mahogany glass-topped table, and the upright piano in a far corner from the windows. The ebony bookcases lined one front parlor wall and a gas fireplace spread over another wall with its mantle shelf on which Mother had placed her French clock and Dresden China dolls. The portrait of P.W. with Booker T. Washington, Emmet J. Scott, and Rev. Taylor was already hanging on the wall to the right of the mantle.

Dr. Garnes came over to welcome us to the neighborhood that first evening in our new home. Antoinette was out of town but he brought a few of the neighbors from across the street and they spoke fondly of their early experiences on the block. Long after the others had left, Garnes sat in the back parlor with P.W., talking, laughing and joking. Minnie excused herself early as she was exhausted.

For the first few weeks every evening was much the same with neighbors coming over wanting to make themselves known or to be of some help. P.W. and Minnie learned a great deal about the history of the black experience on the block during these welcoming visits. The Garnes moved in first, then the Bowman family, who were brown, made the second purchase immediately after the 1919 race riots. The Bowmans had lived in the Englewood Section of Chicago among the Old Settlers but were terrified by the rioting in the scattered outlying areas and felt they would be safer near, or even within, the Black Belt. Even though the white neighbors wrote "No Niggers Wanted" on their door in the 42nd Place Block in 1919 as a warning of their sentiments, the Bowmans were so frightened by the riots near the Englewood Section that the signs made no impact on them whatsoever when they moved. Then came the Thomas family, the Keeble family — and by 1921, in just two years, the block was nearly all colored and the Whites had fled as if from some dread disease, so strong was their antipathy.

These new black families brought their own way of life as railroad employees, bricklayers, and factory workers, all hard-working people with a pioneer spirit regarding home ownership. Some, like the Bowmans and the Thomases, had been homeowners and felt a deep sense of responsibility about keeping up the appearance of their property and performing certain civic duties. Mr. Bowman was the treasurer of his church, Mrs. Bowman was active in politics, Mrs. Wiggins was the assistant precinct captain, and the Thomas family boasted a school teacher or two. Dr. Garnes was the major professional on the block. The distinction which existed between "first settlers" and "newcomers" carried over into this neighborhood. There was an enduring conflict as to which families were really the "first families." My father did not bother himself with such petty squabbles, feeling it was destructive to race loyalty. Everyone suffered from in-fighting and Whites were quick to use it to their advantage. He had moved to get us away from the harrassment and memories of the legal maneuverings, the stripping of the factory, the constant presence of Hummel, the receiver in the Calumet building, and to establish his residence in the First Congressional District. Only one house contained some questionable characters, and we were warned to stay away from it. P.W. could see that Minnie was pleased. Her fears about the bad influences of the neighborhood and the effects they might have on her children were being dissolved as she became acquainted with the friendly people on the block.

But after awhile, Minnie grew tired of Harry's almost daily presence. She voiced the opinion that she was not at all sure how this arrangement was going to work out if Harry was going to spend all of his free time at our house whenever Antoinette was away, and she was away so much of the time.

"Minnie, all of this attention will disappear soon," P.W. assured her. "We have to expect this for awhile." But Minnie had had enough, she wanted privacy with her family right now. "My uncle used to say . . ." Minnie began, refusing to be reassured. P.W. knew by now that any time Minnie reached back to quote her uncle she was very irritated and felt she needed his support to make P.W. understand how she felt.

"What's that dear?" he asked.

"My uncle used to say that the three most important things in life, and I was never to forget them, are *dress, address,* and *redress.* I am beginning to think that address is the most important of the three."

"Oh . . . Harry . . . he's still after me about joining the Ohio Society, Minnie." In view of her mood he knew she might like this conversation, but she was only partly mollified.

"Surely he can see that I am entitled to my husband's help sometimes," Minnie said with a sigh.

The light conversation about Harry had helped him momentarily escape the full impact of yet another blow. Later

250

that evening P.W. pondered a long time as to how he could tell Minnie that his Petition for Review had been denied. When he first learned, a few days earlier, that the bankruptcy charges against him had been refused further review in the higher court, his spirit was almost crushed. He had needed time to pull himself together to carry on. He sat in his Calumet office for a long time looking at the name of Chief Justice William Howard Taft who had handed down the decision. P.W. had campaigned for him in 1908 in Columbus, Ohio when he was running for the Presidency. P.W. remembered that Taft had later become known as "Mr. Disfranchisement" because of his strong segregationist positions and racist views after he was elected President. Again the irony of fate touched P.W. from out of the past.

He wondered if he were to pay an even greater price for not submitting, for trying to battle this charge as an involuntary bankrupt through the higher court? He was a man who loved his race and his people, too much perhaps, if that could be. He was proud of himself and his accomplishments, but he was paying a great price for this pride. However, he believed that this struggle was right. He felt this was the essence of manhood. Slandered all the way to the higher court, he never learned how to be an "Uncle Tom." He had dedicated his life to refute the myth of the basic inferiority of the Negro people. Throughout the trials on the witness stand, in all of his legal depositions and in the community, he carried himself proudly, as was his usual manner. Maybe this was a bigger part of the problem than he realized—not that he steadfastly believed justice would eventually triumph over trickery, but that he let the opposition know he was fully aware of their motives. Perhaps he should have foreseen that this would make them determined to crush him completely, as if it would vindicate and purify them, and this had not been too smart he confessed to himself now. His manner reflected that he knew he was as competent in his field as white people, better than most, and perhaps this hadn't been too smart either. This was 1925 and the Ku Klux Klan, symptomatic of the American psyche, was at its height.

The Circuit Court of Appeals of the United States had

apparently denied him redress for his grievances because he was a black man, in spite of any outstanding personal characteristics or leadership qualities he possessed. He had rights only at the sufferance of the white men, like Taft, in America. Maybe in some ways he had tried too hard to live beyond this American reality, to deny it by association with people such as Stewart, Deneen, and Vice President Dawes. He thought about the Fourteenth Amendment to the American Constitution which guaranteed every citizen equal protection under the law and how he believed and trusted in the sanctity of that law, carrying his case to the high court because of his belief. His thoughts turned to the recent rebirth of the Ku Klux Klan and the continuing expansion of their membership all over the South, steadily invading the North, and swelling to four million members nationwide. Forty thousand of them had just marched down Pennsylvania Avenue in Washington, D.C. holding high the American flag, dressed in their white-hooded regalia.

P.W. reminded himself that his legal team had worked diligently together to present his case, that there were countless frauds perpetrated through bankruptcy procedures and that racism was not the only issue here. Finally he felt that the denial of his Petition for Review did not mean the higher court approved of the preference charge or the bankruptcy decision, it simply meant that the issues of clearing his name and protecting his property rights through the Federal Court would forever remain in doubt. "I must concentrate on protecting my reputation here in the Black Belt and on consolidating my own assets to protect my family and my future," he said to himself, summing up the next steps he would take and searching for the words to tell Minnie about the dismissal.

When he did finally share these facts with her, she accepted the news about the decision stoically, asking no questions. He told her that James was hard at work on an application in the Cook County Court to vacate the order appointing a receivership to be established in her name, the one remaining technicality that could forestall the bankruptcy machinery.

"It will take months to clear up this receivership, Minnie.

252

In the meantime, I am pursuing a Defamation of Character Suit against Hull as it is important that I restore public confidence in my name," said P.W.

"This gets more and more complicated," commented Minnie.

"Yes, I know it does, but there must be justice somewhere," said P.W. "It grieves me to see how the 4716 building is being neglected. The receiver collects rent, but makes no repairs. When I pass by, the tenants tell me about leaky ceilings, cracks in the walls, and other things, but I can't do anything more until that receivership is removed."

"This is draining you, P.W. Maybe it's not for us to have that property," pleaded Minnie. "You're like Job in the Old Testament . . . always crying out for justice, constantly being tested in the wilderness."

P.W. smiled, "Maybe it would be good for you to come to the hearings, Minnie, just to listen."

By early June Minnie felt relaxed enough to go to one of P.W.'s trial sessions, his Defamation of Character Suit. That evening, she talked about their day in court in a factual, calm, and natural way. She had seen Vera Green for the first time in several years and had reacted with mixed feelings of pity and scorn. P.W. and Minnie could be heard in the back parlor talking about the trial. Both were impressed by the way James was handling the case and were hopeful of victory.

"P.W., it does seem this lawsuit has finally gotten to the heart of the matter . . . I want to take the children to some of the hearings to see the inside of a courtroom" she continued.

"Why upset them with this now?" returned P.W.

"You've said you wanted the children to be prepared for life," answered Minnie. She was not going to be talked out of it easily. "All of this action in these trials came to me as a shock and we don't want it to be that way for them," pressed Minnie. "We must educate them to face the realities of this world."

"But we don't want the world to look too dismal to them while they're growing up . . . and what can they get out of it? They're so young," P.W. insisted.

253

"Well, the sooner they know that life can be dismal, the better prepared they'll be. You've said that they will grow up and know why their father had to do some of these things. We want them to know about Negro history . . . well, these trials are Negro history. These trials are a big part of their father's life, and that's what makes the difference. . . . Their father has been making history and these trials are an effort to dishonor him," returned Minnie. She had not forgotten how Wagner had intimidated her, nor the contempt citation that was later issued to her. She thought about how unprotected protected she felt that day when cross-examined by Wagner. She was reared to think a lady is protected by men, and instead she was abused and insulted by the attorney and the judge alike. They did this out of their ulterior motive to ruin her husband. "I want my children to be better prepared than I was. I want them to have as much knowledge as possible to defend themselves in the life that lies ahead of them as American citizens. Besides, it was you who said they have to learn their rights and responsibilities early by participating in what you're doing," she concluded.

"Now, Minnie . . . I didn't mean in a fight to protect my reputation."

"Let's just take our chances that they will learn something, P.W." Minnie replied, and she knew by his silence that he agreed.

The morning we prepared to go to court with Mother we skipped up and down the stairs, restless and excited. The thought of entering the grown-up world of a court room made me ecstatic, another sign I was growing up. As we entered the courtroom full of people, we became serious. Daddy was up front with James; we could see the back of his head.

Hull was the first one to take the stand. James' voice grew louder as he interrogated Hull. I began to remember Mother saying people didn't appreciate Daddy and I grew uncomfortable and restless, squirming about in my seat. Mother was caught up in the movement of the trial, trying not to miss a word. "Shhh . . ."she responded with a finger over her lips. "Let's listen closely."

The more I heard, the louder the question of "why" came

back to me. I fought this question within myself. It seemed Hull was calling Daddy a "cheat" from the witness stand. Then he was explaining his connection with one of the judges in the bankruptcy trial.

"What was this judge's position when you sought his advice?" asked James.

Hull answered in a low voice, "He was the Assistant State Attorney."

"And what is his position now?" quizzed James.

"He is one of the judges on the bankruptcy case!" responded Hull . . . The courtroom gasped, James looked around.

"He advised me to have Vera Green take out a warrant on Mr. Chavers under the Confidence Game Act," confessed Hull.

"Aha . . . Are you saying that this judge, presently sitting and trying the bankruptcy case against Mr. Chavers, did, while he was Assistant State Attorney, advise you to have Vera Green secure a warrant for Mr. Chavers' arrest under the Confidence Game Act, and that you followed his advice?" questioned James, wiping his forehead with his handkerchief. "Then you are saying that three times you used Vera Green to make claims against Chavers for the same parties and the same monies?"

"Vera Green was a voluntary petitioner in a case against Chavers," roared Hull. His words were loud and angry.

I couldn't stand it any longer. I kept hearing the words "against Chavers." I pulled and tugged at Mother. I was a very frightened little eight-year old girl. "What are they saying about my Daddy?" I cried out again.

"Shhh . . . Madrue . . . I'll explain all of this to you later," Mother answered. "They'll make us leave if you won't be quiet, dear."

"Shhh . . ." echoed Bill, as the interrogation started again.

P.W. was sitting at the table with his lawyers, watching his counselor cross-examine Hull on the stand. He was not unaware of the presence of his family in the courtroom. Actually, he was concerned about the children hearing the facts as they came out of the mouth of Hull. The revelation of the conspiracy seemed even clearer to him now. It was as if he were re-examining himself out of a new awareness that some facts had escaped him before. For three long years he had stood alone as the black man in the white man's court, seeking justice from the larger community. Not wanting to add to any depression he was already feeling and yet saddened by these reflections, he steeled himself and did not look back to acknowledge his family's presence in the courtroom.

Hull, still on the stand, answered, "Yes, I've used Price some times in my cases." James was clarifying Price's relationship to Hull. "That's right . . . to get people into these cases against Chavers."

"Then these people have not been, in a strict sense, voluntary petitioners?" questioned James. "Price is not an attorney, of course."

"I have used him in investigations to find out how many people Chavers was defrauding," answered Hull with a smirk.

"Do you know about Price seeing Vera Green to get certain facts?"

"I may have sent Price to get facts for me," answered Hull. "Against Chavers?"

"Yes, I represent creditors against Chavers," answered Hull, still smirking.

I couldn't bear hearing any more of this. I began to cry. Mother rose and walked out with all of us into the corridor to avoid any more embarrassment. Her efforts had resulted in my unacceptable behavior, just as P.W. anticipated.

Later that night, I had a chance to tell Mother how troubled I was about what I heard. "Why are they against Daddy? . . . I just don't understand. What has he done?" I pleaded with Mother to dispel my confusion.

"You have a very gifted and unusual father who has done many things to help people. Others want to take the credit for what he's done." She spoke slowly in her efforts to help me understand.

"But why?" I returned . . . "Did he hurt them?"

"Of course not! The fact that he created the first Negro National Bank should go into the history books. Others have dreamed and talked about it, but he *did* it," Mother replied

256

quickly. "You see, Daddy feels that what he's done will make a better future possible for you and other colored children someday."

"But why are these people calling Daddy names?" I continued.

"They don't want him to get the credit for the wonderful things he's done." Mother was exhausted, but she kept trying to explain, "You have a very brave and good father." She suddenly kissed me good-night and called out to me on leaving the room, "We'll talk more about it tomorrow."

There was little sleep for me that night. I was a very troubled child and couldn't forget the words that were said about my Daddy in the public courtroom, nor the words Mother left with me. "They don't want him to have credit for the wonderful things he's done." These words were to ring in my ears for many years. I now realize my questions couldn't have been answered that night, for how does one tell an eight-year-old of the cruelty, villainy, greed, and inhumanity that motivates some men to destroy others? I would live for years in search of satisfactory answers to those questions I asked that night.

Minnie arranged to keep us out of school, one more day, to take us to court that final day of the Defamation of Character Suit. My questions had convinced her that court exposure was educational. Vera looked forward to this day, hoping to redeem herself. She had rehearsed her lines many times with James who wasn't convinced the opposition wouldn't get to her. After all, she had been disloyal to Mr. Chavers and was easily frightened under pressure. As the judge rapped the court to order, Vera listened eagerly to James addressing the jury.

"Ladies and Gentlemen of the jury, Mr. Chavers asks only for justice. The defendants have said that these were voluntary petitioners against Mr. Chavers . . . Vera Green . . . their chief petitioner, is here to give her testimony. Will you, ladies and gentlemen of the jury . . . decide for yourselves . . . Was she a voluntary witness or did she act under duress? We call now, Mrs. Vera Green."

257

As Vera took the stand to "Tell the truth and nothing but the truth so help me God . . .," she seemed to really mean it. James had prepared her well. "Now, tell the court in your own words what happened to you after you began working in Mr. Chavers' factory."

She spoke first of Thompson's approaches to her in the factory, the offer of employment and her eventual decision to take a job at the bank. Her voice grew softer, the words came slower, so James pressed her further. "What happened to you there?"

"Dey said 'f I made de claim fu my money dat Mr. Chavers'd see ta it dat I got my money and people would 'gan ta talk . . . bu' I dunno why I' lissen ta dem . . . I donno who day wuz talkin' bout. I din' as' . . . I thought dey knew wha' wuz bes' fu people like me ta do."

"Mrs. Green, please explain to the court to whom you are referring? Who urged you to make the claim against Mr. Chavers? Is that person in this courtroom now?"

"Yessuh, that's 'im over there," Vera pointed to Price. "Afta de bank di'nt open in January, I got scared 'bout evahthing 'n' wenta them askin' fu work," Vera paused. "Den it go' so dat evahtime dey wanned someone ta front fu them fu whut dey wanned ta do ta Mr. Chavers, Price needled me. I cin see dat plainly now," continued Vera.

James recognized that she was tense, running through her story too rapidly in her eagerness to clear herself. She had been much clearer in his private office. He also knew she must be worrying about exposing herself as having perjured herself at earlier trials, and perhaps she was still fearful of Hull and Price despite James' earlier reassurances. The Judge gavelled for order again. The spectators were growing restless, unable to follow her easily. James moved in close to her. "Now Mrs. Green, you will have to explain more fully. You admitted you were willing to do these things," he gently summarized for her where she was in her testimony. "Mrs. Green, tell us why you first took action against Mr. Chavers and how did you feel about doing that?"

"I wuz scared of alla dem people. Evahthin' started goin' wrong . . . cause evahtime they'd have me take outa warrant 'gainst Mr. Chavers, I go' real scared," Vera confessed. "I wuz real 'shamed, bu' dey ke'p afta me, 'n' afta me," Vera repeated nervously. "Dey lied ta me, 'bout whut dey wanned outa me."

"Objection, your honor," yelled a voice from the opposition table. "Counsellor James has not established that the witness has been lied to. . ."

"Sustained," responded the bench. "This court must remind you, counsellor, that you're to elicit facts and not encourage conjecture from the witness. You will drop your present line of questioning, or be held in contempt!"

"Yes, your honor," James bowed, then turned to Vera, speaking slowly. "Now please Mrs. Green, tell us . . . just what did happen . . . while you were employed at the bank . . . just the facts Mrs. Green."

"Well, since I'd gone there fu he'p, I felt I owed 'im sonethin' and I wanted ta return a favor, 'n' I wuz angry 'bout de bank not openin' on time, looked like it wuz nevah goin' ta open. Like I said, I wuz happy at first, 'course afta I wuz suspicious 'bout why I wuz so impo'tant . . . 'cause I had such a little money in de Woodfolk Bank. Den, one day when I wuz wohkin' 'round de office dey wuz talkin' 'n' laughin' real loud."

Tell us about that conversation." James was growing weary with Vera's partial answers now.

"I heard dem say dat Thompson 'n' Goldman wuz close friends . . . I knew who Goldman wuz, Yeah . . . dey kep' laughin' 'bout how de whole thing wuz wokin' out fu dem."

"Now Mrs. Green, we have to know exactly what the conversation was all about. What did you hear, and when did you hear it?" quizzed James.

"Dey said dat Goldman, de Woodfolk receiver, planted dat idea ta lease de fact'ry from under Mr. Chavers . . . dat dey wuz good friends, 'n' both o' dem wanned ta see Mr. Chavers lose his fact'ry. Dey jus' laughed 'n' laughed bout de whole things. Now dis wuz 'bout six months afta Mr. Chavers lost his fact'ry."

James nodded his head approvingly, then coaxed the witness again, "Now Mrs. Green, please explain to the court who 'them' is. We will only know if you tell us. Whom did you overhear saying that Thompson and Goldman are close friends and that Goldman suggested to Thompson that he lease the factory from under Mr. Chavers?"

"I 'eard Mr. Hull tellin' Mr. Price, dat day when I wuz wohkin' cleanin' 'round de office, when dey wuz talkin' dey paid no 'tention ta me. Dat day, I wuz very angry wid Price fu botherin' me alla time, 'n' it jus' made me mad to hear 'em keep on talkin', braggin' 'n' laughin' 'bout Mr. Chavers."

"Then what did you do?"

"I kep' on dustin' de furniture, bu' I wuz lissnin' hard, and I 'eard dem say it wuz Goldman who tipped dem off wid de Woodfolk depositors list ta hunt down claimants 'gainst Mr. Chavers."

"So that by now you knew Goldman had hinted to Thompson to lease the factory from under Mr. Chavers, and had offered the list of Woodfolk depositors to Hull to use against Mr. Chavers." Vera nodded as James restated her testimony.

"I 'eard dem say dat Thompson told Goldman 'bout Mr. Chavers payin' off de factory rent which started dese bankruptcy charges . . . an' dey jes' kep' on laughin' even lauder when Hull said dat Thompson 'n' de Landlaud's 'ssociation wuz afta dat Calumet property 'n' it wuz Goldman's idea fu Thompson to lease de fact'ry from under Mr. Chavers. Mr. Hull said all dat as if Price didn' know it, bu' I spect dat Price knew more about it than Hull."

"Objection! This witness is speculating."

"Sustained."

"Mrs. Green, please continue with the facts about what you did and what you heard that day while cleaning around the office," implored James.

"Laud, dis much I know 'cause I 'eard dem say dat Thompson said if Hull hadn't stopped Mr. Chavers in whut 'e wuz trying ta do in de Black Belt, dat Goldman and Thompson would 'cause de Landlaud's 'sociation wuz behind dem 'n' ready to back de fight wid money all de way. Dey wuz afta dat Calumet property. . . Yessuh! I heard dem say dat it wuz de Landlaud's 'sociation dat dey wuz really in cahoots wid. I 'eard dem!" Vera pointed at Hull's table. "Dey wuz carrin' on 'bout how funny Mr. Chavers looked afta he stopped fightin'

Goldman ta try to head dem off'court case 'n' how dey wuz going' a keep cuttin' 'im up in court! Those wuz deir 'sact wohds! Same 'sact wohds!"

James allowed Vera to run herself out on this one, but now he reviewed for clarity. "You are saying that you heard Hull and Price laughing about the fact that Goldman, the professional receiver in the Woodfolk case, who has since been removed and convicted of embezzlement in this and other cases, that this same Mr. Goldman prevailed upon Thompson to squeeze Mr. Chavers out of his factory, to seize control of the Calumet property and that the Landlord's Association was in league with them. Would you say that they acted happy about their plans to get the property away from Mr. Chavers?" James looked across the floor at his opponents.

"Yessuh! Dey wuz happy as two crows in a fresh planted cornfield, dat dey wuz makin' a fool outa Mr. Chavers."

"Objection!"

"Sustained!" The Judge asked to have Vera Green's observations stricken from the record, but it was too late, the damage was done. The spectators roared and the judge finally threatened to clear the court. James smiled triumphantly.

"In other words, Goldman got what he wanted when Mr. Chavers stopped his law suit, that this is what he was after in urging Thompson to undermine Chavers?"

"Yessuh! I 'eard dem say dat 'n' I 'member 'cause I gotta feelin' dat when dey wuz laughin' at Mr. Chavers, dey wuz really laughin' at me, 'cause they'd been tellin' me dat Mr. Chavers could get my money fo me, when dey knew Goldman 'ad da money all along, not Mr. Chavers. Dey plotted de whole thin' 'n' wanted me as a 'scuse ta do dat messin' Mr. Chavers up in court." Vera's words were sharp and clear now. "I 'eard dem say over 'n' over 'gain dat dey wuz goin' ta wreck him in court, dat dey wuz goin' ta make him pay all o' de legal fees for alla dese here court fights. Dey said dey wuz goin' to cut Mr. Chavers up into ribbons in court!! Dem wuz dere very wohds."

"And what did you do when you heard them say these things?" James returned.

"Dat bothered me real bad, I couldn't sleep nights afta dat.

Mr. Chavers had not done nothin' 'gainst me; he been my friend. I thought about evahtime I 'ad testified 'gainst 'im . . . I wuz 'fraid fo my soul. . . I felt real bad . . . mean . . . 'n' . . . 'shamed. I walked de floor all night, 'n' I woudn', I couldn' think days, I wuz so 'fraid." Vera was obviously suffering. She clenched her fists and tucked her head down between them as the full horror of her confession came through to her.

"Then what you are saying is . . . they knew when Chavers agreed to pay Thompson off . . . and they were just waiting to spring this bankruptcy charge when Chavers did pay Thompson in order to make the preference charge stick and to back up the bankruptcy charge." James did not want to lose Vera to self pity, so he drew near to her again.

"Yessuh," answered Vera. She glared at Owens and Hull sitting at the front table with Wagner, their lawyer, feeling James strength behind her.

"Just exactly when did they begin to involve you?"

"I hate ta own up ta it, but I see now I wuz bein' used in Mr. Chavers fact'ry while I wuz wohkin' there. Thompson thought I wuz an easy mark. He wanned me ta stir up things at de fact'ry so's it would close, but de other fact'ry workers, dey believed in Mr. Chavers."

"And now Mrs. Green, will you explain to the court exactly what your connection was with that bankruptcy case? Your name appears on the petition as one of the plaintiffs," asserted James, looking at the jury.

"But I had nothin' ta do wid dat petition. I never signed a petition 'gainst Mr. Chavers 'bout his bein' a bankrupt. I done 'nough 'gainst 'im 'n' I been stayin' 'way from dose people," concluded Vera.

"Then your name on the bankruptcy papers of 1923 was a forgery," responded James slowly, nodding his head. "You may cross-examine," he indicated to Wagner. He was very pleased with Vera; she had come through in the full daylight of the packed courtroom. Wagner rose slowly from Hull's table and walked to the witness stand with a fierce scowl on his face as he approached Vera Green. Then he began condescendingly.

"Now Mrs. Green . . . we realize you have been through many trying times and all of this has been very hard on you." Suddenly changing his pace, "Will you please tell us why you have changed sides . . . you must admit you have changed sides . . . WHY?"

"I's where I belon' . . . on Mr. Chavers' side," returned Vera, growing sullen and brusque. She knew how to get tough too.

"Now, my dear lady, couldn't you be just a little more definite?" Wagner sneered. "You have admitted to changing sides . . . I hold here in my hand statements that you did on three occasions charge Mr. Chavers with conspiracy to defraud . . . I am referring, Mrs. Green, to the fact that you appeared in court against him, just to refresh your memory . . . once in March, 1922, then again in November, 1922, and again in March, 1923 . . . THREE TIMES!"

"Yessuh," Vera admitted at once.

"Now, about your name on this bankruptcy petition. . . Did you forget? Did you lie? You do know what perjury is, don't you, Mrs. Green?"

"Objection," shouted James.

"Slow down a little, Mr. Wagner," instructed the Judge.

"Thank you, your honor. I will rephrase the question," returned Wagner. "You have lied before the court. Is that right?"

"Alright . . . I'm guilty. Bu' whut 'bout the rest o' you? You plotted alla dis . . . sat back 'n' had me say alla dese things 'gainst Mr. Chavers . . . 'cause you think you're too importan'. . . Well, I neva done nothin' like dis before . . . I di'n know how to git outa it . . . bu' you did . . . Yeah, I know your kind . . ."

"Order! Order!" interrupted the Judge.

"Your honor, how can we expect to consider this witness' testimony valid?" Wagner pulled away from Vera now. From her responses, he felt a new kind of determination swelling up in her and realized she was ready to tell more of what she had heard. He couldn't risk that.

The Judge answered calmly, "That is for the jury to decide. Proceed with your cross-examination counselor."

"No more questions," returned Wagner, stalking back to his seat.

James jumped to his feet. "If it please the court, your honor, I would like to re-examine the witness to clarify her motives in appearing here today to tell of her role in damaging Mr. Chavers' reputation." James did not want to leave any loopholes for the jury to debate about or to have any uncertainty continue to hang over P.W.'s reputation if he could possibly avoid it. The courtroom was silent in anticipation of the judge's response.

"You may re-examine the witness."

James paced back and forth before the Judge for a moment or two deciding how he could best draw Vera out. She had been on the witness stand for a long time now and had told of her involvement first with Thompson, then with Hull, Price, and Wagner, but he had to go beyond these confessions. "Thank you, your honor," returned James. Then, looking at Vera intently, he began. "Now Mrs. Green, in your own words please explain to this court why you changed sides . . . why you stayed on even after you knew you were working for someone who was deliberately using you to ruin Mr. Chavers . . . just tell us slowly and in your own words," replied James as he could see she was tired.

"Like I said in de beginning, I wuz 'fraid things wuz 'goin 'gainst Mr. Chavers . . . bu' afta de charges 'gainst him wuz dismissed, I wuz 'shamed fu my part in it dat I know . . . bu' I wuz so 'lone, I couldn' tell nobody." Vera leaned over, pulled a handkerchief out of her purse, put it to her eyes, then bit her lip and took a deep breath as if to steel herself to go on. James smiled at her kindly. "Mrs. Green, why didn't you return to Mr. Chavers? Didn't you know that Mr. Chavers would have given you work? Was there any other reason to keep you in this situation?"

Vera backed into the corner of the witness chair and spoke softly. "Well, yessuh, there was somethin' else . . . yessuh, there wuz." Vera cleared her throat, took a deep breath, and began to twist the handkerchief in her hands. "I didn't know whut else ta do . . . bu' somethin' else bothad me . . . I 'eard dat Mr. Chavers 'ad opened a new tearoom, 'n' 'ad name' it fu

264

Rebecca. I guess I got mad 'cause I 'membered how Rebecca wuz always Mrs. Chaver's favorite at de fact'ry, 'stead 'o me . . . She hated me, 'n' did't like it dat Mr. Chavers wuz good ta me."

"Now Mrs. Green, please explain to the court what the tearoom has to do with this case. Following the opening of the tearoom, what did you do?" James heaved a sigh of relief.

"Well, I got mad . . . I neva did like Mrs. Chavers, wid alla her uppity airs. Not dat she evah done anythin' ta me, bu' she always preferred Rebecca. She wuz her favorite, 'cause she had been the Chavers' chillun's nurse. I usta say ta myself . . .'Why does she 'ave a nursemaid fu her chillun? Why can't she be like otha colaud women 'n' take care o' her own?'"

"In other words, Mrs. Green, after you were working in the factory you became . . . shall we say . . . jealous of Mrs. Chavers and her nursemaid, Rebecca," repeated James.

"Yessuh . . . I knew right 'way it wuz Mrs. Chavers who 'ad Rebecca set up as de head waitress in de tearoom, 'n' had it named fu her too." She looked at Minnie who had just entered the courtroom with us, anticipating the trial was almost over. "Bu' I don't think like I usta, no more," added Vera.

"But, back then, you wanted what Rebecca had, is that right?"

"Yessuh . . ." Vera responded meekly. "I guess I wuz sinkin' lower 'n' lower. I kep' thinkin' only 'bout gettin' my money back, 'n' how I would git even wid Mrs. Chavers and Rebecca. Bu' I wuz only hurtin' myself 'n' Mr. Chavers, not dem."

"It wasn't only that you were scared about a job and the loss of your money at the bank? . . . it was jealousy too . . . that caused you to allow Hull and Price to use you in those charges you made against Mr. Chavers?" James knew his interrogation seemed redundant and harsh, but he couldn't risk a shred of doubt about the credibility of her testimony today. "Had Mr. Chavers ever done anything against you?"

"Nossuh."

"Has Mrs. Chavers ever done anything against you?"

A shake of the head.

"Then between the time you left the factory in January 1922 and the first time you allowed yourself to be used in that

265

charge against Mr. Chavers in March, 1922, in those three months, you thought you had found security? But, all the time before the tearoom was open—about 12 months—why didn't you return to Mr. Chavers to seek work? Why didn't you make some effort to see Mr. Chavers, to say something to him?" James felt himself beginning to ride her heavily. The thought flashed through him that perhaps he hadn't forgiven her, after all...

"Like I said before . . . I di'n know what ta do . . . I wuz too scared by den. . . Laud, I jes' couldn' move . . . I wuz so tied o' dis . . . Hope'd God woulda kill me. I wuz tied o' dis . . . Can't you understan'? . . . I wuz lost . . . I wuz los'." Vera pleaded, reliving her torment. "Bu' now I 'no' how wrong I wuz, 'cause I'm awright now . . . I'm wid Mr. Chavers, where I belon'd allalong . . . I cin sleep nights!!" Vera was drained.

"Thank you, Mrs. Green," responded James, then addressing the Judge, he added, "I believe that is all."

A few hours later, when the jury returned a "Guilty" verdict, and the Circuit Judge Stanley awarded P.W. a judgment of $5000 damages, the session broke up and we saw Daddy coming out of the courtroom. The conversation in the car was jubilant all the way home; Daddy had won his Defamation of Character Suit. Minnie and P.W. talked excitedly, congratulating James, whom we were taking home with us.

"I think they learned their lesson about using slander in the Black Belt to undermine me," P.W. sang out. The feeling of victory permeated the car as we sped along, even though I wouldn't fully understand why we were supposed to be so happy.

I did not pursue my concern or question Mother all the following day. Knowing they were so happy about the victory, I did not bring it up again. But those words she had said a few nights ago kept ringing in my ears. The local newspapers carried an account of Hull's being found guilty of conspiring to damage P.W.'s reputation and the rumor that the Bar Association was taking steps to have him disbarred. Daddy clipped the column out of the newspaper and showed it to company from time to time to prove his point about the value

266

of integrity and a man's responsibility to fight to preserve his good reputation. After I noticed the article was no longer being shown, I pulled it out of the drawer where it was kept with other scrap book material about the bank and other developments. I read and reread it, looking for the same joy in it that Daddy had found, but no matter how many times I read it, or how hard I tried, I couldn't react to it joyfully. To me, somehow, the victory could not compensate for the incomprehensible anguish he had suffered.

I became painfully aware of a longing to be nearer my father and to know him better. I was a child reaching out to a father whom I loved dearly and somehow this article had brought home to me the fact that I had little personal contact with him, that I really didn't know him at all. Perhaps that was why I could find no joy in it, as others had. Finally, I placed the article in a hiding place for safekeeping. I reasoned that no one would miss it now, and by possessing it, I would be spurred on to learn more about Daddy and his world. An awareness had come over me that I had a separate stake in my father's destiny.

That summer P.W. and Minnie were exceedingly happy. The outcome of the defamation suit had renewed their sense of well-being and freed them to enjoy the long trips into the countryside with Frank, Cleo, and various cousins who came along, as well as us children. Sometimes Rebecca, or Cousin Ruth Baker from the Henry County, Virginia side of mother's family, joined us. She was seriously thinking of marrying a dentist and Minnie, ever practical, was advising her about the need to marry a man with a promising future, feeling she set such an example herself. "When I learned about the many enterprises my husband was involved in and how many people he had working for him, I knew P.W. was the man for me," she said to Ruth one day.

Now that the legal battles and the tension had subsided, Minnie felt the urge to do many things she had put off while worrying over P.W.'s career, such as changing our dancing school and taking a more active role in the Willard School PTA after school opened. By mid-fall, P.W. had located land which captured his imagination completely and felt it was suitable for the campsite he had long thought about. The land lay some three hundred miles north of Chicago, near Elcho, Wisconsin, adjacent to a well-constructed highway . . . P.W. was jubilant about acquiring it.

But the Calumet property situation had to be settled first as it was still hung up in the old equity suit of Hummel vs. Chavers. By late fall the condition of that property had deteriorated significantly. It had been seriously neglected since Hummel became Trustee and absolutely ignored since Burtram Buell began collecting rents as receiver. Its restoration and remodelling had been financed by several junior mortgages which P.W. had taken out in the fall of 1923, and again in 1924, but had been discontinued after all the court trials and the cost of litigation. P.W. attended hearings of this equity suit, eventually deciding to resolve the tangled web over the Calumet property once and for all. He supplemented James with another lawyer, Jacob Klappman, who recommended a compromise after reviewing all the vast complexities of the suits interwoven in the equity suit, and outlining what was at stake, including the uncollected $5000.00 awarded by the court for damages he had suffered at the hands of the defendants. Though he had won the case, he had not received the award. Justice had finally triumphed over trickery, but somehow it seemed to P.W. that to pursue collection, chasing the money, would blemish the moral victory he had won. Then too, he pondered, if he pressed for collection, would this only serve as another battleground to deplete his resources? He was forced to review his resources and weigh them against the brilliant, ruthless Hull and his entourage, now fully staffed with "investigators" who could arrange any kind of frame-up he wanted. The Thompson preference charge taught P.W. something about the high risk of an open fight with such men. His energies, talents, and strength could be depleted in another court encounter. He knew compromise meant he would have to avoid taking a strong position on any facet of the case.

In arranging for a compromise conference, P.W requested that Hull serve as the lawyer for the claimants instead of

Wagner. Somehow, he could not tolerate the thought of Wagner arrogantly parading around at such a meeting in his presence. If he must compromise, better it be with his own race, the real instigator, not the benefactor of the instigation. He refused to be manipulated from behind the scenes; it would have to be a full, open, and honorable compromise, he told Klappman when agreeing to this move. In this way, P.W. felt that he had put himself in a better position for compromise as they gathered about the conference table in Klappman's office early in December, 1925.

Arriving early, P.W. and Minnie had a chance to exhange last minute comments about strategy with Klappman. Minnie had steeled herself for this encounter with Hull and Hummel, telling herself it was necessary if P.W. was ever going to be free of that dreadful Douglass National Bank he had created. When Hull entered the conference room, P.W. greeted him cordially, but Minnie remained formal, simply nodding her head, then looking away from him, biting her lip. Hull was flattered that P.W. requested he represent the creditors and made several attempts to be sociable.

"You know P.W. . . We have had a chance to observe each other," he said.

"Yes, for quite a while, as a matter of fact," returned P.W.

Hummel, the party of the fourth part who had entered with Hull, was sitting at the far corner of the conference table trying to appear disinterested, but broke in, "P.W., why can't you see that this is just a personal fight between individuals?"

'I'll be with you in a moment," broke in Klappman, hurriedly assembling papers in the outer office. He sensed that this dialogue could lead to greater tension and complications that might obviate a compromise.

P.W. turned to Hummel, "You of all people should know this is more than a personal fight between two men."

Hull caught the message and felt compelled to speak. "Now P.W., you know everybody is out for personal gain. Business is business."

P.W. put both hands on the conference table. "I have been forced to break a contract made in good faith and there's

269

everything wrong with that. One Negro fighting another, mutual destruction, that's all this can ever be; then the White outsider steps in and takes over. My surrendering this valuable Calumet property would be just as much a defeat to you, Hull, and to your crowd and to the entire community as it would be to me. When will men of color learn to combine forces and grow strong economically?"

Hull was embarrassed with this race talk in Hummel's presence and in Klappman's office. That kind of talk was alright in the Black Belt, but not in this downtown office among the plush surroundings of white men. He glanced towards Klappman, wishing he would hurry in, then commented, "It's dog-eat-dog among all people in this world, and you have to run with the pack."

Minnie had had enough! She rose, excusing herself with the statement that she had left something in the car. Uncomfortable hearing this conversation, she was having difficulty keeping her promise to herself to be silent through the negotiation, answering only when absolutely necessary. Minnie was thinking that Hull was not fit to breathe the same air as P.W. . . . let alone talk to him and query him about his motives which she understood so well, which caused her so much pain and which she had accepted against her own inner motives because she loved him so much. She could not abide her husband sitting there trying to reason with a common thief and a liar.

Klappman joined them, taking his seat at the head of the table.

"Yes," continued P.W., "it is grievous to me that we allowed our feuds to be fought against the backdrop of our community, the Black Belt. Irreparable damage has been done to many innocent, trusting people as a result of all the court trials. My aims for the community have been buried under the rubble of this conflict. If the Black Belt is to grow and prosper, these aims must be uncovered. That's why I'm willing to compromise, and why this is not simply a stalling maneuver."

"Now gentlemen," Klappman broke in, "the business before us today is to work out an agreement. I am very sorry you had to wait for me, but something came up at the last minute." He was hoping their brief exchange had helped move them towards the sought-for agreement but he had difficulty assessing their moods. . .

Hull cut in, ignoring Klappman's apology, "P.W. it is almost impossible to dislike you."

"Thank you, young man." But P.W. realized he had not fully hit his mark. P.W. was thinking of Minnie's sharp questions about the collection of the $5000.00 damages from him when suddenly she returned to the conference table. Everyone stood as she walked into the room and fell as silent as though a judge had walked into a courtroom. Minnie sat down very straight and composed again. Her brisk air had charged the others, cutting short further preliminaries. The business began immediately. Compromise with an enemy was completely foreign to Minnie, so she didn't pretend to be comfortable here. "One cannot compromise with a thief" was the way she put it to P.W. regarding her feelings about Hull.

The agreement hammered out recognized P.W.'s original investment and litigation pending in Superior Court of Cook County to recover his stock in the Douglass National Bank and restored the Calumet property to his control and management, with Buell, the receiver, being removed at once. P.W., as party of the first part, agreed to pay *in cash*: all expenses (in excess of $5000.00 to be paid by The Douglass National Bank) including Hull's, Wagner's, and Price's, the court fees for the various receiverships and mastery in chancery, for the suits brought against him, and from the original Woodfolk creditor's suits to the present expenses incurred in the last equity suit, and finally, in addition, the claimants' cost and 25% of the general claims in the bankruptcy suit. He further agreed to deliver whatever Douglass National Bank stock certificates remained in his possession, if any, and the deed of conveyance of the Calumet property, to be held by Hummel, party of the fourth part, who was authorized to proceed with sale of the real estate if the terms of this agreement were not kept. In the event of a sale, and a surplus, the surplus would be paid to Minnie, party of the second part. P.W. was to have the right and power to object to any claims filed against him during the processing of this agreement.

271

Minnie felt P.W. paid too high a price for control of something he was clearly entitled to. He had been labelled a bankrupt for assuming Woodfolk's debts, but she kept these thoughts to herself. She was physically exhausted from using so much self-control to conceal her emotions. She sat quietly besides P.W. on their way home as he reviewed aloud his hopes that the agreement would work. It was several nights later that she burst forth about P.W.'s compromise with Hull, almost as if she hadn't been there at the conference table. Once more she was reacting to his not having collected the $5000.00 settlement on the Defamation of Character Suit which Hull owed him since last spring. Doggedly, P.W. answered in a soft voice, "Perhaps we had better not talk about it anymore tonight, dear, I see you are upset."

P.W. never expected Minnie to understand his attitude towards money, and he accepted this, but the sharpness of her challenges now did cause him to reflect more deeply on how not collecting the money due him might be seen as an unsound practice. He questioned himself further to arrive at a clearer understanding of his position that he'd expressed to Minnie. He knew that in reaching this agreement he had been considering the anticipated future income of the Calumet property. He knew the apartments were fully furnished and rented for at least $50.00 per week. The building was an income-producing property of at least $500.00 per week, or more than $25,000.00 per year, even with occasional vacancies. His management and furnishings of the property had increased its value considerably; the recent appraisal ordered by the court had assessed the capital value of the property at $55,000.00. He was familiar with the market value of the property and knew its potential, so he felt that if refinancing could be arranged to deal with the cash demands and handle the needed repairs, the agreement worked out might prove very satisfactory to all. After all, this had been bombed-out property when he took it over from the defunct Woodfolk estate just five years earlier. He also knew that the receiver had been in possession of the property for ten months and that his account should reflect at least $20,000.00 in income if he had properly managed it during this period. He

272

knew that exploitation of ghetto people had to stop somewhere, sometime, and he wanted to be the unifying force in
the Black Belt to accomplish this. He reflected on how,
whenever he was chided about allowing Owens to run off with
his bank, he had handled the matter lightly, emphasizing
that he had laid the foundation, and as long as the community benefitted from the enterprise, the actual leadership of the
bank was unimportant. Then too, he learned somewhere in
the midst of the bankruptcy proceedings that people somehow
sensed his integrity.

But Minnie saw him and his position better than he did
himself. She saw that he was blocked off from his creation by
his own people, and that this wounded his pride, perhaps
irreparably. She continued to ponder over his refusal to
collect and his willingness to compromise with avowed enemies. Was it because of his injured pride? Was there a
haunting fear that he would be betrayed once more by his
own people? She knew this would be something he couldn't
tolerate because it would put an end to his life's goal.

P.W.'s fleeting suspicions about the possible bad faith of his
opponents at the compromise conference proved to be well
grounded. As the lawyer's fees and court costs came in, he
sadly realized that Hull flagrantly padded them, possibly to
undermine the agreement and render it meaningless. Early
in January, 1926, Wagner's bill, representing the "Petitioning Creditors" in the action to break the trusteeship of the
Woodfolk Bank, arrived. It alone was $7,000.00, more than
the amount for which he had petitioned. Hummel's fees,
expenses, and liabilities unbelievably read: $1,110.00 ad-
vanced by Jesse Hull on behalf of the creditors in prosecution
of the suit of Hummel vs. Minnie B. Chavers. On and on they
came, fees and costs of Master in Proceedings to clarify the
Woodfolk creditors, costs, fees and Referee in Bankruptcy,
$1,175.00, in addition to administrative costs, court secretar-
ies' fees, publicity, and filing expenses. The legal bills continued to spiral, culminating with Buell's statement at the end
of January for management expenses on the Calumet property covering the ten months of his receivership. This showed
a total rent collection of a mere $2,918.00 with total dis-

bursements of $2,915.00 and a balance on hand of $3.00, listing unpaid boiler repair expenses and fees of $713.00 even though no repairs had been made. Hull's statement listed 68 creditors against the bankruptcy estate which had been pursued by Wagner.

P.W. submitted his questions and objections to the allowances of claims made by 39 of the 68 creditors listed for the reason that the stated amounts were not due these creditors. He questioned whether the receiver had fully reported the rent collection total and whether the receiver had the right to seize possession of the furnishings in the apartments: ten dressers, fifty chairs, eight gas ranges, ten center tables, six day beds, twenty rugs, fifteen beds together with mattresses and linen, lace curtains on all windows, ten kitchen tables, ten pieces of linoleum and small rugs, an office desk, a safe, and other belongings of P.W. which he acquired subsequent to the adjudication; two thirty foot tables and fourteen electric power sewing machines.

P.W. looked over the property many times with a view toward resuming the remodelling of apartments. He obtained estimates from repairmen to ascertain the approximate cost of putting it in good condition, and he requested an extension of time on the agreement. Major repairs could not wait any longer; the furnace had to be replaced, the roof completely restored. P.W. had been in control of it for more than one month now and had made every effort to refinance the real estate in accordance with the agreement, consulting several banks, including the Citizens Trust and Savings Bank, but it was clear that the property was no longer a sound business venture. He had to let it go or bleed to death.

Early in March of 1926, he talked with O. F. Stewart at the Citizens Trust and Savings Bank several times about the issue of refinancing and restoring the property. Stewart, his long time friend and mentor, the white banker who had been among the first to support him in the early difficulties of organizing the bank enterprise even against the harsh prejudices of his white associates, was cautious as P.W. repeated many of the questions boiling inside him now. Why could he not let this white elephant go? The bank was the seed out of

274

which the Calumet property grew. By giving up this building, he knew he would be writing himself out of the bank experience in a final way. "But why hold on?"

Stewart advised P.W. to think about the best way to get out of the morass of disaster it had brought him. "I've thought about restoring my factory. It's been over three years since my business closed down," P.W. spoke indecisively.

"Come on P.W., you are an entrepreneur. You can't make it big in the competition of the sweat shop," returned Stewart. "Times are prosperous again with all these new enterprises, like radio and air travel; optimism is everywhere." They talked a long time about general conditions in the country since Calvin Coolidge had entered the White House. The get-rich-quick mood was sweeping through the land. "You've always been in the forefront of such a mood with your people. These are happy times. Everybody is hitting the road in a Model T Ford. I say, get what you can out of it and clear out of that Calumet property, once and for all!"

"Well Stewart, I have an option on a tract of land near Elcho, Wisconsin where I would like to promote a children's camp someday. Maybe I should pick up that option right now and go ahead with that venture," returned P.W.

"That sounds promising," exclaimed Stewart. "If you need money, we can talk about that too." Old friends were agreeing again as they smiled and puffed heartily on their cigars. The decision was made. P.W. was pleased with the prospects of the new course he was about to pursue and was eager to share all the details of the decision with Minnie as he hurried home.

Minnie pondered over his new objective for a long time, never fully comprehending many dimensions of the decision. But as she watched him striking out with vigor she knew he was relieved of the tremendous burden he had carried for so long. She admired the finality with which he was able to turn away from all that was connected with the bank after he had put so much work into creating it and defending its use, even after his ouster . . . even after all the personal cost and suffering for which he would never be repaid. Once again she marvelled at the total commitment and the enthusiasm of this man who was her husband.

Protect Depositors—Abolish Bank Failures

Important Mass Meeting Concerning Bank Failures in 1st Congressional District.   Every BANK VICTIM

should be present to hear **Hon. P. W. Chavers**

Author of House Bill No. 8977, now pending in Congress before the Banking and Currency Committee, will explain to you a plan for your protection.

Other Speakers—Hon. P. J. Zisch, Hon. A. J. Buntin, Member of the Wisconsin Legislature: Hon. Chas. C. Roe, Hon. Benj. W. Clayton and Hon. Nathan Taylor, who will preside.

Sunday Afternoon at 4 P. M. at 430 E. 43rd St.

Under auspices of **Voters League, 1st Congressional District.**

Abolish Bank Failures, 1926

13

The Compass

Now that the decision had been made about the Calumet property, P.W. was free to pour all of his energies into new directions and was pleased to have shared his thoughts with Minnie all along the way as he needed and appreciated her support. He had considered getting into Chicago politics for two years while working on the final draft of his bank proposal. He had just met recently elected United States Senator Charles Deneen, the powerful leader of the reform wing of the Illinois Republican Party, who was then compaigning for this national office and subsequently served as senator from 1925 until 1931. In his several conversations with Deneen, they had discussed providing more security for banks and bank depositors and had agreed that Congressman Doyle should be approached about introducing the bank bill in the House of Representatives. Deneen, favorably impressed with P.W.'s ideas and interest, had urged him to join the reform forces as a candidate someday. They spoke only briefly, but P.W. never forgot Deneen's early interest in him.

Deneen, as States Attorney, had built a strong reputation for himself as a reformer as far back as 1896, sending criminals to jail, convicting bankers for fraud, and later, as Governor of Illinois from 1905 to 1913, appointing honest men to high influential positions. Under his cool, dignified, well-meaning leadership with its special appeal to the "respectable" element, the reformers gained control, splitting off from the rest of the Republican Party including the Thompson forces in Chicago. While out of office, Ex-Mayor William Hale Thompson and his buddies claimed credit for helping to elect Deneen, but later accused him of being "pro-British." Thompson projected himself as the "champion of the people," but he

277

was known for his spectacular genius in campaign clowning and "buffoonery" in public office. This included his rampant spoils system, police and gangster alliances and school board scandals. Now, eager to regain control of patronage and power, Thompson sought strategies to appeal to the German elements in Chicago, using campaign slogans such as "Kick the snoot of King George out of Chicago," playing the clown, and handling the campaign like a grand circus, while the crowd roared with laughter. But Deneen, a proud leader of the reformed forces, tried to keep a balanced ticket with all racial, linguistic, national, religious, economic and neighborhood groups represented. Later, the flamboyant William Hale Thompson was re-elected mayor in 1927, and was tabbed as the man to keep a Negro out of Congress.

Over a year ago, while lying in bed recuperatng from his bout with pneumonia in December, 1924, P.W. had had considerable time to dwell more seriously on the possibility of running for election to Congress. After he had moved his real estate office into the newly acquired 49th Street building, he would sit at his desk gazing out of the big window where he could see the "Elevated" rushing past. He would meditate about conditions and opportunities and muse about what others were telling him of late, that now was the time to take the political plunge. Martin B. Madden would be running for another term in Congress from the First Congressional District of Illinois. P.W.'s political sponsors were urging him to enter the race, pointing out that his name had become a household word synonymous with someone who had the community interest at heart, that he knew the issues and wouldn't be entering this new endeavor as an unknown.

In preparing for his campaign, P.W. met with Deneen and renewed contact with Charles Dawes who had been helpful in his efforts to secure the bank charter and had supported his philosophy about the potential positive effect on the American economy of purposeful political activity among the urban black masses. Together with like-minded political leaders, P.W. would discuss the issues currently at stake: the incumbent Congressman Martin B. Madden, P.W.'s opponent, who had reigned like a county squire over the First Congressional District and was viewed as a venerable statesman by the Blacks who faithfully returned him to Congress term after term for twenty-six years. From 1900 until that point he had also been their Second Ward Committeeman as well as their United States Congressman from the First Congressional District which was comprised mostly of the Black Belt. As Ward Committeeman, he was a political czar wielding extensive patronage and oiling his political machine with eager aggressive precinct captains and their assistants through favors and fixes. This powerful political organization had been organized early during the Great Migration and was geared to deliver the Negro vote to the straight Republican Party, the party of Abraham Lincoln. It had served to reinforce Madden's sense of "inalienable right" to return to Congress. By now, at age 70, Madden had grown comfortable in his estimation of his power to remain in Congress and he no longer bothered to campaign among the voters. Some black leaders who considered themselves militant had extracted an understanding about a general change: when the time came that Madden would decide not to run for Congress anymore, a Negro would be found to replace him. And thus they agreed to go along for the time being, with this white control of an almost totally black area.

Such mindless following by the community leaders and voters, and such indifference displayed by Congressman Madden, stirred P.W. to a vigorous schedule of meetings, speeches and rallies. In his literature and speeches, P.W. stressed how he had organized and brought into being the First National Bank, owned and operated by Blacks and how that experience had led him to the authorship of House bill #8977, now pending in Congress, the legislation to protect all bank depositors in national banks. "Vote for Chavers and your race will have real representation in Washington," P.W. told his potential constituents. In 1926, these words spoken in the Chicago Black Belt were frightening to many and tantamount to revolt for others. But Senator Deneen was delighted to have P.W. on his team. Deneen's strong reform reputation was in complete harmony with P.W.'s political aims.

Minnie objected to the campaign only once. This was while

279

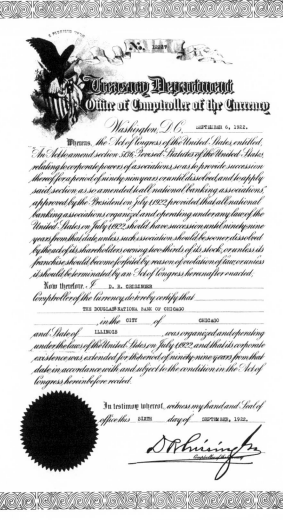

Treasury Department
Office of Comptroller of the Currency

Washington, D.C. SEPTEMBER 6, 1922.

Whereas, the Act of Congress of the United States, entitled, "An Act to amend section 5136, Revised Statutes of the United States, relating to corporate powers of associations, so as to provide succession thereof for a period of ninety-nine years or until dissolved, and to apply said section as so amended to all national banking associations," approved by the President on July 1, 1922, provided that all national banking associations organized and operating under any law of the United States on July 1, 1922 should have succession until ninety-nine years from that date unless such association should be sooner dissolved by the act of its shareholders owning two-thirds of its stock; or unless its franchise should become forfeited by reason of violation of law; or unless it should be terminated by an Act of Congress hereinafter enacted;

Now therefore, I D. R. CRISINGER Comptroller of the Currency do hereby certify that _____

THE DOUGLASS NATIONAL BANK OF CHICAGO

_____ in the CITY of CHICAGO and State of ILLINOIS _____ was organized and operating under the laws of the United States on July 1, 1922, and that its corporate existence was extended for the period of ninety-nine years from that date in accordance with and subject to the condition in the Act of Congress hereinbefore recited.

In testimony whereof, witness my hand and Seal of office this SIXTH day of SEPTEMBER, 1922.

D R Crisinger
Comptroller of the Currency

Certificate of charter, Douglass National Bank, 1922

68TH CONGRESS
1ST SESSION

H. R. 8977

IN THE HOUSE OF REPRESENTATIVES

APRIL 30, 1924

Mr. DOYLE (by request) introduced the following bill; which was referred to
the Committee on Banking and Currency and ordered to be printed

---

A BILL

To provide for the furnishing of surety bonds by national banks
for the protection of depositors

1   *Be it enacted by the Senate and House of Representa-*

2 *tives of the United States of America in Congress assembled,*

3   That all national banks now organized or hereafter

4 organized under the National Banking Act shall file in the

5 office of the Treasurer of the United States a surety bond

6 with an approved surety company as surety thereon, con-

7 ditioned for the payment by the bank upon demand to the

8 depositors of said bank the full amount of their deposits. And

9 no national bank hereinafter organized shall receive depos-

10 its until it shall have filed and had approved by the Treas-

11 urer of the United States the surety bond hereinbefore

THE GUARANTEE: P.W.'s H.R. Bill #8977 To Provide
protection of bank deposits, introduced by Congressman
Doyle, 1924

1 stock from any surety company acting as surety for said

2 bank; nor shall the directors or officers of such national

3 banks hold directorates or other offices in such surety com-

4 pany.

5   SEC. 7. All sections and provisions of the National

6 Banking Act now in force inconsistent with or repugnant to

7 the provisions of this Act are hereby repealed.

68TH CONGRESS } H. R. 8977
1st SESSION }

A BILL

To provide for the furnishing of surety bonds by national banks for the protection of depositors

By Mr. DOYLE

APRIL 30, 1924

Referred to the Committee on Banking and Currency and ordered to be printed

The Chavers Plan of Guaranteeing Bank Deposits

P.W. was setting up his headquarters to use the entire first floor of an old mansion on Michigan Avenue, with its large foyer, for the public meetings and the numerous rooms for his working staff. Before he rented the headquarters he had banners, campaign stickers, and posters printed and delivered to our home. "P.W., about your elaborate office on Michigan Avenue," Minnie began one night, "It's so expensive. It might have been better to use our address at home for your headquarters."

"You have no idea of what goes on in a campaign, Minnie. The volunteers knock at the door asking for help, asking for material to distribute, and raise questions that have to be answered immediately. There is a constant flow of people and chatter in and out of the headquarters. You wouldn't want that in your home, dear. You would have no privacy. Some of the people involved are not discreet enough to know when to leave you alone. Then too, I need a place where I can get away from the excitement of the campaign. Peace of mind is the most important thing a candidate's home can contribute to his campaign," P.W. explained.

"Well, I am just thinking about all of the additional expenses," Minnie answered. "If you had collected the $5000.00 from Hull, that would have helped."

"Now Minnie, let's not go over that again. We've pulled out of all that litigation . . . If I press for payment, they would open it up again with an appeal to a higher court and they could keep me in court for the rest of my life as they threatened to do years ago. Remember, it almost went that way . . . and remember another thing . . . The Federal system questioned the capability of colored men to conduct a national bank from the beginning. The challenge for Owens and Hull now is to keep the bank open and running. They could never repay the debt they really owe me. Without me they would have no bank to run . . . and besides, I have finally rid myself of those vultures, frauds, and parasites. Is that too hard to understand, Minnie?" P.W. questioned.

Minnie turned around and looked directly at him, "P.W. . . . they stole the bank you created, they labelled you a bankrupt, they dragged your name through the mud in many courts . . . they plagiarized many of your ideas . . . they grabbed all of the credit and drained your energies for years!! And now you're not going to collect even though it's just a symbol of what they owe you!!"

"Don't worry, Minnie. Those people tried hard to bluff but they won't try to get in my way again." P.W. was reassuring her again.

"Well, I could use the money around here," Minnie answered softly, suddenly embarrassed by her persistence.

Although the campaign headquarters were open Monday through Saturday and closed late each night, many neighbors and well-wishers would occasionally stop by our home for a chat about the campaign. One day a stout, elderly, colored lady, strangely visionary in appearance, arrived at our door announcing herself loudly as Miss Mattie.

"Good afternoon," she grinned at Bill who had answered the door bell. "Is Mr. Chavers in? I just want to speak with him for a few minutes," she asked as she moved at a swift pace through the door, almost knocking Bill down. She was dressed in a patchwork skirt nearly reaching the floor. Her long, grey, kinky hair, piled high on top of her head, bobbed up and down as she spoke, her pink, freckled skin and blue eyes belied her age and race. She took a seat in the parlor as if she had been to our home previously.

Edwina and I approached her with timidity and curiosity and her grin broadened even more as we drew near. "You children should be real proud of your father. He's doing a great thing," she began as she bent closer to us. We looked at each other, too transfixed by this odd figure to speak. Her blue eyes sparkled brightly and the long whiskers sprouting from her chin jiggled up and down as she spoke, smiling broadly, revealing many gold-rimmed teeth.

"My children, mark my words, Africa will rise again!" Miss Mattie continued.

Edwina and I rolled our eyes at each other and then we broke out laughing. We tried to hold back our feelings of hilarity at the sight of her, but her words about Africa "rising again" sounded peculiar and amusing. Africa, in the popular notion of the time, was a vast space occupied by primitive

284

Edwina, standing on the Velie-8, 1925

"cannibals," wild animals, jungles, and drum-beating savages hooting voodoo deliriously at the moon. It was perceived in America as a land of backward, naked, ugly, painted black tribesmen, a strange people whose customs and behavior hardly seemed to connect them with black Americans. We shrieked with laughter.

Miss Mattie repeated even louder, "Africa will rise again!!" Bill ran to get mother. Miss Mattie was not to be laughed down or ignored; she was a dedicated Marcus Garvey follower and had come to tie Daddy's campaign in, somehow, with Garvey's "Back-to-Africa" movement. Marcus Garvey, a grandiose West Indian from Jamaica, had initiated this "Back-to-Africa" crusade as the answer to the oppression of Blacks. He had been strongly influenced by the self-help philosophy of Booker T. Washington and had migrated to the United States in 1915. Once established here, he had gained nationwide attention and support, including that of the Ku Klux Klan who entertained the idea of a mass exodus of Blacks back-to-Africa through the Garvey movement. Attracting millions of followers and raising ten million dollars in the name of African nationalism for the 400,000,000 Blacks around the world, he crowned himself "Provisional President of Africa," wearing resplendent uniforms in parades. However, he was sentenced in 1923 on the charge of illegally using the mail to defraud in connection with the sale of stock in his Black Star Line (of ships that were declared "unseaworthy"), imprisoned for five years, later deported to Jamaica, and died in London in 1940. Although his movement had fizzled out by the time of Miss Mattie's visit to our home, it had fired hope in the soul of the black masses in America.

Miss Mattie was one such enthusiast and was trying to convince us of our destiny. "Why children, I want you to know that the alphabet was invented in Africa, the numbers were invented in Africa, and all the great advancements of mankind came from Africa. Africa may be down now, but watch my words, dear children, Africa will rise again and be free!!" Sometime I think back to how her prophecy has been partially fulfilled (in that after World War II many African nations

286

obtained independence) and I wonder if her message of our African heritage was planted in my sister's mind at the time. Edwina, as an adult, became a professor of Black Studies, a pioneer in the field as a learned scholar of African culture and history, and brought black history into the curriculum of the New York City public school system.

We children became more involved as the campaign moved on, especially my brother Bill who would go riding in a horse-drawn covered wagon with Billy Parker, an old Indian, every opportunity he got. Parker was a resilient, hard-working man of many talents. He had a sense of humor, enormous energy, chewed tobacco and wore old clothes that smelled musty most of the time. He had volunteered to campaign for Daddy. He was jovial and effective, always drawing a crowd as he stopped at the street corners and shouted to passersby . . . "Chavers for Congress!"

As was the custom of the era in which TV was not yet invented and radio not pervasive, the political campaign was conducted in the public eye much like a carnival procession. The horse-drawn covered wagon with cow bells strung along its sides went "clang, clang" up and down the street, over the cobblestones, advertising that Daddy was running for Congress. Bill would tell us of his adventures, feeling pretty important to be with Billy Parker and going everywhere in that wagon. They distributed pamphlets that told about Frederick Douglass and the bank, why Daddy was running for Congress, and why he deserved their votes. We grew accustomed to seeing our father's picture all over the area . . . on the telephone posts, in store fronts, and in parlor windows. Eventually all of us were drawn into the campaign . . . Daddy's strategy was to go to as many churches as possible with his family to reach the voters. We went to meetings, church services, and played a part in many programs. The big picture of Fredrick Douglass in the back parlor would be carefully loaded onto the covered wagon. Then it went down the street, "clang, clang, clang" with Billy Parker calling out "Chavers for Congress," on its way from one meeting to another. The picture moved from platform to platform to form a back-drop

Chavers for Congress, 1926

for Daddy's speeches about Fredrick Douglass, the protester, and how he had inspired Daddy to want to help his people.

We responded to Daddy's call for help with mixed feelings of pride, wanting to help, and being a little apprehensive about having to speak in front of so many varieties of strange people. Minnie prepared us for our part and rehearsed our lines in the little speech the three of us would recite, a short story about Fredrick Douglass. Before long, it was time for the windup rally at the Wendell Phillips High School in the heart of the Black Belt. When Mother began to prepare us, she planned to have Bill play the violin and me the piano. But Bill refused to play the violin and in a torrent of protest he told Daddy, "If I have to play that old violin, nobody will vote for you." Daddy agreed with Bill that the violin was inappropriate and though Mother was disappointed she gave in to Daddy's decision, also excusing me from having to play the piano, for which I was grateful to Bill.

Edwina was now 6 years old, an appealing youngster sought after by women's groups to recite poetry at their church and social affairs. I can still remember her voice ringing out her most successful recitation of "It takes a heap o' livin' in a house t' make it home" from the poem "Home" by Edgar A. Guest, popular at the time. But mother felt this would not be appropriate for a political rally, so she spent days searching for the right selection. Then she came upon a speech by Wendell Phillips in tribute to Toussant L'Ouverture, the liberator, which she thought most appropriate because the rally was to be held at Wendell Phillips High School. She felt the poem expressed so clearly and fully the message of Daddy's campaign, pride in Black achievements, Negro History, and the equality and rights of all men. Mother decided that we had recited about Fredrick Douglass enough so I could write my own speech. Bill could serve as master of ceremonies for our part of the program, introducing Edwina and me. For weeks we practiced and prepared. That Sunday afternoon on the platform of Wendell Phillips High School, sitting with Daddy and many renowned dignitaries, we were acutely conscious of the importance of this rally. It was Daddy's last chance to project his message to the voters. Two days later was Primary Day and the school auditorium was packed with people sitting in the aisles and standing at the back . . . even out in the corridors. Mother sat in the front row of the audience, close enough to coach us if we forgot our lines.

Bill was introduced as the master of ceremonies for the Chavers children's tribute to their father. He moved slowly to front center of the stage and looked briefly all around the huge auditorium as if looking for something or someone. Then he began:

"Good afternoon, ladies and gentlemen . . . " he paused and began again. "Good afternoon, ladies and gentlemen . . . we are proud to present this part of the program; we are proud of our dad, P.W. Chavers, and we know you will be too." He looked down at Mother who was mouthing words to him from the first row in the audience. I looked at Daddy, getting annoyed with Bill's groping, but Daddy was beaming with pride. Bill then called on me. I took a deep breath and stepped forward eagerly, smiling, looking to the far corner of the auditorium over Mother's head and made the curtsy as I had so often rehearsed.

"Ladies and gentlemen, I am pleased to speak to you about my Daddy and to tell you why you should vote for him to go to Congress as your representative. My Daddy is a very kind man who is interested in children. Not just his children, but everyone's children. He knows so much about so many important things, and he is very brave. My Daddy wants everyone of you who is old enough to go to the polls on Tuesday and vote. Be sure to vote for P.W. Chavers for Congress. A vote for him is a vote for yourself and a vote for your children too."

I curtsied low. People clapped and waved their programs around in the air. I looked at Mother for the first time as I turned to go to my seat. She was beaming. Bill introduced Edwina, explaining that she would read the "Tribute to Toussaint L'Ouverture" by Wendell Phillips, the famous American lecturer and essayist for whom the high school was named. He added that Wendell Phillips was a great abolitionist who spent his life agitating for equal rights for all men and that Toussaint L'Ouverture was the great liberator of

Haiti where black slaves were held in bondage and that the great pride Daddy had in Negroes and their history would be spelled out in the reading of this tribute. Bill spoke with clarity and feeling and did not look at Mother once.

Edwina moved gracefully to the center of the stage, looking like a beautiful little doll, her black ringlets circling her head. She cleared her throat and waited for total silence, looking out at the audience. Then she began to recite as if she were a mature actress. Her voice rang out melodiously and she formed each word slowly, distinctly and perfectly as she read:

"A Tribute to Toussaint L'Ouverture"
By Wendell Phillips

"I am to tell you the story of a Negro, Toussaint L'Ouverture,
Who has left hardly one written line.
I am to learn it from the reluctant testimony of his enemies
Men who despised him because he was a Negro, and a slave,
hated him because he had beaten them in battle."

Her gaze was steady, her voice sure and clear. The audience was entranced as she continued her recitation. She concluded resonantly:

"Fifty years hence, when truth gets a hearing,
The Muse of History will put Phoebus for the Greeks . . .
. . . will write in the clear blue above them all,
The name of the soldier . . . the statesman . . . the martyr . . .
Toussaint L'Ouverture."

She bowed low, then smiled, as a thunderous applause began. Minnie was watching each of us, lovingly and proudly. We were so pleased and preoccupied with the reaction of the audience to our part of the program, that we didn't notice Daddy walk forward to the speaker's rostrum. His voice soon stopped the applause and drew our attention to him. He was in the middle of his first message before the audience quieted down completely.

"We have been part of the rich fabric of this country since our first ancestors arrived in 1619. A Congressman of color is no new thing for our race; our history shows two United States Senators and twenty Congressmen.

I now call your attention to the issues created in this Congressional campaign . . . between Madden, a white man, and myself, a colored man. I say to you that we must respect our God-given skin color, the skins with which we were born. We cannot, and we must not, accept the doctrine that white is the only official color in America and that a white man can represent us better than one of us can. No white man can feel the sting of uncivilized lynchings and the constant assaults of discrimination and segregation that we suffer simply because of our God-given color. If we accept the doctrine of white representation, then we are forever condemned, for we are not asserting ourselves as we should.

We have helped to build this country with the sweat of our brows for over 300 years, and we will continue to do so, but we must chart our own course as other groups have done here in America. We must fulfill our own destiny in this country. The future belongs to those who plan. Other societies have been divided by religion, language, and custom, according to history. Our country is divided by skin color, even more than by class and custom, but we are free men, in competition for rights and privileges, for goods and services, and yes, even for survival.

We are competing in the economic arena and must rise to this challenge and earn our place in this society, side by side with the white man. This is our right and our responsibility. We must protect what we achieve . . . and never let them take away what is rightfully ours."

A murmured wave of muted sound swept through the audience as though his words were a pebble hurled into a deep lake. P.W. went on, "The white man says he does not understand what we want so how then can he represent us? Our Congressman is a white man, born in England. In coming to this country as a young boy, he had none of the heavy burden of skin color to endure that you and I had and yours and mine will have. Every door of opportunity was opened to him as he climbed the ladder of achievement on the backs of the colored masses. How can *he* really know what we need, or

292

feel the humiliation we feel in every action to achieve, every day, every night, everywhere in the land of our birth, when he is white and foreign born and we are neither? We want an equal opportunity, a fair chance and respect, no more than what he wants. Slavery is to blame for the brutal discrimination we continue to suffer.

We are pictured by many white people as being happy-go-lucky, living a hand-to-mouth existence. Well, we must change that picture. We must learn to save some of what we earn for the future and learn to store our own capital for our own security. We are already changing money-wise. We have insurance companies with resources worth $500 million; we have church property worth $100 million... Yes, we are rising financially, but we must rise politically too. We must learn to use our ballot to work for economic freedom.

Pending in Congress is a bill I wrote to insure your bank deposits. Guaranteeing your money is guaranteeing your freedom for the future. Yet my bill, introduced by Congressman Doyle, has been in the House of Representatives Committee on Banking and Currency for almost two years. To date, no session has ever been called to discuss it. If you send me to Congress, I will promote this bill which will advance you and all of our people... and indeed all people, by safeguarding our bank deposits in national banks... Send me to Congress to represent you and I will agitate to free this bill for action and open other doors to new opportunities for us.

Potentially, we hold great political power in this First Congressional District. We have eight colored votes to each white vote. United we stand, divided we fall! Fifteen million Negroes in America wait... to see what we will do at the polls on Tuesday... here in the First Congressional District where it has been openly admitted that a colored man can be elected to Congress.

Vote for me, P.W. Chavers, when you go to the polls on Tuesday and I will proudly be your voice in Congress."

P.W. backed away from the rostrum while the crowd gave him a standing ovation. He raised both hands high over head and clasped them together to symbolize the hope for victory.

293

Many came up on the platform to talk to him following his speech. Minnie collected us lest we be overwhelmed by the crowd swarming around P.W. We went out to the car with Frank, waited a long time for Daddy to join us, then drove home. We were excited, tired and bewildered. All the way home, Mother was talking softly to Daddy and leaning on his shoulder occasionally in the front seat. She had been greatly stirred by the rally.

However, our jubilation was short-lived. A cynical and self-destructive force had been underestimated. In those days, voters, especially in the Black Belt, did not trust middle-class reformers. They felt that black leaders were more interested in personal aggrandizement than opportunity for the masses. Chicago, in 1926, was a bloody city running wild with Al Capone's gangsters, murderers and grafters. They prowled the streets with their machine guns, shooting up saloons while sluggers, killers and crooked politicians roamed City Hall. Vote thievery, ballot stuffing, voter intimidation and pay-offs dominated the polling places on Primary Day. Some reformers spoke the language of freedom but were bought off, others talked political salvation but were wholly ineffective. Perhaps some saw P.W. as too innocent to maneuver in the rough and tumble of smelly political deals. Ironically, three years later, when Congressman Martin B. Madden finally died in office at age 73 from a heart attack at his desk in the room of the Appropriations Committee at the Capital, he was replaced by Oscar DePriest, his powerful black assistant and 3rd Ward Committeeman. At the time, DePriest was under Special Grand Jury indictment for conspiracy in aiding, abetting, and inducing gangsters and racketeers to operate gambling houses and houses of prostitution as a result of a special investigation into vice and gambling conditions in the 3rd Ward. It was commonly known that he had been indicted eight times previously on similar charges, including bribery of police in connection with protection of houses of ill-repute, and that Madden had paid $5000 at the time of his trial when he was ably represented by Clarence Darrow. Though found "not guilty," DePriest was never fully exonerated from this blemish on his public record. In such a notorious environment, the infamy of Chicago increased and the masses believed that anyone who projected civil rights issues was just using such idealistic causes as devices to deceive the public.

On that Primary day, our parents went to the polls early and P.W. spent most of the day at his headquarters. He came home for dinner a little later than usual and listened to the radio far into the night. The manual ballot count in use did not allow for rapid reporting and it was several days before the results of the Primary were finalized. P.W. was hurt because he made a much poorer showing than he expected. On Friday morning he recovered sufficiently to talk with us about it on the way to school.

"Children, I never would have let you participate in the campaign if I hadn't trully expected to win. I want you to be brave about my defeat," he explained. Bill and I were quiet about our hurt and disappointment as we listened to him. He realized that by permitting us to have such an active role in his political ambitions, he unwittingly exposed his children to the raw edges of defeat and placed upon them the responsibility of having to bear their own hurt.

Our parents talked together about this experience for many evenings, staying longer in the back parlor, their favorite place for discussions, since they thought their voices could not be heard by us upstairs. "You did a wonderful job, P.W. You put the issues squarely before the people," Minnie told him many times. He needed these healing words. His haggard and depressed expressions troubled Minnie as she kept reminding him he had achieved at least part of his objective. "You have challenged Madden as an independent reform candidate in our district. He will never feel safe again." Minnie loved a fighter, and though her husband had not won, he had fought determinedly in the apathetic, indifferent, corrupt political arena that was the Black Belt.

"But I really thought I was going to win. I had it figured out mathematically . . . eight Blacks to one White, even if only half of them voted," commented P.W. at one point. He followed her around the house as she worked. "I only got 6,000 votes out of 20,000. Even considering how the political machine tampers with the vote count . . . I must face the fact that our community is not ready to use the ballot to answer their problems." P.W. came up against the bitter reality of his oppressed people again. "Others will have to follow in my wake, and some may do a better job. At least I have started something for others to measure themselves by."

Later, when neighbors and friends stopped by to talk about the results, some voiced the feeling that P.W. did very well considering he was still new in the community and that Chicago people did not readily go along with "upstarts" challenging the old ways of doing things. Many were surprised to find Minnie and P.W. ready to talk about the defeat and able to analyse it openly.

But we were deeply hurt. Mother would say to us in various ways over and over again, "Children, your father is a man born before his time. His far-reaching values and visions are beyond many people, beyond anything they dare to dream." Bill took Daddy's defeat better than the girls did for he had secretly feared he might have to give up playing with the neighborhood boys when Daddy won and we had to move to Washington. Edwina complained that she didn't want to go to the private school anymore because the children were teasing her about her father's defeat. But Mother would not consider her request to be transferred to Willard School where she could be with Bill and me. Mother and Cleo observed that I was becoming secretive, pensive, sensitive, and subject to crying spells. They thought the changes in my behavior were due to the scars on my hands. One day Cleo commented to me that my hands were beautiful and I should not try to hide them. I hugged her for being so concerned, yet I knew it was not my hands that bothered me. The sadness I was feeling was about what was again happening to my father, but I could not admit, even to Cleo, how deeply I was hurt over his defeat, so I added left-over copies of Daddy's pamphlets and campaign literature to my growing treasure of material about him. At age nine, the world seemed a strange and cruel place.

By late May, Mother was caught up in preparing us for our first appearance in a dance recital and showing our neighbors and friends the many costumes she had designed and made for us. She was especially pleased with the sequin-bodiced full winged butterfly costume I was to wear. But on the day of the recital I announced I had decided not to be in the recital. It may have been that I did not really want to perform before a cruel world that had not chosen my father to represent it. None of the statistics about how many people had voted, nor my parents' post election rationalizations, had really helped me. I repeated, "I just cannot dance tonight!" then went to bed to prove it.

Mother was beside herself as she spoke to Daddy about my refusal early that evening. "Madrue must dance tonight!" she insisted.

"But I don't feel well," I protested at the dinner table.

"Now Minnie, maybe we should call the doctor for her," Daddy proposed.

"Oh, I don't need a doctor, I just can't dance because of my headache," I rallied.

Mother listened as Daddy questioned me further. "If you're not sick enough to need a doctor, maybe you feel well enough to come to the recital and watch the show with me." Then he added, "Madrue will learn, give her time."

I smiled, feeling relieved. "Yes, I can go . . . but I can't dance tonight." I could not change my stance in all of this now. My headache disappeared almost as soon as I was relieved of the pressure of being in the recital.

That night, I sat proudly with Daddy and his friends in our box watching the other children perform and secretly wishing to be up there on the stage sharing the applause, the attention, and the flowers. I did learn. That night I decided that I would never be left out again if I did not feel well and that I would suffer any feelings to be a part of the show.

Early in the year, even before he had become involved in the political campaign, P.W. had purchased the 6,000 acres of virgin timberland in Langlade County near Elcho, Wisconsin.With its many lakes and an altitude of more than 1,600 feet above sea level, it was to be developed into a campsite and resort. The big lake on the property he named for Mother.

297

Come to the Magic "Charmed Land" at Camp Madrue
Being Developed for the Colored American Boys and Girls

AS the Winter breaks and Spring and Summer creep upon us it is most natural that our boys' and girls' thoughts instinctively turn to the vacation days of recreation and pleasure.

We invite you to come where you can find rest and dream away the most pleasant and healthful vacation that you have ever enjoyed; close to nature, amid the green fields, the tall pine forests, silver lakes and bubbling brooks and bracing air at Camp Madrue.

P. W. CHAVERS
President

Dear Reader:

May I ask for a few minutes of your valuable time to acquaint you with a very helpful, philanthropic work which concerns the welfare of the colored school children of Chicago?

This Wonderful, Beautiful Camp for You and Your Boy or Girl

Enjoy Life Amid the Pines on the Shore of a Clear, Cool Lake at Camp Madrue in Northern Wisconsin

A SERIOUS PROBLEM

A close check-up shows that approximately 30,000 colored school children are turned loose in the street in this great city every summer. The good they have learned in school is too often lost in the vacation period by the city "gang life." The boy of today is the man of tomorrow. He may become a useful citizen or a worthless criminal.

CONSTRUCTIVE DEVELOPMENT

We feel that if the colored child is given the opportunity to study nature, learn the value of the soil, the dignity of labor, the training of the heart, hand, and mind, which we teach them at Camp Madrue, we will plant in him the first principle of good American citizenship.

In Seach of Adventure on the Cool Northern Lakes at Camp Madrue

Hotel Accommodations for Adults At Camp Madrue

Come to the Magic Charmed Land-Camp Madrue literature

It was a great span of quiet, clear blue water and was framed by deep green pine trees with a 200 foot long sandy yellow beach, just off the main road. The campsite was to be named for me.

"Camp Madrue and Lake Minnie Bell," he would say to himself over and over again, liking what he heard. P.W.

298

IDEAL MODERN OUT-DOOR RECREATIONAL CENTER OF AMERICA.
A WONDERFUL PLAYGROUND.
HAPPINESS AND REFINEMENT FOR GIRLS AND BOYS AT CAMP MADRUE

MRS. M. B. CHAVERS
*General Superintendent
of Camp Madrue*

CHILDREN'S PLAY GROUND

Our plan is to develop one of the finest children's play grounds in the country, where every year the churches and various societies can send hundreds of kiddies to spend a part of their summer vacation.

The clear waters and sandy shores of Wisconsin's lakes are ideal for bathing at Camp Madrue

With this idea in mind, we have set aside approximately 150 acres of rich farm land facing on a very large lake, in Langlade County, noted for its high latitude of 1,697 feet above the sea level, the highest in the state. And the various lakes in this area are practically at the same level; the tract is really the divide where the waters of the north eventually drain into the Atlantic and the waters of the Southern Slope eventually drain into the Gulf of Mexico. It is because of these environments and opportunities that no parents should neglect to see to it that their children get the best. Camp Madrue affords the best in America for outdoor training for colored boys and girls. It's the garden spot of the world.

The Camp Madrue Society is composed, in part, of what is known as a committee of arrangements. Our race must feel proud of them for all have borne the burden of motherhood with honor. Each and every one stands as a great monument for higher racial development. You will not go wrong if you follow their advice. They have been at Camp Madrue; they will all be there again this summer. They want to meet you there, for the great good it will do you and your children. For any information you may desire concerning Camp Madrue, please write or phone direct to any member of the committee.

Horseback riding where the trails never end

AN OBLIGATION

Every parent owes the child a chance to fight life's battle; health is the cornerstone for all that follows. Years take their toll or bring their rewards, according to wisdom of the parent or society. The bracing air—clear mineral water and sunshine, with plenty of clean, wholesome country food is what my boy and your boys and girls receive at Camp Madrue, the wonderful playground surrounded by the silent old forests, filled with its great pine trees and health-giving odors which serve as a great tonic that strengthens and builds the physical youth on a sound foundation.

It has been the paramount question for years just where the better class of colored citizens of the nation could find just such a place. This problem has been solved, and our President, Mr. P. W. Chavers, has interested a large number of prominent social and religious leaders in sponsoring this great national co-operative fishing, hunting and pleasure club where only members and invited guests can come.

*Where all outdoors is opened as though it were Nature's book
at Camp Madrue*

thought of the thousands of black children playing in the dingy alleys of Chicago and how his camp, with its clean, unspoiled environment, beautiful acreage, mineral water, pure air, and plenty of sunshine, which was sorely needed by so many, would provide a respite from the harsh reality of the urban slums in which they lived. Some of the men who worked in the political campaign, like Billy Parker, were now retained to start clearing away the forest. Billy Parker drank hard liquor, chewed tobacco, and seemed like a wild smelly

animal to Minnie who hoped P.W. would dismiss him after the campaign. But P.W insisted that Billy was a talented Indian who knew nature's wonders intimately, had grown up among the Oklahoma Indians, and most of all was enthusiastic about the camp project.

P.W. arranged for Billy to move into the 49th Street apartment house, behind the office, where they talked over plans to clear the forest, how to start, and what to order first in the actual construction of the camp. Billy had been a Past Patriotic Commander in the Spanish-American War and continued as Veteran Camp Commander. "Give a man of talent, like Billy Parker, an opportunity to show what he can do in civilian life, show him that his efforts are appreciated and he will not let you down," P.W. emphasized to Minnie. Billy took a fresh crew of workmen to Wisconsin to finish clearing the campsite, set up the tents, living quarters, a mess hall, and an open camp fire not too far from the open ball field. A big all-purpose tent to house thirty or forty girls, equipped with collapsible cots, would serve as an indoor recreation center during rainy weather. Three smaller tents were set up on the outer rim of the camp, each to accommodate 10 to 15 boys, not far from the workmen's tents.

Pleased with his design of the camp featuring the central-ized campfire, P.W. was keeping his lifelong promise to him-self to do something really important for colored children and to bring happiness into their young lives. He imagined the children singing songs in the cool evenings while sitting around the camp fire roasting marshmallows. He saw his camp as a great tonic for city children where they could have outdoor, healthy, happy experiences, and he would jot down notes for his brochure, describing the camp, as inspirations occurred to him during the planning and construction that went on that spring . . .

I clearly remember the night before we left for camp when the first group of children began to arrive at our house, about thirty of them eventually, and many from dancing school. They bunked all over our house that night. Excited and impatient for the day break, we slept fitfully. Before sunrise we were off in the big bus and sang throughout most of the long journey as the bus weaved its way over the highway through Milwaukee to Fond du Lac, and on to Oshkosh, where we stopped briefly for lunch. We rode through Antigo, then suddenly began the last uphill 5 miles, a long climb at the end of which we saw a huge sign, "Camp Madrue."

The road curved sharply to the left at this point so that only the entrance was visible as the bus neared the top. We screamed with joy as we pulled inside the gate and the bus came to a sudden halt. The land was level and clear. Rebecca, Vera, and Mother ushered us out of the big bus. The workmen

Approaching Camp Madrue

Crew of workers

greeted us with warmth and pride; they had caught many porcupines for the welcome dinner. This was our first experience with game, but we were hungry and fell to it with gusto.

Many thrills opened up to us as days went by. Our program included exploring the forest underbrush for raspberry patches, hiking down the winding back roads, and bathing in the clear waters of Lake Minnie Bell. At night, we sat around the open fire place talking, singing, joking, exchanging stories, watching the stars, and on special occasions, roasting marshmallows and frankfurters. Our presence in the mid-Wisconsin area soon became known; farmers from near and far heard about us and came to get acquainted. We found out that most of these farmers were Scandinavian, Swiss, and German, born in Europe but newly arrived in the United States. They were hardy farm people, open to new experiences and pleased with the excitement the city children in camp brought to their rural isolation. They marvelled at our talents as we talked with them about some of the things we did and the places we went to in the city. They made us welcome wherever we went. P.W. bought a little pony from Farmer King so we could learn to ride horse back. The warmth was genuine and spontantous and we reciprocated.

P.W. travelled back and forth between camp and Chicago, taking care of his business affairs, raising funds for the camp and promoting the sale of some of the property. He visited as often as he could in order to oversee the camp's development and to enjoy the outdoor life. As soon as he arrived at camp he would become "one of the boys," going swimming and fishing, and doing the calisthentics with them. He kept up fairly well with the hand springs, the push-ups, and head-stands that Billy Parker would make them go through every morning. He enjoyed these experiences with the boys as if absorbing some of their youth. For their part, the boys were proud to have "Mr. Chavers" in their midst and they tried harder at their games and talked about what a good sport he was for days after he left.

Minnie worked long hours to supervise the girls and to help out in the kitchen with planning and scheduling the meals and other operational details for Rebecca and Vera to carry

Dancing At Camp Madrue
Marie Bryant, Madrue, and Ernestine Ford.

At the lakeside

out. Though it was difficult (she was not really the outdoor type), she was pleased to see how much the experience meant to her husband and her children. It was deeply satisfying for her to watch P.W. run through the woods with the boys and swim with them in the lake.

We Chavers children romped and played and exalted in the freedom of space and pines, in the wonders of nature and the many camp activities. Those were happy, carefree summer days when we would run with the pack through the forest, loosing ourselves to the mysteries of the underbrush and searching out treasures amidst the stately evergreen trees. We would romp up and down the roving hills, even in the heat of the mid-day sun, while hiking back to camp from the morning dip in Lake Minnie Bell. I almost forgot my sense of obligation until one day it was brought back to me forcefully. The Williams' family had been helpful to Daddy in raising funds for the camp. Mr. Williams was a prominent Negro lawyer with a sickly wife and two whining, demanding children. He heard about P.W.'s plans to develop a camp for colored children geared to promoting good citizenship through the study of nature and learning the values of the soil, and wanted his children in a camp where they would be safe and their behavior would not embarrass him. He also thought of the camp as a wise investment.

Mr. Williams' daughter, Loretta, was a well-developed 12 year old girl with a cream-colored complexion, sky-blue eyes and black curly hair. She was acutely aware of her physical beauty and its power to attract the attention of the crew working around the grounds most of that first summer. Watching her flirt with the workmen and behave nastily and arrogantly with the girls, I developed a strong dislike for her. One day, Loretta and I were bent over two basins outside the big tent washing our long, curly hair, the one activity we shared. Her brother, Warren, and mine, Bill, were pitching horseshoes close by. Warren was 13, large, almost 6 feet tall, and awkward, with a stupid expression and protruding frog-like eyes. We watched them pitch horseshoes for a few minutes in between soaping our hair and refilling our basins with water . . . We would hear them calling the scores. For days Loretta had been trying to tease Bill, as she did with the work crew, to gain his attention, but he remained unresponsive. Nothing she did seemed to interest him. Now, suddenly, while she was soaping her hair, she snapped at me loudly.

"Your brother is a liar and a cheat!"

"He is not," I protested. I didn't know what had provoked her outburst. "You can't see what he's doing," I shouted, getting mad.

"Oh yes I can . . . he's a dirty liar" she yelled.

In a flash of temper, and trying to stop her from screaming, I threw my basin of suds in her face. She ran into the open field and was struck by one of their horseshoes as it was hurled. She lay on the ground screaming and kicking, blood running from her mouth, and soap all over her head. The others gathered around her showing their anxiety and concern. The entire scene occurred within a few minutes. I walked over to her slowly and looked down thinking, "she brought it on herself." But the adults and other children were distressed. Her two front teeth had been knocked out by the blow of the horseshoe and I felt the first twinge of remorse for what I had done. In the end, I was to pay a heavy price for having contributed to this disaster.

The Williams' family took their two children out of camp and never expressed an interest in the camp again. Mother reminded me of the affair on and off for the rest of the summer, and periodically during the following winter, telling me what my responsibility was, both as the namesake of the camp and as the daughter of the proprietor. She spoke of how influential the Williams' were and how much they had helped Daddy. I had spoiled all this; their daughter was now toothless and would have to go through life with artificial teeth. I had mixed feelings about the incident as I had defended my brother's character and felt I was right. Since the results of my actions had caused Daddy great pain, I was sorry for my rash behavior and vowed to make it up to Daddy. Somehow, though, I was glad to be rid of Loretta.

The camp season ended all too swiftly after that episode. To brighten our farewell, the boys suggested we put on a show in the big tent for the farmers. Bill directed the rehearsals, giving orders as though he knew exactly what he was doing. Daddy joined us for the last week of camp to supervise the closing. He brought a carload of costumes which Mother refreshed and repaired for the show.

The night of the farewell party the curtain opened to a full tent of farmers who had come from miles around to see us. Bill handled the spotlight and directed the show out front, Frank strummed the ukelele, Billy Parker worked the improvised stage curtain, and Vera and Rebecca helped the girls in and out of costumes as we changed for the different scenes. The farmers were impressed by Ernestine's soft shoe dancing, Alvina's acrobatic feats, Marie's saucy jazz rendition, Edwina's "Rich Little Snob" act, and my toe dancing around the big tent. After the show, a barn dance began. The farmers had a night that they would remember all through the cold Wisconsin winter and they gave us a sense of worth about our talents to last many of us for a lifetime. They marvelled at our dancing feet and entertaining personalities and we heard them congratulate Daddy on the camp and speak in glowing words about how nice it had been to have us in their midst. They would eagerly await our return next summer.

The next three summers were spent in much the same way. We ran carefree in the great north woods and knew very little of the difficulties P.W. was having in arousing the interest of Chicago people to help finance the camp. P.W. charged minimum fees for campers and adults to encourage as many as possible to benefit from the camp, and to attract adult interest in purchasing lots for summer cottages. Minnie questioned the low rates when he set them up, pointing out that she spent as much for a single dancing lesson for one of her children as he was charging for a full week with room and board at the camp. P.W. maintained that his people were poor and that the camp would eventually be sustained by his promotion of summer cottages and the philanthropy of the Committee of Goodwill he was organizing in Chicago. He saw his camp movement as a partnership of business and philanthropy, rather than a luxury, as Minnie implied.

He thought of incorporating the entire camp effort, organizing and floating stock as he had in the Douglass Bank experience. After weighing this possibility, he realized that corporate structures required a degree of sophistication about money investment that his people did not have. In the late spring of 1927, to prepare for the second opening of his summer camp, P.W. redoubled his promotion and at the same time took out a substantial loan using his 49th Street equity as collateral. The economic boom was on its way, following the earlier recession, and P.W.'s natural optimism and the national mood were in tune once again. The camp promotion began to move well after he subdivided some of the land for year-round cottages and the volunteer committees to protect the camp benefit idea began to function.

One committee included a physician who examined the children before camp and the wives of several businessmen who reviewed applications for camp scholarships. The Goodwill Benefit Committee eventually included the recently re-elected Mayor Thompson, the owner of the Chicago White Sox, the President of the Dixon Transfer Company, his friend Stewart, and many others who made consistent contributions. He launched several money-making schemes, one a "Moonlight Boat Ride" with Mayor Thompson announcing that a playground on the campsite would be named for him. Charles Comisky donated the proceeds of one day's admission at the White Sox Ball Park and named that day in honor of the Camp Madrue Outdoor Life Society.

That summer I made up for the damages I had done the previous year when I had fought with Loretta. Mother's words had left a heavy weight on my growing conscience. I was promoted to the sixth grade showing promise in mathematics, often helping students having difficulty, and staying after school to coach children at the teacher's request. When a few parents inquired about the camp and raised the question of having their children coached in arithmetic and spelling while there, I offered to help the younger ones with these subjects. Mother and Daddy were proud of my offer. I gathered old books from my teacher and outlined the study course. It was a make-shift course at best, but I conducted the coaching sessions that summer and emerged with a new awareness of my abilities. I was ten years old now and beginning that stretch of awkward years, too young for boys and too old for dolls. Teaching that summer redeemed me in my mother's eyes and kept me out of further mischief. I lost myself in the thrill of seeing the children grasp the knowledge and acquire new skills in multiplication and long division from my special way of simplifying and making meaningful the numbers on the page. It seemed almost magical that I could teach them so readily.

P.W. was proud and pleased with the outcome. He subsequently pursued this much further and in following summers several teachers from the Chicago Board of Education came to camp and developed classes in a more formal manner. The camp activities eventually expanded to include not only elementary school subjects, but woodworking, taught by Billy Parker, and farming and poultry, taught by local farmers. P.W. arranged for the credits earned at Camp Madrue to be accepted on the same basis as those earned in any other summer school.

Jack, our former chauffeur, had been assiduously studying and learning the real estate business. In many ways, he and P.W. became business colleagues. Jack, rather than P.W., broached the question of whether or not it was time for them to break off their present relationship. "I think I'm ready to go into business for myself," he said one day as he was driving P.W. to Stewart's office at the bank to negotiate a loan for the camp development. "I been goin' to night school at the "Y" takin' English and Declamation, like you told me. You're right! I cin see that a businessman mus' be able to speak well 'n' present himself in a proper manner if he wants to be a success with the public," he added, giving P.W. an immediate and practical demonstration of what he had learned there. He squared his shoulders ostentatiously as they whipped around the corner.

"Now, course I done learned lots from you too ... P.W. ... 'n' I'm grateful for what you done for me ... bu' I gotta do things that's mine ... jus' like you do, suh. Camp Madrue is yours and you are workin' at it! I been watchin' all these years how you take an idea 'n' the next thing I know, it becomes somethin' real. I gotta be like that, have ideas and make them grow for me and mine!"

Jack looked up into the mirror to catch a glimpse of P.W.'s face as he sat pensively in the back of the car where he was going over some papers, preparing for the loan request. P.W. smiled and leaned forward to slap Jack on the shoulder to show his affection for him. "I'm going to have to watch you, Jack. Now you're my competitor," he said jokingly, then added, "You will do very well on your own. I know you will."

"I've been savin' money too," Jack said proudly, glad it had been so easy to tell P.W., as they pulled up in front of Stewart's office. "I learned a lot 'bout the importance of bankin' from you, P.W. I put my money in the Binga State Bank to keep it here in the neighborhood, jus' like you always say we should do."

P.W. got out of the car, shaking hands on the new deal. "I'll be back for you when you say, suh. I still enjoy drivin' you 'round like old times," Jack offered.

"Well, then pick me up in two hours," responded P.W. He chuckled to himself, "He'll do all right. I'll give him a small loan to help him along until he gets settled." Watching the Velie—8 spin down the street, P.W. thought of how close they had been, then felt a twinge about the forth coming separation, but smiled as he turned to enter the building. He knew Jack was ready; the apprenticeship was over.

14

The Crossings

Jack left us shortly before our Filipino cousins arrived. Mother told us that they were on an ocean liner crossing the Pacific Ocean, coming to America. Over the years, she had told us that Uncle John lived far away, unlike Uncle George who came in from Washington or some other part of the country to visit us. We knew that Uncle John had been an officer in the United States Army during the Spanish-American War and had been stationed in the Philippine Islands where he settled and married a Filipino girl after the peace treaty. Our only first cousins were Filipino because they lived in the Philippine Islands, but Mother always talked about her family as Virginians. We noticed the family resemblance in Uncle John's pictures. This same proud bearing showed through all of the photographs we received from him.

P.W. sat in the big velvet-covered chair, puffing contentedly on his cigar and reading his newspaper while we talked with the family album between us, as before, during one of Minnie's sessions about her side of our family. We were impressed by the latest picture of twelve children clustered in three rows around Uncle John and his wife wearing the lowcut balloon-sleeved Filipino dress. At their feet sat their youngest child Richard, four years old, blond and smiling, with the Calloway streak clearly showing. He was coming to America with his two older sisters, Elisabeth and Petrita. Minnie pointed them out. "That's Elisabeth, she's nineteen and very smart. She's been teaching school in Manila and is coming here to finish her education in English literature and journalism. She inherited her father's literary talent." Then Mother pointed out Petrita. "That's Petrita who is twenty-two years old and coming to make her home in America as a

311

THE FAMILY TREE

BAKER—BANNISTER—CALLOWAY—CHAVERS— PANNELL ROOTS

FREE BORN OF COLOR
NORTH CAROLINA

Descendants of WILL CHAVIS,
French Huguenot mulatto indentured
servant, The Immigrant, 1700

KATIE CHAVERS, b. 1815
d. 1860 +

Chatham County, North Carolina

FREE BORN OF COLOR
VIRGINIA

BETTY BANNISTER, b. 1800
Patrick County, Virginia

EUROPEAN FREE BORN, Cornwall, England

JOSEPH CALLOWAY, The Immigrant, 1704

had 5 sons

COL. WILLIAM CALLOWAY ═
b. 1714   d. 1778
Bedford County, Virginia
had two wives, nine children

ELIZABETH TILLEY, m. 1735
1st wife

COL. JAMES CALLOWAY ═
b. 1736   d. 1809
Bedford County, Virginia
had 3 wives, 22 children

ELIZABETH EARLY, m. 1777   b. 1759
2nd wife   d. 1796

JOHN CALLOWAY ═
b. 1781   d. 1865
had 14 children by
3 unions including:
George Hairston Calloway,
b. 1822, brain injured, 1832
d. 1894, Henry County, Virginia

Mary Polly Hairston, m.1809   b. 1793
1st wife,   d. 1819
had 3 children
America Hairston, m. 1821   b. 1801
2nd wife   d. 1826
had 2 children,
Bedford County, Virginia

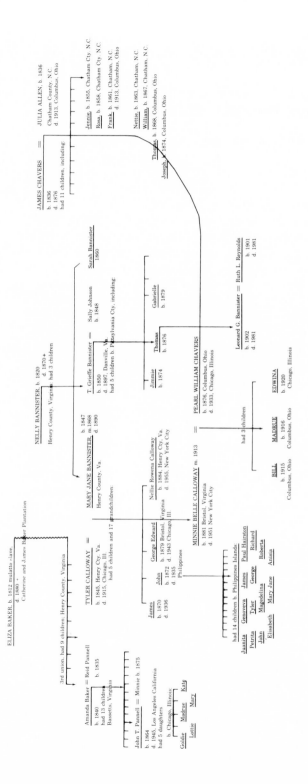

ELIZA BAKER, b. 1812 mulatto slave.
d. 1880 +
Catherine and James Baker Plantation

JAMES CHAVERS =
b. 1836
d. 1876
had 11 children, including

JULIA ALLEN, b. 1836
Chatham County, N.C.
d. 1913, Columbus, Ohio

Jennie b. 1855, Chatham Cty. N.C
Rosa b. 1858, Chatham Cty. N.C
Frank b. 1861, Chatham, N.C.
d. 1913, Columbus, Ohio
Nettie b. 1863, Chatham, N.C.
William b. 1868, Columbus, Ohio
Thomas b. 1874, Columbus, Ohio
Joseph, b. 1874, Columbus, Ohio

3rd union, had 9 children, Henry County, Virginia

NELLY BANNISTER, b. 1820
d. 1870 +
Henry County, Virginia had 3 children

TYLER CALLOWAY =
b. 1845, Henry Cty. Va.
d. 1915, Chicago, Ill.
had 5 children and 17 grandchildren:

MARY JANE BANNISTER b. 1847 m.1868
d. 1890
Henry County, Va.

T. Grieffe Bannister =
b. 1850
d. 1897, Danville, Va.
had 5 children b. Pittsylvania Cty. including:

Sally Johnson
b. 1848

Sarah Bannister
1860

Jimmie
b. 1874

Thomas
b. 1876

Gabrielle
b. 1879

PEARL WILLIAM CHAVERS
b. 1876, Columbus, Ohio
d. 1933, Chicago, Illinois

Leonard G. Bannister =
b. 1902
d. 1981

Ruth L. Reynolds
b. 1901
d. 1981

MINNIE BELLE CALLOWAY m. 1913
b. 1881 Bristol, Virginia
d. 1951 New York City

Nettie Rowena Calloway
b. 1884, Henry Cty. Va.
d. 1955, New York City

George Edward
b. 1879 Bristol, Virginia
d. 1943 Chicago Ill.

John
b. 1872
d. 1935
Philippines

James
b. 1870
d. 1936

had 3 children

BILL
b. 1915
Columbus, Ohio

MADRUE
b. 1916
Columbus, Ohio

EDWINA
b. 1920
Chicago, Illinois

Amanda Baker = Reid Pannell
b. 1840   b. 1835
had 13 children
Bassetts, Virginia

John T. Pannell = Minnie b. 1875
b. 1864
d. 1945, Los Angeles California
had 5 daughters
b. Chicago, Illinois

Goldie Madrue Katy
Lottie   Mary

had 14 children b. Philippines Islands:
Juanita Genoveva James George Paul Hairston
Petria Tyler Richard
John Magedelina Roberta
Elisabeth Mary Jane Anisia

bride." She spoke of the others in the picture: "John, James, George Edward, Paul Hairston, and baby Richard are the boys."

I suddenly realized that none of the children looked like us, not even the four-year old. "Our cousins looked Chinese." Bill picked this up too. "Do you think Uncle John and his wife will come later with our other cousins?" I asked.

"I don't know, Madrue," she replied. "Perhaps, but your Uncle John has twelve children . . . a big family with many mouths to feed and many shoes to buy." She knew he had a strong sense of family and the will to make sacrifices for their sake. She too had these values, so she knew he would not return to the United States until all the children were grown.

Petrita's husband failed to meet them at the boat in San Francisco. They were crushed, despondent, and stranded without money in the midst of the excitement and all the people who swarmed about them. Suddenly Elisabeth thought to wire P.W. who answered by return wire, sending the fare for them to come on to Chicago. They arrived at our house together. Mother had prepared us for their similarities, but not their differences. They were trilingual; they had grown up speakng English in school and with their father, Spanish at home with their mother, and Tagalog with their classmates and some of their friends.

Elisabeth, the tall, more Chinese-looking of the two, with the light yellow skin, had finely-textured brown hair that curled a bit. She was the intellectual, very class-conscious, and the favorite of her father. She spoke frequently of their high status in Manila, based on Uncle John's important government position, and their rich cultural background on their mother's side, intermixed with Spanish blood and heritage. Petrita was petite, brown, more Filipino looking, with a quality of humility perhaps brought on by her recent crushing let-down by her husband. They vowed over and over they would never forget the benevolence of "Uncle Chavers and Aunt Minnie." Richard was a bright-eyed happy youngster, smiling constantly, involved in all adventures . . . by now we were calling him "Dickie."

314

We went along on the sight-seeing trips and heard Daddy brag about Chicago being the first city to build skyscrapers, "the first in this" and the "first in that." Mother bragged about our experiences in camp last summer and showed off our dancing costumes. We noticed how proud she was to introduce our cousins to the workers at the office of the *Chicago Defender* where she took them to see the printing press of a large American Negro newspaper. She knew this would interest them, since their father had set up the Bureau of Printing in Manila years ago and had fulfilled his calling as a printer and writer.

During one dinner conversation, Elisabeth spoke of how impressed she was that everyone at the *Chicago Defender* recognized Aunt Minnie immediately as "The Mrs. Chavers." They talked about the litigation and publicity over the Woodfolk Estate and the Douglass National Bank, including the Calumet property fight. "Who got the property?" questioned Elisabeth.

"It was eventually sold at an auction to Wagner, the attorney," explained P.W. . . . "He got it for $880 cash. Can you imagine buying a twelve flat building in Chicago, with an appraisal value of $55,000, for that amount?"

"Was he White?" asked Elisabeth who took an analytical interest in skin colors and skin discriminations of people she met or talked about, eager to fully absorb status detail of her new environment, America.

"Why, yes, he is," answered P.W.

"I thought so," she answered. "They know how to work every angle, I've noticed," continued Elisabeth. After two weeks with us, she left for New York. P.W. took her to the Baltimore and Ohio Station where he bought her a Pullman ticket for Washington, D.C. There was going to be a reception for Lindberg returning from his solo flight to Paris and Elisabeth wanted to be a part of this first big event to happen since she had arrived in America. She had aspirations of becoming a journalist, hence her interest in news-worthy events.

After considerable deliberation, Petrita decided to go on to

315

New York like Elisabeth, in order to help her sister. P.W. had encouraged Petrita to stay on in Chicago where she could work for him in his 49th Street office while making new plans for herself. He wanted her to feel welcome in her father's native land about which she had heard so much during her developing years. He knew that she had many adjustments to make now that she had been deserted by her husband. But she said that under the circumstances she wanted to help Elisabeth in whatever way might be necessary for her to complete her studies. She also looked forward to meeting Nellie, and perhaps she was still secretly hoping that her husband would seek her out in New York, through Nellie, where he knew Elisabeth would be for at least one year. Thus, after a six week stay with us, Petrita and Dickie prepared for the last lap of their journey and P.W. again advanced the train fare to New York.

Shortly after they left us it was time for us to pack and leave the city for another summer in camp, where not only did I coach the children in mathematics and spelling, but I learned to row a boat by myself. I would venture alone far across Lake Minnie Bell, just for the thrill of mastering the boat, paddling one oar after another rhythmically, absorbing the beautiful view of the evergreens surrounding the cool still waters and feeling a oneness with nature.

Autumn, with its grey skys and red-yellow leaves, encircled us once more and we returned as usual to Chicago. The fall of 1927 saw the return to power of William Hale Thompson as Mayor and his victory was considered beneficial to Al Capone and his gangs. When Thompson had decided not to run for office in 1923, William Dever was elected Mayor of Chicago.

The politics of the Chicago underworld was also changing, albeit, not so quietly. Johnny Torrio, king of the underworld (ruling brothels, gambling houses, opium dens, and bootlegging operations) had returned to Italy and assigned Al Capone, then operating in New York, to Cicero, a suburb in West Chicago. But Capone moved swiftly to enhance his reign, and within two years, by 1925, he ruled all of Chicago's underworld, challenging Torrio upon his return to Chicago from Italy in a notorious gangland battle. Torrio quit, leaving his territory to Capone who now controlled an army of 700 sluggers, some 10,000 speakeasies, and the bootlegging fortune from border to border, and Florida to Canada. On Valentine's Day, 1929, Capone's gangsters, masquerading in policeman's uniforms, raided a garage where they gunned down 7 rival mobsters with a blast of Capone-led machine-gun fire. None of the killers were apprehended in the chase. Thompson, who controlled the police, apparently looked the other way. Sluggers and killers did the dirty work for employers, workers in their disputes, and for politicians in their campaign battles as they paraded around city hall after Mayor Thompson returned to power.

The Chicago that Mayor Dever had inherited for four years in 1923 had been bloody with gang wars, averaging 400 murders per year, but determined to crusade, he had appointed William McAndrew school superintendent in 1923 to improve the chaotic Chicago school system. He had no patience with civil-service incompentents and loafers and demanded periodic ratings of teachers. He instituted time clocks for all school employees of the Board of Education and started a program of 100% mastery of reading, writing, spelling and arithmetic.

Upon return to power, Mayor Thompson was quick to charge McAndrew with insubordination and being pro-British. He was forced to defend himself in the courtroom. Teachers participated in his trials, calling him a cruel taskmaster. In reality, McAndrew had introduced progressive ideas, improving academic standards for teachers and students. Schools became more efficient, but McAndrew was unpopular, a threat to the incompetent, considered autocratic, and lacking tact in his methods of implementing his ideas.

The controversy about McAndrew's charges was shaking up the complacent school system of Chicago in the fall of 1927, the very time Minnie decided to remove Edwina from private school. It was at this time that we children first learned that Daddy had loaned the private school the money

317

to purchase the bus which Edwina had boarded every morning to go to school for the past three years. The director, when confronted by P.W. about repaying the debt, had defaulted on the loan sometime during the spring of that year.

Minnie felt that a transfer was the correct thing to do in the face of the school's failure to repay the loan, together with Edwina's request for a change of schools over a year ago, and even more important, the need to curtail household expenses. She realized that no matter what P.W. said, available money was growing scarcer with P.W. continuing to invest in the camp. A transfer would solve several problems. P.W. would have converted the loan into Edwina's tuition to allow her to continue at the private school if he had been convinced that this was the best source of education for his little girl.

P.W. accepted Minnie's decision to remove Edwina from the private school, so that fall we three enrolled in Willard School together. Edwina, seven years old, was beginning fourth grade at Willard, an integrated school with an almost totally white teaching staff, and deeply embroiled in Mayor Thompson's thrust for the German vote in Chicago. There were a few black teachers, but they did not seem to want to be Black—one was quoted directly as saying such. They sought close association with the entrenched white teachers, fearing that something might go wrong with all of the racial turmoil encircling the school. After it became known that a majority of the children in the public school system were of German-born parents, the Mayor geared his appeal to the devaluation of the pro-British emphasis in curricula and tests, ordering all school books rewritten to reflect this bias. He was fanning his political ambitions with old unhealed scars of World War I. The Board of Education was the prime exhibit for his pro-German thrust, and Willard was one of the target schools for the change.

I don't remember Edwina complaining about the changes although she probably was feeling the differences strongly. The private school she had attended had been an all-black private school catering to upperclass Negro families, emphasizing an intense exposure of the children to black culture and black history. Edwina apparently took it all in stride and seemed to enjoy going along with us in the car; Bill rode up front with Daddy while Edwina and I rode in the back seat. Every morning Daddy drove us to school, then went on to his 49th Street office or to other business engagements. We had lost our second chauffeur, Frank, when he went to work in a garage as an automobile mechanic which he had always wanted to do. Daddy decided not to replace him. Daddy now drove us to and from school regularly, stopping to chat with the teachers on occasion.

A few months after school opened, an incident arose between Bill and Miss Zeller, his elderly spinster teacher, a recent arrival from Germany. I remember that day after school when Daddy asked in his usual way, "How was everything in school today, son?" as Bill climbed in the front seat of the car.

"Hmmmm, alright . . . I guess," Bill grumbled and scowled. P.W., for reasons of his own, did not question Bill further. He was always concerned about knowing Bill's thoughts, aware that Bill was outnumbered by his sisters at home. Talking and giggling in the back, Edwina and I barely noticed that Bill was unusually quiet in the car all the way home.

Entering the house, Bill ran upstairs to his room and closed the door. Hours passed before he came downstairs to be with us. After much prodding by Mother, he finally told us that his teacher, Miss Zeller, had attacked him in front of the entire classroom, and that she had hit him so hard with a ruler he had banged his head against the blackboard. Miss Zeller, a strict disciplinarian who tolerated no sign of childish pranks in the classroom, was referred to by the children at Willard as "the terror" because of her fierce temper. At this time, Bill, age 12, was still small for his years, and to compensate for his lack of height he would show off with smart answers. Daddy questioned Bill about his behavior "Were you rude, son?"

"No, dad. She is just a mean old woman," Bill explained.

Daddy surmised that Bill probably had displayed some of his childish wit to Miss Zeller while he was at the blackboard, provoking the teacher, who then tore into him. He calmly looked at Mother as he suggested, "Minnie, you had better find out more about this the first thing in the morning. If I go to see Miss Zeller about it, she may get the wrong impression at this point. I'll see her later about this incident, if you are not thoroughly satisfied with the answers you get from her."

From his chats with them, Daddy knew that the pro-German appeal within the school system was something that had been distressing all of the Willard School teachers. He realized that Miss Zeller, the sole German teacher at Willard, was least prepared to be embroiled in the political nationality background fight that was sweeping Chicago. His going to see her would only increase the stress she was undergoing as a new arrival in a foreign country which had set her up as a scapegoat for the other teachers as well as the students who resented the aggressive pro-Germanism in the school. P.W. knew something about the struggles of new arrivals in the City of Chicago, and therefore was not quick to overreact to this incident.

Mother went to school the following day to get the facts from the principal whom she knew well because of her P.T.A. participation. She learned all of the circumstances as she discussed the attack on Bill with the principal who called Miss Zeller into the conference. "Now, just what did happen?" questioned the principal.

"Villiam knew ze answer to zat problem . . . but he vanted to clown, to make ze children laugh. . ." Miss Zeller began her explanation to the principal in her heavy German accent.

As she talked, Minnie realized that Bill had provoked his teacher, that his pride had been injured by the blow with the ruler before the entire class; and that he had felt embarrassed. Minnie did not consider this incident as racial discrimination, but she was clear in stating that she would not tolerate a physical attack on her child. She told them, "Reason prevails in our home, and I expect Miss Zeller to control her annoyance like the other teachers do. When Bill is rude or contrary, your can tell his father when he comes to school to pick the children up in the afternoons, or tell me when I come to school for P.T.A. meetings." Minnie was frequently at the school, oftentimes too frequently for the children's liking.

Our parents felt less concerned about the incident after Bill

320

told them that Miss Zeller had begun to single him out for special achievements. Although Minnie remained close to our school setting now that we were all in Willard, it was easier for her to become more active in other community activities.

Over the years, the aloofness of the Negro elite leaders began to change. Minnie had always been involved in social affairs as a luminary in this elitist group that felt they had a stake in their community and sought recognition in Chicago as Americans, rather than as Negroes, with a distinct ethnic identity. Minnie was part of the Berean Baptist Church, the backbone of the social life, and one of the pioneers in defining the lines of social structure among the Negroes in Chicago of these early days. The new arrivals and the poor of the Black Belt may not have been aware of it, but Minnie never lost her sense of the difference between the "Old Settlers" of which she was one, and "the others." The presence of her brother's children during that brief visit did serve to reawaken her inherited class consciousness, yet, she too had begun to drift away from friends who were primarily interested in the arts as a means of self-indulgence.

She increasingly leaned towards groups committed to social and civic betterment of the community. This change may have been due to the rise of the Chicago Negro "shadies" in social and economic influence, or to P.W.'s preoccupation with "saving the race," or to Minnie's involvement in "saving the youth" in the community which sprang from her concern that our development be "proper." P.W. was pleased with the change in Minnie's interests and activities. Soon after his political campaign, she joined the Federated Club, a group of civic-minded women selected by the community because their life stood for something substantial. She would raise funds for various social services, the Phyllis Wheatley Home, and the Jacksonian Community Center, as a popular chairman of committees, urging membership, preparing programs, and inviting friends to increase their support. This new affiliation brought her into contact once again with Emily Brown, her former employee, whom she met at a fund-raising cake sale. Emily had been working as a caterer after P.W.'s factory closed. Minnie urged her to join the movement, to rekindle

321

their friendship, and to bring her talents and steady influences to bear on the community.

Early in 1928, Minnie's club member, Annie E. Oliver, spoke to her about joining a group of ladies being formed to commemorate Chicago's first settler, Jean Baptiste Point DeSaible, and to keep alive the memory of this man, a black fur trader who had been born in Haiti. Mrs. Oliver had made this discovery in her library research as a part of a committee selected by Mayor Thompson to plan for the Chicago World's Fair, projected for 1933. The movement to commemorate DeSaible's memory was timely. There was current agitation about the status of Haiti and plans for the World's Fair were being focused on commemorating the history of Chicago's rapid growth. The *Chicago Defender* had been full of the agitation about Haiti. Just a few weeks previous there had been a lengthy article about the Haitian people and how they resented having the United States Marines occupy the islands for the past decade and their distaste of the indefinite U.S. control.

Almost immediately, Minnie became an officer of the De Saible Society. The women made trips to City Hall, the Board of Education, and to the original site of DeSaible's log cabin on Michigan Avenue and Wacker Drive, accompanied by city officials. They located original sources of information and discussed their research and programs at regular meetings. Interestingly, although much was discovered relating to De Saible's life, the spelling of his name still lies in controversy. It is spelled "DeSaible," "duSable," "deSable" and "auSable." Their findings substantiated that DeSaible, a handsome, well-educated, French-speaking black man, who came from Haiti all the way up the Mississippi River, was the first proprietor in Chicago; that he built a log cabin in which he lived from 1779 until 1796 on the bank of the river where the wigwams of the Pottowatomy Indians stood, and that because of his prosperous trade with the Indians, the place "Checagow," meaning "place of the wild onion," was well-known to the Indian fur traders. He was the first to see the commercial potential of this location. Some accounts explained his prosperous fur trading and good repute on his father, a member of an ancient and noble French family, Dandonneau DeSaible, who travelled Canada and the American Northwest. We know nothing about his mother who was black. Other accounts reported that he spoke the Indian language, courted an Indian maiden named Kittihawa, and joined the Pottowatomy tribe in order to marry Kittihawa by whom he had two children. He travelled five hundred miles to have his marriage solemnized in the Catholic faith. The birth of his daughter is considered the first recorded birth in the Chicago area. The DeSaible home was built at the present site of the Wrigley Building and was 40 feet long and 22 feet wide. The furnishings were described as rather elaborate for the times: French walnut cabinet, large feather bed, mirrors, tables, chairs, and 23 large pictures. It was the scene of the first solemnized wedding, the first election, and the first session of court to be held in the Chicago area.

"The history books will have to be changed for our children in elementary school to learn that a Negro was Chicago's first settler and first citizen," Mrs. Oliver, their President, would say to the ladies. In reviewing her club activities with P.W., Minnie could be heard saying "It was not a white man as the history books would have you believe, it was a Negro, who first saw and used the possibilities of this location and had his ownership recorded legally." Sometimes she would comment, "Our children must learn these facts in school." Her awareness of the existing vacuum in Negro history increased as a result of her participation with this lively, spirited group of women who felt an intense kinship with this man who lived over a century ago and whose memory and acts would be immortalized by their efforts. Around the house we children heard a lot about the DeSaible Society, the Federated Women's Club, and the importance of being a "Federated Woman."

One day, we stopped by the assembly hall at our school to meet Mother. We were surprised to find her standing and speaking to the crowd at the P.T.A. meeting. Mother was good at lecturing us at home, but she always left any public speechmaking to Daddy. Now, here she was lecturing to a large crowd.

"How can you expect these children to have any self respect when they have to look at that mural on the wall every time they come into this assembly hall?" She was challenging the principal, teachers and parents who were there and her voice rang out in anger. "That mural!" she pointed up to it. "It is almost the full length of this assembly hall. There you see the many white ethnic groups and nationalities living together in America, portrayed in their native costumes, proudly walking and dancing with joy across this land of liberty. But," she paused for emphasis, "If you look in the corner of that mural, there is a little black boy, almost naked, down on his knees, almost crawling on his belly and grinning." She took a deep breath and continued.

"Now I ask you, what does that mural do to those black children whom you say do not know how to behave? What does it do to them every time they come into this assembly hall and see their ancestor portrayed as a little black idiot child, down on his knees and grinning? I'll tell you what it does to me. Your mural is an insult to me and my children. . . ."

We stood frozen at the Assembly door, wondering what had happened to our Mother to provoke this public display. She continued, "You of all people should know that respect is mutual. Respect is more important than money or love! That little crawling black boy down on his belly in that mural is a symbol of your lack of respect for the children in this school. Disrespect breeds disrespect! Mark my words . . . someday that little boy will develop a back-bone . . . he will stand up proudly with all the rest of the races and nationalities walking across America.

"Give these children a mural to inspire them, not to degrade them!" Minnie took her seat in the audience as the applause began. Suddenly she remembered she had wanted to announce that Chicago was about to honor its first settler, Jean Point DeSaible, and that the City Council had just appropriated $20,000 for the erection of a monument in his honor. She was a little annoyed with herself for having left this out, but she smiled in recognition of their applause. We ran to her and found her trembling from her outburst.

324

"You alright, Mother?" Bill asked, concerned about her even though she was smiling, looking around, and once again our calm sedate mother.

"You certainly are a woman on the go Miz Chavers," Mrs. Essie Wiggins, one of our more observant neighbors, commented one day after noticing Minnie rushing back and forth. "I don't see how you can do it, jus' turn off you' work round the house 'n' make all those meetin's 'n' children's rehearsals 'n' such." Since we moved on the block, she had tried hard to know Minnie better, but Minnie would just smile and say nothing. Mrs. Wiggins, the assistant precinct captain on the block, had come from Atlanta, Georgia twenty years earlier and had mingled in the local political circles, getting occasional jobs, and acting as boss of the judge and clerks at the polling place on election day. This gave her special status all year long and ready access to the local gossip. From the political point of view, she was the ideal assistant precinct captain: articulate, beautiful, and skillful in the use she made of her natural charm and talent to observe others, especially their weaknesses, and to pass these observations on to the proper person when it could be most useful. She kept making overtures for Minnie's friendship and could not understand Minnie's cordial though aloof responses.

Minnie held it against Mrs. Wiggins that she had not helped, when her help would have made a difference, during P.W.'s political campaign several years ago. Minnie had not forgotten that Mrs. Wiggins had spread her opinions around, letting it be known that she felt Mr. Chavers had not been in the neighborhood long enough to earn the right to ask people to work for him in the Second Ward; that it was popular for Whites to hold office in Congress and she did not trust colored reform candidates like Mr. Chavers.

But Minnie and Essie Wiggins were eventually drawn closer together when the neighbors decided to plan to improve conditions on the block. Mr. Bumpas, the retired Pullman porter who lived across the street and had a beautiful front yard, offered to fix up the neighborhood front gardens and worked long hours digging and replanting the flowers, making beautiful arrangements, cutting hedges and trimming

325

lawns to improve the appearance of the entire block. The idea of a block club came to Mr. Bumpas as a way he could find out what would inspire the neighbors to achieve a more beautiful block and increase the neighborly feeling. Dr. Garnes was the first to pick up on Mr. Bumpas' idea and he convinced Mrs. Wiggins to have the first meeting in her home in the fall of 1928. The Bowmans, Garnes, Bumpas' and Helen Nixon, daughter of Mr. and Mrs. Bowman, now married and the mother of two children, were early arrivals. Mr. Smith, the cranky neighbor with the two-flat buildings on the corner, came late, chiefly to protest the constant ball-playing by children near his property. P.W. and Minnie were unable to attend the first meeting. Since no one else volunteered, Dr. Garnes accepted the Presidency and Mrs. Wiggins agreed to be Vice-President; only property owners were eligible for membership. Thus, the Five Hundred Block Club was born.

P.W. and Minnie became active. The Keebles attended few meetings because they worked nights, but paid dues and got the news from different neighbors, especially Mrs. Wiggins, who made all the meetings. This neighborliness resulted in the children organizing their own "Willing Workers' Club." I was made President, Edwina, Secretary, my best friend Gwendolyn Keeble, Treasurer, and her sister Constance, Sergeant-at-arms. Helen Nixon's children, Bobby and Willetta, were allowed to come to meetings, but were too young to become members. We had to have some exclusions too. Gwendolyn and I were close even though we went to different schools. She was always in my house or I in hers, playing games, dressing up and entertaining each other with shared secrets. Our club prospered and within one month we staged a Halloween party, making enough money to buy a basket of groceries for a "poor family" which was eventually selected by Mother and Mrs. Keeble. I remember we delivered the basket the day before Thanksgiving and Daddy and Mother were proud of our spontaneous efforts to be helpful, recognizing this as an outgrowth of the good feeling on the block.

On December 6, 1928, Gwendolyn Keeble was killed instantly while on her way home from a music lesson. Constance usually went with her for the music lesson but did not feel well that afternoon. "Mr. Chavers . . . Oh Mr. Chavers, Gwendolyn has been killed," Mrs. Wiggins cried out dashing towards him as he climbed out of the car that evening. "The poor child was struck down by a wild car while crossing Forrestville Avenue, jus' around the corner!"

I was at the dining room table doing my homework as Daddy entered the house. He knew this would be a terrible blow to me. He patted me gently on the shoulder, then holding me in his arms, told me Gwendolyn just died and that I must be brave. I froze with panic and terror. This first encounter with the death of someone about whom I cared, and the utter finality of loss, completely immobilized me. I cried for three days, almost continuously, in my helplessness over the loss of my closest friend.

Our spray of flowers was prominently displayed at the funeral held in the parlor of the Keeble home. Daddy wanted all to know and understand what their little girl had meant to me . . . "Playmate" was all the ribbon on the big heart read, but that was enough for me and I loved my father even more for respecting the friendship Gwendolyn and I had shared. This tragedy brought the homeowners even closer and after this they watched over each other's children as well as caring for the property on the block.

The Coolidge era ended in March of 1929 with Herbert Hoover's inauguration. Alfred E. Smith, a Catholic, had been defeated for the presidency. Since P.W.'s political campaign we were interested in national politics and felt sad thinking that like Daddy, Al Smith had fought against tremendous odds. There was talk in our home about the changes that must someday come to this country for all people, unshackled by racial and religious bigotry, free to achieve self-realization to the limit of one's capacity. We were old enough to join in with this adult conversation and occasionally were permitted to do so. But there were other more subtle changes occurring which we were too young to realize.

Financial disaster was being forecast on the basis of too much borrowed money, easy credit, over production, and stock market speculation. America had been a nation of giddy consumers obsessed with reckless optimism since the mid-twenties. In an ever increasing manner, banks had supplied the money to brokers, manufacturers, and land speculators. Customers had bought merchandise, land and stock, everything on time. 10% down on the purchase price could buy anything: cars on the "pay-as-you-ride" basis, clothes and furniture on the "pay-as-you-wear" basis. Speculators bought land on margin, known as a "binder," which granted the "right-to-buy," the "right-to-develop," and the "right-to-sell" the right to buy at a profit. The binder took on value and with each land transaction it increased in value. Everybody was buying, but nobody owned, or had the responsibility of ownership . . . the whole economy was moving on an ever mounting pile of worthless paper . . . getting rich in a make-believe world. This Wall Street speculative fever and gambling psyche prevailed across the land and spread overseas, yet wages remained low and the economy lacked any governmental control or accountability to check the fever. But the disquieting news about the economy was beginning to surface in the spring of 1929.

P.W. was preparing for the forthcoming season at Camp Madrue when he read in the *Chicago Defender* that serious changes were taking place in the Black Belt as firms were firing more and more of their Negro employees. Because of this, P.W. had to wait for the rent from more of his tenants for longer periods of time. This brought his concern about the economy a little closer to home. He knew that growing unemployment in the ghetto was a warning of the possibility that the country was financially shaky; Blacks were the first to be fired when money was tight . . . Besides providing the cheap labor, the backbone of the American economy, Blacks were the barometer of the economy. The growing unemployment in the Black Belt was indeed the first symptom of the nation's failing economic health.

For us children, everything was going along as usual. Bill graduated from Willard and was now attending the intellectually elite Hyde Park High School. I was enjoying an especially happy year with my favorite teacher, Mrs. Ora Morrow, who had been Bill's teacher and had recognized his

YOUR GENEROSITY WILL BE OF GREAT BENEFIT TO THE COLORED SCHOOL CHILDREN OF CHICAGO

AN OUNCE OF PREVENTION IS WORTH A POUND OF CURE

CAPT. WM. PARKER
Past Patriotic Commander of the Spanish American War Veterans Camp Commander.

Camp Madrue outdoor life society is advocating and promoting the great benefits that will accrue to the underprivileged youth of our race by giving attention to their needs when it will do them the most good. The "gang" life of Chicago paints the picture.

DANGER LINE
By G. W. DIXON

We reprint from The Chicago Tribune, March 24, 1929, the following statement, according to George W. Dixon, President of the Chicago Boys' Week Federation. "Statistics show that approximately 85 percent of Chicago's crime is committed by boys under 21 years of age," Mr. Dixon said yesterday. "It costs taxpayers about $14,000,000 to maintain the police, court, and jail machinery. Of this amount, therefore, nearly $12,-000,000 is due to juvenile crime. These youthful criminals are at the age when corrective influence would be effective, if intelligently applied, in four-fifths of the cases, thus saving the city $10,000,000.

Promotes Good Citizenship

"One dollar spent in giving leadership and opportunity to underprivileged boys will, in the long run, save two or three dollars required for capture and punishment after neglected boys become criminals. In addition, priceless good citizenship is also saved."

The old maxim is as true today as it ever was and "an ounce of prevention is worth a pound of cure." Help us to teach the love of soil and the dignity of labor to our youth; to teach him respect for the flag and love of country, and to mold his character higher than the "gang" life of Chicago, which welcomes him with open arms.

HELP NOW!

We will need $25,000.00 to carry out our present program to give 2,000 colored school boys and girls a two-weeks' vacation.

The boys and girls eligible are from the ages of seven to fourteen. The children who are to be the beneficiaries of your generosity are chosen by the public school teachers in the various schools, and the civic leaders in the various city organizations, and they are made to understand that this outing comes to them as a premium in recognition of their school records.

Please mail in your subscription at once.

We thank you very kindly for your favorable consideration of this effort.

Motor Route to Camp Madrue

Chicago—West on Milwaukee Avenue to Route 19

Niles Center—Take 42-A to 41-U. S. Continue through Milwaukee to Fond du Lac and Oshkosh to Route 26 to New London, Wittenberg Antigo to Elcho 5 miles Northeast to Camp Madrue.

By Rail—Northwestern Railway from Chicago to Elcho, Wisconsin. to our property about five miles from the station. Bus to Camp Madrue.

CAMP OUTFIT

Each one will be required to take—
2 blankets
1 pillow
1 tin plate and cup
1 knife, fork and spoon
Everyday clothing for camp life for girls.

RATES:

BOARD and LODGING

Children, 7 to 11 years—
Per week . . .	$5.00
Adults—Per week .	9.00
Visitors—Per day .	1.50

Cottages extra.
Round trip bus—
Children . . .	5.00
Adults	7.00

CAMP OPENS
Tuesday, June 25, 1929

CAMP ACTIVITIES	Recreational Summer School.	Woodwork.	Credits earned at Camp Madrue will be accepted
	Educational Chautauqua.	Poultry Raising.	on the same basis as those in any other summer
	Domestic Science.	Botany, Farming.	school.

Motor route to Camp, 1929

keen intellect. She was my first black teacher and a kindly soft-spoken woman who lived around the corner from us. There was something comforting about seeing her on the street, or being able to run into her house on occasion. Bill and her son played in the street together. For me, she unified

329

the two worlds of home and school which had previously been so divided.

When school closed, we went off to camp for the entire summer again. Most of the children now left after their brief two week vacations. A small core of children, mainly from dancing school, stayed the summer with us. Each year, P.W.'s camp promotion would bring more requests for scholarships from needy children whose pleading letters only served to sustain his conviction about the importance of the camp movement to developing youngsters.

The summer of 1929 passed quickly. The forests and star-filled nights surrounded us with their deep quietude and beauty. Vera, now pardoned and reinstated into the family milieu, was there for the two months and the beloved Rebecca also assisted us at the camp. P.W. visited less frequently, but he arranged to spend the final week with us. In the big tent, on the last night, we children sang and danced in our prettiest recital costumes for our country neighbors who saw one another infrequently in this sparsely populated country. They enjoyed each other's company and bid farewell to us as they had done over the past four years. The farewell party had become a tradition. After our presentation we square-danced with the young, awkward farmers and we laughed together about our many experiences. The warmth was genuine and plentiful. Packed for the trip, except for the costumes we were wearing, we would be heading south the next morning to Chicago and school.

We children went to bed while our neighbors lingered to talk to P.W. and Minnie; their voices lulling us to sleep. I was the last to doze off as my curiosity and excitement over Daddy being with us during this week kept my eyes open long after the other girls stopped chattering and giggling, succumbing to sleep. I lay staring at a tiny hole in the ceiling of the tent; the bright moonlight made it into my private little star that shifted slightly from time to time as the sumer breeze wafted in and gently rocked the canvas. I remember having paused and fallen silent several times during our frantic last minute activities on this happy day; it had always been so when Daddy was around. I remember stopping and looking up at him lovingly, and then quizzically, several times. The last thoughts I had before the muted voices and the merry music of the grown-ups finally lulled me to sleep were of the long trip to Chicago and my being able to see Daddy everyday once more.

In the morning, we discovered that Daddy had had a massive cerebral hemorrhage. He had fallen to the floor of the big tent in the middle of a heated conversation. A doctor was hurriedly called and most of the neighbors stayed to find out if there was something they could do to help. He was now stretched out on the porch of the large tent, in a coma, breathing heavily. We walked out to Daddy and looked at him silently after Mother explained what had happened. We were shaking with fright. I don't remember crying. I think I was completely numbed by the sight of my father, lying there breathing so heavily, incapable of moving his body as he struggled for each breath. Mother rallied herself enough to make the necessary decisions about how the camp was to be left. The farmers came over early that morning to help. Shortly after noon, the big bus was loaded up with Vera in charge to see the children home safely, all except the Chavers children. We remained behind with Rebecca, looking around sadly at what had been our happy playground, now deserted. We were lost in our feelings of helplessness.

Several hours after the bus left, Daddy regained consciousness and was moved on a stretcher to Farmer King's home. Mother went with him while Rebecca stayed with us at the lonely campsite and later took us to the home of the Switzers, an elderly couple who lived down the road in an old frame house. She left us there and immediately went to join Mother at Farmer King's place. The Switzers were friendly, and welcomed us to their home. Mrs. Switzer was toothless and laughed frequently, sometimes without reason. Mr. Switzer smelled of hay and tobacco. After dinner, which we had scarcely eaten because of our concern for Daddy, we went to sleep. Edwina and I slept in a small bed and Bill slept on the floor near us. Staying in the home of strangers for the first time in our lives, I could not feel confortable. Daddy's condition continued to be grave. Eventually it was decided that Rebecca would remain with Mother in the King home to help watch over Daddy and we would return to Chicago to be met by a cousin at the railroad station.

As we neared Chicago on that long ride, we began to talk, perhaps the steady unchanging rhythm of the train lulled our fears.

"Do you remember when we went to Washington?" asked Bill.

"What about it?" I asked flatly, still looking out the window.

"Don't you remember we met the President in the White House?" Bill persisted, trying to cheer us up. As he talked on, I felt better and began to listen. "We met the President," Bill smiled and went on. "There were hundreds of people standing in that long line and the East Room was painted green."

"Yeah . . . I guess I do."

"Daddy said . . .'This is my son and he is going to be the first colored president'," continued Bill.

"Wasn't he the President who was in that Teapot Dome scandal?" I asked.

"That's what the newspapers said," responded Bill.

Suddenly we grew quiet, our thoughts and fears now overcame us again. The Switzers were very good to us, generously sharing their home and the discomforts had helped us avoid talking too much about our worry over Daddy and what would become of us now. In that train on our way to our Cousin's home, we again felt frightened and abandoned.

Cousin Madrue and Cousin John, her husband, and their two children, Ted and Hugh, met us at the railroad station. Riding in their car to their Morgan Park home, Cousin Madrue seemed genuinely happy, but there was something forbidding about Cousin John. He talked very little to his wife and children, and we later noticed that he never looked at us. We stayed in Cousin Madrue's home for several months, but we never got used to the silence which was so different from the atmosphere in our home, always bustling with activity, conversation, music, dancing, and confusion. Some of the silence may have been due to Cousin John's real worries; unemployment had struck many of his neighbors and customers. He was a real estate broker and land speculator, like Daddy, involved in land promotion in Morgan Park, the valley section of Beverly Hills where the rich lived. Their servants, and some aspiring factory workers in Chicago, were beginning to purchase land and build homes through Cousin John's real estate promotion. It was while we sojourned at his house that news reached us that the stock market had finally collapsed completely on Thursday, October 24, 1929. The bottom fell out, pulling everything else down with it. As a child, this bit of news which seemed to occupy adult minds rather feverishly, filtered through me without much impact. The collapse of my father was my total concern; it signaled the close of childhood for me.

Cousin Madrue enrolled us in school and taught us how to travel to Willard School via the Cottage Grove Street car, a very long, monotonous ride so early in the morning. I remember enjoying our young cousins, Ted and Hugh, with their constant whispering to us whenever Cousin John was in the house. The days dragged on slowly until at last, by mid-November, we were reunited in our home on 42nd Place. Cousin Madrue and Cousin John wanted to handle the reunion as painlessly as possible, but there was no escape; our Daddy was not the same.

P.W. was still bedfast. Minnie had stayed in Wisconsin until he had recovered sufficiently to be moved by stretcher and to take the same long, slow train ride, still unable to talk. We children tried to help Mother by studying hard and by tip-toeing and whispering around the house when we felt it was best; our experience at Cousin John's was good preparation for us after all.

Gradually strength returned to P.W., first his speech, then locomotion, until at last he was able to limp around the house and eventually even go up and down the stairs unassisted. But Minnie became more tense. His constant limping and dragging of the right foot, his clumsy groping and his persistent massaging of his right arm to hasten the return of circulation, only served to deepen Minnie's irritation. Mrs.

Wiggins, who knew what it was to care for a sick husband, had managed to keep hers working on a "good paying bricklayer's job" even with his "bad stomach." At last she had something in common with Minnie who now listened to the advice she offered.

I remember resenting Mother's attitude toward Daddy's efforts to get well. Somehow I felt she was avoiding him. To me he was the same Daddy he'd always been. His eyes still brightened as he spoke to us, never looking over us, as Cousin John did. Even if his right leg did drag, it was his. I could sometimes sense his determination to recapture his former strength and overcome the paralysis which still engulfed him. "Mind over matter," he would say as he exercised up and down the stairs and around the house, enjoying each minor return of his former power and strength. He would rub his right arm vigorously and exercise to limber up his fingers for a long time while I watched, but after his comment, he would smile at me and move away. This was the crushing part for him; it was what drove him to keep trying. He was our giant, our hero . . . and now every glance, every expression on the faces of his children, told him he was limited.

As P.W.'s strength gradually returned, it was not too surprising that he began to think of taking a trip somewhere, to seek out new opportunities and get out of the confined situation he was in. He also wanted to release Minnie from some of the burdens that overwhelmed her.

Nellie wrote to Minnie regularly after P.W.'s stroke, rekindling their old relationship. Minnie's spinster sister, once a school teacher in Bordentown, knew how to be effective if she wanted to be helpful. Nellie had been busy all winter making contacts in New York for P.W., especially after she learned that Reverend Roberts was living there. At least her letters made it sound that way. The same Reverend Roberts who was part of the Douglass National Bank, knowing P.W.'s abilities, could open channels for him to make a new start. Nellie wrote to Minnie suggesting that P.W. visit New York to try out new possibilities. All of this sparked hope in P.W. . . . . providing his life with some direction again, even if it was just a thread of a chance. Chicago was broke. The Great

Depression had ruined business. Even the regular city workers, teachers, firemen and policemen worked with payless days. P.W. was being threatened with foreclosure on the Camp Madrue property and he was hopeful of raising additional funds to keep it going now that he was stronger.

Roberts was a promoter and would know others who were. P.W. was grasping at straws, taking more than the usual calculated risks, especially with his health, but he felt he had to go. He felt that any plan, even a poor one, was better than none. Minnie feared for his health in attempting to make this trip alone after such a devastating illness. She no longer had confidence in Nellie's promises as her experiences with Nellie had taught her that you could always count on something going wrong somewhere, but she went along with his plans because she knew he needed the purpose and meaning in his life; these plans were stirring hope in him once again. She approached the situation stoically with full awareness that she would have to deal with any disappointment that resulted from the trip. Early in March, 1930, P.W. left for New York.

As soon as Daddy left, Bill willingly assumed responsibility as man of the house, stoking the furnace, shovelling the snow, cleaning the porch, even cleaning the car, although no one used it now. The handy man had been dismissed. We could not determine how much our family's financial situation had changed. Edwina and I continued taking dance, dramatic art and piano lessons. Mother continued to remind us that "all things pass, but art alone endures." She arranged for me to teach dancing two evenings a week at the Willard School Community Center in the large kindergarten room with Edwina playing the piano and accompanying my student's efforts. Bill would play basketball in the gymnasium while we conducted dancing classes and Mother collected the fees and took attendance, but complained that I taught the class too much in each lesson.

"You teach them as much for 25¢ as it cost me $10 to have you learn," she would scold. "Don't give your knowledge away." Later, I opened a bank account at the Binga State Bank and this pleased her more than anything else I did. "You will make it in life, I can see that now, Madrue," she

335

would say, delighted that at least one of her training lectures hit its mark.

Then Bill offered to sell the *Chicago Defender* to make some money. Minnie thought about this for a long time. Instead of her first-born having a carefree childhood with all the fine education he needed for a solid future, he was now proposing to go out in the street and sell newspapers. She was already worried about her decision to let him go to the neighborhood high school, Wendell Phillips, even though thus far he was doing all right. She thought of the irony of fate. Bill would go out and begin selling newspapers just as P.W. before him had begun, in spite of her best efforts, not for the experience in growing up but out of his need to help his mother. Bill always wanted to be just like any of the boys in the neighborhood; he never wanted to be as special as P.W. and Minnie had hoped he would be. He liked it at his new school. Although the teachers at Phillips were pleased Bill was attending their school, he did not completely understand their attitude since he felt he never did anything special to please them. Eventually, Minnie went along with Bill's wish to sell newspapers, watching every week for his reaction, thinking that after he tried it for awhile he would decide to give it up.

"I've got to sell the *Defender,* Mother. I've got to make my own money now that Daddy is sick," he would insist. After he had tried it for awhile he explained further, "The really hard part is trying to sell the newspapers like the kids do who've been selling papers a long time. I've got to learn how to out-scream them in the street . . . how to throw my voice so people will look out the window and call me to buy my papers."

Minnie looked at Bill and her heart ached. She knew he was beginning the long struggle to achieve manhood and nothing in his childhood had prepared him for the way he now had to go. She realized her son had been sheltered, all of her children had been sheltered. She knew that P.W.'s illness was somehow robbing Bill of the companionship and protection he needed at this very important time in his life. He was 15 years old. "Yes, I agree, there is much for you to learn, son," she said as she let him go with her approval out into the roaring March blizzard.

Nellie was excited about P.W.'s arrival in New York. He did not appear disabled or impoverished as she feared he might. The evening of his arrival, they talked a long time in the living room of her apartment. "He has changed, become thinner, but he's still dreaming the same dreams," she said to herself as he spoke of what he hoped to do while visiting in New York.

P.W. went on at length about his ideas of staging a national contest between colored children in different cities to raise funds for the camp. With the proper social sponsorship, perhaps an intercity social club like the New York Girls Friends, founded a few years prior, and the proper financier to translate his ideas into action, he could stage his contest finals in Town Hall. With the aid of radio announcements and good newspaper coverage, he felt confident this would move quickly in time for the opening of Camp Madrue early in July. As he talked on, Nellie thrilled at being in on his planning. She was thinking that she could take him to church and show him off to her Ladies Club even though he didn't look as prosperous as he once did. She felt more comfortable in his presence now than she used to, but she couldn't decide if she liked this.

Before the end of the week, she realized P.W. was no longer his former self. He no longer looked like somebody big and important, nor did he carry himself as a moving force, a physically influential person certain of his prowess. The old strength had gone out of him and she began to fear he might grow comfortable in her home and become dependent on her. P.W. decided to make the most of Nellie's eccentricities while he was in her home. He admired her purposefulness, thrift and singlemindedness. Regarding her previous association with his persecutors in the "Creditor's Petition," he felt she was merely misguided. "If only she could point her compass differently," he often thought, "What a boom such tenacity would be."

Nellie had reneged on her promise to help Elisabeth finish

Columbia University. Petrita and Elisabeth left Nellie's house with Dickie after realizing the terrible price demanded for her help: tolerating her stinginess, her badgering, her gossiping with neighbors in the coop apartment, and general obtrusive nosiness. Elisabeth became ill and went off to Virginia where she could regain her health, teach school, and look up her father's family. Petrita firmly decided which path to take toward her identity following Nellie's atrocious behavior and the failure of her American Negro husband to communicate with her in any way. She gravitated toward the small Filipino community in New York and took a job in the garment industry utilizing her skills in the fine arts of Phillippine embroidery. After divorcing her American husband she married a Filipino.

When P.W. arrived, Nellie attempted to mend the break by calling Petrita. Although three years had passed since the final outburst, Petrita immediately set aside any reservations she had about seeing Nellie again, and rushed over to see "Uncle Chavers." Surprisingly, the visit was pleasant. Nellie was at her best, solicitous about providing food, tea, and chuckling like a hen over the wellbeing of Petrita's new husband and the success of his podiatry practice. They talked of Elisabeth who would be returning to New York soon, after having her fill of blatant segregation in the South. Petrita didn't visit Elisabeth in Virginia because she felt the social customs would be unbearable. Nellie spent most of the time between the kitchen and the parlor, thus minimizing any discomfort Petrita might feel. P.W. was relieved that the visit went along so well after hearing Nellie's account of the troubles she had with Petrita and Elisabeth. Petrita's gracious style certainly reminded him of Minnie. He felt this character trait, in contrast with Nellie's brusqueness, was the main contributor to the breach between the two women.

A week later, Elisabeth returned from Virginia and immediately went to see P.W. She told of the severe illness she contracted on her arrival in New York three years earlier and the doctor's advice to go South as a means of easing her physical and emotional strain. Unlike Petrita, she could not move as comfortably in the same Filipino group because of her physical appearance and her strong identification with her father and his lineage. P.W. was pleased to hear that she felt at ease in Virginia among Minnie's family and friends of color. She left Dickie in Danville to visit longer with the Bannisters.

When P.W. finally located Roberts, he was shocked to see him a frail, grey, balding man, just a shadow of his former self, coughing, swallowing and grasping for breath throughout their visit. "I've been unable to preach for the past ten months because of poor health. My wife is pretty bitter about my sickness, working to support both of us . . . an awful blow to me, P.W.," explained Roberts. He seemed genuinely happy to see a familiar face from Chicago. After the initial amenities, P.W. wanted to talk about his new idea, his search for sponsors to ensure the future of Camp Madrue, but he was drawn into Roberts compelling need to talk about the bank.

"I'm glad you are here in New York and proud you came to see me," Roberts repeated. "I have wanted to talk with you, by yourself, for a long time. I keep thinking backward, not forward."

"I have been ill too, Reverend," P.W. responded but did not dwell on it.

"I have had bronchial asthma ever since we moved here four years ago, and now emphysema is setting in," Roberts continued, meanwhile coughing and swallowing painfully. "I'm just a 'has-been,' P.W. That's what my wife keeps telling me."

P.W. knew what illness could do to a man's hopes and his self-esteem, but he decided that maybe the change in Roberts was for the better in some ways; the old arrogance and pompousness were gone. "We had our bad days," responded P.W., compassion overcoming him, "but that doesn't mean it's over for us."

"That's just like you, P.W., to keep on pushing," said Roberts, then added, "You know P.W., I've been wanting to ask you for a long time about those early days when we were starting the bank in Chicago . . . what a mess you put me in."

"How can you say that? I am the one who endured the

attacks on my integrity and reputation, and at a terrible cost to my family." P.W. was becoming annoyed with Roberts, but he didn't want to jeopardize any possibility of gaining Robert's help by letting his feeling show. He tried to change the subject but Roberts interrupted. "You were about to make a calamity of the bank when Owens stepped in with the money."

Suddenly P.W. realized that Roberts hadn't really changed at all. It was just that opportunities to continue to exploit others had now disappeared. "As long as you want to go over it Reverend, why did you involve me in a completely false bankruptcy charge?"

"I guess we were all after different things back in those days," Roberts reminisced. "Your way of sticking to the rules was ruining the whole thing. You would not play along."

P.W. was startled at the pathetic picture Roberts conveyed to him, then rubbed his right hand to stir circulation as he searched for a response. "I'll never understand why you and Morris turned on me after all the work I put into creating the bank," returned P.W., sick at the thought of what happened to his hopes for the bank. "It was my idea, my dream, my hard work, and my time taken from my family as well as my money that went into it. You know I paid for the bank fixtures and financed those out of town trips from my personal funds. You all knew, but especially you knew, that I put much more into it than anybody else." There was more P.W. could say about what he felt but held back and simply added, "What is it you want me to know that I don't already know about the shameful betrayal I lived through with the men in whom I misplaced my trust?"

"You should have taken that vice-presidency . . . None of us really wanted Owens . . . We were about to repudiate him when you filed that Federal suit to investigate the legality of the bank. When you did that, you forced us to back down about Owens," returned Roberts.

"Are you finished?" questioned P.W.

"No . . . I hear from Morris that there is unrest on the Board." Roberts was gasping for breath now but he was determined to share his thoughts with P.W. "Owens has been

340

in hot water with his associates for several years . . . I knew it would come to this . . . They are accusing him of bad judgment, bad leadership, bad management, and the rumor is going around that top-heavy expenses are wiping out the bank's surplus altogether. Three board members have resigned. Did you know about the companies he started after he got you out?" Roberts continued, stopping to catch his breath.

P.W. sat silently for a moment, then backing away from this conversation, he calmly said, "I have been too busy myself to follow Owens and the bank."

"Well the Board got fed up . . ."

"Why are you telling me all this?" interrupted P.W. "I left that charter with you men so you could run the bank soundly. My only concern was that you run it with some regard for the community people, the depositors." P.W. had forced himself to listen to Roberts long enough, now the old hurt was coming back and he simply did not want to hear anymore about the bank or anyone connected with its early days. He could see the struggle Roberts was having with himself and decided to hold on a little longer in the hope that the afternoon would not be a complete waste.

Roberts squinted his eyes, taking in P.W.'s obvious irritation, but as soon as he caught his breath, he started up again, determined to get it all out. "Well P.W., I am glad I am not there now, it must be worse. You should have mixed around with us more . . . we needed you . . . we really did, and if you had mixed with us, you would have known how we really felt about Owens."

"You could have reached me if you wanted to. You knew what I was doing, especially when I was running for Congress . . . You knew I was crusading for the protection of the small bank depositors. All of you knew what I stood for, what I still stand for." P.W. no longer cared whether or not he ruined the afternoon, he wanted Roberts to realize once and for all that his coming there did not mean he would compromise his principles; Roberts had succeeded in bringing back the past. P.W. shook his head and continued, "The way I see it, a bank represents stability, confidence, faith and hope for the people who live and work in a community. As in a family,

341

someone has got to make sacrifices, and the more people involved in making the sacrifices, the brighter the future for all . . . That is what I hoped for all these years. If we are someday to be a strong people, we must make sacrifices for each other. We have got to think beyond our own little lives . . . we must be creative and productive . . . we must put our resources in motion for the benefit of all our people of color. Larceny, shady deals, and double-crosses are not for the leaders of a people with a future." P.W. did not want to discuss individuals; this was never his way.

"That's what I liked about you, P.W." responded Roberts, smiling. "You always had so much class and such strong character . . . but it's over for both of us, P.W."

"Speak for yourself, Reverend," returned P.W. sharply. "I came here today to talk about a new idea I have."

"That's you P.W., never say die!"

"You should know that Roberts. You're the preacher, not me." P.W. smiled and went on, "I am looking for sponsors for my summer camp and I thought perhaps you might make some connections for me."

Shaking his head now, Roberts leaned back away from P.W. and slumped helplessly in his chair. "I've been a big disappointment to these New York people," he responded.

"Too bad, I have some leads from my Chicago contacts and I thought you might have some additional connections. My time in New York is limited."

"You may try some leads I have, but it won't help to mention me," Roberts went into a long coughing siege.

P.W. knew he had exhausted himself with their conversation and he thought, "What's the use?" But he said instead, "I'll take the names and let you know how I make out with these people."

On the way back to Nellie's apartment, P.W. reviewed how he misguessed their moves in the bankruptcy charge. They had seen him as a powerful force, even more effective than he realized. The afternoon had not been a complete waste, he now knew how far behind him all of this was. Also, he could see their machinations much more clearly and was glad he no longer concerned himself with any of those people. He felt

342

there was a lot to be thankful for; there was the future and he had things to do.

Nothing was developing from Roberts' leads but those from the Chicago lists brought him in contact with the Town Hall officials and others with whom he met in preparation for the nationwide camp benefit show he planned. He spoke to Nellie about his negotiations but noticed she grew less interested. Beneath her façade of hospitality she was becoming annoyed with P.W., feeling he was using her home to advance his Chicago interest rather than planning to set down stakes and move his family to New York. P.W. knew that Nellie had made a tremendous effort to be friendly, in the beginning, while he stayed in her home. He also knew it was her pattern to shift her feelings about among different relatives because the closer she came to any of them, the more frightened she became. He gradually ceased to speak with her about his business activities. He mentioned his concern about Minnie and the children, how much he missed them, and his thoughts about how they might be getting along without him. Paradoxically, Nellie began to resent his silence about his daily activities and feared that he might get sick again while in her home.

One day when they were talking, she jokingly added that she would like to have me stay on in New York after the Town Hall benefit was over. "Helen Madrue is my favorite, you know," she added. Nellie wrote to Minnie about the possibility, saying P.W. had presented no objections and this might even help relieve Minnie's burdens if things continued as they had for the past six months. She also hinted that she had reason to feel that whatever P.W. had came to New York to accomplish, was not working out as he had hoped.

P.W. was in New York almost two months before he finally had dinner with Petrita, her new husband Dolph and Elisabeth. Dolph was a brown skinned Filipino, plump, pleasant, and assertive. P.W. could see that Petrita was happy in her new apartment as she went about preparing the elaborate Filipino dinner. She had looked forward eagerly to "Uncle

343

Chavers" visit. Dolph was comfortable with P.W. and spoke freely of his humble beginnings in the Philippines, working as a deck hand on a ship, crossing the Pacific some ten years ago to get to America, his hardships in getting located in New York, of finding work as a bus boy, and going to night school. After enrolling in Chiropractic School, he made his way into the Filipino West Side social set around Columbia University's International House, where he met Petrita . . . They had been married almost one year. Petrita was pleased by the way he spoke of her help, understanding, and financial cooperation in making his plans come through faster. P.W. felt that Dolph knew where he was heading and that Petrita had a husband who would amount to something now.

Turning to Elisabeth, P.W. asked, "Now, tell me about your plans." Before Elisabeth could answer, Petrita raised a question, "Have you seen any of the good shows downtown, Uncle Chavers?" She was so excited that Uncle Chavers and Dolph liked each other, she wanted to prolong their discussion.

"I'm afraid not, not this trip." P.W. answered. "I am thinking about returning to Chicago soon, children." Then he told them that his work in New York would soon be over, but he would be returning again for the camp benefit in late June. "I have set up a few more appointments but the rest of my affairs here I can handle by correspondence."

"Oh Uncle Chavers, we would have invited you over much sooner if we knew you were going back to Chicago so soon." Petrita's voice revealed her disappointment.

"How can I enjoy New York without Minnie? Then, too, you know how Nellie is, she's getting on my nerves . . . I don't want to sound ungrateful to her," P.W. smiled.

"Oh yes, we know about her alright," answered Petrita quickly.

"It's not that she's been mean, it's just that, you might say, she is not used to having a man around the house. My cigar smoking, my way of clearing my throat, even the way I gargle in the morning disturbs her, but when I speak of it, it sounds as though I don't appreciate her hospitality."

Petrita frowned; she didn't even want to think of Nellie.

344

"Uncle Chavers, you are so kind, how could anyone not be kind to you?"

"Well, I am homesick too. I want to go home," P.W. continued.

"If Aunt Nellie weren't so mean and stingy, you wouldn't be thinking of going home so soon, Uncle Chavers," Petrita insisted.

Elisabeth interrupted with, "I will visit Aunt Nellie occasionally after you leave, Uncle Chavers, for papa's sake. He always asks about her in his letters. When I was growing up and asked questions about his relatives in America, he would always mention his last memories of his little sisters Minnie and Nellie and how they were asleep in their beds the night he ran away."

"Someone has to keep in touch, and show an interest," responded P.W. He tried to move from the discussion about Nellie and her eccentricities, but thoughts of her continued to monopolize the converstaion. "Nellie hinted that she would like it if I were to re-establish here to get a new start, but I don't see it that way."

"Why not?" questioned Elisabeth. "That would be wonderful!"

"Minnie loves Chicago, her many friends and interests. There is nothing like that social life here . . . everybody is just a 'striver' in New York. Then, too, if I settled my family here, I would want to live in Harlem. There is no real business community in Harlem for colored people; there is no real social structure either." P.W. was thinking of how slowly his plans were moving in New York and how many contacts were necessary before he could get to some of the effective groups. "Oh, I like the port-town atmosphere," he went on. "It's rugged and I like it. But Minnie wouldn't and then there are the children."

"How soon will you be returning to Chicago?" Petrita asked after insisting P.W. accept the repayment of the train fare loan and realizing his plans were definite.

"About the end of the week," he answered. "Well, my money is running out too. I have to get back to look after my business there. You know you can't stay around Nellie without money," laughed P.W., attempting to take the edge off their disappointment.

Elisabeth felt she had had no chance to talk with Uncle Chavers about her concerns. Even on the long walk across town, Petrita insisted on walking with Uncle Chavers and she had to walk with Dolph. "The dinner was delicious, the conversation stimulating, and the company refreshing," commented P.W. as they approached Nellie's door. "Thank you for a lovely evening, children." P.W. shook Dolph's hand. "Take good care of your fine wife, young man!" he said, turning to go into Nellie's apartment alone.

15

The Rescue

Immediately on return to Chicago early in May, P.W. arranged for prominent speakers to assist him in broadcasting announcements over radio station WIBO about his "Camp for Colored Children" and the work of the Outdoor Life Society. Edwina and I found ourselves drawn into radio broadcasts with Daddy and were billed in the newspaper advertisements as "Mr. Chavers' daughters, Madrue age 12, Pianist, and Edwina age 10, Reader."

By mid-June, 1930, financial panic and rumors of further disaster in the Black Belt were flying thick and fast. Daddy was neglecting his health, overstepping the boundaries of his physical strength, and limping again. He had to realize that the response to his radio broadcasts and other camp promotion activities were insufficient; the Town Hall benefit would have to be cancelled. The Citizens Trust and Savings Bank, his staunchest supporter for years, was threatened by runs on their reserves. Between the poor response to his camp promotion and the squeeze on his major sponsor, he would be unable to open the camp. All that was left was how to make the announcements to the registrants, to his public, and how to handle this final blow with his children, which troubled him most. He no longer shared his thoughts and feelings with Minnie who immediately involved herself with our preparations for Madame Daley's Dramatic Art Recital when she learned the Town Hall benefit was cancelled.

In late June, Nellie arrived for my Willard School graduation. In some ways, her arrival was a relief. P.W. gathered the courage to explain to us children that he was not going to reopen the camp this year and tried to make it sound like a temporary change, but our lives had altered so in the past ten

347

months, since Daddy's illness, that we no longer expected things ever to be the same again. Aunt Nellie's presence did help to cushion the impact of the sad news. She and mother would take long walks together and hold deep conversations . . . Time and again she pressed Minnie that I be allowed to go to New York with her to relieve the family situation, implying that I was the one whom Minnie could most easily give up.

Eventually she gained my parents tentative permission to take me to New York. I told Mother I felt it would be fun to see Broadway and live in New York for awhile and I would find a way to get along with Aunt Nellie. Daddy had been to New York and I wanted to go where he was all the time he was away. The trip sounded like a great adventure, a new world would be opening up for me. Then P.W. began to present Minnie with second thoughts about my leaving home. "Nellie is difficult at times."

"Yes, but she will be able to give Madrue the guidance she needs right now," answered Minnie as she reminded him how happy the invitation had made me. My response resulted in Mother's feeling that this was the correct decision, not only for me, but for the entire family. "After all, Nellie has worked with adolescents, this is a time of great temptation," continued Minnie. "The only thing that troubles me about letting her go is that no one has been able to stand living with Nellie. She almost ruined John's children after promising so much," reflected Minnie.

"Those two months I spent with Nellie were a strain on me, and I'm an adult," Daddy commented. "I wouldn't want my little girl hurt by what Nellie might say or do. Nellie can be difficult, and Madrue is sensitive."

"What can we do about it now? Madrue is in there packing her trunk every spare moment."

Mother talked over some of their reservations with me and I promised I would be good in Aunt Nellie's home. "You will be proud of me, Mother, just wait and see." She smiled; confusion and doubt stirred in her as I pleaded with her not to change her mind.

Madrue graduating from Willard School, 1930

And so it was that Aunt Nellie left for New York immediately after my graduation and Madame Daley's recital with the understanding that I would follow shortly. It was a tearful Saturday morning in July when I boarded the train to New York to make that 28-hour trip alone. At the railroad station, I was overwhelmed with a great pain at the realization of actually leaving home alone at the age of 13 for the first time in my life. Daddy helped me onto the train as best he could and waved from the platform, with Bill and Edwina beside him, as Mother escorted me to my seat. Edwina cried hysterically as I looked out the train window and the tears that follow the separation of loved ones welled up in me and ran down my cheeks. Uncle George had made the arrangements for my ticket, saw to it that my luggage was labelled and handled properly, and sent a Western Union telegram to Aunt Nellie giving her the time and details of my arrival. Mother pinned a little sack of money in my bosom and severely cautioned me to watch out for anyone trying to be unnecessarily friendly and to ask the conductor for information if I had a question.

As the train pulled out of the station, I sat with my face pressed against the grimy glass of the coach window. Many hands were waving to me; then my eyes caught Mother's. She held them for a while and slowly waved back at me. Father was standing there beside her, just looking in my direction. Hot tears welled up in my eyes. I could see the last hand waving to me; I believed it to be Daddy's. I waved back at a sea of people and caught Father's eyes for a split-second.

I was numb with the sense of strangeness all about me, the rhythmic clicking and turning of the wheels speeding the train toward the great city, New York. This and this alone lulled me out of my fears until I again began to feel the thrill of expectation and excitement about the adventure that lay before me. The train blared out a long, loud whistle and I forced myself to look back toward Mother and Father, but I couldn't see them any longer. I closed my eyes, feeling the warm tears rolling down my face.

"So, my little girl is leaving me?" I recalled my Daddy saying as he had stood in the doorway watching me pack.

"Oh Daddy, don't say it that way! I'm not really leaving you, I'm just going to live in New York, just for a little while," I smiled back happily.

Now the train rushed onward.

The journey seemed endless. I slept fitfully through the night, not venturing to the diner for supper, my thoughts altering now and then, anticipating what was to come. The train pushed on past a sunset and a dawn. When the conductor announced "Harmon" I was sure he had said "Harlem," this word Daddy said many times. I ran off the train but saw only open space, no people around, then realized I had made a mistake. The conductor had been watching and rushed me back before the train moved again. "Little girl, I'll let you know when we get to Harlem," he said laughingly in answer to my question. After a long stretch, the landscape faded from fields to clusters of buildings as we entered the city limits of New York.

All of Mother's instructions about not talking to strangers remained with me, but I remembered none of her reminders about where Aunt Nellie would be waiting for me. "New York, the doorway to America is now opened to me!" I thought as I took my first step off the train at 125th Street. Two hours later I was still waiting in that busy station where strange people were rushing back and forth. I finally looked at the telephone book rack to locate Aunt Nellie's number, but I was bewildered by the sight of a whole row of telephone directories. "New York is many cities," I thought. It never occurred to me that my aunt was too parsimonious to have a telephone and Mother overlooked the possibility of my getting lost since she had given me explicit instructions. Finally I decided to reach my aunt's home on my own. Asking for directions, I was told to follow the numbers as she lived only five blocks away. Feeling by now like a thirteen-year old vagabond and looking around at my strange new world, I walked along 125th Street, dragging my luggage and passing the stores, to Madison Avenue. I followed the numbers, passing brownstone townhouses and the tall exclusive-looking apartment buildings surrounding Mt. Morris Park. Though I

351

was walking swiftly, I was impressed with the compact elegance of the neighborhood. Finally I reached my aunt's home.

The widow and son who roomed in my aunt's apartment welcomed me in and deposited me in the kitchen explaining that the parlor door was locked. Aunt Nellie had gone to Grand Central Station many hours ago to meet me. They warned me she would be furious. After they went into their room and locked the door, I sat quietly, feeling I was trapped in a house of locked doors until Aunt Nellie burst into the apartment. At first she was relieved that I was safe, sound and unharmed. Then her anger surfaced but it was directed at the Western Union Telegraph Company. I sat in her dark kitchen listening to her complain in great detail that Uncle George's telegram had not been delivered. She went to Grand Central Station not sure when I would finally arrive. She envisioned a tragedy befalling me so she called Chicago, which cost her a lot of money. She stormed about the poor service in the Harlem area. So many words were flying around the kitchen, I kept quiet, realizing that if I had remembered Mother's instruction to go to Grand Central, Aunt Nellie would have met me. But since Aunt Nellie was so pleased with my presence, I decided not to spoil her mood with this confession. Finally, she said she was too tired to cook, suggesting that we go to "Father Divine's Heaven." By this time I was prepared for most anything. I dragged along Seventh Avenue beside her, gazing around at the smart looking, well-dressed people. Aunt Nellie explained that on Sunday evening everybody dresses up to promenade up and down Seventh Avenue, to meet and socialize with everybody else. There was an excitement, gaiety, comaraderie and prosperity about it which I felt as we walked along, until we came to that strange place "Father Divine's Heaven."

I sat gazing at all of Father Divine's "angels" serving chicken and cabbage for 15¢ a plate, rushing back and forth in that huge, noisy church dining hall. Here the place swarmed with hungry people, thousands it seemed, all eager to get their plates full for 15¢. They kept saying "Peace . . . It's truly divine." Some spoke to my aunt, calling her "Sister Nellie." I promised Mother faithfully I would be good so I ate that horrible 15¢ dinner as best I could and then walked home with Aunt Nellie. I had come to the fabulous city of New York, the citadal of jazz and gaiety, laughter and rhythm, the home of "Shuffle Along," "Green Pastures," and of the "Cotton Club," only to have it begin in "Father Divine's Heaven!!

It was July and school was out. Aunt Nellie planned my days, verbally admonishing me to complete whatever duties she could think of on her way out the door to work. Before I went to play, I had her stockings to wash, the rice to pick and cook, the stove or ice box to clean, the water tray under the ice box to empty, and the long hallway to polish. Each day I had either forgotten something or "half-did" my assignment. "Minnie hasn't taught you how to do anything," she would comment. I was allowed to visit in the homes of only two children, hand-picked by my aunt. After awhile I grew bored by such restrictions, yet, in looking back, I realize my subsequent life was influenced by one, Barbara Watson, the daughter of James S. Watson, a West Indian, who the following year became New York's first Negro Municipal Judge. Through conversations with Barbara I developed an interest in being admitted to the high school she was attending, Hunter College High School, because of its special requirements of high scholarship and its emphasis on developing citizenship participation.

Although my aunt's restrictions depressed me, I refused to complain. One night she came into my room for a confidential "little talk."

"I've been worried about you, Helen." She began walking slowly towards me and rolling her eyes mischievously, still refusing to call me "Madrue."

"Why?" I asked innocently.

"You are so moody!" she charged.

"No I'm not, Aunt Nellie!" By now I knew I could not please her regardless of how hard I tried.

"You are so absent-minded," she continued.

"I try very hard to remember all of the chores you give me." I was not going to let her overlook my efforts.

"Minnie has not taught you how to do anything," she repeated.

I bristled; she was talking disparagingly about my Mother again. She observed my unspoken reaction and responded by moving closer, sitting on my bed.

"What I mean, Helen, is that maybe there is something bothering you," she started again.

"What do you mean?" I asked puzzled. If she understood that something was bothering me, she should have realized it was she. I gave her no reason to be worried; I took all her orders and restrictions uncomplainingly.

"Well, sometimes when little girls start letting little boys play with them, you know what little boys like to do, well, when little girls start letting little boys do things with them, they get sort of absentminded." She finally got it out, pinching her lips, squirming on the bed, rolling her eyes knowingly, and looking at me suspiciously. Curiously enough, her statement recalled Mother's lectures about the physical changes I could expect, but her tone and underlying suspicions contrasted vividly with my Mother's tender compassionate words. I was shocked and fell silent for a moment. Then I looked at her with anger and said, "I don't know what you're talkng about!"

Aunt Nellie left my room at once. The finality with which I had spoken ended our confidential chat, though it didn't end her suspicions. I had a fairly well-developed sense of self-worth for a 13 year old and while I was determined that I would show my aunt respect, I would not allow her to accuse me of misconduct when I tried so hard to please her in every way. Mother may not have taught me how to do housework, but she had taught me that "pretty is as pretty does" as the popular saying of the day went.

Early in August, Mother wrote that the Binga State Bank had closed, letting me know that I had lost the little money I had saved from my Willard School Community Center Dancing School. She added how proud she felt of my saving habit even though it ended this way. Actually, despair had swept through the Black Belt on July 31st when the state bank

354

examiner closed the doors of the Binga State Bank. It was the first bank in Chicago to be closed, but it was soon followed by many others. Jesse Binga had been the financial wizard of the community, emerging from meager beginnings as a peddler, around the turn of the century, and then amassing a real estate fortune of some 300 units of property in the Black Belt. He opened a private bank and then rose ever more swiftly after his marriage to the heiress of a $200,000 fortune, the sister of "Mushmouth Johnson," the foremost of Chicago's notorious black gambling lords. Law enforcement officers had rarely raided the place of "Mushmouth Johnson" where he made a fortune gambling in his State Street emporium in the late eighteen nineties. The elaborate Johnson-Binga wedding in 1912 had symbolized the arrival of Chicago Negro shadies into leadership position in the elite society of the Black Belt where Binga was to reign supreme for twenty years, especially after he reorganized his private bank into a state institution known as the Binga State Bank. His opinion was sought in all financial and social circles of the Black Belt. His endorsement had even been eagerly sought by P.W. in the early days of developing the Douglass National Bank because of his far-flung influence, which eventually included collaboration with Samuel Insull, the utility magnate, who was now too involved in trying to save his own financial empire and reputation to help Binga forstall the collapse of his bank in July.

Mother did not tell me that the despair crushing those who had over-mortgaged their property and the collapsing economy had sealed my father's fate. P.W. was busy straightening out his financial affairs, coping with threatened foreclosure of Camp Madrue and other holdings. Then, on August 5th, Stewart's Citizen's Trust and Savings Bank closed its doors after a half million dollar run on its reserves. With this, Daddy's equity in most of his real estate was wiped out. By September, charges of fraud and treachery were all over Chicago; the Black Belt community was dying.

That fall, I enrolled in the 9th grade of Julia Ward Howe Jr. High School in New York City, an all-girls-school across

Seventh Avenue from Aunt Nellie's home on 120th Street. Lower Harlem at that time was very ethnically diverse, predominately German Jewish, Irish, and Black (mostly new arrivals from the Islands). This was the time that Harlem was in transition, when Blacks were moving south from 136th Street. Landlords eagerly rented to them because they could get much higher rents than from Whites, although white residents attempted to stop the Black "invasion." Certain groups even went so far as to try to pass laws preventing Blacks from owning or renting property in Harlem. Banks were petitioned to cut off loans to homeowners and to speculators who sold or rented to Blacks. However, these efforts were unsuccessful and compared to Chicago, the atmosphere was quite calm and free of racial upheaval.

Perhaps Aunt Nellie was there the day I registered, but I don't remember her ever going to school with me. I felt very much alone in a strange atmosphere standing around waiting for some attention in the busy school clerk's office. She appeared harried and brusque as I timidly asked questions about enrolling myself. She could see that I was frightened by the constant stream of youngsters swarming in and out of the corridors around her office, competing for her attention. As I gave the identifying information, she commented in a reassuring way, "If you say you are from Puerto Rico, getting started here may be easier for you. After all, you are beginning in the final year of this school." I was puzzled. I didn't know what had prompted the clerk to make such a remark as I hadn't hesitated about giving information. Again I felt my sense of self-worth was being challenged, and this time by a stranger. Bristling with indignation, I answered "I can't do that. You are asking me to deny my father. I was born in Columbus, Ohio and that's the way the record must read."

I often wondered if she was trying to tell me that racism prevailed in that school. But I was never to know from my own experiences because the students and teachers quickly absorbed me into the friendly atmosphere of the all-girl school, a new and exciting educational experience for me with the changing of class rooms, subjects and teachers. I was delighted with the curiosity I provoked in some of my classmates. They seemed thrilled to think of my coming from Chicago and assumed that I was far more worldly than I really was, a message I got when the comment was passed one day, "Oh, you're from Chicago, that's Al Capone's Town." I didn't confess that I really did not know he owned the town, but I realized that his fame added to their interest in me. Even though there must have been a quality of innocence about my responses to my new classmates, they were pleasant and friendly and seemed to genuinely welcome new experiences and new people, one of which I represented. Before long, I wrote home telling how pleased I was with my new school and friends.

In the middle of the general collapse, P.W. and Minnie were receiving my letters now asking that they send Edwina to join me in New York. All through September P.W. had kept busy. The Board of Directors of the defunct Binga Bank consulted with him about developing a plan for reopening the bank and organizing mass rallies of the Binga depositors and thousands of depositors of other banks. Once again he was the community motivator, talking about the "great struggle," "the sacrifices needed," and "the Negro shouldering greater responsibilities for his fate." He was everywhere setting up committees, reliving his experiences of ten years ago except that now he was disabled and poorer financially. The same words came forth, but they took greater effort. There were other differences too. At night, when he returned home, he would tell Minnie about the day's events, but he would stop short when it came to speaking of his hopes. He could not expect her to listen now, fearing she might remind him he was too disabled to be as effective as he once was. But he was greatful to Minnie, even during her most irritating moods, because she had remained a concerned wife and a devoted mother to his children. He appreciated these qualities even more when he read in the *Chicago Defender*, early in October, that Binga's wife was filing a petition in Probate Court charging Binga with being feeble-minded and incompetent and requesting that a conservator be appointed to handle the affairs of his estate.

357

My letters from New York telling how well I was doing in school but giving suggestions of how lonesome I was, were eating away at Minnie. She could not reconcile herself to the disaster all around. Her fears for Bill mounted each day as he went off to Phillips High School. He mingled with so many dangerous and rowdy children, was beginning to be more secretive, and was taking on some of their mannerisms, such as swearing under his breath. She moved about the house, outwardly calm, but deeply concerned about facing the winter with her family and P.W. with their assets down to a minimum. Minnie conversed with P.W. as little as possible now, wanting to spare him the anguish she felt so keenly. It did help some that George dropped in more frequently, yet Minnie knew it would not be long before George would be leaving for his annual trip South. She remained immersed in her own helplessness. A silence grew between them which was alien to both them and their children. Finally, because of their financial pressure, P.W. and Minnie sent Bill, the most provocative of the three of us, to New York instead of Edwina. He arrived during the day when I was at home and Aunt Nellie was at work.

"Mother made another error!" I thought as I looked at him standing in the doorway weary from his bus ride to New York. But I was delighted to see him and ushered him quickly into the kitchen where we talked about Chicago. I told him of my new school, of how happy I was with my new friends, many of whom were from different countries, and assured him he could be happy here too. I wanted Bill to know all about the good things in New York first, then I told him that getting along with Aunt Nellie was not easy but that I had found the best way to handle her was to keep quiet when she got angry.

"Just don't answer her back," I repeated, trying to prepare him for the inevitable encounter.

"I'll make out O.K., sis, don't worry about me," he said with a weary smile while slouched over the kitchen table, dismissing my warning with a wave of the hand. But my fears soon became real. Bill was immediately entered into DeWitt Clinton High School, a new all-boys school in the far north Bronx, requiring him to travel two hours a day. One week after his arrival, Aunt Nellie found a job for him across the street delivering Chinese Laundry for $3 per week. She believed in work for adolescent boys, knowing that this was one way to keep them out of mischief.

With two adolescents in her home, Nellie ran the place like a boarding school. Lights out at nine o'clock became the rule, leaving Bill little time to study after making his laundry deliveries. Loud quarrels began between Aunt Nellie and Bill about his earnings, his grades in school, in fact, about everything Bill did, or did not do. Because of the constant bickering, the widow threatened to move away as the confusion was affecting her son. At one point, late in November, Bill became so angry that he chased Aunt Nellie around the apartment with a broom and we both wrote to Chicago giving our respective versions of these fierce clashes.

P.W. and Minnie were increasingly troubled by each letter they received. Edwina, lonely for both of us now, withdrew even more from our parents, spending long hours alone in her room brooding and day dreaming. The distress caused by constant financial crisis kept P.W. busy and out of the house most of the day, but at night he pondered over each facet of the family dilemma, seriously considering that the only solution might be for Minnie to go to New York. Minnie and P.W. did not speak directly about the contents of Nellie's letter until one evening after a pleasant visit with the Garnes next door. Edwina was spending the night at the Nixons' across the street.

They walked hand in hand into the living room and as they settled down on the sofa, all their upspoken fears rose to the surface. They talked first of the distress Harry and Antoinette had revealed to them that evening, Antoinette having learned she would be losing her job because the Chicago Opera House was closing down. Nothing could save it. "They are really worried," remarked P.W.

"So am I," confessed Minnie.

"About Bill?" P.W. knew the letter from Nellie had been uppermost in her mind since its arrival that morning.

"Yes, I don't know what got into me that I permitted him to go to her. I am sick with worry, P.W." Minnie bit her lips.

A few days later, Bill's version of the broom incident arrived. Apparently Nellie became aware that Bill had finally written his parents and she hurriedly penned a rebuttal, threatening if Bill misbehaved again, she was going to call the police and have him locked up. Minnie could not sleep for several nights after Nellie's letter arrived. She began grinding her teeth most of the day and all through the night in her worry and fear for Bill until she woke up one morning with a swollen jaw.

"That does it, Minnie!" said P.W. looking at her swollen face. "You have to go to New York to see what's really going on and bring the children back if necessary."

"But P.W., I can't leave you here in the house alone."

"Yes you can . . . I will be alright. Harry is right next door and I'll find Billy Parker to stay with me and to help around the house. I won't be lonesome."

Minnie shook her head. "I don't like leaving you under these circumstances. I belong here at your side but I can't desert our children either." She wiped her tears away again. "I'm so unnerved," she confessed. "I can't sleep. Sometimes I walk the floor all night thinking of the terrible times Bill must be having . . . what is this going to do to him?"

Over and over he reassured her. He would try to join her in New York if everything worked out well here in Chicago where he still had important work to do.

It took a great deal of courage for P.W. to let the last of his family go to New York, remaining to face a bitter winter in Chicago. He turned away from the railroad station after seeing Minnie and Edwina off to return to an empty house for the first time during his marriage to Minnie. He knew how difficult it would be to get used to being alone. They had been separated before when he went away on business trips in his efforts to promote the bank stock campaign. He had gone to Washington to obtain the Douglass National Bank permit, and later to Michigan and Wisconsin to search for land, but always it was he going forth, filled with plans and hopes for

360

the future; even his recent trip to New York was drastically different. This time it was Minnie leaving him behind and going forth to salvage the family situation. There was little hope anywhere in Chicago and even less in P.W.'s heart that night.

He entered the empty house, removed his hat and coat slowly, hanging them on the hall tree carefully, then went into the living room. As he sat there silently, the room seemed to echo Minnie's voice; the warnings she gave him came back. "There's many a slip between the cup and the lip," she had said many times, cautioning him about his optimism, which he would have to remember. Tomorrow would be Christmas Eve, the first Christmas alone since their marriage. There would be no unwrapping of gifts, no excited expectations of little children, no trimming of a Christmas tree, no laughter or joy as there had been all of those previous years. But the thought of Minnie being together with the children warmed him somehow. He gathered himself for the long climb up the stairs to his lonely room, concluding that for now this would have to be enough for him.

In the days that followed, he dragged himself up and down the stairs, growing accustomed to the silence in the house. He put in more time organizing groups concerned with the fate of the collapsed Binga Bank. Some evenings were spent in the company of Harry Garnes who came over to listen to the radio, pass the time away, and share views of the tight economic situation. They still lived in separate worlds, but comfortably tolerating each other's differences, as long-time friends often do. Mrs. Wiggins would come over with a special dish of food when she had not seen P.W. for a day or two. "Thought you would enjoy a dish o' home cookin'," she would explain as she walked through the house with a steaming plate, directly into the kitchen. The Five Hundred Block Club had helped P.W.'s neighbors to know him better. He took pleasure in their warm, folksy, comforting efforts even more after learning that Billy Parker, whom he had searched for, had moved to California seeking employment.

During the Binga Bank meetings he would think of the cries from the Black Belt and how the cries grew louder now than in 1921. In spite of all he did, all he had tried to do, and all the things his family had given up, the cycle of misery was repeating itself. Did the cries seem louder because he too was helpless and out of control? His active mind no longer determined his destiny. It was irreversibly encased in the great weight of his crippled body. He could no longer lift his right leg which felt leaden. Each morning he would reach for his right leg, lift it off the bed with both hands to get started dressing, prepare his own breakfast, gather notes for meetings and leave the house for the day. With this dreary routine, Harry Garnes' regular visits and Mrs. Wiggins' neighborly interest were welcome interludes. P.W. would repay the Wiggins' for their kindness by spending more time with Mr. Wiggins in the evenings outside on the porch of their building. They had little in common, but Mr. Wiggins was pleased to have P.W. pass the time with him for he saw P.W. as a man who had aspired and achieved.

During one cold spell early in February, Mr. Wiggins came over to see how P.W was doing as they had not seen him in several days and the fierce winter snow had encircled the house. P.W. had been ill and had become engrossed in his thoughts, thinking, thinking. A feeling of utter futility had swept over him after the last Binga mass meeting. The meeting was well attended, but no community leader had been willing to take responsibility for further effort. The one chosen at the meeting spoke eloquently of the challenge and the great desire on his part to serve in whatever way possible in this crisis to aid the thousands of depositors whose life savings were tied up in Binga Bank. He had said someone "had to make the sacrifice in the interest of the lost fortunes of the community" . . . but that was two weeks ago and nothing had happened. Mr. Wiggins' call cheered P.W. . . . He stirred the fire in the furnace after bringing several bushels of coal over to P.W. until the coal delivery arrived. Human companionship rekindled his courage. P.W. reproached himself for giving way to self-pity and read Minnie's last letter over again.

She wrote almost daily. The first letter told him that the family was well and each additional letter told him of the children's progress in school, but very little about how she was getting along financially. He sensed she was waiting for the word about their future plans from him. He saved her letters, reading them over and over again. How could he suggest she return to Chicago? After the Binga Bank rally resulted in silence, P.W. became more indecisive regarding his family. Looking around the house, now in disarray, was a painful reminder of his helplessness. "It's like I'm living through a nightmare" he said to himself. All of his many physical and financial limitations were pressing in on him. The fear of falling down the stairs increased, the risks he was incurring by straining to pull himself around the house became clearer to him. "I see more, because I can do less," he told himself.

It was now one month since P.W. had received the letter from Minnie with a new address on the envelope, telling him she had rented an apartment across the street from Nellie on 7th Avenue, assuring him the move was for the best. He was now worried about how far away his family was from him and how they were putting down roots in New York without him. His helplessness as the head of the family became excruciatingly apparent to him.

Minnie wrote that she had found a job sewing for the Edison family in New Jersey and no longer had to tolerate Nellie's oppression of her children. The more P.W. thought about the situation, the more desperate he felt about being unable to change any of it. She told him the children were making much progress in school; both girls were taking dancing lessons at the Grace Giles Dancing School and would soon be preparing for a June recital at Rockland Palace. He could not understand . . . "Minnie can't possibly be earning enough to cover their expenses. How is she managing to do all of these things?" he questioned repeatedly. "Is George helping out, I wonder?. . . . I'm sure Nellie isn't."

These months in New York were not easy for Minnie although she phrased her letters to make them sound cheerful. After two weeks in Nellie's home, Minnie made up her mind that staying on in New York was her only choice for now but that eventually she would have to move out of her sister's home with her children. Minnie did not tell P.W. about the constant irritation she felt having to put up with Nellie's incessant bickering about how much the children ate, how much electricity they used to do their homework, and her constant intimidations and criticisms of the way they either had or had not been taught to do something. But Minnie reached the final level of endurance; she moved out.

Mother explained to us that this was only a temporary move until she and Daddy got settled. Actually, only Bill questioned the move. Edwina and I were busy with school and our friends, happy to be away from Aunt Nellie's constant harrassment. Our new home was furnished, a four-room apartment on the top floor of an apartment house with an elevator. They were the most barren surroundings we had ever experienced, but considering the lack of freedom and confusion we had left behind, we were elated. We even enjoyed Mother's employment which allowed us more freedom than we had ever known, especially after school. At last we felt like real Harlemites!!

During the Roaring Twenties, the era of Prohibition, black entertainment in the performing arts was the rage of America. Before he left New Orleans for Chicago in 1917, Joe "King" Oliver had taught Louis "Satchmo" Armstrong, as a teenager, to play the trumpet. Armstrong had played the bugle and cornet in the school for wayward boys prior to his release. He replaced "King" Oliver in Kid Ory's band for several years before he came north to Chicago. In 1923, King Oliver's Creole Jazz Band, together with Johnny Dodds, the clarinet player, made Chicago's South Side, midst the violence of the gangsters and gun-toting mobsters, the place where true jazz, that "Great blue New Orleans sound", was first appreciated. Later, Armstrong came to New York, joined Fletcher Henderson's band, then Erkine Tate's, doubling with Earl "Fatha" Hines at the piano, and subsequently organizing his own band. The nation had been dancing the "Black Bottom," the "Charleston," the "Shim-Sham-Shimmie," and the "Lindy Hop," one Negro-oriented dance after another, ever since Nobel Sissle and Eubie Blake produced "Shuffle Along," a smash hit in 1921 which was rapidly followed by "Runnin' Wild" and many other all-Negro Broadway musical shows. The downtown theatre-goers in New York would flock uptown to Harlem in their full dress, top hats and tails, where the jazz and the good times rolled, to see and hear the statuesque "high tone, high yeller gals" sing and dance at such night clubs as the "Cotton Club" and "Connie's Inn" where great entertainers began or enhanced their careers. Such jazz immortals as Duke Ellington, "Fats" Waller, Cab Calloway, Louis Armstrong, Chick Webb, Fletcher Henderson, and many others, such as performers like "Bojangles," The Nicholas Brothers, and Lena Horne, a young singer just starting out, appeared there. They were all to enrich America with their innovations and fantastic melodies. Harlem boasted the famous Savoy Ballroom where only the best bands played: Chick Webb, Lucky Millinder, Count Basie, Earl Hines, Benny Goodman, Lionel Hampton, and Erskine Hawkins, among others. The Lafayette and Apollo Theatres, the most popular musical stages, presented only the blues and jazz greats: Bessie Smith, the "Empress of Blues," Earl "Fatha" Hines, Jimmie Lunceford, and countless others. Harlem eventually had eleven exotic night clubs and 500 jazz places. Those owned by bootleg gangsters were occasionally subject to their rowdy behavior and bomb throwing. One time the mob wrecked a whole place during rehearsal, tearing up the band's music and instruments in a violent outburst to show their authority over the performing artists who laughed it off and kept on singing and dancing with the knowledge that the crowd came to Harlem to see and hear their jazz flow with "sophistication in bronze."

Paul Robeson, the Phi Beta Kappa scholar and all-American athlete, had already appeared in the male lead of Eugene O'Neil's "All God's Chillun Got Wings." Roland Hayes had cracked the color curtain all over Europe and America for colored concert singers, paving the way for Marion Anderson, who was just beginning to attract contracts, and leading to her appearance with the New York Philharmonic Orchestra. Josephine Baker had starred in

"Chocolate Dandies," Florence Mills in "Blackbirds of 1926" and "1927", Ethel Waters in "Africana" and Bill "Bojangles" Robinson in "Hot Chocolate." This sparkling decade of Harlem creativity in the performing arts was coming to a close with the production of "Green Pastures" whose struggles to secure sponsorship I had heard about even before leaving Chicago, probably because of my childhood involvement in dancing school. Harlem was still throbbing with creative excitement early in 1931, which even we as children could perceive.

I remember being thrilled when Mother enrolled us in Grace Giles Dancing School, located over the Lafayette Theatre, where I was selected as a front line dancer to set an example for the beginners and intermediates in the middle and back rows, which seemed endless. There was an atmosphere of mass production, the floors swinging and swaying with the beat of the hundreds of children tapping and prancing. I felt my years of training had paid off with this front line position which put me in with the group of better dancers who also happened to live on or near our block, 120th Street, and had already formed a club known as the "Modernistic Rhythm Girls." We thought we were the snappiest adolescents in Harlem wearing our red and white club costumes, fully chaperoned by one of the mothers, Mrs. Seaman, when we went to Coney Island and to the neighborhood parties together. We called ourselves by such nicknames as "Bubbles" for Dorothy Seaman, "Gwenie" for Eloise Walker, "Tessie" for Theresa Frazier, "Pinkie" for me, and "Toots" for Edwina, the mascot. Enjoying every minute of being included in her big sister's activities, Edwina graciously took on the duty of tagging along with me wherever I went, in accordance with Mother's wishes, especially after she started working every day. Most of the group were in the Rapid Advance Class, upper classman at the Junior High School on 120th Street, where I found myself again preparing for yet another graduation as part of this class of "31." Here I was in my element, reacting to the creativity of Harlem which was all about me and having a delightful experience attending a neighborhood school, knowing my classmates on multiple

366

levels as friends, neighbors, club members, and dancing school partners, therefore having more time and intimacy with my classmates than ever before. They seemed happier and freer than the well-programmed children of the bourgeosie I had known in Chicago. But my elation may have really been due to the fact that I was emerging from the cocoon of childhood and fully aware of the changes I was experiencing.

It may also have been that I was reacting to the fact that Harlem had become a mecca of the Black American world, longing for expression and recognition of its energies and artistic gifts, and bursting with creative forces throughout the Roaring Twenties and even before. Decades ago, Paul Lawrence Dunbar, the poetic genius, had made his contribution of poems in dialect and Henry O. Tanner had won major honors for his famous religious paintings in Paris and later in America. W. C. Handy, "The Father of the Blues," through his compositions, performances and music publishing business as well as his company of musicians, had established the blues of rural southern Blacks as part of this country's musical heritage, producing and conducting a musical history of the Negro at Carnegie Hall by 1928. Carter G. Woodson, "The Father of Negro History," had already popularized the study of Negro History, organized the Association for the Study of Negro Life and History, started The Journal of Negro History, and initiated "Negro History Week."

Some say the Harlem Renaissance, with its fiery protest motif, began with the publication of Claude McKay's book of protest poems in 1922, followed by James Weldon Johnson's *Book of American Negro Poetry*. In 1923 in New York, the first major work of black fiction, *Cane*, by Jean Toomer, with its short stories and poems describing life in rural Georgia was published. A few years later, Dr. Alain Locke, a Phi Beta Kappa at Harvard and a Rhodes Scholar at Oxford, published an anthology of poems, stories, essays and pictures entitled *The New Negro* which sparked the vogue of Negro Art among serious white art patrons in New York, then spread across the country and encouraged black artists to perceive of their work as a new approach to the old color problem. The same year, Countee Cullen's volume of poems, *Color*, appeared and he eventually became the prize-winning, nationally acclaimed, leading poet of the Harlem Renaissance. Arna Bontemps was the young scholar from California who mingled with these creative writers, known as the "New Negro Renaissance Figures". He went on to become one of the most prolific writers of verse, fiction, nonfiction, history and biography, then later, head librarian and publicity director of Fisk University in Nashville, Tennessee. Langston Hughes, one of the most honored authors in the land, and the poet laureate of Black America, had already produced his first book of poems, *The Weary Blues*, by 1926. That same year, the Carnegie Foundation purchased Arthur Schomburg's rich collection of Negro books which were presented to the New York Public Library and are now housed in the Schomburg Center for Research in Black Culture in the midst of Harlem. During these rich years of cultural emergence, James Van Der Zee, the photographic biographer and a Harlem artist, took photographs of everything: the weddings, the funerals, the family life of the black middle-class, capturing on camera the prosperous and exciting life style of Harlem in the 1920's and early 1930's.

I don't remember studying very hard for the achievements I was beginning to accumulate. Everything seemed to come to me so easily with my new freedom of motion and the recognition by peers and teachers that I was receiving. Before long, there was talk at school of my being in line for the Algebra and Biology awards. Mother was pleased and she began to speak of Daddy joining us in New York as soon as everything could be worked out that way.

One evening, Elisabeth came over around dinner time. Mother was happy to have her join us. Elisabeth understood the situation we had fled, even though Nellie was not discussed. After Mother showed her around the apartment, Elisabeth announced she would be leaving New York in a few days to enter LaGrange College in Illinois and planned to contact "Uncle Chavers" since LaGrange is not far from Chicago.

"Oh, your plans sound so good! Tell me, how did all of this

come about?" Mother questioned as we sat down at the table.

"Well Aunt Minnie, as soon as I returned to New York from Virginia last summer, I knew I had to do something about my situation and I wrote to different colleges to see where I could earn my room and board. LaGrange College offered me employment and accepted my credentials from the Philippines," responded Elisabeth. She had lost some of her heavy foreign accent living in Virginia where she had been speaking English constantly.

"Elisabeth, you are a brave girl. I know your father must be proud of you," Minnie smiled, then grew quiet for a moment. She felt distressed about her beloved brother's favorite daughter moving about America like an outcast in a loveless world. "I do hope you and your sister will remain close and not pull apart as Nellie and I have done."

Elisabeth perceived Minnie's concern. "I don't usually speak of this to anyone, but it is very different between Petrita and me now that she is married to a full-blooded Filipino, Aunt Minnie. It is not pleasant for me living in my sister's home with her passing as a full-blooded Filipino." Elisabeth took a deep breath and went on, "As far as I'm concerned, Petrita has cut all Calloway family ties here."

Mother, in the midst of all her many concerns, now had to concentrate on future plans for my going to Hunter College High School in the fall, but she was not being specific. She had talked all the time about our staying in New York and of Daddy joining us, but now, suddenly, she was speaking indecisively. Somehow I got the idea that she was not thinking of me, but had begun to focus on the attention Daddy might be getting from Elisabeth in her absence, especially after she voiced some of her feelings to me which sounded ridiculous to an eager adolescent.

"After all, your Father is a man, and Elisabeth is a young woman," she had said. The strain that Mother was under seemed to induce strange forebodings in her. I could not comprehend what Elisabeth's going to live near Chicago had to do with my future. I was too young at the time to realize that Mother's decision to stay on in New York was motivated by trying to keep Bill away from the "low life" in Wendell

Phillips High School in Chicago where he had been attending. When she saw he was failing in New York too, and Edwina was having trouble, this forced her to realize that she was doing no more or less for her children in New York than in Chicago. Nellie's menacing presence on the heels of Elisabeth's visit, brought to the surface Minnie's old fears of losing her man. Under the pressure of separation and financial difficulties which were new and strange to her, she was subject to suspicions which were rather far-fetched. These events only served to crystalize her thinking and finalize her decision to return to Chicago.

What Minnie did not know was that by late February disaster was everywhere in Chicago. Even the powerful owner of the *Chicago Defender* was being plagued with misfortunes; his white wife had deserted him and was publicly charging him in the courts as being abusive to her. As P.W. read the news, he felt that he could not ask Minnie to return to him or offer to go to New York to stay with the family because he could do so little for her now. But, as he reflected on their relationship, he was consoled that his Minnie had brought him no scandal, no public recriminations and that she had endured everything and was now as alone as he was, with the additional burden of the three children.

In March, the news broke that Binga was being held in the Infirmary at the County Jail. One of the main speakers at the last Binga Bank rally, a man whom P.W. had sponsored just one month ago in the fading hope of having the bank reopen, had been apprehended and taken into custody with Binga. This was another overwhelming blow for P.W., now feeling a profound sense of failure in every effort he had made.

When P.W. received a post card from Elisabeth telling him that she was fully enrolled as a student at LaGrange College and would be visiting him soon, he was exceedingly happy about her plans developing so well and the possibility of a visit from one of Minnie's family. He needed family contact desperately now. The loneliness of the house, the worry about Minnie and the children, and the horrors of the financial depression were closing in on him from all sides.

On one of her visits to the Filipino Club in Chicago, Elis-

370

abeth met a young mestizo student, Basilio Hawkins, an American Negro Filipino, whose father too had fought in the Spanish-American War, and had visited in the Calloway home in Manila. They felt an immediate kinship. Basilio took Elisabeth to visit her Uncle Chavers in mid-May. P.W. looked thin and shabby and limped heavily now. The neglect of the house reflected Minnie's absence and his weakened condition appalled Elisabeth . . . But P.W. was oblivious to all but Elisabeth's presence. "I will offer you whatever I have, daughter," he said as they approached the kitchen. Shortly after, Elisabeth wrote a brief note to Minnie telling of her visit and hinting about P.W.'s situation. This letter heightened Minnie's realization that her place was at her husband's side.

Minnie did not wait to hear from P.W. She wrote to him about her return. By the second time Elisabeth visited "Uncle Chavers," they both knew Minnie would soon be on her way home. P.W. was beside himself with joy that the family was returning home, now aware of his great fear that Minnie might not ever return, and that this had been a part of the distress he had felt all these months. He also became aware of how profoundly he feared her abandonment of him, wondering if this was what had plagued him most of his married life. At last he acknowledged to himself that he had always feared Minnie might desert him because of his causes. Preparing for Minnie's return brought new hopes to P.W. Elisabeth would help him prepare for his family's return and he would make this a very special homecoming. He was radiant with expectation and talked of nothing else.

Minnie, Edwina and I left New York the day after school closed in June. Bill had failed geometry during the last term and was showing a growing disinterest in school. Minnie was determined that her standards be maintained, so she worked out an arrangement for him to stay on with Petrita and repeat geometry in summer school with the understanding that we would all be together again in eight short weeks in Chicago. I had fought against the idea of returning to Chicago and continued to hope for some last minute miracle to alter

371

my fate . . . either by bringing Daddy to New York or by making arrangements for me to remain in New York where I had spent a happy and productive year in school. "Outstanding in every way . . . work and conduct" had been written all over my report card. Mother had been proud to speak with the teachers who reported on the promise they saw in me, telling how they had recommended me for admission to Hunter College High School, a distinguished public school. In New York I had grown into adolescence, responding to the freedom I felt, enjoying the rugged competition, and mingling with my classmates in the neighborhood. Most did not envision going on to college, many were new arrivals from the Caribbean. The fact that I came from Chicago gave me a strange glamour that I felt in school, at play, at dancing school, and in the clique with which I was associated in the Harlem of those days. At last I had found my own place in the sun, here my unique drive and determination was given special acclaim and I had thrived on it.

I felt I had earned the right to stay in New York. During the last few weeks, Mother had become enraged by my attitude and obvious resistance to the move. She accused me of caring only about my own future, having forgotten all about my sick father. This pained me, as there were certainly elements of truth here. So far from Chicago, a change was occurring within me that I had not consciously noticed; a new independence that intoxicated me. I had coped with a series of "crises" on my own. In this exciting new milieu, my thoughts of my father were, for the first time, secondary. We heard more about Uncle George and what a blessing he was to Mother during all these years. Bill supported me in my efforts to change Mother's mind, grumbling about the way she lauded Uncle George. "To Mother, he's old St. Christopher." But it was a lost battle for me. I had to listen over and over again about Mother's early years, interspersed with comments about family tradition and family loyalty, as exemplified by Uncle George's devotion to her. Each ended with reaffirmation of her decision that she was returning to Chicago, and the decision was irrevocable. Neither the Depression, Daddy's illness, the opportunities in New York, nor our emerging adolescence would affect her reign. Minnie was the queen, and she knew her responsibilities. Her lifestyle had to be maintained at all costs. Everything Daddy used to have to listen to about her coming from the "FFV's" (The First Families of Virginia), her background and her values was now being foisted on us. It had not helped my cause any when Aunt Nellie reported that she had seen me walking down 7th Avenue holding hands with one of the neighborhood boys. As the day of the departure neared, I began to accept the inevitable. I realized now that Mother was fighting against a knowing sense of the threatened loss of her children. She was regretting ever having allowed any of us to come to New York. Her sense of relief was great as we boarded that Greyhound bus for Chicago, home and P.W. It had been six months for her, and a year for me.

Daddy was overjoyed to greet us that hot July afternoon when we arrived in Chicago. Uncle George, Elisabeth, and Basilio were with him at the Greyhound Terminal. All of the smoldering annoyance I had felt about being dragged back to Chicago and all of my dreams about growing up in the fabulous city of New York vanished completely the moment I saw Daddy waiting for us in the station. I was home, and Daddy's girl once again. The joy our presence brought him was undeniably obvious. On the way home in Uncle George's car, he spoke of his eagerness to get acquainted with us again and he told of the plans he had made to celebrate our homecoming.

Together with the manager of the local Metropolitan Theatre, he had planned a "Homecoming Event." These were Depression days and management was eager for any attraction to bring in additional business. P.W. had special tickets and posters printed for the event. He was still glamourizing his daughters, listing us as the returning "juvenile wonder stars," and was delighted with the way Edwina and I responded to his plans for our "Homecoming."

373

WARNER BROS. THEATRES, INC.
1307 SOUTH WABASH AVENUE
CHICAGO, ILLINOIS

WARNER BROS. THEATRES, INC.
METROPOLITAN THEATRE 47 & SO. PARKWAY
MONDAY, TUESDAY, WEDNESDAY, THURSDAY, FRIDAY
  AND SATURDAY
JULY 27, 28, 29, 30, AUGUST 1st

  PRICE 25¢—ADULT TICKET—25¢

FIRST PERSONAL APPEARANCE AND HOMECOMING
OF MADRUE AND EDWINA CHAVERS, CHICAGO'S OWN
JUVENILE WONDER STARS IN STAGE ENTERTAINMENT

The event stirred Mother to enroll me in a dancing school she had heard was being developed by Katherine Dunham under the tutelage of a Russian ballerina. Mother and Uncle George knew Albert Dunham, Katherine's father, in their youth, and heard that his daughter, Katherine, while working as a librarian, had studied dancing seriously and was now developing a new dance form. Mother quickly revived the friendship so I could be in the first group of students. Before long, I was travelling to the Loop and rehearsing with this group which included many of the students I already knew from other dancing schools we attended in younger years.

P.W.'s assets continued to dry up and the Velie-8 had to be sold by late fall, 1931. Mrs. Neal, who held the mortgage on our home, threatened to foreclose. Minnie wanted to speak with George about the foreclosure, but hesitated, feeling George had already invested heavily in many of P.W.'s enterprises and feared this request might be the one to jeopardize their family relationship forever. She continued to be driven by her greatest fear that Edwina and I might somehow be drawn into the "low life of the trash and riff-raff" around us, that we might absorb the values of those disreputable men and boys hanging around pool halls, candy stores, police stations, or street corners either fighting or loitering about as we passed by, or calling out and whistling after us. P.W. realized that all of Minnie's worries were serious and pressing to her, but he would say confidently, "Throw my children into the Atlantic Ocean and they will come up swimming! Remember blood will tell!"

One day we were out riding in Uncle's car, Mother and Dad were in the rear, and I was sitting up in front with Uncle. It was Mother who turned the conversation to the mortgage on the house. "Well, I guess we'll have to take in roomers," Mother said desperately. "Oh, my poor children . . . my poor children," she went on, bemoaning having to share our home with outsiders to meet the mortgage payments, forgetting momentarily that Uncle George and I were in the car. "Worse! I might have to move my children into a rooming house if we're evicted."

Uncle's face froze in horror! Daddy laughed out loud at the thought of the paradox, Mother's dramatics in contrast to the fact that she had just enrolled Edwina and me in dancing and music schools and I had just entered Englewood High School, an out of area school, involving additional expenses. He was not laughing at the pain Mother dramatized as he knew it was real to her, but at the fact that Minnie refused to alter her standards for the development of her children even one iota. He laughed so spontaneously that Mother became furious.

"I don't see anything funny," she snapped.

Uncle continued to drive with a frozen face. I listened to them as long as I could.

"Why can't Uncle George take over the mortgage?" I burst out as if they were discussing a problem in geometry. Silence fell over the car as I continued, "Uncle is rich." I said it very simply as if I expected Uncle would know his responsibility and recognize the logic of my suggestion.

"Madrue, we are not speaking to you!" interrupted Mother quickly. There was another silence which Uncle George broke into this time.

375

"That's a possibility. You're a smart girl, Madrue, very smart," he continued, winking his eye at me. Then he began to whistle as if he were happy he was being asked to help again. My suggestion opened up Pandora's box of problems in the family. I was to hear from Mother, years later, how I had hurt Daddy's feelings that day by being so blunt. This was a workable solution. Uncle George was happy to be able to ensure that we had "a roof over our heads," as Minnie put it, and he insisted that Minnie let him know when the family needed money from then on. His little sister and her children would again feel safe and secure.

As things turned out, we three children grew to adulthood in that home. Uncle George assumed the mortgage payments and we never learned about the dreaded life of a rooming house boarder which Mother had spoken of so dramatically and fearfully that day in the car. Yet the situation grieved Daddy, for it signified his complete loss of status within his own family. George was now the one Minnie looked to for financial support and the one who took her and the children for rides. P.W. suffered in silence now, knowing that when George returned from his long Southern trip in the early summer, he would not be going to the Ganaways as he had always done, he would be moving in with us.

16

The Harvest

P.W. was not alone in his distress. The deep Depression, crushing business over the entire nation and spreading frustration and shame over a once proud and happy land, had extended to Europe with major financial crises in Austria, England, and Germany, now devastated by unemployment. The worldwide jobless had swollen to over 30 million and the nationwide idle to 15 million of the usually employed. Mortgage foreclosures and bank failings were widespread; by 1932 more than 5000 banks had closed nationwide. The philosophy of government had been: "Let the depression run its course; it cleans out the inefficient people and is a necessary part of the capitalistic economy."

The City of Chicago was paralyzed and the Black Belt was riddled with total defeatism. It is said that Samuel Insull, the utility magnate, more than any other man in Chicago was responsible for the degradation of the municipal government, now unable to pay the teachers and other city employees, hopelessly caught up in its traditions of the "quick political fix," the tax racket run by leaders of both parties, entrenched favoritism, and corruption. In his quest for economic power, Insull had courted the Democratic and Republican parties alike, providing huge campaign contributions to both for the privilege of pursuing his own financial conquests, the cost of which was inevitably passed on to the general public in the form of increased utility rates. The Chicago leaders had been defiant of moral codes, lacked concern for social order and social responsibility, and vehemently resisted any kind of control of business and industry.

During those expansive free-wheeling Roaring Twenties, Insull, the wizard of finance, had built a vast empire of nonworking trusts and holding companies which he mass-marketed, using these monies to buy up other companies, one of which sustained the Garnes and the Bingas. Insull had built the Chicago Opera Company and made a present of it to the City of Chicago. But the stock market crash of 1929 had brought down the City of Chicago, the House of Insull, and along with the disastrous collapse of the Binga State Bank, the Chicago Opera House, thus ending Antoinette's career as an opera singer. Some men had been hopelessly destroyed, like Jesse Binga, now imprisoned for embezzlement. For the most part, the Chicago financial and political leaders had been ruthless, self-made men, dependent upon large campaign contributions from these utility interests, and hopelessly incompetent to lead the city out of the chaos of the Depression. The national government had no program to relieve the wholesale suffering. Samuel Insull, who had financed many of Mayor Willian Hale Thompson's circus-like political campaigns, was now facing charges of shady corporate deals and embezzlement, and was, therefore, in no position to rescue his vassals.

During the previous winter while their wives were out of town, P.W. and Harry had spent many evenings together discussing Harry's dilemma. Harry, one of those professionals hit early in the Depression, was crippled financially because his clientele, unable to pay his fees, now stood in long bread lines and marched in the parades of the unemployed. Antoinette, being a resourceful woman, found work as a music teacher at Fisk University after the closing of the Chicago Opera Company. Harry had finally closed his dental office in the early part of 1931 almost immediately after Antoinette went to work at the college in Tennessee without him. Once at Fisk, a black university, she no longer had to put on the pretense of being white.

As they discussed their situation, P.W. pointed out to Harry that Antoinette, like Minnie, was a real fighter; he doubted that she would permanently desert Harry. However, Harry resented Antoinette and her ability to cope with the threatened foreclosure on their home. He would speak of the comfort P.W. was to him and that he never wanted to move

378

from the peaceful privacy of 42nd Place where even he, at last, had learned to love his neighbors with their simple, earthy values . . . P.W. assured him that Antoinette would find a way for them to hold onto their home. Indeed, Antoinette did find a way. She canvassed the area for a suitable tenant who would sub-lease their home, furnished, and allow Harry to have the use of the back bedroom. Mrs. Nixon from across the street heard that she could rent the Garnes' house fully furnished and rushed to complete the transaction.

When the Nixon family moved into the Garnes' home, Mr. Nixon, the pullman porter, succeeded Dr. Harry Garnes, the dentist, as the head of that house. Harry, living in the back bedroom of his own home, now felt he had lost even more status and control than P.W. Even with Antoinette's job at the college, everything seemed to be sliding downhill for Harry. He endured the humiliation of living in the back bedroom of his own home where he and his wife had entertained so lavishly, and had never invited the Nixons. Now, sometimes, Antoinette would have to ask Mr. Nixon for the rent ahead of time because she was embarrassingly short of money.

P.W. kept busy with the local merchants as his strength permitted, sometimes giving away his promotion ideas in exchange for their companionship. He continued active with the thought of developing still another money-making idea, using his creative energies as he circulated in the community among the local merchants. When he listened to Harry's troubles, he would tell him that at least he still had Antoinette; many men were more unfortunate. Harry felt P.W. was deluding himself and joked about the way P.W. dragged around, talking big money among people who had their own problems now. "Brother, Can You Spare a Dime?" had become the national theme song.

"The whole world has gone to the dogs," Harry would say.

"Where there's life, there's hope," P.W. would insist. "With my children about me everyday, I have to keep going. I have to make them see that life is worthwhile."

Harry could not reach P.W. with his pessimism, nor could P.W. reach Harry with his optimism.

"P.W., you will have to admit that your great American dream for the Negro people has led nowhere."

P.W. would smile, looking out into the distance, and not bother to reply.

During the Depression, any item that could make money had a special appeal to local merchants, and P.W. saw possibilities even in these dismal days. He decided to arrange a local business fair which he called "The South Side Food and Home Show" and coupled this idea with a "Crown the Queen Contest." Once again, he went into the community with his plan to secure local clubs to sponsor contestants for the "Crown the Queen Contest" and to locate merchants to sponsor booths who were willing to distribute coupons which served as votes to be cast the night of the contest. P.W. knew that in the Black Belt the Old Settlers and the upper-class that had emerged during the twenties had been dethroned by the Depression, had gone into hiding, except for the gambling lords with their underworld wealth, and had been replaced by the pullman porters and postal employees with their job security. They could at least pay the rent, buy the groceries and continue church membership. P.W. saw a gold mine in the many social clubs and organizations of the South Side . . . a way of inaugurating business promotion efforts to keep the community money inside the Black Belt.

Shortly thereafter, Bill transferred back to Hyde Park High School because he felt he wasn't learning anything at Wendell Phillips. Then I began to pressure Mother about becoming a professional dancer with Katherine Dunham's Dance Troupe, now planning a night club engagement on Chicago's North Side at the "Chez Paree." Mother objected vehemently, forbidding me to discuss it with Daddy. "You know your father wouldn't want you to show your legs on the stage as a professional dancer," she declared during one of our heated exchanges which went on for several weeks. But it all culminated in a compromise: I would be allowed to develop a dancing school, using the front and back parlors on Saturdays . . . Before long, a sign, "Madrue's School of Dancing,"

Madrue's School of Dance, 1933

was displayed in the front window of our home and everytime I looked at it, I glowed with pride.

Now, like Daddy, I had my own enterprise and I began seeking out customers in the community. Every Saturday afternoon the rugs were rolled back and the students arrived. Edwina would play the piano while for hours and hours I taught the neighborhood children to dance. Sometimes in their fascination of the dance, one would bump up against Fredrick Douglass in the back parlor, to Mother's alarm. Little did I know when I began my homemade dancing school that one of my students would someday be the great American playwright, Lorraine Hansberry, or that the father of another child, in a few short years, would become one of the most powerful black politicians in the United States, Congressman William L. Dawson, the man who was eventually able to deliver the black vote to the Democratic Party in Chicago. My dance school, with its numerous recitals, lasted six years. I literally danced my way through the twin crises of adolescence and the Depression.

The big family occasion of the year before, after Bill returned home in August, had been the quiet wedding of Elisabeth and Basilio. They were joined in Holy Matrimony in our parlor, with P.W. giving Elisabeth away to Basilio. They set up housekeeping "out South," at the very edge of the Black Belt, near the University of Chicago, where only a few clusters of colored families lived and where Minnie had once wanted to live while bringing up her family. Basilio would soon get his Bachelor's degree in Business Administration and face the challenge of securing employment where he could use his education. He was straining to leave the Post Office job. Where would opportunity open up for Basilio? He knew competition was keen for positions everywhere.

One Sunday morning in May of 1932, they visited church with a Baptist friend. After the sermon, the Reverend introduced a Mr. Jesse Hull as the President of the Douglass National Bank who was going to make a brief announcement. Everyone shifted noisily. The congregation seemed surprised. Elisabeth and Basilio eyed each other, vaguely recalling what Uncle Chavers had said about a Mr. Hull. Then, Hull began a barrage of angry words, loud and threatening, about foreclosure on the church which was indebted to the Douglass National Bank for $8,000. It seems that special fund raising events given by the various groups throughout the past year had not raised enough money to meet the church debt.

"Let's go, Basilio," Elisabeth whispered nervously, reacting to Hull's ugly words. As soon as they shut the church door, Basilio commented that they had not seen P.W. in a long time.

"That's right! Let's stop by before we go home," agreed Elisabeth.

For years our family attended the fashionable Grace Presbyterian Church. We children graduated from the Primary and Junior Sunday School classes and throughout our growing up years we spent many Sunday mornings there with the children of other well-to-do black members. However, the neighborhood had deteriorated; the financial resources of many of the once prosperous families like ours had been swept away. As a result, Mother had affiliated with the nearby Metropolitan Community Church. P.W. rarely went to church now.

He was expecting us momentarily, but when he opened the door, there stood Elisabeth and Basilio instead. They had been involved in a conversation with each other, trying to recall P.W.'s comments about the organization of the bank and P.W.'s connection with the court fights and trials. "We didn't know what to make of such an outburst in church," Elisabeth began. P.W. could see they were puzzled, and obviously expecting him to clear up this confusion.

"Mr. Hull was very demanding," added Basilio. "He shouted that 'If your doors must close to keep the bank open, we will close them.' He was really threatening the congregation right in the middle of the Sunday morning services. Is that the way black businessmen carry on their business?"

"The bank must be in great difficulty," remarked P.W.

"Hull certainly shocked the people," continued Elisabeth.

"We were strangers there," explained Basilio, "but we could feel the shock and irritation of those around us. He was accusing them of taking their personal accounts downtown to white banks, telling them it was the little fellow in the 29th Street and Dearborn areas who was keeping the bank doors open, not this congregation, and those little people weren't even welcome in this church."

P.W. could scarcely believe his ears as he thought of what he had told Owens and the bank Board years ago about the importance of the little people and urged the bankers to encourage confidence in local banking. Though Owens and the others had turned deaf ears to P.W.'s beliefs then, it seemed as if Hull was now repeating the exact words P.W. had said over and over again during their bitter battle years ago.

"I really felt sorry for the minister who allowed him to speak; you could see he was very uncomfortable. The congregation seemed trapped into listening to Hull's ranting about 'the little people who put their money in our bank being used by people like you who refuse to meet your obligations.' Then he ended up by saying that he was not going to allow them to suffer," Basilio continued.

P.W. mentioned an article he had read a few months ago in the *Chicago Defender* about Hull becoming the new President of the Douglass National Bank, about the fact that the bank was facing another financial crisis, and that Hull was spearheading a campaign to raise $30,000.00 from the community in order to save it. Elisabeth and Basilio listened eagerly as P.W. counseled them about business conditions on the South Side. "Business in the Black Belt is very tough, much tougher than in the white world," explained P.W. "We are all forced to live here together, isolated, walled off by the Whites. Of course, Hull's attack was not only discourteous, it was poor business, but he was always short-sighted and grasping. His getting angry and abusive with those church members was the wrong way to handle the situation. He should have explained why the congregation should support the bank as depositors and what happens to their money when they take it downtown to the white banks. That it leaves the community, never to return."

"I wonder why he didn't put it that way then," questioned Basilio.

"Because he has done nothing to teach the people about how they can increase their own buying power by depositing their money in the Douglass National Bank, that it is as important to think about where you save as how much you save, for all banks are in the business of buying money to increase purchasing power somewhere. Basilio, community leaders have to teach people how to live, or bear the fruits of their ignorance." P.W. shook his head thinking about how these people had used the bank to build monuments to themselves. "Basilio," he continued, "you are going to have to understand a lot more about the colored people in America, the extra burden we carry, the suffering we know, and the forces in the economy that keep us outside the upward stride so that even the prosperous black man is viewed as lower than the most illiterate white foreigner in the caste system of this country. In America it is our historical suffering of slavery that unites us; that is all!"

"But, after all, business is business. Why is it so difficult here?" questioned Basilio.

"Aha! There is a vast difference between what you learn in school about the economy and the harsh realities of the business world. There is a great gap between theory and practice which is bridged only by experience," returned P.W. "The Negro community has not learned the importance of supporting its own business enterprise. During the last decade, when everybody had money or thought he had money, very little of that prosperity was going into this community. Partially, it is our ignorance of the dynamic economy of this country that keeps us down."

The telephone rang in the dining room and P.W. limped over to answer it. It was Jack. "Haven't heard from you in sometime," said P.W. responding jovially. "Come on over."

P.W. felt more like his former self than he had since his stroke as he returned to the living room, explaining that Jack, who had also been in the congregation of the same church that morning, would soon join them. He told them

385

briefly about Jack and how he had come into the sewing factory one day, many years ago, looking for work, how he had become his chauffeur and later, because Jack had shown promise as a businessman, P.W. had encouraged him to enter the real estate field. P.W. spoke proudly of their relationship over the years and was delighted that Basilio would have a chance to meet Jack because of his extensive knowledge of the practical side of business in the colored community.

Within five minutes Jack drove up to the house in a brand new car. He greeted P.W. with a ready smile and a warm hand-clasp, acknowledging that it had been a long time since he had stopped by. After being introduced to Basilio and Elisabeth, he filled them in about the bank having loaned the church the money for a mortgage, that the members were doing what they could to meet this obligation, and that the bank had been shaky for a period of several years. He had heard that they had applied for a Reconstruction Finance Corporation loan, but he had not heard how the bank had made out on their application.

"Yessuh, Mr. Chavers, I think back on those days when you struggled all alone. I'm almost 'shame o' belongin' to the same church they do. It's the one part 'bout joining that bothers me, but like I always told you, suh, a fellow has got to have a little practicality . . . if he's goin' to make it in this here town. Yessuh, I will never forget how much you cared about your fellow man and how your believin' in me gave me my start. I won't forget that you was responsible for all I have been able to do."

P.W. beamed. Jack and Basilio were about the same age, both in their early thirties, and beginning their careers. P.W. thought, with regret, that he had just turned 56 years old and it occurred to him that they now stood where he had stood at the start of the real big events of his business career when he had first met Minnie and his heart sang out with all the promise he had felt for their future. "Was that just 20 years ago?" he wondered. So much had happened.

Minnie and the children came in talking about the church services being unusually long that morning. Elisabeth left the men to join Minnie and the girls in the kitchen and help

386

prepare dinner. Looking at the two men, P.W. said, "It's up to you young men working in the community to get the message across to black businessmen and to the people at large.

Our people have to learn that there's no disgrace in making money," P.W. continued. "They are not on the plantation now . . . They have to learn how to handle money . . . how to hold on to it and be quiet about having it. I used to think the Whites should 'give' us the opportunity, but now I feel it's our responsibility to 'see' opportunity . . . it's all around us. We've got to go after the money and the opportunity to make money. Opportunity is everywhere in this brand new country and we are a 'brand new' people! Now, you take the camp I had up in Wisconsin; that was a beautiful piece of land and it was open for Whites or Blacks to develop. It was a shame I had to lose it. There was so much up there to spark a new life for our families and children, but I couldn't hold on to it because of this Depression and the lack of solid backing from our people . . . Young men like you must teach them how to grasp the opportunities that lie all around us."

Jack smiled, but Basilio was serious as he listened attentively to P.W.

"I have said all of my life that if we're going to get any respect as a people in America we must begin right here where we live, and we must unite. We must learn to enjoy competition, to see it as a challenge, and to stop settling for second place; to stop behaving like beaten horses!"

Jack's smile broadened as P.W continued talking, speaking once again as he used to, sharing his clear thinking.

Basilio repeated how sorry he felt for the minister who so graciously allowed Mr. Hull to speak to the congregation this morning. Basilio, a sensitive, soft-spoken, dark-skinned man, had had enough encounters with abrasive black and white co-workers at the Post Office and knew how it felt to be poorly defended in the face of an unexpected onslaught.

"Yes, I'm sure it was shocking to you, Basilio," responded P.W. He was thinking of what Roberts had told him in New York about the internecine fighting going on among the bank's board members, and about how Owens was ousted by his own son-in-law, Hull, now president of the bank. But he decided not to speak of these things; they were too shameful. He said instead, "Hull is not sensitive enough to know how to talk to people persuasively; he only knows how to scheme. His main concern has always been 'What's in it for me?' When I think about my long lonely fight to hold the community together through the Chavers Contract, to establish that bank, to get the permit, to sell the stock, to obtain the charter, and the double cross of that Calumet property fight with the eventual seizure of that property by Wagner at an auction for a fraction of its worth . . . I realize the victims get no justice. . . it was all a rape of the community people!" P.W. was wound up now. "All of those people were victimized. Many were just learning to trust a bank, a Negro bank, at that! . . . instead of keeping their money under their mattresses. I knew that seeds of trust had to be planted in this community, but I was a minority of one, pushing on in that bitter fight, blind to my own destruction."

He paused briefly. Jack and Basilio pretended not to see him rub his right hand to increase the circulation and waited patiently until he started up again. "Now, at last Mr. Hull stands facing the real truth! The truth that he is no mightier than the little man on 29th Street and Dearborn Avenue on whom he is completely dependent. What you saw this morning was the same raw terror at the imminent loss of the bank and the status that goes with it that I faced for years in the courtroom!"

"Yessuh, Mr. Chavers! But you know I tried to get you to stop and think of yourself and your health in those days." Jack struggled for a thought that would cheer P.W. He wanted to reassure him that all of his faith in the small man had not been a total waste. "Mr. Chavers, I want you to know that I been one of the lucky ones!"

"How's that son?" asked P.W.

"Well, a couple years ago I drew all my savin's out o' the Binga State Bank, just before it closed. That was luck! I had to have the money to meet a big down payment on my apartment buildin' over on 44th and Indiana. I heard it was bein' foreclosed by one of them downtown banks. As soon as I got wind o' that transaction, I pulled all my savin's out o' the bank for the deal, an' that's how I didn't get caught in the bank collapse," explained Jack.

"You always had a way of moving in on opportunity just in time! That's what I first noticed about you." P.W. was now fully recovered from his sorrowful reminiscences and happy to see his protege so successful. "You're not letting this Depression get you down, and that's good!" He beamed with pride, then suddenly reflected, "I hope you haven't forgotten your family in Alabama, with all of your new found prosperity, Jack."

"Oh, nossuh. Fact is I drove home last fall to talk things over, hopin' one of my brothers would come up to give me a hand with the buildings. They're afraid it would be worse here."

"Well, keep your family as close as you can," advised P.W.

Jack struggled to voice the thought he had wanted to share with P.W. when he telephoned as now it surfaced again. "I'm plannin' to git married 'n' settle down, suh. I wanted you to be the first to know," he added in a low voice. "I'm sure I found the right girl. Mamie's her name. She's got class and style, just like Mrs. Chavers. She's for me . . . and I'm for her, all the way."

"Congratulations, Jack," P.W. said, glowing.

"Well, like you always said . . . a man needs a good steady wife to watch over him! I see Mrs. Chavers is still right here with you just like she always been."

"When do you plan to marry?" questioned P.W.

"Not 'til spring o' next year. I'll bring her over soon, suh. I know you will like her. Mamie wants to wait until next year so we can have a big weddin'. It seems her family expect this of her, so it's alright with me," Jack smiled, a little embarrassed at the thought of a big formal wedding.

The dinner and the spirited conversation sparkled. It had been a long spell since our home was the gathering place for a lively good time.

A fortnight later, P.W. sat alone in the living room for a long time holding a copy of the *Chicago Defender*. The headlines seemed to scream out at him!

389

"DOUGLASS NATIONAL BANK FAILS"

"Executive Says Failure Due to Lack of Community Confidence"

The article went on,
"Following a steady withdrawal of deposits from the Douglass National Bank over the past nine months, the capital at the bank dwindled from $2,000,000 to $408,000, making conditions so desperate that the Board of Directors voted on May 20, 1932 to close the institution. . . Saturday the bank's doors failed to open. Three weeks ago, the bank launched a prosperity drive to get more deposits; this would have saved the bank had it been successful, but the people lacked confidence and the bank had to close."

P.W. read and reread the article, meditating about the sorry state his bank had come to, hesitating to show it to Minnie. At last, he went into the back parlor where she was sitting with her sewing basket and showed her the article. A long silence passed between them before she broke it to say, almost vindictively . . . "You told them this would happen! Ten years ago you told them that community confidence was needed. You were too good. Too *understanding*, P.W."

During the next week, P.W. pushed on, spending every waking moment preparing for the Food and Home Show. I clearly remember the many attractive booths with beautiful displays of merchandise and the enchantment of the colorful pageantry in the bright new ballroom of Bacon's Casino on the night of June 1st, 1932, which culminated in the "Crowning of the Queen." Many of our friends, some of whom we had not seen in several years, like Rebecca, Frank, Cleo, and Emily Brown, were there along with our neighbors, the Nixons, the Bowmans, the Wiggins and Dr. Garnes. Some were interested in every detail; others came out of curiosity. Mother's club ladies and many of Daddy's present and former business associates were there, mingling with us and the community people. I recall seeing Jack, Attorney James, and Attorney Lucas, sitting with the contest judges. The affair was a tremendous success. Elisabeth and Basilio were everywhere that night, helping out wherever they were needed, taking care of details, checking the door, answering questions, and in any way they could, relieving P.W. of the physical strain of moving about in such a large crowd.

After the Food and Home Show, Daddy stirred less and less. Slowly the mood in our house changed. Minnie sensed he had given up and had begun to live in the past completely, thinking back on what happened to his dream of economic freedom for his people. At night Minnie sat in silence with P.W., her sewing basket nearby, close to the full length, life-size portrait of Fredrick Douglass, the oil painting that dominated our back parlor ever since we had moved into the house seven years ago. It had been unveiled at the Armory to inspire the community during those early days of the bank-stock campaign and was destined to hang in the lobby of the bank when it opened. Instead, it travelled with P.W. on his unsuccessful political campaign and came finally to rest on the back parlor wall where it comforted him. The painting of Douglass, the great protestor against oppression and exploitation of his people, symbolized his dream, and it was all that remained now. The Douglass National Bank had closed for the lack of community confidence, the one thing he was so determined to build when he began to work on the bank.

When Uncle George moved into our home during the summer of 1932 with his many valises, selling paraphernalia, and huge collection of toiletries, occupying Bill's room, relationships and routines seemed relatively undisturbed at first. Bill slept out on the back porch most of the summer, except during rainy weather when he used the couch in the back parlor. He did not seem to mind since the arrangements gave him a kind of migratory status at home, which being 17, he appeared to enjoy. Uncle George set up his usual busy schedule of going to the race tracks, playing cards, and attending garden parties, when he was not measuring customers for suits and coats. We did not see anymore of him than we usually did during the summers, but we were aware that when he was in the city, he would be coming home to us at night. As the summer lengthened into fall, Daddy had another attack and spent more hours upstairs in the front bedroom, some days coming downstairs only for meals. Occasionally, he would sit at the front window for hours just staring outdoors. Or he would sit in a corner of the kitchen while Mother prepared our meals, quietly listening to her constant chatter, watching her move gracefully around the kitchen.

A few months before, P.W. had learned that at long last a sub-committee of the Banking and Currency Committee of the House of Representatives was meeting to consider taking measures that would guarantee bank deposits. As the Depression deepened, there was more talk about the need for governmental help and regulation of business and pressure to nationalize the banks as available money dwindled. Franklin Delano Roosevelt was campaigning for the presidency, using expressions like "the forgotten man at the bottom of the economy" and "the need to rebuild the economy to protect the purchasing power of the people and to improve bankruptcy procedures to decrease fraud and exploitation."

During the fall of 1932, P.W. thought again of his banking regulation bill still being held up in a Congressional Sub-committee. He had wanted to revive interest in his proposal after the Depression had begun several years ago, realizing that his idea had been considered premature when he originally submitted it to Congress, through Congressman Doyle, in 1924. Those prosperous years had promised so much easy, pay-as-you-go, ever-expanding credit, and so much free floating, available money to the public that deposit guaranty legislation was unpopular for political reasons. But now, since the Depression had started, he was talking more and more with colleagues and associates about the principles involved in his legislation. Just a few months before, he had appeared as a guest speaker at a neighborhood rally sponsored by the Voters League of the First Congressional District, along with representatives from the Illinois and Wisconsin Legislatures, who were agitating for Congressional action to protect depositors and abolish bank failures. He knew that his bill had been the first one submitted to Congress that would require national banks to guarantee deposits by surety companies in the full amount of the deposits and to provide for inspection of banks to guarantee financial stability on a regular basis. If there had been action on his bill long ago, at least the national banks and their depositors would have been spared the disgrace of financial failure. But P.W. no longer had any effective link in Washington, since his friend Charles Dawes, former Vice President of the United States who had been appointed by President Hoover as the Chairman of the Reconstruction Finance Corporation, had resigned in mid-summer of 1932 because he was needed in Chicago to assist the bank in which his family firm had large investments. Dawes did subsequently secure a $90,000,000 RFC loan, but a storm of protest was unleashed about political influence and the need to publicize these loans which intimidated prospective borrowers from seeking aid from the Reconstruction Finance Corporation.

The world seemed to be sinking in a quicksand of insolvency and confusion. Sometimes Minnie would say, "P.W., you should have known that there are thieves and troublemakers everywhere." He knew she had become bitter about all of the many sacrifices she had had to make because of his preoccupation with the bank and the needs of the community. He was pained when he considered that there would be no accumulated wealth to leave his children and this made him all the more sensitive to Minnie's many worries. He felt the least he could do was to be in her presence whenever his physical strength would allow.

Uncle George was as gentle and considerate of Minnie as always, and this was probably why he remained out of family discussions and gatherings unless specifically asked to talk over some issue. He might well have thought that in these hard times Minnie should relinquish her determination about her children's education, but he never made mention of it. Mother's only relief from the daily strain she was under was her club activity. She was active in the DeSaible Society's plan to have a Log Cabin Exhibit at the "1933 Century of Progress," Chicago's forthcoming World's Fair. We children knew we were expected to concentrate all our energies on school and our future, which she constantly assured us would be bright.

By mid-November, Uncle George left for his Southern route, a little later than usual. Mother was sure she had something to do with his delayed departure, but P.W. realized that George's business, too, was finally beginning to feel the impact of the Depression.

When Roosevelt won the presidency by a landslide vote, P.W. pointed out to Minnie that hope was on the horizon; that Roosevelt, as the hero of "the forgotten man," would lift the curse of the Depression from the entire world.

About one week after Uncle George left, Uncle James, Mother's eldest brother whom we had never seen, suddenly appeared at our door with a little bundle of clothing. Minnie had not seen him since he ran away from their Uncle Grieffe's home more than 40 years ago, almost immediately after their mother, Mary Jane, had passed away. It was James who had lured Minnie's brother John away from home, with his glowing letters about adventure, so many years ago. Minnie had never really forgiven him for luring John away. Now, he stood there in the door sheepishly asking Bill, "Is Minnie Chavers at home?" Minnie recognized him at once.

There he was, a bent, wrinkled, sixty-year-old man with blond curly hair and blue eyes. We children gazed on him with amazed fascination, for he looked like a white version of our Aunt Nellie, whom we knew so well. After Mother invited him in, he explained that he had been walking across the country, from state to state, making cabinets wherever he could find work, and one day had gotten the notion that he would look up his sister Minnie.

In the beginning, Minnie made the most of an awkward situation, even though she didn't really want him there. The next three weeks proved very exasperating as Uncle James busied himself scraping and painting all of the floors and woodwork. He insinuated that she had not taken proper care of the furniture and grew increasingly demanding about his need for special soaps for his feet, talking about the remedies he had developed for the care of his teeth, and bragging that he was in excellent condition for his age. Minnie found his eccentricities brutally reminiscent of Nellie's, so that daily he became a greater source of irritation to her.

Uncle James somehow learned about Uncle George's helping the family out financially, and this had increased the demands he made on Minnie, feeling he was entitled to some of his brother's help too. P.W. and Bill found Uncle James' brotherly heckling of Mother somewhat comical, if not refreshing. His constant busy work around the house was certainly further proof of what Mother had always said about industry being a Calloway family trait, as we watched Uncle James in action. Minnie, on the other hand, felt that he had been a tramp all his life and became angrier each day at the thought of James, her brother who had shared none of his life with her, having the nerve to suddenly show up at her door and want to live in her home because of the emptiness of his own life, now that he was facing old age. She was relieved when he finally decided to walk to New York and visit Nellie. Minnie felt that James and Nellie deserved each other.

As Christmas neared and Uncle George's expected letter with money to cover Christmas expenses did not arrive, Minnie was crushed to think that the fears for her children which had plagued her years earlier were becoming a reality. She would voice her regrets over and over about ever having insisted that P.W. move the factory to Chicago: "We should have stayed in Columbus." This confession became a sort of refrain she would repeat at times of crisis. Just before Christmas, a receiver was appointed to take possession of all the belongings in the Garnes' household and Mrs. Nixon was ordered to stop paying rent to the Garnes. "The wolf is really at their door," Minnie could be heard saying in thought of the Garnes. She recalled how she had dismissed James and sometimes reflected on her three brothers: James, the tramp, John, the genius, and George, the devoted, and how their lives were spinning out so differently. Of all, George was the rock of her world, just as he had been during their childhood.

Before long, Uncle George's Christmas check for us did arrive. On Christmas Eve, we children left the house to do our last-minute shopping, ending up at Neisner Brothers' 5¢-$1.00 Store on 47th Street where we heard that the prices dropped just before the store closed on Christmas Eve. Making a game of it, we followed the manager around the store that night, shopping for gifts as he marked down the prices. We bought Daddy a pair of beautiful lavender garters to hold up his socks, which of late seemed to be always falling down. He kept those garters in their gift box, propped up on his bureau, so he could look at them, lovingly, everyday. Sometimes when he was lying in bed, I would stop at his door and ask jokingly "Daddy, when are you going to wear your garters?" He smiled in reply. He just enjoyed looking at them; they were a constant reminder that we loved him very much.

The mortgage on the Garnes' home was foreclosed; Harry moved away quietly without letting us know where. Now, when P.W. thought of Harry, he felt very much alone. He spent more time, long hours every day, sitting and staring out the front window. He no longer cared to play his favorite victrola records. We hadn't heard "Among my Souvenirs" since Harry moved away. P.W. sat there, thinking back that only yesterday he had been a boy playing in the street whenever there was time to play between daily chores and his news route. Only yesterday he had been young and firm of limb like those boys out there playing ball right now. He thought of the choices he had made in life and now he questioned whether he had chosen wisely. He looked at the boys playing in the street on 42nd Place and wondered if they would soon be making the same effort and meeting with the same harsh obstacles. How far he had gone up the ladder of success, and how far he had fallen, crossed his mind many times. Whenever he thought of it, he rubbed his right hand, as if for reassurance. He remembered that his first decision was to turn away from playing in the street. He had always been in a hurry, confident of making it up that ladder. Then he would come back to the present, recalling all the choices he made, the choices that had led him to where he was now.

Over the past six months, his habit of sitting at the parlor window gradually lengthened. I just could not get used to it. Mother told us repeatedly that Daddy was not himself ever since he read the news about the closing of the Douglass Bank. She said that the bank had finally managed to drain him of his last energies. She said that he needed to think these things through undisturbed, and cautioned us not to bother him. Sometimes she would tell us that the fate of Harry Garnes and his misfortune was distressing him. At other times, she would say she really didn't know why he sat there so long. It might have been because of his inability to send Bill to a private college, although he seemed proud that Bill had graduated from Hyde Park High School, had registered at Crane City College, and then had taken the Civil Service examination for the Post Office, which he passed, beginning to work shortly thereafter. His working helped support the family through the Depression. Ironically, what my father had hoped to prevent had occurred: his children having to grow up prematurely and take on adult responsibilities at an early age.

Mother always ended up by saying that it was good he enjoyed watching the children in the street. Their play seemed to distract him from his physical suffering. I don't know what came over me that day, but I stood in the doorway for a long time watching him. I was absorbed in my own activities for a long time before I stopped and began to ponder about him. We all had grown accustomed to his severe disablility long ago even though he kept on fighting back with some kind of activity, pushed on by his great determination. I felt that same spirit stirring in me, the drive to conquer whatever adversity beset me, as he did. But suddenly that day, I seemed to fear the tremendous drive he had always shown was gone.

"What's the matter, Daddy?" I questioned, approaching him slowly. As he became aware of my presence, he reached out for me.

"Come here, Madrue," he said, responding to the solemn concern on my face. I walked towards him, reaching out my hands to him, and was pleased he had not hurried me away, knowing that Mother had cautioned us not to disturb him with our questions. Yet I felt strangely compelled to talk to

397

him, if only to ask if there was anything I could do to comfort him. I had always longed to be old enough to be of real help to him and now, perhaps because I was a big girl standing taller than Mother, I felt confident there would be something I could do or say to help him. Always in the past, when I felt alone or bewildered, his expression of concern quickly revived my well-being. I wanted to pay him back in some small measure for the comfort he held out to me.

"Is anything the matter?" I asked again as I sat beside him at the window.

"No, dear," he smiled. Then there was silence.

I was puzzled. "I was watching you," I confessed.

"Yes, I know dear," he answered. Then there was another long silence as if he were searching for some special words he wanted to say to me.

"Daddy, why do you watch the boys out in the street all the time?" I inquired, almost as if to confirm that he was actually all right. I looked deep into his eyes. We all were aware that he had had several minor strokes during the past few months, each one causing temporary loss of memory, and that these strokes were the reason for his long days and nights in bed.

"I am all right, dear. I was just watching the children at play," he answered lovingly, stretching out his left hand to me. The next thing I knew, I was cuddled in his lap, shrunken as it was. The big girl that I was wanted to be close to him, to make him feel my affection for him, and accept my attention.

"You looked so far away, Daddy; I was worried." I whispered to him. He knew I had been watching him for sometime.

"Well, Madrue, I have been thinking about the way things are with us. All of you children help Mother a great deal and this pleases me very much," he said, wanting to reassure me.

"But you always look so far away," I insisted.

"Well, sometimes, I think of all the things I wanted to give you when you would be this age, and how I've failed to give you anything. Maybe when I think of that, I look far away." He smiled, then looked past me again, out the window.

"You miss Dr. Garnes, don't you?"

"Yes, but we will see him as soon as he gets settled, I am sure," Daddy responded.

"The Douglass Bank closing bothered you too, didn't it Daddy?" I persisted.

"Yes, Madrue, it is closed like all of the others, and there is nothing I can do about it."

"But Daddy, the way those people treated you, you should be glad they failed," I returned, trying to cheer him up.

"No, I can't feel that way about it," he answered, shaking his head. "The Douglass National Bank was my idea; I created it and was proud of it even though I had to fight the men who took the bank away from me. Yes, I was proud of it."

"Even though they treated you the way they did?"

"Yes, now it is as though I lived only to see my creation die. It's great pain to see my life's work crumble."

For the first time in my life, I saw my father cry. Big clear tears were running down his face; he looked at me unashamed and spoke again. "As long as the Douglass National Bank remained open and running, it provided hope for the community and for me. The Douglass Bank was a beacon light, holding out hope for our people, and hope is the only guarantee of life, Madrue," he emphasized, wiping his tears away. "If I were able now, I would help with the Douglass Bank. I am not ashamed, and I'm not defeated, even though those men in the bank labeled me a bankrupt and fought me so hard, I'm not ashamed . . . I would go back to help with that bank." I looked at him in silence.

Daddy spoke again, "Maybe I shouldn't talk to you this way, Madrue. You're so young and all of life is stretched out before you."

"Oh, Daddy, why do you want to stay in Chicago with all these awful people?" I questioned. "Why do we have to stay here?"

"This is our home, Madrue," he answered.

"Well, I still don't see why you feel you have to stay here now!" I continued, as if he could still pick up and do whatever he wanted to.

"It's not that easy, dear," he went on. "This Depression has

399

everybody stalled right where they were when it began . . . Besides, I like Chicago. For me this is the 'big city' . . . and I have many friends here."

"But where are they" I inquired. "When the telephone rings, it's always one of Mother's club ladies wanting something." I was thinking that only the neighbors stopped by the house to ask about Daddy and pass the time of day with him now.

"When I speak of friends, Madrue, I'm talking about those who helped me in the past to do the things I was able to do. Even now, they would be willing to back me."

"But what good are those people to you now, Daddy?"

"I am proud of the things I've done and what I stand for, Madrue." Daddy's eyes were shining. It seemed incredible to me that he could believe in himself this much, even now, as shrunken and wasted away as he was. I tried to change the subject. "Why don't we see some of your relatives sometimes?" Perhaps I was thinking that Daddy's sisters and brothers could help him as Mother's were always helping her. But he only shook his head slowly.

"Where are your kin?" I asked again.

"Well, I couldn't look them up now, dear," he finally responded. "My mother and father are dead. As for my brothers and sisters, I don't even know where they are, Madrue. The brother I was genuinely close to, Frank, died before I left Columbus. As for the others, we haven't kept in touch for many years now. Anyway, they never did agree with the things I was trying to do. They just weren't interested in what I was doing, even long ago."

"Daddy, I want to meet your brothers and sisters," I persisted.

"I couldn't do that now, Madrue," he replied. "When I watch the children play, I think of the time long ago when I was a boy and would play with my brothers out in the street; sometimes they would play on and on, but I would stop to take care of my newspaper route. I never took enough time to play when I was young. My brothers used to tease me about not having played more. They felt I wouldn't get any place, no matter how I tried. If they saw me now, they would feel they

400

were right all along; they would think that I hadn't gone any place after all. They would say, 'I told you so'."

"That's not true, Daddy!" I returned in his defense. "It's just that you're not feeling well now."

"I know, darling. I've been places and done things, almost everything I ever wanted to do, thanks to the help of your Mother. Making money was always like a game to me. Your mother understood the joy I felt in making money and watching it grow, grow right out of the dreams I had. That joy for me was the same as other children felt watching their scores go up in a baseball game."

I kissed him. "I love you, Daddy!" I had never before been able to bridge the gap between us during all those years when he was so busy, so well-known, and so important.

Many evenings, P.W. would play his favorite records on the victrola again with Minnie in the back parlor near the Fredrick Douglass portrait. Sometimes he played the Hawaiian records and would rock to the lilting rhythms, then he would return to "Among my Souvenirs," finding strange solace in the words and music. Bill noticed that the records brought a certain comfort to his sick father for whom he now wanted, more than ever, to do something big to prove himself. Sometimes P.W. would limp slowly over to the ebony bookcase and look through some of his newspaper clippings, or thumb through a few of his books on banking legislation. He looked over the brochures he had written in preparation for the building of the bank that had been his dream, of which nothing was left but these few "souvenirs."

Although Roosevelt had been elected, a lame-duck transition government followed for four months while Hoover remained in office. The financial picture worsened, although that hadn't seemed possible. The daily papers were full of distressing news about our lame-duck Congress, our lame-duck President Hoover, and panic runs on banks all over the country. In late February, Hoover was still declaring that a bank holiday to investigate the stability of banks was unnecessary, yet the panic was draining the money out of the banks, and with it, the gold out of the Federal Reserve Bank, especially in Chicago and New York areas, and the clamour to nationalize banks was mounting.

The day before Roosevelt's Inauguration, an order went out that all banks in Chicago would have to close to save the banking system. News of devastating withdrawals of currency and gold in New York, and the hysteria, was blasted constantly over the radio. By the time Roosevelt uttered his now famous words to the nation to rally the American citizens around him, "There is nothing to fear but fear itself," on Saturday, March 4th, twenty states had declared bank holidays. A few days later, Roosevelt, in his first official act as President, declared a National Bank Holiday as a national emergency, closing all banks for investigation as the only way of restoring public confidence in what the government was doing and confidence in the future of the American banking system itself.

On March 14th, several days after the national emergency was announced, Daddy collapsed while down in the basement of our home. We were sitting around the radio, entranced by Roosevelt's melodic voice, when Daddy went down in the basement to look over some of his official court records and papers, where the overflow was stored.

"Minnie . . Minnie . . Minnie!" we heard Daddy's voice calling out from the far corner of the basement.

Mother, in the kitchen preparing dinner, stopped at once and ran to him. He was slumped over among his papers, almost lifeless, breathing heavily and with great difficulty. Minnie knew at once that P.W. had had another massive stroke.

"Bill, get help and come quickly!" she cried out in panic.

Bill ran next door for Mr. Nixon and together they carried Daddy very slowly upstairs to the second-floor bedroom. We stood terrified as the doctor came again to check his blood pressure and to advise Mother how best to keep him comfortable. Mother soothed him, watching constantly for a return of consciousness. As each day passed, she clung more desperately to the hope that if he could know the Bank Holiday in Chicago was lifting, this might somehow make a difference. But Daddy lay there, frozen in a coma. Each time we children would tip-toe into the room, we felt more helpless. His once powerful body, now wasted, was caught in a great struggle, breathing loudly as if each heave were the last, his deep rales resounding throughout the house day and night.

It was raining and hailing for almost a week now, the grey clouds constantly hovering overhead, as if nature herself were shedding tears for P.W., lying in a deep coma. Our father was dying. Occasionally he would seem to be regaining consciousness, but he sank back into a final coma, that Saturday night, as the fierce March winds and freezing sleet beat down and the house itself rattled and shook. It was Sunday, March 19th, 1933. The morning unveiled a spectacle of icy crystal. The March rain had frozen over during the night, and a light snow had left a pure and glistening clean look over all of Chicago. That Sunday, there was a strange calm about the house when we awoke and looked out the window to marvel at the cottonwood tree outside, hung heavy with great long crystal icicles. On that day, according to the newspapers, more Illinois banks were authorized to reopen, but far across the ocean, other events of grimmer portent were occurring. Hitler had seized power in Germany, marching across Europe to the drumbeat of racism and nationalistic militarism. On that beautiful, glistening, ice-encased Sunday, in the early afternoon, my Daddy began to breathe his last, and before the day was over, he died. Bill was almost 18, I was 16, and Edwina was 13. Daddy left us. We felt orphaned and defenseless in that jungle of frightened, hungry, forgotten people of the Black Belt of Chicago whom he had loved so very much, and for whose betterment he had spent himself. The sounds of the imminent spring, the birds, and the wind, echoed across the frozen, ice-encased terrain.

"Wasn't that a memorable day; the day he passed away?" commented Elisabeth many years later in reminiscing about these experiences. "The ice gleamed like crystal, hanging from the branches of all of the trees. I will always remember how unusual the trees looked that day: clear as glass, glistening in the sun. Every winter, as I think of Uncle Chavers, I think of that day! There has never been another winter day exactly like that day, here in Chicago."

I remember the well-meaning relatives being obstructionists, for the most part, during their few days stay with us for the funeral. Aunt Nellie, in particular, with her long black dress and black veil, whimpering at the grave site. Everyone was in dark and formal attire, the morbid seriousness of the funeral costume. Cousin Gabrielle had been especially overbearing with her constant lamenting of "poor little Minnie." Bill, Edwina and I huddled together in the big black car. A solemn Uncle George sat beside Mother who was clothed in black, covered with a dark veil, moaning softly, and shaking periodically, dealing as stoically as she could with the situation. George's comforting presence shielded her from the other more intrusive relatives who were full of advice for her.

I was shocked into a death-like numbness. I fell into a deep depression after our relatives left the house, engulfed by the silence that was everywhere, unable to get used to Daddy's absence. Always before, when he had gone away so many times, he had come back. Although I was sixteen, at first I kept thinking he would come back, in spite of Mother's explanations. As though I were a young child, unfamiliar with the ultimate loss that death brings, this fantasy of his return obsessed me for an indefinite period. But as the days and weeks passed and I dragged myself to school, returning only to cry each afternoon, I realized he would never come back. "Madrue is going to cry her heart out," I heard Mother say to brother Bill.

For months now, Mother had been setting the example for us, that life goes on, as she kept busy with her household chores and the winding up of Daddy's affairs. She prepared for participation in the 1933 Chicago's World's Fair, "A Century of Progress," serving as Vice-President of the National DeSaible Society which was planning a log-cabin exhibit in this big event, soon to open in the city along the lake front. We were now involved with our own school pursuits and studying harder, even more bent on making others proud of

404

Minnie in Century of Progress, National De'Sable Memorial
Society Log Cabin Exhibit, Chicago, 1933

our accomplishments, recognizing our duty to be a creative part of the experiences that were made available to us. Then, one day in June, we were all at the dining room table, just the four of us, as it had been for months now. I sat across from Edwina and to Mother's right while Bill sat across from Mother who had grown accustomed to sitting in Daddy's place at the head of the table, under the Tiffany chandelier, a symbol of our former affluence. The blessing was said slowly and calmly, the plates were passed, dinner was served, and then Mother began to speak, saying she had a special message for us and wanted us to listen carefully.

"Children," she began, "I want you to always remember that your father was a great and good man." She had spoken of him, though infrequently, during the past few weeks; she had been so busy with her club commitments and the expectation of Uncle George's arrival from the South anyday. But now she was speaking slowly and with great concern, as if to give us a message we should retain for life. "I know this has not been easy for you, for any of us . . . to keep going on. But remember that you had a great and good father. He did the things he believed in, although he did not live long enough to see many of his ideas come to fruition. His great crusade for the safety of bank deposits has not been in vain. His ideas about protecting and preserving depositors' bank accounts have now become a part of Federal Law."

P. W. CHAVERS, DOUGLASS BANK FOUNDER, DIES

RELIABLE FOR 27 YEARS

Passes Away

P. W. CHAVERS

Former political leader and founder of the Douglass National bank, who was the victim of a stroke Sunday. For more than a decade he was a leading figure in commercial and civic life. Friends paid their last respects to him Wednesday when funeral services were held at Charles Jackson's undertaking parlors.

Funeral Services Held at Charles Jackson's Parlors Wednesday

An illness of four years, which culminated with a stroke Saturday, brought death Sunday afternoon to Pearl W. Chavers, for more than a decade a leading figure in the commercial and civic life of the city. Mr. Chavers died at his home, 527 E. 42d Pl., with his wife, Minnie, and three children, William, Madrue and Edwina, at his bedside. He was 56 years old.

A host of friends, including many political leaders, attended the funeral services Wednesday afternoon. Charles Jackson undertaking parlors. Interment in Mt. Glenwood cemetery.

Born in Ohio

Mr. Chavers was born in Columbus, Ohio, and came to Chicago in 1917 with his wife whom he married in 1911. His first contact with Chicago was when he came here at the age of 21 as a delegate to the Republican national convention. At that time he was editor and publisher of the Ohio State Journal, an ...arding newspaper, with wide distribution throughout Ohio. In addition he edited papers in Cincinnati, Ohio, and Pittsburgh, Pa.

Built Apron Factory.

In 1905, Mr. Chavers published several books concerning the economic and social conditions of the Race.

Mr. Chavers operated an apron factory in Columbus and when the ...ne came to Chicago he established a branch factory here on 43d st. Difficulties which arose at the beginning of the war forced him to sell his ... Columbus factory and Mr. Chavers devoted all his time to his enterprise here.

...jungle the business of the Woodford bank thus resulted in the founding of the Douglass National bank of which he was the first president.

Has First Stroke

In the fall of 1929, Mr. Chavers suffered his first stroke while at the children's ...amp. He partially recovered his health.

At the age of 4 he was christened and joined the Baptist church in Columbus. He later became a member of St. Paul and retained that membership until he came to Chicago. He received his education in the public school of his home town and studied banking and business at Hulson Business college.

In Chicago, Mr. Chavers got into the newspaper business for a short time when he took over the Chicago Evening Bulletin book. In 1927, Francis Alexander and P. H. Pace, who started the daily newspaper, ... a great deal of money and were unable to carry on. Chavers stepped in and guaranteed the payroll for two weeks. It is said he would have gone further with the proposition but the original owner refused to give him the controlling interest.

P.W. finally had peace, 1933

407

Epilogue

Although as developing teenagers, and later as maturing adults, we remained aware of our father's efforts which, to some extent, guided us in our ultimate choices in our own careers, it was many years later that we were to realize the significance of his thinking in regards to bank legislation. Each of us took from our unique experiences that part of his value system and commitments which we perceived as meaningful in our own lives. I was drawn into the health care and human services fields, Bill into the recording industry, and Edwina into the emerging field of the scholarly study of black history. But it was not until I began the research for this book that we were to learn the implications of Daddy's bank legislation, HR 8977, which was introduced in the 68th Congress by Representative T. A. Doyle of Illinois in 1924, and about which Mother spoke that day in June, long ago.

HR 8977 was the earliest bill introduced into the Congress providing for protection of bank deposits by requiring banks to purchase surety bonds in the amount equal to their deposits. It guaranteed deposits in full. The Banking Act of 1933 did not require banks to purchase bonds guaranteeing deposits in full; the deposit insurance coverage was limited to $2,500 per depositor, but it was a beginning. It was a composite bill with features of one or more of the many deposit guaranty bills introduced into the 72nd Congress beginning in 1931. The Federal Deposit Insurance Corporation, an independent agency of the United States, was created by this Banking Act of 1933 to restore public confidence in banks by protecting the nation's money supply through insurance coverage for each depositor's funds in national and some state banks. This new bill began the long task of establishing sounder conditions in banking. Gradually, the insurance coverage has been increased from $2,500 to $5,000, to $10,000, to $15,000 and then to the current $100,000 coverage per depositor. Full coverage has not yet been attained, but a revolution in the nation's banking system has gradually taken place so that it is generally recognized that the government is prepared to deal with economic warnings of runs on banks as one mechanism to forestall another Great Depression. Long ago, my father envisioned this depositor insurance coverage as necessary to stabilize and humanize the banking system in America.

Minnie lived almost 20 years after P.W. passed away, continuing, as before, to center her activities in family, home, and community. She remained involved in her neighborhood and local clubs and assisted Elisabeth, as much as possible, in dealing with the arrival of the remainder of our cousins coming from the Phillipines, after World War II. She was there for our marriages and the birth and early years of the grandchildren, Benjamin, Ina, and Edward, that came into her life before she passed away in 1951. Shortly after she suffered a massive stroke, my husband, Bill Wright, brought her at my request to live in our home in New York. I wanted only to comfort her, but her time had run out. She had a final stroke one afternoon, and a few hours later was dead. The funeral service was planned to be held in Chicago. Our Uncle George had bought, prior to his death, eight plots in the Chicago Burr Oak Cemetery to eliminate the anxiety of funeral preparations for our family. But Aunt Nellie's jealousy prevailed even at the end. Although we had had a grave site designated for only Mother next to Uncle George (who died in 1943), Aunt Nellie argued ferociously for the site to be moved so that *she herself* could rest between them, next to her coveted brother. We acquiesed in memory of our Mother who had disliked senseless arguing and favored dignity and grace. She was laid to rest in Chicago, amongst her beloved Chicagoans.

For many decades, it has been said that Chicago as the "great generator of black hope" is no more, that the once hopeful black masses streaming into Chicago from the southern farms and villages in search of a better life, pursuing the American dream, . . . that they are no more and that the dynamic spirit of the inner city of Chicago is dying by design. Some said that power brokers, with their institutionalized racism, had won the struggle for Chicago's soul. In 1947, John

Gunther, the journalist and author, called Chicago "the chief breeding area and headquarters of Fascism in the United States," and as such is "the most Fascist City in America." Yet other historians and observers began to predict that white supremacy was over in America; it had done its work and was finished. One anthropologist maintained that Blacks had reached the numerical majority in Chicago and questioned why they had remained relatively powerless. We know that the Black Belt has survived the Great Chicago Fire, the Great Northern Migration, the fierce Race Riots, the Great Depression, the social upheavals of world wars, post-war riots, civil rights demonstrations, recessions, the epidemic of drugs, and the slavery of addiction. And it lives on, spreading across the sprawling South Side and multiplying, while the housing and employment discrimination continue.

The flags of foreign ships in the harbor of this huge metropolis now connect to the Atlantic Ocean by the St. Lawrence Seaway, but it was Jean DeSaible, a black man, who 200 years ago first visualized and demonstrated the commercial trading post possibilities of this site near the mouth of the Chicago River. In ceremonies opening the Seaway in 1960, Mayor Richard Daley of Chicago underlined the contributions of DeSaible "who gave the city the germ of the idea." Yet Chicago, throughout these 200 years, has remained ambivalent about its people of color. The era of Mayor Daley, with the well-publicized brutality of his police, had only recently drawn to a close when a tremendous grass-roots movement of voter registration and black participation in the political process began to gradually emerge.

Eventually the Latins, the Asians, the Lakefront liberals, and the poor Whites joined with the Black Belt, under the leadership of the Reverend Jesse Jackson, and formed the "Rainbow Coalition" to overthrow the ancient fiefdoms of the white, blue-collar, ethnic ward bosses in the most astonishing municipal campaign in American history. Sixty years earlier, P.W. had warned the voters that "We must learn to use the ballot to work for our economic freedom" and now they had learned. In a historic economic and political freedom struggle, the campaign process was rough, but the 90% turn out of the

411

black vote, and a high turn out all over the city, prevailed. On April 12, 1983, for the first time in the history of the city, a black man, running on a reform platform, was elected Mayor of Chicago, after a bitter racist campaign. With the assistance of Reverend Jackson's "Rainbow Coalition," Representative Harold Washington had proved the enormous power that black voters have and became Chicago's first black Mayor. It is anticipated that the democratic process in America will never be the same again.

The myth of Chicago as the "Promised Land" remains. Perhaps this is because it is the place where some of the "firsts" and the "greats" of the people of color emerged from the ashes of slavery and where the black impact on the nation has been profound, transcending the boundaries of color discrimination and segregation, and making national and international contributions in the fields of politics, medicine, art, business, and sports, to name a few. Equally important, this is the place where a tradition of achievement among enterprising, well-educated black families was established and perceived as a stabilizing presence for on-coming generations. There always was a mid-Western determination of spirit blowing in the "I Will" City, swirling in the Black Belt, which made for a tough, rugged, and courageous people, sustaining them. For me, no matter where I roam, Chicago, land of my childhood, is always in my heart, and in that sense, I have never left it.

Notes on Sources

This abbreviated bibliography is prepared for those readers interested in knowing more about the sources used in writing this book. No attempt is made to document all of the sources or to verify all of the facts presented. My hope is to supply readers with some references with which they may not be familiar, and may want some credentials of conditions cited in this historical novel.

I. BOOKS, JOURNALS, MAGAZINE ARTICLES AND REPORTS

Ackerly, Mary Denham and Lula Parker,*"OUR KIN" THE GENEALOGIES OF SOME OF THE EARLIEST FAMILIES WHO MADE HISTORY IN THE FOUNDING OF BEDFORD COUNTY, VIRGINIA.* 1929.

Anderson, Jervis, *THIS WAS HARLEM, 1900–1950.* New York: Farrar Straus Giroux, 1982.

ANNUAL REPORT OF THE FEDERAL DEPOSIT INSURANCE CORPORATION, 1950, "History of Legislation For the Guaranty or Insurance of Bank Deposits." Federal Deposit Insurance Corporation,Washington, D.C.

A BRIEF HISTORY OF DANVILLE, VIRGINIA, 1728–1954, "The Founding of Danville."

Chavers, Pearl William, *CONDITIONS THAT CONFRONT THE COLORED RACE.* Columbus, Ohio, 1908. Microform Reading Room #41182E, Library of Congress.

Chicago Commission on Race Relations, *THE NEGRO IN CHICAGO.* Chicago: University of Chicago Press, 1922.

Cochran, Thomas C., *THE AMERICAN BUSINESS SYSTEM: A Historical Perspective, 1900–1955.* Cambridge: Harvard University Press, 1957.

Drake, St. Clair and Horace R. Cayton, *BLACK METROPOLIS, A Study of Negro Life in a Northern City,* Vol. I & II. New York and Evanston: Harper & Row. Revised edition 1962.

Early, Ruth Hairston, *CAMPBELL CHRONICLES AND FAMILY SKETCHES EMBRACING THE HISTORY OF CAMPBELL COUNTY, VIRGINIA, 1782–1926.* J. P. Bell Company, 1927.

Early, Ruth Hairston, *THE FAMILY OF EARLY,* 1920.

Franklin, John Hope, *THE FREE NEGRO OF NORTH CAROLINA, 1790–1860.* Chapel Hill: University of North Carolina Press, 1943.

Galbraith, John Kenneth, *THE GREAT CRASH, 1929.* Boston: Houghton Mifflin Co., 1972.

Gerber, David A., *BLACK OHIO AND THE COLOR LINE, 1860–1915,* Urbana Chicago London: University of Illinois Press, 1976.

Hill, Judith Parks America, *A HISTORY OF HENRY COUNTY, VIRGINIA WITH BIOGRAPHICAL SKETCHES OF ITS MOST PROMINENT CITIZENS.* Baltimore: Regional Publishing Company, republished, 1976.

Hughes, Langston and Milton Meltzer, *A PICTORICAL HISTORY OF THE NEGRO IN AMERICA.* New York: Crown Publishers Inc., 1963.

Journal of NEGRO HISTORY. "Booker T. Washington and the Negro Press." Jan. 1953.

Lester, Julius, *TO BE A SLAVE.* New York: Dell Publishing Co., Inc. 1970.

Meier, August and Elliott M. Rudwick, *FROM PLANTATION TO GHETTO.* London: Constable and Company, 1966.

Miller, Loren, *THE PETITIONERS, THE STORY OF THE SUPREME COURT OF THE UNITED STATES AND THE NEGRO.* New York; 1966. Pantheon Books.

Moley, Raymond, "The Great Bank Rescue of 1933, "*THE BANKER MAGAZINE,* Vol. 151, No.1, Winter, 1968.

Pedigo, Virginia and Lewis, *HISTORY OF PATRICK AND HENRY COUNTIES, VIRGINIA,* Roanoke, Virginia: The Stone Printing and Manufacturing Co., 1933.

Price, Edward T., "A Geographic Analysis of White-Negro-Indian Racial Mixtures in Eastern United States," *ANNALS OF THE ASSOCIATION OF AMERICAN GEOGRAPHERS,* Vol. XLIII, #2, June, 1953.

Quaife, Milo Milton, *CHECAGOU, 1673–1835, FROM INDIAN WIGWAM TO MODERN CITY.* Chicago, University of Chicago Press, 1933.

Ray, Worth Stickly, *"List of the Earliest Inhabitants of Granville County, NORTH CAROLINA 1754" COLONIAL GRANVILLE COUNTY FAMILIES*. Baltimore: Southern Book Company.

Sinclair, Andrew, *THE AVAILABLE MAN, THE LIFE BEHIND THE MASK OF WARREN GAMALIEL HARDING*. New York, 1965.

Turner, John, Bill Stanton, Mike Valhala, Randall Williams, *THE KU KLUX KLAN. A HISTORY OF RACISM AND VIOLENCE*. Montgomery: Klanwatch, The Southern Poverty Law Center, 1982.

Virginia HISTORICAL MAGAZINE, Vol. 31, "Will of Nathaniel Harrison, July 15, 1728: 1923.

Wendt, Lloyd and Herman Kogan, *BIG BILL THOMPSON*. New York: The Bobbs-Merrill Co., 1953.

II. NEWSPAPER ARTICLES, PAPERS AND DOCUMENTS:

BROAD AX. A black weekly newspaper published from 1899 to 1926, credited as presenting the most perfect file of the Chicago Black Belt, and the most dramatic reportage of P.W.'s public career during the years of the bank development. See especially: Aug. 25, 1906; July 30, Sept. 3, 10, 17, Nov. 12, and Dec. 3, 1921. Reference Section, Library of Congress.

Chicago DAILY JOURNAL, "Negroes Start National Bank," May 25, 1921.

CHICAGO DAILY NEWS. "National Colored Bank . . . Charter for First Institution of its Kind Given Chicagoan," April 27, 1921. "New Negro Bank Here Seen as Boon to Race," Dec. 6, 1921.

CHICAGO DAILY TRIBUNE. "Goldman Target in Damage Suit Filed by Banker," May 16, 1923.

CHICAGO DEFENDER. A black weekly newspaper founded in 1905, the oldest and most widely known, very helpful resource, used to trace the activities of the Ku Klux Klan; the lynchings and mass murders by vigilante groups; the Race Riots of 1919; the economic, political and housing conditions resulting from the migration of Blacks from the rural South to urban Chicago; the history of black banking in Chicago; the impact of the recession and unemployment during 1921 and the 1929–1933 Great Depression on the life style and well-being of the citizens of the Black Belt. See: Oct. 19, 1918; Feb. 1, 1920; July 8, 1922; July 15, 1922; Nov. 8 1924; Dec. 6, 1924; April 10, 1926; Feb. 14, 1931. Schomburg Collection.

CHICAGO WHIP. "Douglass National Bank to Open Soon." May 21, 1921. "Celebration Banquet in Honor of Permit to Organize the Douglass National Bank," May 28, 1921 "Large Audience Hears O'Donnell Discuss Economic Problem." Sept. 6, 1921. "Chicago to Honor DuSaible," Dec., 22, 1928. Chicago Historical Society.

COLUMBUS DAILY PRESS, Sept. 1903. "Prominent Men Address Emancipation Meeting" Ohio Historical Center.

COLUMBUS EVENING DISPATCH, Jan. 19, 1909 "Lincoln Ohio Training School for Colored Youth," Ohio Historical Center.

COLUMBUS PRESS POST, Feb. 1 and Feb. 16, 1907 Ohio Historical Center.

COLUMBUS STANDARD, July 27, 1901. University of New Orleans, Microfilm Division.

JAMES M. COX, GOVERNOR'S PAPERS, "Pearl Chavers to 'Dear Friend'" Feb. 6, 1913. Ohio Historical Center.

HOUSE OF REPRESENTATIVES BILL #8977, 68th Congress, 1st Session, April 30, 1924. Copy on file in Chavers family records.

LESSON PLANS IN AFRICAN AMERICAN HISTORY, "Pearl Chavers Pioneer in the Banking Field," United Federation of Teachers of America, AFL-CIO Local #2, New York.

GEORGE A. MYERS PAPERS. "Letter from the Ohio Republican State Executive Committee," Sept. 18, 1903. Ohio Historical Center.

OHIO DAILY SUN, "Colored Men Organize For Uplift of Race," Nov. 29, 1906. Ohio Historical Society.

OHIO STANDARD WORLD, Vol. XIII, July 31, 1909. On file in Chavers family records.

Other newspapers carrying the bank story include: *Detroit Leader,* May 13, 1921; *New York Age,* May 7, 1921; *Kansas City Sun,* Aug. 21, 1921; *Negro Star,* Wichita, Kansas, Aug. 12, 1921; *Cleveland Call,* June 11, 1921; *The New Era,* Charleston, South Carolina, Aug. 13, 1921; *Wilmington Delaware Advocate,* May 21, 1921; *Times Plain Dealer,* Birmingham, Alabama, May 21, 1921.

BOOKER T. WASHINGTON PAPERS, 1906-1912. "Letters to and from Booker T. Washington or Emmett J. Scott to and from Pearl W. Chavers." Box 808, 317, 343, and 831. Manuscript Division, Library of Congress.

III. Bureau of Census, City Directory, and Genealogy Microfilms.

Bureau of Census, used to trace P.W.'s ancestors: Federal Census in 22 counties of North Carolina from 1790, *FIRST CENSUS OF THE UNITED STATES* through 1860, in total of North Carolina eight census all Chavers were identified as "FCP" Free Colored Persons, tax-paying, and therefore listed. *NINTH CENSUS,* 1870; *TENTH CENSUS,* 1880; *TWELFTH CENSUS,* 1900: Franklin County, Columbus, Ohio. Schomburg Collection.

Bureau of Census, used to trace Minnie's ancestors: Federal Census in both *Free and Slave Schedules* in Henry County, Bedford County, Franklin County, Pittsylvania and Patrick Counties from the *THIRD CENSUS OF THE UNITED STATES,* 1810, through the TENTH CENSUS, 1880. In this way, the movements and interlocking relationships of the Calloway, Bannister, Pannell, Baker, and Hairston families were documented. Schomburg Collection.

Bureau of Census, *TWELFTH CENSUS OF UNITED STATES, 1900. Illinois, City of Chicago,* Town of Lake. (Minnie's ancestors)

Church of Jesus Christ of the Latter Day Saints, Genealogical Microfilm:

HENRY COUNTY, VIRGINIA WILL BOOKS, 1777–1856, #0031956; 0031957

HENRY COUNTY, VIRGINIA PROBATE & WILLS, 1865–1867, #0031958
HENRY COUNTY, VIRGINIA LAND & PROPERTY BOOKS, 1838–1860, #0031970-0031972
HENRY COUNTY, VIRGINIA DEED BOOKS #4-5-6, 1789–1805, #031967
PITTSYLVANIA COUNTY, VIRGINIA, DANVILLE CITY LAND & PROPERTY, 1861–1880, #0870577
Columbus, Ohio City Directory From 1867 through 1920.

INDEX

420

Housing in Chicago's Black Belt, 2, 31, 54, 206
Hudson College, 14
Hughes, Langston, 368
Hunter Bank, 45, 52
Hyde Park Property Owners Association, 4

Insull, Samuel, 355, 377, 378

Jackson, Jesse, 411, 412
Jamestown Colony, 14
Jefferson, Thomas, 17, 18
Johnson, James Weldon, 367
Johnson, "Mushmouth," 355
Journal of Negro History, 367

Keystone National Detective Agency, 170
Ku Klux Klan, 10, 168, 251, 252, 286

Lafayette Theatre, 365, 366
LaGrange College, 368–370
Lake Minnie Bell, 97, 303, 305, 316
Liberia, 17
Lincoln, Abraham, the party of, 279
Lincoln Ohio Industrial Training School for Colored Youth, 22, 25
Lindberg, Charles, 315
Locke, Alain L., 367
Louisiana Territory, the purchase of, 15
L'Ouverture, Toussaint, 15, 289–291
Lucas, J. Grey, 45, 132
Lunceford, Jimmie, 365
Lynchings, Springfield, Illinois, 12 See also Race Riot.

McAndrew, William, 317
McCormick, Medill, 85, 92
McKay, Claud, 367
Madden, Martin B., 85, 92, 278, 279, 294, 295

Madrue's School of Dancing, 380–382
Marshall Field Department Store, 39
Mason School For Children, 242, 318
Metropolitan Community Church, 383
Metropolitan Theatre, 373, 374
Migration, Black, 1, 6, 10, 12, 14–19, 22, 31, 47, 48, 179, 206, 279
    European, 1, 6, 10, 47
    Hispanic, 10, 12
Millinder, Lucky, 365
Mills, Florence, 366
"Modernistic Rhythm Girls," 366
Morrow, Ora Lee, 328, 329
Municipal Court of Chicago, 229

National Association for the Advancement of Colored People (NAACP), 11, 12, 66
National Bank Holiday, 402
National Negro Business League, 10, 11, 20
New York Age, 106
New York Girl Friends, 337
New York Philharmonic Orchestra, 365
New York schools:
    Dewitt Clinton High School, 358
    Hunter College High School, 353, 372
    Julia Ward Junior High School, 355–357, 366
Niagara Movement, 11, 12
Nicholas Brothers, 365

Ohio Society, 143, 211
Ohio Standard World, 19, 53, 80, 83
Old Settlers, 1, 2, 52, 113, 179, 249, 321, 380
Oliver, Annie E., 322, 323
Oliver, Joe "King", 364
Oxford University, 367

Pacific Islands, 10, 12
Phelps-Stokes Fund, 9
Philippine Islands, 112, 311, 410
Phillips, Wendell, 18, 289, 290
Property Owners Protective
    Association, 4
Prostitution, houses of, Chicago, 90,
    294, 316

Queen Victoria, 10

Race Relations Commission Report,
    168
Race Riot of 1919 (Chicago), 6, 31–
    33, 168, 249
Rebecca's Tearoom, 186, 265
Reconstruction Finance Corpora-
    tion, 386, 393
Republican Party, 10, 19, 25, 148,
    277–279, 377
Roaring Twenties, 364, 367, 377
Robeson, Paul, 365
Robinson, Bill "Bojangles", 365, 366
Roosevelt, Franklin D., 394, 401,
    402
Roosevelt, Theodore, 10
Rosenthal Fund, 9

St. Lawrence Seaway, 411
St. Mark's Methodist Episcopal
    Church, 2
Savoy Ballroom, 365
Schomburg, Arthur, 368
Schomburg Center for Research in
    Black Culture, 368
Scott, Emmett J., portrait, 248
Sissle, Noble, 365
Slavery, American, 1, 9, 13–19, 109
Smith, Alfred E., 327
Smith, Bessie, 365
South Side Food & Home Show,
    380, 390
South Side Savings Bank, 244
Spanish American War, 16, 311,
    371

Taft, William Howard, 251
"Talented Tenth," 11, 113
Tanner, Henry O., 367
Tenant farm system, 17, 27
Thompson, William Hale, "Big
    Bill", 32, 90, 277, 316, 322,
    378
Toomer, Jean, 367
Torrie, Johnny, 316
Town Hall, 337, 343, 347
Turner, Nat, 17
Tuskegee Institute, 9

Underground Railroad, 1, 66
United States Circuit Court of Ap-
    peals, 239, 251
United States Constitution, 18, 252
United States Supreme Court, 18
University of Berlin, 11
University of Chicago, 382

Valentine's Day Massacre, 317
Van Der See, James, 368
Vice and crime, Chicago, 90, 179,
    294, 316–318, 355

Waller, "Fats," 365
Warren, Furman B., 166
Washington, Booker T., 8–12, 19,
    22, 63, 143, 286
    portrait of, 248
Washington, Harold, 412
Waters, Ethel, 366
Watson, Barbara, 353
Watson, James S., 353
Webb, Chick, 365
Wheatley, Phyllis, Home, 321
Wilson, Woodrow, 30, 151
Women's Federated Club, 323
Woodfolk Bank Trusteeship, 49, 51,
    53, 54, 73, 78, 85, 123, 181,
    182, 189–191, 196, 199, 200,
    219, 220, 222, 225, 270
Woodfolk, R. W., 2–4, 7, 38, 52, 272

423

ABOUT THE AUTHOR

Madrue Chavers-Wright grew up in Chicago, received her professional training at the University of Chicago, School of Social Service Administration, and has lived most of her life in New York City. She gained her clinical experience as a medical social case worker at the Hospital for Joint Diseases, a supervisor at Montefiore Hospital, and a Public Health Social Work Consultant at the New York City Department of Health working with all kinds of people of various ethnic and socio-economic backgrounds. For nearly twenty-five years as Consultant Supervisor to the Health Insurance Plan of Greater New York, she developed and implemented programs and systems, and for almost thirty years has been a member of the Executive Board of the Mental Health Association of New York and Bronx Counties. As Vice President of the Association, she continues her work for improving family life education, community mental health services, and race relations. She recently joined the Board of Directors of the William Hodson Community Center, bringing her expertise in the field of geriatric health services with her. She also has worked with Citizens' Committees of Countee Cullen, P.S. 194 in Harlem, the Urban League of Greater New York, the New York City Departments of Health, Hospitals and Welfare, and the Department of Mental Health, Mental Retardation and Alcoholism, encouraging improved linkage of health, education and human services throughout the city.

By appointment of the Governor, she is a Member of the Board of Visitors of the Bronx Children's Psychiatric Center. She is a charter member of the National Association of Social Workers, active with the Social Workers for Peace and Nuclear Disarmament and a Representative to the United Nations for Servas International, a Non-Governmental Organization, in a consultative status with the Economic and Social Council. Recently she became a Corporate member of the Schomburg Collection of Black History, Literature, and Art, Inc. Madrue Chavers-Wright has two married sons and three granddaughters, and continues to make her home in the Pelham Parkway section of the Bronx, New York.

Comments About The First Edition

During my researching and writing period my brother, Bill, would share his memories and thoughts about Daddy's perception of Chicago as the "pivotal city" in America, prevailing attitudes, forces our parents coped with as they transmitted their standards to us. Always supportive, he urged me to produce a book worthy of public readership and appreciation. "Make it a classic, Madrue." He stimulated me to become a self-published author, and sent an article "How To Publish Your Own Book." When it was finished, his pleasure was emphatically conveyed: "*Your book is a classic!*"
The Late William Chavers, Chicago

"An introduction to your book is not necessary. It stands on its own merits. P.W. Chavers' mentor was Booker T. Washington whose contribution to the development of our people must be reassessed in relation to where we are today. Had we heeded to the need to build community unity back in those days, national unity would have been much further along today. You can't build a nation until you build a community."
Dr. John Henrik Clarke, Professor Emeritus, Africana & Puerto Rican Studies, Hunter College, City University of New York
The Guarantee is the biography of P.W. Chavers, banker, enterpreneur, philanthropist in Chicago's Black Belt of the Twenties. He founded the Douglass National Bank, the first of its kind, owned and operated by Black people. He named the bank after Fredrick Douglass because Douglass stood for integrity, dignity and self-respect for Black people, and the bank was designed to lead our people out of *economic slavery*. The author's research on her family, and on the politics and economics of the Twenties has enabled her to write a well-rounded narrative. For this reason, as well as its intrinsic human interest, *The Guarantee* is highly recommended."
Jean Blackwell Hutson, former Chief of the Schomburg Center for Research in Black Culture

426

"What a beautiful memoir, a tribute to your father . . . the most pleasure was learning about you; and how your life was shaped by the forces of family, racism, politics, economics and your personal strengths. My enthusiasm spread to my friends who witnessed my reading your book."
Janis Brodie, Psychotherapist

". . . a marvelous job of presentation in an historic setting in the mecca of the 20's and 30's, showing the family forces which shape us and set the tone for life in the 'outer world.' The story is visible and imaginative on an involvement level . . . a sharing of the experiences and happenings. The author has graciously shared her life and that of her family in an exciting way."
Madrid Turner Hamilton, Ph.D., author of *Erosive Health*

"Your book enabled me to visit your home and meet your family. I could for a time become a part of the life of a cultured, prosperous black family. Your scholarly attention to historical detail helped me to understand some of the world-wide forces, as well as the prevailing national customs and attitudes which helped to shape the lives of those whom you wrote about. Prior to reading your book, I had had no inkling of the fact that national laws which make our bank deposits secure had been first proposed and drafted by a black American, your father, P.W. Chavers. What a true visionary he was!"
Aclen B. Lewis, Retired Elementary School Principal

"P.W. Chavers, entrepreneur, established the first black national bank in the United States in 1922, also helped develop legislation that led to modern banking laws for insuring depositors. This family saga provides much information about the Black and white Chicago of the 1920's."
Essence. December, 1985

". . . an enlightening account of a wonderful and dear man . . . a work tastefully done with a fine sense of style. This will touch all who possess the good judgement to choose an inspiring book. It teaches you and it touches you!"
Rochelle Shapiro, New York.

427